You Are Your Child's

supported by

North Lanarkshire Council

culture NL

Hawthorn Press

You Are Your Child's First Teacher copyright © 1989, 2000, 2006 by Rahima Baldwin Dancy

Rahima Baldwin Dancy is hereby identified as the author of this work in accordance with Section 77 of the Copyright, Designs and Patent Act, 1988.
She asserts and gives notice of her moral right under this Act.

First published in the United States by Celestial Arts.
This edition published in the UK by Hawthorn Press, Hawthorn House, 1 Lansdown Lane, Stroud, Gloucestershire, GL5 1BJ, UK
Tel: (01453) 757040 Fax: (01453) 751138
info@hawthornpress.com
www.hawthornpress.com

Cover photograph by Stock4B
Cover design by Hawthorn Press
Design and typesetting by Lynda Smith at Hawthorn Press, Stroud, Gloucestershire
Printed in the UK by Woolnough Bookbinding Ltd
Printed on paper sourced from sustained managed forests and elemental chlorine-free

Every effort has been made to trace the ownership of all copyrighted material. If any omission has been made, please bring this to the publisher's attention so that proper acknowledgment may be given in future editions.

British Library Cataloguing in Publication Data applied for

ISBN   1 903458 65 X
        978-1-903458-65-5

Contents

Foreword

I was first introduced to *You Are Your Child's First Teacher* 12 years ago when my son was 3 years old. I still have my book from that time, stained, battered and so well used. How I wish I had known about Rahima Baldwin Dancy's work even before I had become pregnant. It was the one book I turned to again and again when I began to lose faith in my abilities to be a 'good enough' mother, when I needed inspiration, when I was at my wit's end to know what to do in a particular situation. In my gratitude for Rahima's sound advice in my years of early motherhood I have, in my work as a Parent and Child group leader and course organiser, always put her book at the top of my recommended reading for all those who care for the young child.

However, it was only when I was asked to edit this new edition of the book for English readers that I fully began to realise the profundity of what Rahima has managed to do. As I read through the book from beginning to end, I slowly feel an inner waking-up. I realised that the reader is being gently guided through a process of re-membering the true nature and purpose of early childhood and the task of parenthood. I realised that the book is also like a chalice, in which many mysteries of childhood development and parenthood are contained and simply explained. And it is written in a way that is absolutely relevant to our task as parents today.

But being a parent these days is no easy task. We are right out at sea. The safety of the harbour, with the traditional knowledge of the tasks of motherhood and a simpler way of life, has been left behind. Parents are now faced with many complex dilemmas and choices – the traditional extended family is all but gone, the nuclear family is fragmenting, there are many pressures to return to work in early infancy. There are demands for early academic learning, the double-edged explosion of technology, the loss of traditional skills and know-how, our loss of contact with nature and natural rhythms and the speeding up of our lives. Many parents, for many different reasons, are giving up their very young children to the 'professionals' to take care of. There are many hazards that threaten fundamental child health and well being. Thankfully alarm bells are being sounded by researchers and experts in many different fields – politics, psychology, education and health. There are lighthouses out there.

Rahima Baldwin Dancy is a lighthouse in stormy seas. She has given us a great gift by bringing together the timeless wisdom imparted by Rudolf Steiner, the particular dilemmas that we face as parents today, the most up to date research on child development and practical, compassionate, non-judgemental advice. Through her understanding we can clearly see choices that are truly healthy for the young child, and which also empower us as parents.

She describes every aspect of raising the young child, from pregnancy and the very early months right up to school readiness. Each chapter is packed full of well distilled, digested research and practical suggestions. She explains Rudolf Steiner's spiritual understanding of early childhood and shows how modern research is in agreement with his insights. She explains the different stages of early child development and how as parents we can develop our child's imaginative, artistic, musical and cognitive abilities. She gives us advice on discipline, sleep, play and bodily health. At the end of each chapter are resources for further study. She is a mother who has experienced the journey in all its joys and difficulties.

I feel the last great taboo is around our understanding of ourselves as spiritual beings and our purpose on this beautiful planet. One problem is that we can feel so suspicious of anything 'spiritual' that we can get blindly caught in purely materialistic ways of interpreting everything in our lives. For those with open eyes and ears I believe that Rahima Baldwin Dancy's book is able give new understanding, freedom, confidence and joy in the parenting journey. Her advice helps us to allow our children to unfold and blossom naturally. I often say to the parents I work with – 'If there is one book you ever read as a parent, let it be 'You Are Your Child's First Teacher.' I really mean it!

Dorothy Male, February 2006

Preface

When I was a mother with young children, I was carrying questions shared by so many parents today: How can we help our children to develop the skills needed for life in today's world? What can we do with and for our children from birth to age six that will enhance their development without having negative effects at a later age?

These and other questions – together with a feeling of being totally lost at sea – led me to an in-depth exploration of early childhood and parenting. My search led me to study the work of Rudolf Steiner, an Austrian educator who founded the first Waldorf School in 1919. (See Appendix B for further information on Steiner and Waldorf education). I found that using the insights into human development provided by Steiner enabled me to see children in a new way and completely transformed the quality of family life.

Although this book makes many concrete suggestions of things you can do with young children, it is not offered as a formula for raising children! Rather, I hope that some of these new ways of seeing and understanding the child between birth and age six will provide fertile ground for your own creativity, help to increase your own perceptions and confidence, and deepen your relationships with your children.

Today there is even greater urgency for parents to understand the developmental needs of young children and ways to create a nurturing environment for them. Childhood has increasingly come under assault as products and activities formerly reserved for adults and teens are marketed to younger and younger children, and computers and academic demands squeeze imaginative play out of the kindergarten curriculum.

The universality of these and other problems facing families today is demonstrated by this book having already been published in Japan, Korea, and Thailand. So it is with great pleasure that I am able to write a preface to the British edition , which will take this information to many more parents throughout the English-speaking world.

In wrestling with the gender difficulties of the English language, I finally decided to attempt balance by usually referring to the child under three as she and to the older child as he. Because this is a personal and practical book, I have also addressed you in many places throughout the book and hope that you will find it a helpful guide on the path of parenting.

Being a parent today is one of the most important and challenging tasks you will ever face. It is my hope that the insights in this book will deepen your understanding of the importance of honoring the unique world of early childhood. This new understanding can not only enrich your personal and home lives, but it is vitally important for giving our children the wellsprings of health and creativity they will need to meet the challenges of today's world.

Rahima Baldwin Dancy
Boulder, Colorado, 2006

Acknowledgments

Both this book and my work as a parent and early childhood educator take their greatest inspiration from the work of Rudolf Steiner, an Austrian philosopher and educator who founded the first Waldorf school in Stuttgart, Germany, in 1919. Steiner's understanding of child development and his reverence for life have enabled me to be with young children in ways that complement the natural unfolding of their capacities. I would also like to thank Werner Glas, who served for many years as the co-director of the Waldorf Institute, for inspiring me to undertake the task of making the wisdom of Rudolf Steiner more accessible to parents, so they can apply it in home life.

I would like to acknowledge the work of Burton White, founder and director of the Center for Parent Education in Newton, Massachusetts. While director of the Harvard Preschool Project and the Brookline Early Education Project, he observed mothers in their homes to see what parenting practices were being used on siblings of 'wonderful children' rather than starting from some theoretical or laboratory base. His observations and conclusions about the first three years of life strongly support many of the principles set down by Rudolf Steiner a half-century earlier. His book *The First Three Years of Life* and his 'New Parents as Teachers' project, which was so successful in Missouri, have encouraged me in writing this book and developing ways of working with parents and children during these vital years.

I have found similar support from the work of David Elkind, Professor of Child Study at Tufts University, who has described the current crisis in education and parenting in *Miseducation: Preschoolers at Risk* and *The Hurried Child*. Characteristic of Waldorf education are activities that are developmentally appropriate and take into account the whole child – in mental, emotional, physical, and spiritual development. Our rapidly changing society needs more than ever to protect early childhood and to assure children's healthy development of inner resources so they may successfully assume their places as adults.

The research and work of Jane Healy on developmental neuropsychology and the effects of computers on brain development and education have also been of tremendous help to me. It is wonderful to have someone completely outside the Waldorf movement provide a synopsis of the current research that ends up being so supportive of the indications of Rudolf Steiner. I originally shared the insights of Rudolf Steiner in this book because I found them so valuable in family life and in my teaching young children; it is satisfying to find, twelve years later, that Steiner's insights – far from being dated or anachronistic – are, in fact, on the leading edge of developmentally appropriate education. Healy's books provide parents with the latest information on developmentally appropriate learning (*Your Child's Growing Mind: A Practical Guide to Brain Development and Learning from Birth to Adolescence* and *Endangered Minds: Why Children Don't Think and What We Can Do About It*) and on how to guide our children in the digital revolution (*Failure to Connect: How Computers Affect Our Children's Minds – for Better and Worse*).

I would like to thank my own grown children and stepchildren, Leif, Seth, Faith, and Jasmine, for leading me on this path through parenting and for providing me with so many opportunities for growth!

My husband, Agaf Dancy, also deserves hugs and kisses for his continual support in all areas and for his editorial skills. Thanks also to Katherine Czapp, Susan Howard, Wahhab Baldwin, Mary Lynn Channer, Ann Pratt, Joan Almon, Barbara Stern, and others who read and commented on the manuscript. Special thanks also go to Judith Johnstone and the late David Hinds at Celestial Arts for their help in making this book available for parents.

I am delighted that the book is now going to be available as a UK edition and wish to thank Erika Bradfield at Celestial Arts and Martin Large, Rachel Jenkins and Carole Richards at Hawthorn Press for making this possible. Special thanks also go to Dot Male for her gentle touch in customising the text for a UK readership.

CHAPTER 1

You Are Your Child's First Teacher

A Unique Opportunity

The time between birth and age six is a time of growth and learning unparalleled in later life. Tremendous physical growth and learning occur between birth and age three. The four-year-old continues learning about the world through his play, imitating all that goes on around him and expressing his own unique personality and approach to the world. The six-year-old evokes in us a picture of a grinning child with missing teeth who is well-oriented in time and space and eager to exercise his emerging skills in reading and writing. From this time on most people assume that the child will do his or her primary learning at school, but we cannot forget that what the child has learned in the home forms the necessary and irreplaceable foundation for all that comes later.

The formative power of children's experiences in the early years has been recognized by thinkers and educators throughout history. However, in the United States the importance of the first three years has only gained scientific backing since the 1960's. The Head Start Programme in the US, which the UK Sure Start initiative is based on, was launched in 1965. This programme, developed by a panel of child development experts commissioned by the US government, was devised to help communities meet the developmental needs of disadvantaged pre-school children. Follow up studies carried out on three- and four-year-olds showed that it was necessary to start assisting families much earlier, if children were going to be helped to achieve their full potential. Early Head Start launched in 1994 now specifically caters for the particular needs of infants and toddlers. Brain research that became available in the mid-1990s also re-focused attention on how critical the first three years are, not only for the development of intelligence, but also for building social and emotional foundations for everything that comes later. An important indicator of this interest in the US was the publication of a special edition of internationally acclaimed *Newsweek* magazine in 1997, entitled 'Your child: From Birth to Three', which featured essays by leading early childhood researchers. One report stated 'New technology, such as positron emission tomography (PET) imaging of the brain, has provided hard data on the importance of these years. Simple activities, like cuddling and rocking a baby, stimulate growth. The long-term effect of inadequate nurturing can be devastating. In profoundly deprived children – for example, orphans left to languish in an institutional nursery – critical areas of the brain remain undeveloped.'[1]

The renewed interest in the first three years in the US , sparked by the landmark 1994 Carnegie Corporation study 'Starting Points' and furthered by the 1997 White House Conference on Early Childhood Development and Learning, has its modern roots in the 1960s and 1970s. While many researchers at that time were focusing on programs for poorly developed preschool children, Burton White and his associates at Harvard University undertook a thirteen-year study of how children develop in the first six years of life. White states:

> In our studies we were not only impressed by what some children could achieve in the first years, but also by the fact that a child's own family seemed so obviously central to the outcome. Indeed, we came to believe that the more informal education that families provide for their children makes more of an impact on a child's total education than the formal educational system. If a family does its job well, the professional can then provide effective training. If not, there may be little a professional can do to save a child from mediocrity. This grim assessment is the direct conclusion from the findings of thousands of programs

for remedial education, such as the Head Start and Follow Through projects.[2]

In the Brookline Early Education Project in Massachusetts, White continued his studies by focusing on the question of what helps children to develop into 'wonderful' people. First he found 'great' six-year-olds – children who were not only intelligent and well-developed, but also well-balanced and a pleasure to be with. To try to determine what parental factors and experiences in the early years had helped to make them that way, he involved their families in the study when a new baby was expected so he could observe the ways these parents interacted with their children before the age of three. White's work is especially interesting because he truly observed and learned from mothers and babies in their own homes, and he was concerned with the children's overall balance, not just intellectual development.

White discovered that most families get their children through the first six to eight months of life reasonably well in terms of overall development. Unless a child was part of the small percentage of children who are born with a significant handicap or acquire one within the first year, there was little measurable difference in development among babies in their first eight months. But White and others have shown the period that begins at eight months and ends at three years is uniquely important in the development of a human being. White feels that perhaps not more than 10 percent of American families get their children through the ages of eight to thirty-six months as well educated and developed as they might be.[3]

White also observed that 'raising a bright three-year-old is much easier than raising a pleasant unspoiled three-year-old.'[4] Therefore, he developed educational programs for new parents that emphasize more than just intellectual development. One such program based on White's work, the Missouri Project, was offered to couples from before birth until the children turned three. Group sessions for parents were supplemented by home visits in which trained workers answered parents' questions and offered suggestions from what they observed. Not only was parent satisfaction with the program 99 percent, but studies done after three years of the pilot program showed a positive impact of parent education on children's development in many spheres.[5]

Another educator who recognized the importance of the early years in the development of the human being was Rudolf Steiner. Steiner, a scientist and visionary as well as an educator, founded the first Waldorf School in Stuttgart, Germany, in 1919. Albert Steffen, who attended many of Steiner's lectures, reports, 'Many times in his writings Dr. Steiner has shown that it is in the earliest years of childhood that things happen which are the deciding factors in later life. Whatever is done well or ill to a child in its earliest age will reappear in the grown person as faculties or failings, health or disease. On this account we should feel it our duty at the outset to gain an understanding of the whole course of life.'[6]

Parents' Dilemma Today

All parents want to do what is best for their children, to give them the best possible start in life. But what is best? Many parents feel that they ought to be doing more with their eight-month-old. But what? Or parents want to spend 'quality time' with their child but find it boring to sit and do puzzles together. That we are plagued with so many questions, doubts, and guilt about how to raise our children is the result of living in a time of tremendous changes. Our culture no longer provides a strong and unified message about how children should be reared. In addition, most of us live separated from our own parents or other extended family who traditionally provided wisdom, help, and continuity in rearing children. The art of mothering was replaced by the science of parenting, yet many parents have come to question the values their own parents embraced in such practices as bottle feeding every four hours and letting the child 'cry it out.'

As members of modern Western society, it is appropriate that we question everything, that we bring things to consciousness and go on to create something whole and nourishing. For example, we found in questioning modern practices of technological intervention in birth that there is no such thing as 'natural childbirth.' All childbirth is influenced by the culture in which it takes place. It is not possible to just do it 'naturally'; rather, we have to re-educate ourselves and try to bring our minds, bodies, and feelings into a new harmony, a new integration that will allow us to birth as complete human beings, with body, mind, and emotions working together.

The same is true of parenting. It is appropriate that we question what we are doing and that we discuss our attitudes and intentions with one another – but not in front of the children! It is beneficial for children to think we know what we are doing even if we aren't so sure ourselves. They don't need to be involved in the intricacies of adult considerations and thought processes. Rather, they need to feel that mother and father are united in what they are doing.

Being in a state of 'not knowing' and 'questioning' can be very positive, but it can also be frustrating because children don't wait until we have it all figured out! They demand constant interaction and decisions that will influence them in both the present and the future. Just as babies don't wait until the world and our lives are in perfect order before they are born, children don't wait until we are 'perfect parents.' Indeed, we will be better off if we can give up the idea of perfection in regard to parenting. Parenting is a process of mutual growth, in which parents and children grow in different levels through their interactions and through the elements they bring into one another's lives.

Because everything has come into question, many of us find ourselves as new parents in a real quandary about what to do in various situations. And we often find we have no way of foreseeing the effects of our actions on our children – especially the first child! Should we encourage our child to express all of his emotions and perhaps end up as a little tyrant, or yell at him and risk producing a repressed and resentful adult? Neither alternative is very inviting! Should we start teaching our nine-month-old to read or swim? Does our three-year-old need to be computer literate in order to get ahead in today's world? We don't seem to have any way of judging, and therefore find ourselves at the mercy of whatever notion comes along. We need to listen to our own inner knowing. And we need to acquire knowledge about how the young child develops, so we can make choices with confidence and receptivity. Many of us as new parents have no knowledge of child development, and we haven't even been around children since we grew up. Many of us have forgotten what children are like and find ourselves on the path of parenting without any knowledge of the landscape.

Cultural Dilemmas

We need to begin to see the child in a new way, one which takes into account physical, emotional, and mental development, as well as the less tangible spiritual dimension of the human being. Once we begin to perceive the whole child and how he or she unfolds, then our choices will begin to have coherence. No longer wanting a cookbook of 'how to's,' we will trust our own decisions, based on our understanding of the developing child and observation of the resultant flowering of our own children.

We need to realize that there are many cultural norms working against seeing the child in such a way. First of all, western society tends to regard children as little adults, so we are encouraged to reason with them as if they were grown-ups and to teach them with techniques appropriate for much older children. Despite years of studies by Piaget and neurophysiologists, educational politicians determine curricula and textbooks seemingly without any regard to the way children actually think and learn. The 'new math' fiasco of the early 1960s illustrates how professors and book companies tried (and ultimately failed) to introduce an approach that was far too abstract for primary-school students.

Our western culture also tends to regard children – and human beings in general – as machines. The human brain is likened to a computer, instead of reinforcing that the power of modern computers – to process data, not to think – is a product of the human brain and involves a very simple 'on-off' process occurring at remarkably high speeds. The computer culture permeates our values, so that popular articles on brain research refer, time and time again, to children being 'hard-wired from birth' for certain capacities or tendencies.[7] We also see the mechanized model in the sphere of medicine, in which worn out parts are replaced as they would be at the auto repair shop. And it permeates the materialistic psychology of behaviorism, in which the individuality of a person's soul and destiny are reduced to a complex series of conditioned responses.

We also need to recognize that western society values intellectual development above all else and tends to ignore other aspects of development, both as to their own value and the impact they have on learning. In an attempt to produce more intellectual and literate students and adults, the American elementary-school curriculum has been pushed earlier and earlier, so that kindergartners are now doing what used to be taught in first grade, when children are six and seven years old. The fact that many children are now failing kindergarten and functional illiteracy continues to rise in this country has only led to starting 'reading readiness' with four-year-olds in an increasing number of school systems. The fact that there is a difference between kindergartners and first graders – that is, that there is a major developmental change that goes on around age six or seven – is being ignored as parents and educators continue to 'hot house' preschoolers into academic channels.

This disregard for the natural development of children has resulted in what David Elkind, a leading writer in the US on child development, calls 'miseducation,' or practices that put preschoolers at risk and have no real benefit. His books *The Hurried Child* [8] and *Miseducation: Preschoolers at Risk* [9] detail the cultural forces that are jeopardizing the healthy development of our children.

We have lost touch with natural processes in child development, convinced that we have to 'do something' rather than allowing the child's own inner process or unfolding. Pediatricians try to reassure mothers that each child has his own timetable with regard to walking early or late, but educators do not reassure parents or try to maintain the self-esteem of a child who does not learn to read until age nine. Rather, he is labeled 'learning disabled' and put into remedial classes, in which the basics are drilled to the point where he loses out on the richness and excitement of learning.

Rudolf Steiner had tremendous confidence in the natural processes of development and reminded us that 'That which is asleep will awaken.' [10] That doesn't mean we do nothing – it means the things we do need to be consonant with the child's own developmental stages as they unfold. It is unhealthy to skip stages or to rush the child through various phases. While it is sometimes possible to do so, just because something can be done doesn't mean that it should be done! Again, we need an understanding of the development of the human being to be able to judge what is in harmony with a child's development and what violates it.

In summary, many of the factors working against our knowing

how to parent are a result of our unique position in time and culture. We are not part of a culture that dictates the way things are done. We question many things as we look for value and meaning in our lives. And we live in isolation from children and more experienced parents who can share with us what children are like. We are also influenced by a cultural tendency towards distrust of nature and the desire to control nature with the mind. We tend to be unaware of the fact that children have a completely different consciousness from adults.

Lack of Support for Mothering

Compounding the dilemmas faced by parents today is the changing nature of family life. An increasing number of women find themselves being single mothers, forced economically to juggle one or more jobs in order to make ends meet. Many other women today enter marriage and motherhood later in life, having already completed undergraduate or even graduate degrees and/or having been in the workforce for several years. Today's economic situation often requires incomes from both parents to maintain high mortgages and the lifestyles to which they have become accustomed – and not many people want to sacrifice financial comfort for their children.

But even without economic necessity, some women prefer to work for relatively low wages and pay childcare rather than be home day after day with their child or children. Why has it become so difficult for many women to be with children? The answer lies partly in the changing nature of our society. In rural yesteryear, life for women centered around survival tasks that took most of the day – gardening and canning, washing and ironing, baking and cooking, sewing, chopping wood, or other farm chores. The children tagged along, helping their parents as soon as they were able, but life never centered around them.

To expect a thirty-seven-year-old Ph.D. candidate, or a woman who has had an exciting career, to be fulfilled spending her days in an apartment with a two-year-old is idyllic but hard to find in reality. In the nuclear or subnuclear family, far too much energy gets focused on the child because he or she is the most interesting subject around (try getting excited about cleaning the kitchen floor!). But after a time many mothers find themselves getting 'cabin fever'. It becomes increasingly difficult, both emotionally and intellectually, to be home day after day with this child because there is a lack of adult stimulation and lack of perceived value.

The wide variations in family life today were brought home to me when I was a midwife offering home birth and delivery at an urban birth center in Dearborn, Michigan, USA. I got to know families from all ends of every spectrum! There were recent immigrants who were still trapped in 'biology as destiny': they were exhausted by having babies every year, yet their husbands wouldn't let them use birth control. But there were also American women who were having their sixth and seventh babies. They felt that children were the jewels in their crown – they were not only having a lot of them, but they were often home schooling them, as well. They didn't feel as if they were sacrificing themselves, but seemed genuinely fulfilled in their roles as wives and mothers. For the most part, these women seemed to have a strong religious faith that still infused all areas of their lives (most were Mormons, practicing Catholics, or fundamentalist Christians whose world view still held for them).

Women today who lack such a framework often find themselves trying to balance many conflicting forces. Many women don't want to feel as if they are sacrificing their own individuality to their marriage or their children. But they don't know how to balance this impulse with the often contradictory pulls of family and work outside the home. The women's movement in the USA helped women develop their individuality and fought for their right to be equal with men in the work force. But it disparaged women's place within the family and neglected family issues (this has not been the case with the women's movement in developing countries, which has helped women primarily by strengthening the family and women's and girls' positions in it).

When I was in my early twenties, I found myself a feminist outside of the main women's movement. Despite having been laughed out of the newly opened feminist book store in 1972 for asking for a book on pregnancy, I knew that women's reclaiming their bodies, health, and birth had to be key feminist issues! Women slightly younger than myself, who entered into careers right after college, were told that they could 'have it all.' But many found that they were pursuing a career and still doing the majority of the housework and tasks relating to raising the children – despite the men's movement and greater participation and support by many husbands and fathers. A realization arose that it might be healthier to 'have it all sequentially,' and the current generation of new mothers seems much more interested in 'phasing' and demanding changes in the workplace. They not only watched what their mothers went through trying to juggle family and full-on careers, but they experienced the stress and disappointment as children of parents who were too busy for family life. This change is also being reflected in some areas of feminist thinking, with leaders such as Betty Friedan advocating moving beyond gender issues to issues such as parenting, daycare, and quality of life for all members of the family.[11]

While it is my own conviction that support for mothering is a feminist issue, neither present society nor the feminist movement supports 'at-home mothers.' Mothering, like so much of 'women's work,' is both invisible and undervalued by our culture. Strong economic forces are still working against mothering, just as they did during World War II. At that time society needed women to enter the work force in droves. This goal was supported by the medical community's dictum to replace breastfeeding with the modern, scientific practice of formula feeding, for when women were not as bonded to their babies and not tied to feeding them, they were more willing to enter the factories. Similarly today, bottlefeeding, widespread use of epidural anesthesia, and other obstetrical practices work against maternal-infant attachment, enabling many women to blithely plan during pregnancy to return to work at six weeks postpartum (although some are shocked by the unanticipated strength of their feelings when it comes time to put their infants in daycare).

But sometimes returning to work is an economic necessity. Unlike countries in Europe, the United States does not value or offer extended paid maternity leave. In Denmark, for example, a woman is given six months maternity leave and can apply for another six to twelve months with benefits at 70 percent of the initial six-month period. This is a far cry from the six weeks an American woman receives – if her job even provides that much! A survey of executives reported in *Fortune* found that concern about their children was the biggest problem facing both men and women executives – perhaps with good reason![12]

With 55 percent of new mothers in the USA returning to the labour force in 1995 within twelve months of giving birth, there is a tremendous strain on the daycare system. The strain is being increased by the growing demand that mothers on welfare benefits go back to work. In New York City, there were 2.9 million children eligible for 22,000 Early Head Start positions for children under three; and for those with money, full-time care at the well regarded Bank Street Family Center for children six months to four years cost $16,000 in 1997, and there was a long waiting list.[13] A national study of daycare centers was conducted by the University of Colorado Economics Department in 1995. It found that many programs are unlicensed and most are staffed with untrained, underpaid adults. Apparently the report found that: 'Ninety-one percent don't have basic toys, books, hygiene or enough adults to respond to each child. A full 40 percent are downright hazardous, both to a child's health and safety as well as to her social and intellectual development.'[14]

Fortunately, society is finally having to consider how it can support families – both by supporting quality daycare for mothers who work outside the home and by supporting mothers who want to stay at home to do so. There aren't any good solutions yet, but at least the questions are being asked. On the grassroots level, a number of support groups for stay-at-home mothers have arisen in the past decade (see the list at the end of this chapter, and refer to Chapter 6 for what to look for when evaluating a daycare or preschool center). Whether a mother finds it the most wonderful thing in the world to stay home with the children, whether she is struggling to make a go of it, or whether she is trying to juggle a work schedule with a child's needs when he is sick, she needs to get more support for her mothering!

A Way of Seeing Children's Development: Children Are Not Tiny Adults!

One of the keys to avoiding many of the problems that accompany parenting today is to have an understanding of children's development. If we can understand the nature of the young child as it unfolds, we will be able to meet the child's real needs for balanced development of mind, body, and emotions.

Although children are obviously very different from grown-ups, our culture tends to treat them as privileged but miniature adults and to rush them through childhood. Many problems arise when we fail to realize how different a three-year-old is from a nine-year-old, a teenager, or an adult. That sounds obvious, but many parents take all their children to the same film in an effort to be fair, or they reason with their five-year-old as if his ease with words ought to translate into control of his actions in the future.

The hurried-child syndrome is apparent in all spheres of activity today. It is obvious physically that children's bodies are not mature, yet we try to speed up their development with baby walkers and baby gymnastics. Designer jeans and Barbie dolls for young children contribute to the ever younger entry into the teenage world of makeup, clothes, and dieting.

It is also obvious that children are not emotionally the same as adults. A young child can smile through his tears when given the simplest distraction. The basically happy four-year-old stands in sharp contrast to the brooding adolescent. How does the one turn into the other? It is clear that the emotional inner life only gradually develops the complexity and texture with which we are familiar as adults. Yet many parents try to develop their children's emotions and their awareness of emotions by naming, expressing, and even practicing emotions with them. And we tend to expose young children to situations that are far too powerful for them emotionally – notice the unhappy children in the theatre at the next film you attend!

It is obvious that children do not reason as adults do. They are able to come up with amazing statements, both about how the world works and about how something they shouldn't have done managed to happen. Logical thought and problem-solving ability are slow to develop. Very young toddlers lack 'object permanence' and will look for an object where they have repeatedly found it hidden rather than in the place where they have seen you put it. Children before the age of six lack the ability for what Piaget calls 'concrete operational thinking.' Rational thinking does not develop until age ten or eleven, as observed in Piaget's studies. So it has long been documented that the ability to reason and to think logically is a gradually unfolding power that children grow into. As adults we have forgotten what it was like to live in a nonlinear, nonsequential world. We expect to be able to reason with our children as soon as they are verbal. We reason with them about everything from their behavior and its consequences to why the sea is salty. And indeed, some five-year-olds show great ability to conduct such conversations with their parents – but they have learned it through imitating years of that type of interaction with their parents. Young children do not yet think rationally, and reason has little impact on changing their behavior.

Similarly, we offer lengthy scientific explanations as answers to children's questions, when a direct experience of something similar or an image that can live and work in their imagination would be much more satisfying to them. Rational explanations are like giving a hungry child stones instead of bread. Elkind points out that when young children ask questions like, 'Why does the sun shine?' they are really asking about purpose rather than mechanics and are much more nourished by an answer like, 'To keep us warm and to make the grass and the flowers grow' than a lecture on thermodynamics.[15]

The Child's Changing Consciousness

Differences in physical, emotional, and mental capacities between children of various ages and adults are easy to recognize, though they are often ignored. Differences in consciousness are equally apparent when we observe different-aged children's awareness of themselves and their surroundings. For example, the infant has what can be called 'participatory consciousness,' with no differentiated sense of self and other. Between the second and third years a major change in consciousness occurs with the development of memory and the first saying of the word 'I.' This change is the reason most people can't remember very much before the age of three. Most young children are fairly dreamy, living in a stream-of-consciousness state that follows whatever comes into awareness without adult concern about intentionality and 'task completion.' If you send a four-year-old to get ready for bed by himself, you can expect to find him playing with the toothpaste or the water when you join him. Young children have a completely different orientation to time and space. They live in the present, without adult perceptions of the past and future. Hence, they find waiting so hard and don't understand 'ten minutes' or 'three days' when told they must wait that long.

The achieving of adult consciousness is a gradual process. It does not happen at birth or age eight or even age fifteen. The preschool child, elementary-aged child, adolescent, and adult are very different – they perceive the world differently, think, learn, and feel differently. We can call the gradual process of achieving adult consciousness incarnating, which literally means 'coming into the body' or into earthly life. This incarnating process is an important one, for, if it does not occur, the person remains childlike, not fully able to seize hold of life on this earth. This process unfolds according to its own natural order and time and should not be either rushed or hindered.

If we recognize that the process of incarnation is a gradual one, we will interact with and teach children differently at different ages. For example, the preschool-aged child is centered in the will and in the limbs, in movement. The tremendous growth of the first seven years is accompanied by nearly constant movement as muscles and bones grow and coordination is gradually achieved. During these years the child learns primarily through repetition and movement and by imitating everything around her. Sitting still for long periods is unhealthy if not impossible for the young child, who desires to experience everything through her body.

The primary-school-aged child is obviously still growing physically, but his 'center of gravity' is shifting to the feeling sphere. As the emotions mature between ages seven and fourteen, the child learns with the greatest enthusiasm when a picture is given of what life was like in ancient Greece or on the American frontier. Artistic or imaginative presentations of topics taught in school appeal to this child and make them easy to learn and to remember. Instead of being centered in the movement of the limbs, as was the young child, the child between seven and fourteen is centered in the 'rhythmic system' of the breathing and the heartbeat. This means that music, which always involves rhythm and often involves the breath, (as in singing or playing a wooden recorder), is especially important for the child in the middle years. The breath and heart are also associated with emotions, which we can see in the way our breathing and heartbeat change when we are excited or afraid. Thus artistic and imaginative presentations engage this aged child.

Not until puberty is the child really centered in the head, in the sense of exercising his newfound capacities to analyze and criticize the world. Certainly major changes are still going on in the body with the maturing of the sexual organs, and the adolescent's emotions can also seem overwhelming at times. But rational and abstract thinking is the exciting new element, which now needs to be engaged by subjects such as the proofs of analytical geometry or the laws of physics. Similarly, an ability to see causes and patterns emerges for the first time, so that courses such as 'Trends in Western Civilization' are also vital to the high-school student. It is during these years that independent judgment begins to be born.

With the gradual maturing of the body, emotions, and thinking, the vehicle is ready for the person to assume the responsibilities of adult life. The traditional age of twenty-one as the age of majority coincides with Rudolf Steiner's perception that the will (movement, imitation) dominates development between birth and age seven, the feelings between ages seven and fourteen, and the thinking from ages fourteen to twenty-one. At age twenty-one the body, emotions, and thinking are ready for further stages of adult development.

Steiner was one of the first to share this perception that the human being is threefold in nature, consisting of thinking, feeling, and willing. If we are truly to understand the growing child, we must understand how these three aspects shift in dominance and how they influence the child's consciousness during different stages of development.

Whose Consciousness Is Changing?

Steiner also discussed the incarnating process in terms of who or what is ready to be responsible at age twenty-one (not that twenty-one-year-olds always behave responsibly!). Once the body, emotions, and thinking have reached a certain level of maturity, what Steiner calls the *Ego* can live out its own biography without guidance from the parents. Steiner does not use the term Ego as Freud did, but uses it to mean our unique individuality, or *I*. He perceived the human being as having an individuality that is capable of breaking the bounds of stimulus-response mechanisms and manifesting the unpredictable: free behavior and the possibility of fulfilling a particular destiny on earth.[16] This individuality has been variously described and named by the great religions and by psychology as the self, I, ego, spirit, observer, or consciousness. By whatever name, it is this presence that is felt so strongly in the newborn child and that evokes feelings of awe and wonder in all but the most jaded souls.

Rudolf Steiner speaks of this presence as the spirit, or I, of the human being and asserts that it is in a continuing process of incarnating (coming into the physical body) that is only in its beginning stages at birth. The spirit at birth is, in a sense, hovering around the body, loosely connected with it, and gradually, over the course of development to maturity, becomes more and more the master of (and slave to) the body. Perhaps you have had the experience of walking into a room where a newborn is sleeping and wondering how the room can feel so filled by such a tiny creature sleeping over in the corner. This individuality is present from before birth, which explains the feeling many parents have of a child wanting to come to them around the time of conception or the perception that a pregnant woman has that this second baby is certainly going to be different from the first. Perhaps the glow that we experience around a pregnant woman is really the being of the child that we are vaguely sensing.[17]

Steiner believes that the child is a knowing, spiritual being. Whether or not you have ever thought of children (or yourself) in this way, you have no doubt had the feeling that your children are their own people, not copies of siblings or extensions of you. Often it is not until parents have more than one child that they experience how different children can be. They seem to bring their uniqueness with them when they come, and we have to adjust our parenting accordingly. Perhaps you have had a sense of your own individuality at important moments of decision when you needed to be 'true to yourself.'

Even if the language of this discussion doesn't match your vocabulary, the phenomena of the incarnating process are still observable: the progressive mastery of physical processes as they come under the young child's control and the simultaneous narrowing and focusing of the child's initially diffuse consciousness. These phenomena will be explored further in the next chapter.

How Children Learn in the First Seven Years

The child between birth and age seven experiences the world primarily through her body. The senses are completely open, without filters or buffers, beginning with the moment of birth. The newborn continues to experience each sensation with her entire body and being. This is easy to see in the infant, who is all hunger or the pain in her stomach, or all the blissful sensations of nursing that cause her eyes to roll back and her toes to curl. The three-year-old is also much more open to impressions of the world coming through the senses than is an adult. We can even observe that children's eyes stay open longer between blinking than do an adult's.

Two things are happening through sense impressions from birth through age seven. One is that the child's growth and development are being shaped by the impressions she takes in, just as a sculptor might work with clay. This phenomenon does not occur very often with adults, who are less open and responsive to the environment than young children, but we can see a similar phenomenon in the molding of the features that the elements of light and weather etch into the face of a seaman or farmer.

This 'sculpting' effect of impressions on a young child's developing organs was pointed out by Rudolf Steiner in the early 1900s, and was not meant to be taken metaphorically. Current research has demonstrated that this is physically true for the young child's brain, which is still forming, not just growing larger:

'Only 15 years ago,' reports the Families and Work Institute in the just-released study 'Rethinking the Brain,' 'neuroscientists assumed that by the time babies are born, the structures of their brains [had been] genetically determined.' But by last year researchers knew that was wrong. Instead, early childhood experiences exert a dramatic and precise impact, physically determining how the neural circuits of the brain are wired.[18]

What happens is that at birth, only the primitive brain stem is fully functional. It has been estimated that the higher functioning cerebral cortex contains about 100 billion neurons and 50 trillion connections (synapses) at birth. In the first months, the number of synapses increases twenty times, to more than 1,000 trillion. This process of synaptogenesis, together with myelination (or insulation) of nerve pathways, forms an interactive process with the environment: experiences help certain parts of the brain to 'come alive' and certain pathways to strengthen, while others, which are either not used or which are affected by stress and trauma, fade away. Dr. Bruce Perry of Baylor College of Medicine Texas, USA states: 'Experience may alter the behavior of an adult, [but it] literally provides the organizing framework' for the brain of a child.[19]

The second thing the child is doing through sense impressions is learning about the world. Through the body the baby learns about near and far, attainable and unobtainable, as when she learns that the wooden ring can be grasped, but the brightly shining moon cannot. As she begins to learn the names of things, memory, language, and thinking develop so she can give expression to her own and the world's emerging complexity. When the child reaches age three and beyond, what is taken in with the senses is also transformed and comes out again in the creative play and imagination of the young child.

The child's major task in this first year is taking control of the body. Sitting, crawling, and walking are quickly followed by running, jumping, climbing, and other feats of dexterity as fine and gross motor coordination increase. Everything is done for the first time – using a shovel, sewing with a needle, cutting with a scissors – the list is infinite – and then it is done over and over again. The child loves to move and to imitate, learning through doing something along with someone else or after seeing it done. And the young child loves repetition, hearing the same story over and over or playing the same circle game, no matter how simple or boring it may seem to an adult.

The young child is also learning about the world emotionally, learning the fundamental lessons about trust and attachment, and later lessons about sharing and consequences. It has long been known that babies and young children in institutions where they are denied the love of a primary caregiver suffer 'failure to thrive syndrome' and can die, even though their physical needs are being taken care of. Now photographs of PET scans of the brains of Romanian orphans, who have been institutionalized from shortly after birth, show that the temporal lobes, which regulate emotions and receive input from the senses, are nearly quiescent.[20] Such children suffer emotional and cognitive problems resulting not only from a lack of stimulation, but also from a lack of love and bonding.

The baby is love. Bonding is less a process of babies loving their parents, because children will love even parents who abuse them, but of parents establishing the connection that will enable them to make room in their busy lives for another being who needs attention twenty-four hours a day! Children enter the world with a great deal of love and trust. They are not yet able to perceive good and bad, but take everything as good and appropriate to absorb and unconsciously imitate.

Our Task as First Teachers

One of our primary tasks as our children's first teachers is to provide them with impressions of the world that are appropriate for them to copy. This means guarding and protecting them from sensory overload in a world of urban frenzy, and surrounding them with experiences that teach them about the world in a gentle way by letting them do things directly themselves and later act them out in their play.

We also need to strive ourselves to model appropriate behavior – that our emotions are under control with our children, that we don't spank them while admonishing, 'Don't hit!' and so forth. Our actions speak louder than our words with the young child, who cannot help but imitate. Through us, children learn whether or not their initial love and trust in the world was well founded.

Another of our main tasks is to understand our children's physical, emotional, and mental development so we can guard it and let it unfold without hindrance. No one would want to stop a child from walking, but it is also something we don't have to worry about teaching the child. The child will walk when she is ready, as expression of her mastery of her own body – an achievement of verticality in the face of gravity that has kept her horizontal for so many months. There is a task for us – to guard, to protect, to understand, to share, and to enjoy with the child the unfolding of his or her abilities. We can also do things to enhance abilities by providing an example and allowing the young child to express them freely from out of his own being. We can also note discrepancies in development and areas at risk and take gentle steps to help assure balance. But with the young child much more is achieved indirectly through example and imitation than head-on through lessons.

No matter what our family situation or lifestyle, we as parents are our children's first teachers. The importance of what they learn in the home and through their relationship with us cannot be underestimated. By understanding how children develop and some things we can do to help their balanced and healthy growth – physically, mentally, emotionally, and spiritually – we will not only help our children, but also increase our own enjoyment and growth as parents.

Trusting Ourselves

Sometimes we can become overwhelmed as parents when we contemplate the momentous nature of the task before us. Contradictory advice from books and friends can leave us feeling frustrated or annoyed. Becoming painfully aware of the times we fall short of our own ideals can be downright discouraging!

As a first-time mother, I fell into most of the pitfalls of mothering today. Although I had prepared myself for labour and delivery and my first child's birth went smoothly enough, parenting (and boys) were a gigantic mystery to me. Fortunately, children are resilient, and my son has developed into a fine man despite my confusions and shortcomings. But I've realized through the years that much frustration and grief could be avoided by keeping in mind a few basic principles.

1. *We need to accept who we are and build up the support we need.* Today there are as many lifestyles and possibilities as there are people. Not working outside the home when your children are young, managing a home business, working flexible hours, having your mate be a househusband, living communally, inviting grandma to live with you, going back to work when the baby is six weeks or six months old – all of these approaches have their difficulties and rewards. No matter what you do, you will find you need and deserve support.

    The real difficulty comes when we are doing something that we don't want to be doing. For example, if we must work when we want to be home or if we are staying home when it is driving us crazy, then our parenting will tend to be influenced by guilt, resentment, and a whole range of other emotions. We need to make our best choices at each moment. We can't always have what we feel would be ideal, but we can actively do the best with the options as we see them.

    In my own life, I ran Informed Homebirth out of my home and lived with other adults and children when my children were young, so I had support to be a midwife or to write *Special Delivery* without overly disturbing my children's lives. This situation brought other complications along with it, but I am grateful for the parenting support I received.

2. *We need fathers to become actively involved with children.* Fathers need support for their fathering, not for babysitting while mother steps out for a few hours. When both parents assume responsibility for care of the children, everyone benefits – especially the children. The different styles in parenting and their importance have been wonderfully explored in the book *Mothering and Fathering: The Gender Differences in Child Rearing* by Tine Thevenin. As a professor of psychiatry at Yale

University, Connecticut, USA, aptly stated, 'Even when they are the primary caregivers, fathers do not mother.'[21]

In addition to developing their own nurturing aspect and becoming more active with the children, fathers need to support mothers in their mothering. This support is partly financial, but it is also emotional. Fathers need to be sure they are actively involved with and in harmony with their wives concerning basic issues of discipline and parenting styles. This includes actively supporting the mother with trite-but-true statements such as, 'You heard your mother,' or 'Don't talk back to your mother,' when necessary.

In single-parent families, support needs to come from a wider circle of friends and social agencies. The parent (most often the mother) not only needs other significant people in the child's life, but also needs the perspective that another adult can provide for her parenting and relationship with the child. Perhaps the most important thing a single parent can do is to find or create those connections with other adults that can keep her (or him) from being so single in her parenting. Single parenting is a momentous task and involves special stresses and needs.

3. *We need a true understanding of children and their world.* When we have an understanding of children's real developmental needs, we can respond to them in ways appropriate for their age level that can lead to their balanced development. In my own floundering as a first-time mother, I turned to a US parenting course called 'Effective Parenting', but found that they were really geared to the child who was six or older. The instructor said, 'Well, try these things with the younger child as well to start building up good habits.' But it was clear to me that parenting a two-year-old was of a completely different order of magnitude and required something entirely different.

When I began studying Rudolf Steiner's indications for Waldorf education and child development, lights began to go on. For example, I had three children but still hadn't realized that up to the age of six they learn primarily through imitation! It seemed so obvious once I had read it. Why hadn't I thought of that? I found in Steiner many things of that nature – and many other things that made no sense whatsoever on first reading. But I approached the ideas with an open mind and in a pragmatic way. Could I observe the same things? Did this new approach improve the situation? I found that Steiner's understanding of the developing human being provided me with ways of seeing children that made a difference. When I saw children in those ways, suddenly everything worked: home life became more harmonious; I was able to enjoy young children and relate to them more confidently; I was even able to become an early childhood teacher, something that I never would have foreseen under other circumstances.

4. *We need to trust the natural process of development and not interfere with it.* By understanding a child's physical, mental, emotional, and spiritual development, we will be able to avoid doing things that are appropriate for a child at one stage of development but can possibly be damaging for a younger child. Just as children need to crawl before they can walk (to establish the neurological pattern), so we need to let children be children and unfold according to their own inner timetable, which always demonstrates both pattern and individual differences. If we see each child as a unique individual, we will be able to do things to enhance gifts and to work on weaknesses with a view toward a balanced development of thinking, feeling and physical abilities.

5. *We need to trust ourselves and our children and to let go of guilt.* Because we usually live isolated from young children and other families before starting our own, we don't have much knowledge about parenting. The discrepancies between expectations and reality are often shocking to new parents. I know when I was pregnant for the first time I felt that I would never put my child in preschool because no one could possibly do as good a job as I would. So I was discouraged when I found my two-year-old and I at constant odds at home and so put him in preschool where he was the model child. At that point it seemed that anyone could do a better job than I!

As mothers we tend to feel that 'it's all our fault.' Naturally,

I did things differently with my third child than with my first, based on my increased experience as a mother and my increased understanding of young children. If I hadn't done things differently, maybe I could be accused of not having grown. But it is fruitless to feel guilty for what I did earlier—because I was doing the best I could at the time! If we can see parenting as part of our own inner growth and development and see our children as unique individuals with their own personalities and lives to live, we will be less likely to fall into feelings of guilt. The problem with guilt, aside from being bad for your health, is that it takes you out of the present moment where your child lives and where you need to see and act clearly.

6. *We need to trust our children as individuals.* We are not the only ones participating in our children's development. They also have something to say about it, albeit not consciously! If this were not so, how could children growing up in the same family be so radically different? Each child is unique, neither merely the sum of its experiences in the family, nor the product of our skill as parents. Sometimes it is only when they have a second child that parents realize how different children can be and how they help create what happens to them.

   You can neither take all the credit nor all the blame for how your child turns out. We cannot consciously select the children who come to us, which is no doubt a blessing. Our task is to do our best, and trust in the best. We need to trust our children to be resilient, to be able to heal, to be terrific people despite our flawed efforts and our most regretted actions. We can, however, strive to help each child's experience (and our own) be as positive and rewarding as it will be varied.

7. *We need to value our parenting.* There is a way in which no one can do a better job than you of raising your child. No paid caregivers, however skillful and loving, can feel as much excitement as you do over your baby's every accomplishment. Parents have a unique involvement with their offspring that is nourishing to the child. Especially in the first year, the child's connection with the mother is so strong that she needs to be

close to the mother and frequently held. Taking a child under three out of the home and putting her in a group situation is stressful for the child – and many children will have been in several such situations by the time they are three.

Not everyone can stay home with their children in the first three years, and childcare options are discussed in Chapter 6. But we need to reject the notion that it's all the same. What the child experiences before the age of three has a tremendous effect on him. 'Quality time' is not the same as the everydayness of being together. Let's neither glorify nor undervalue it.

Recommended Reading

(Because many of these titles are difficult to find, first check the catalogs of the mail order services listed in Appendix A, or see if your local bookstore can order them.)

The Incarnating Child by Joan Salter (Hawthorn Press). An excellent book covering conception through the age of two by the founder of the Gabriel Baby Centre in Australia. Steiner-oriented. Highly recommended.

Miseducation: Preschoolers at Risk by David Elkind (Knopf). Discusses the personal and cultural reasons parents and preschools 'miseducate' young children and what is age-appropriate for them.

Mothering and Fathering: The Gender Differences in Child Rearing by Tine Thevenin (Avery). Increase your understanding of why you and your spouse/relatives/and 'the experts' may often be at odds in your approaches to parenting. Honors both the male and female principles that both parents bring to the child and family.

Mothering with Soul by Joan Salter (Hawthorn Press). Shares the experiences of mothers at the Gabriel Baby Centre who are exploring 'raising children as special work.' Steiner-oriented.

Natural Childhood by John Thomson, et al (Gaia Books). An excellent holistic and practical guide to child development by several Waldorf and other writers (this author served as a consultant on the North American edition).

The Spiritual Tasks of the Homemaker by Manfred Schmidt-Brabant
(Temple Lodge). A short and valuable essay by the chairman of
the General Anthroposophical Society and one of the organizers
of the annual 'homemaker's conference' at the Goetheanum in
Dornach, Switzerland. He invites all of us to bring spiritual
knowledge and vision to the career of 'carer for home and
family.'

Resources for Aware Parenting

Association of At-Home Mothers, 406 E. Buchanan, Fairfield, IA
52556. Provides 'practical information, inspiration and support
for mothers at home and those who would like to be.'
Memberships, quarterly journal (*At-Home Mothering*), and
resource catalog.

The Compleat Mother, an excellent quarterly journal on pregnancy,
birth, and breastfeeding. From P.O. Box 209, Minot, ND 58702.

Fathers' resources: The Fatherhood Project (www.fatherhoodproject.org);
the National Center for Fathering (www.fathers.com); the National
Fatherhood Initiative (www.fatherhood.org).

FEMALE (Formerly Employed Mothers at the Leading Edge) is a
support and advocacy group with more than fifty chapters
nationwide, a monthly newsletter, and other resources. P.O. Box
31, Elmhurst, IL 60126.

Mothering, award-winning magazine published six times per year
from P.O. Box 1690, Santa Fe, NM 87504. Everyone needs
Mothering.

National Association of Mothers' Centers, 336 Fulton Ave.,
Hempstead, NY 11550. (800/645-3828). Provides nationwide
information on how to locate or start a mothers' center.

The Peridot, P.O. Box 97, Gainesville, Fl 32602. This quarterly
journal on Waldorf approaches to parenting and education is a
real bargain, full of great articles!

Welcome Home, monthly journal from Mothers at Home, 8310A
Old Courthouse Rd, Vienna, VA 22182. 1-800-783-4MOM;
www.mah.org.

Work-at-home moms can find support at www.WAHM.com.

Resources for Aware Parenting in the UK

FathersDirect. National information centre on Fatherhood. Herald House, Lamb's Passage, Bunhill Row, London EC1Y 8TQ
Tel no: 0845 634 1328
www.fathersdirect.com. Email: mail@fathersdirect.com

Full Time Mothers. A UK organisation supporting mothers who wish to stay at home. PO Box 186, London SW 3 5RF.
www.fulltimemothers.org. Email: info@fulltimemothers.org

Juno, an excellent quarterly magazine for parents wishing to explore Steiner/Waldorf approaches to family life. PO Box 592, East Grinstead, West Sussex RH19 3AQ.
www.junomagazine.com Email: editor@junomagazine.com

Steiner Waldorf Schools Fellowship. Lists courses on parenting, kindergarten teacher training and school teacher training and contacts for Schools, Kindergartens and Steiner Parent and Child groups around the UK. Kidbrooke Park, Forest Row, East Sussex RH18 5JB Tel no. 01342 822115
www.steinerwaldorf.org.uk. Email: mail@swsf.org.uk

CHAPTER 2

Receiving and Caring for the Newborn

What Was Birth Like for Your Baby?

The French obstetrician Frederick Leboyer helped the world to understand the affront to the baby's senses on going from womb to world. Is it possible to gain further insight into the baby's experience of this event, which many psychologists hold to be so primal? In *Birth Without Violence*, Leboyer ironically describes birth as a life-and-death struggle with the mother, who is like a monster needing to be overcome.[1] While this may have been his experience, which he was able to recall through work with an analyst, it is by no means everyone's experience. The birth experience is as individual as we ourselves are, and natural birth is not as traumatic for the baby as doctors have presumed. In fact, research by Lagercrantz and Slotkin has shown that the catecholamines (enzymes associated with stress response) in a newborn's blood are actually part of an adaptive mechanism that helps the baby withstand low levels of oxygen without damage and start to breathe on its own.[2] These studies explain why cesarean babies, who are born without the 'stress' of contractions and the passage through the birth canal, often have more trouble breathing and adapting to life outside the womb.

Birth is physiologically sound and all right for your baby. This is even more true the more aware you are of the baby's experience. What can we intuit of his or her experience? Let us envision what life is like in the womb, an environment that protects the baby from many of the influences of ordinary life. The uterus, strongest muscle in the human body, is rounded, and its concave shape serves to concentrate forces so the baby can develop (just as a magnifying glass focuses the rays of the sun). Indeed, a metaphor that has been used to describe the incoming spiritual being is 'like a falling star that then becomes a sun glowing in your womb.'[3] The baby is surrounded by nine layers of substances, including the waters, membranes, uterus, muscles, tissue, fat, and skin. At birth the baby truly becomes an earthly being, coming fully under the forces of gravity. Thus birth can be seen as an unveiling process, a taking away of the sheaths that have surrounded the developing baby inside the womb.

The Experience of Space, Time, and Gravity

In the womb the baby has a different experience of space, time, and gravity from what it experiences after birth. The baby's experience of physical space changes dramatically throughout pregnancy and birth. At first it floats like an astronaut in inner space, supported by the waters and tied to the mother through the umbilical lifeline. In the uterine space the baby is hidden and safe in the fetal position. As the baby continues to grow it feels the mother surrounding and protecting it and has its first possibility of body awareness through encountering the resistance of the uterine walls. Then space becomes more confining, making movement less free as the months go by. Sometime around the eighth month the baby usually finds that it cannot get out of the head-down position due to gravity and the heaviness of the head, so there it stays until delivery, approximately ten lunar months from the time of conception.

With the birth process, the baby's experience of physical space again changes. It goes through a narrowing process as contractions make its space smaller and propel it through the birth canal. Then suddenly the baby is born into seemingly endless space, where it encounters nothing when it flails its arms and legs. This is why giving a warm bath, holding a baby's arm, or swaddling it can be so consoling for a newborn or a young baby. Having been used to the security of surrounding touch, babies need to be reassured by touch after they emerge from the womb.

Turning next to the baby's experience of gravity, we bring to mind Archimedes' discovery that an object floating in water has about 1/50 its usual weight. Thus, the baby in the womb is protected from too strong a dose of the earthly influence of gravity, but suddenly becomes about fifty times heavier at birth![4] Imagine yourself floating in a warm swimming pool when someone pulls a huge plug and you suddenly find yourself lying on the concrete bottom, helplessly moving your arms and legs, and unable to get up. At birth the baby truly becomes an earthly being, experiencing the full force of gravity. Indeed, it must spend the next year gradually overcoming the forces of gravity so that it can hold itself upright in balance between the forces of heaviness and lightness.

Birth brings with it not only an experience of gravity, but also the experience of time. Although a baby seems passive to the course of birth and when it will be born, in fact labour seems to start through an interaction of the fetal and maternal hormones. To the extent that there is a spiritual reality hidden within real astrology (not the horoscopes in the daily paper), it makes a difference when one is born, and the time should not be chosen according to the attendants' convenience. It may be that we choose the planets and stars and those influences that will enable us optimally to take hold of and live out our destiny on earth. I don't know, but I think this possibility is more valid than the practices of inducing labour because the doctor has a golf game, or setting a 'convenient' date for a scheduled cesarean.

Birth as an Experience of Temperature and Breath

We have seen that birth also brings the baby's first experience of temperature change. As warm-blooded creatures, we feel good only within a narrow range of internal body temperature. A low-grade fever makes us feel out of sorts, and a high fever results in our being unable to distinguish reality: we become delirious and unable to move. People who lose their body heat and experience hypothermia also lose their relationship with reality and often die from making decisions based on delusions.

Thus we see that only within a narrow range can our 'I' be in right relationship to the outer world. Steiner calls the circulating blood and other elements that maintain our bodily warmth the 'warmth organization,' which gives our consciousness the possibility of controlling our body and our emotions. The 'I' cannot interact properly with the external world when our internal body temperature becomes too high or too low.

The change in temperature from womb to room is a cold shock for the baby. When you are in a shower that suddenly runs out of hot water and turns icy cold, you inhale sharply and then usually voice a loud complaint. The baby does the same thing when thrust from womb to world. It responds by drawing inward and taking in the first breath, so vital to the process of coming into the body and earthly life.

We can see in our own lives how cold tends to be 'incarnating,' or makes us feel strong and able in our bodies. Think how fresh and ready for work we feel on a crisp autumn day; we feel invigorated and ready to tackle all of the projects we've let slide over the summer. Heat, on the other hand, tends to be 'excarnating.' We find ourselves driven slightly out of our bodies and into sleep when we're in a room that is too warm, to give a simple example. We need equilibrium to be in right relationship with the world, and the baby especially needs to be helped to maintain a constant temperature, one that is slightly warmer than we adults prefer.

In addition to temperature, stimulation of the baby's skin plays a role in the first breath. The massaging of the baby's body by contractions and its passage through the birth canal help to start the breathing process. Changes in oxygen and carbon-dioxide levels as the placenta ceases to function also help trigger the first breath.

What happens with this first breath, in which the baby exchanges the water sphere for the air sphere? Many things happen physiologically as the lungs expand for the first time, the foramen ovale in the heart closes, and your baby changes from dusky gray to pink right before your eyes. But many things are also happening in terms of the incarnation process during this vital first breath. To understand them, let us first consider the nature of breath itself.

Breath, with its rhythmical in and out quality, is the mediator between a person's inner and outer worlds. It is the medium through which our emotions, or what Steiner calls soul life, are expressed. When we are afraid, we hold our breath; being happy is exhaled in laughter; contentment is expressed in a sigh. All emotions are expressed on the breath, which is the physical realm for the unfolding of our soul activity in the life of feeling.

With the first breath, inner emotional life begins, and the breath serves as the connection between the inner and outer worlds. With the first in-breath, the possibility exists for the soul life to enter into a deeper relationship with the body, a relationship it will keep until the last expiration.[5] Although the baby is both spiritually present and physically responsive to stimuli while in the womb, the soul cannot come into the body without the breath. Then the soul gives expression to our emotions through the breath as sound and speech. The breath thus forms the link between body and soul until death, when we breathe out the soul with the last breath. In fact, we incarnate and excarnate a little with each inhalation and exhalation, and many meditation practices focus on that still space between the inspiration and the expiration.

Everyone senses how important the first breath is for the baby. Those present at a birth tend to hold their own breaths until the baby breathes and pinks up. The baby is still receiving oxygen through the placenta, but we need to remember to keep breathing ourselves! The breath marks the true time of birth, for the first breath means that the baby has successfully completed the journey from fetus to newborn and accepted earthly life outside of the womb.

The Contraction of Consciousness at Birth

Birth involves a narrowing of consciousness for the baby from the dimensionless 'space' of eternity, or whatever you want to call it. As spiritual beings we are dimensionless, as 'large' as the whole spiritual world. From this limitless, macrocosmic existence we find ourselves bound to a physical body and born into the earthly realm of space, time, and gravity. Just as the baby's physical body passes through the narrowness of the pelvis and the birth canal, so the spiritual being experiences a narrowing of consciousness which culminates in the incarnation of the spirit and soul into a physical body.

The contraction of consciousness from the cosmic to the earthly is a dramatic event for the being who experiences it. Usually the cosmic or spiritual world is forgotten, though we feel echoes of it in myths and fairy tales. The Greeks described this threshold as the crossing of the River Lethe (or River of Forgetfulness), when we leave or enter this world. This forgetfulness allows us to have ordinary earthly consciousness and be full citizens of this planet, though at times we may sense a dim memory, feel a yearning for something that can guide us back to God or our original nature.

This passage from one level of existence to another is a very significant and holy time, and anyone who can maintain some awareness of what the baby is going through during this time is a real midwife for the baby. Karl König, the founder of the Camphill Movement for working with handicapped children and adults based on the indications of Rudolf Steiner, gives a detailed and highly recommended description of the baby's experience during pregnancy and birth that integrates a spiritual perspective with embryological development. In the book *Eternal Childhood*, he shows how the various stages of development of the baby inside the womb can be likened to the creation story in Genesis, with birth being like the expulsion from paradise into earthly existence, for suddenly the baby must 'work' for its food instead of all its needs being automatically provided for via the umbilical cord.[6]

König also states that scientists have shown that fetal movement decreases in the latter part of pregnancy, and he likens this to the baby being in a state similar to deep sleep. Birth thus can be seen as a transition from sleeping to waking (or daytime) consciousness, and he states, 'To the child the pains of labour are like the sound of trumpets calling the sleeper to awake and make ready.'[7] The earthly birth is at the same time like a spiritual death, just as physical death is simultaneously a spiritual birth or awakening (this is why some of my friends in the hospice movement refer to themselves as midwives for the dying).

The birth process thus involves both physical narrowing through the birth canal and a narrowing of consciousness for the being coming into this life. This densification of consciousness into matter can be a painful experience for the one who is coming into this life, which is so much more limited. Steiner says that the mother, if she consciously experiences the discomfort of labour rather than being anesthetized, is strengthened in her bond with the being of the child and has a much closer understanding and compassion for what the child is experiencing in the process of incarnation; others present can only try to hold it in their awareness.[8]

The process of birth is painful for the new being from only one perspective, for it is also a joyous participation in the pendulum swing between expansion and contraction that permeates all of life. As parents and birth attendants, we rejoice with this first breath, thankful that a new being, so full of promise, has decided to join humanity.

Pondering the tremendous threshold that birth involves can help us to better understand our children and ourselves. For a young child who has only recently crossed this threshold, the door to the spiritual world is not yet closed, as it is for most adults. The fact that young children still have access to the spiritual world helps to explain why they can 'see' things we can't and why true fairy tales, which are descriptions of the spiritual world and the incarnation process, are so nourishing to them (more on that in Chapter 8). Understanding this concept – that incarnation into earthly life is a gradual process – can clarify how we perceive our children, how we interact with them, and how we help them to realize their full potential.

Working with the perception that there is a vertical stream of knowing individuality as well as a horizontal stream of hereditary characteristics in each child can help in our parenting. It can help us to realize that, while we are important in our children's lives, they are unique individuals and not extensions of us. It can lend credence to the possibility that our children choose us as parents. The movie *Back to the Future* expressed elements of this idea in its comical portrayal of the main character's need to bring his parents together so that he could be born. If we are having particular difficulties with a child, it can provide the reassurance that we may be together for particular reasons and particular growth.

A view that takes into account the vertical stream can also help to explain certain behaviors, fears, or characteristics that children seem to bring with them rather than acquire from any experiences of which we are aware. For example, Steiner said that one explanation of particularly difficult children is that the 'fit' between the spiritual and material elements isn't quite right and is frustrating for the child.[9] One of our tasks as parents and educators, then, can be to help harmonize these two streams, without one dominating at the expense of the other. Being open to the possibility that there may be more going on than meets the eye helps to keep the spiritual potential open for the growing child.

Gentle Birth Choices

If you are in the position of still being pregnant while reading this book, you may want to consider the many options you have to optimize the birth experience for your baby, yourself, and your partner. Many parents are clear that they want the most natural birth possible, in an environment which honors the hard work of the mother and the sensitivity of the baby – hence the rise in LDRP rooms in hospitals in the US (where Labour, Delivery, Recovery, and Postpartum occur in the same room), birth centers, home births, and the midwifery model of care. But other mothers are so permeated by our culture's fear of birth as a terrible, medical event from which women need to be saved, that they are signing up for epidural anesthesia in record numbers. Such fear of pain and lack of trust in a woman's own body can be lessened by reading and attending childbirth classes.

Another thing that couples need to consider is the high rate of unnecessary cesarean births in this country. In the US the cesarean rate is among the highest in the world, without all the surgery having improved our ranking in perinatal mortality. It is important to be informed and prepared and to know that the choices you make do make a difference in your own and your baby's experience of birth. My books *Special Delivery* and *Pregnant Feelings* can provide you with valuable information and emotional preparation, emphasizing informed choice and making your own best decisions.

Many parents are also interested in ways to welcome their baby that take into account the newborn's experience of birth. *Gentle Birth Choices* by Barbara Harper provides an excellent discussion of various ways to welcome the newborn. Most couples insist that the baby be brought right up on the mother's stomach – often by the mother and the father themselves, whose hands can help the midwife or doctor in the final moments of birth. Skin to skin contact, low lights, immediate nursing, no separation – all of these provide the best possible welcome to earthly life for your baby.

On the other hand, if you really get into alternatives and plan to have a water birth, I'd like to include a few words of caution. Water is wonderful during labour – getting in the tub at 8 centimeters dilation can actually take about half the pain away! And if the mother is so comfortable she decides to stay in the tub, there is certainly no problem with the baby being born in the water – if he or she is immediately brought up onto the mother's stomach. But letting the baby swim around for a few minutes before bringing it up is, to my mind, as much of an intervention as many medical procedures, because it interferes with the normal birth process and this baby's efforts to become an earthly being and take its first breath. As a midwife, it is my experience that water births are very different from normal hospital births because no one can cut an episiotomy or run off with the baby. But they aren't very different from gentle home births in the mother's bed. I've experienced some lovely water births, and others where the mother was insistent on having a water birth and then discovered when she was pushing that she wanted the resistance of solid ground and the help of gravity. Each mother, each birth, and each baby are different, so please remain flexible in your planning!

With all the above discussion about gentle alternatives to standard birth in this country, what if your baby has already been born and the experience was less sensitive than you would have liked? All is not lost! While birth is a tremendously powerful experience and can have a profound effect on both the mother and baby (and their developing relationship), it is possible to become aware of and let go of psychological pain that may have been caused by the birth. If you were separated from your baby due to a cesarean section or other medical complication, you have not 'failed to bond' with your baby or done irreparable damage to his or her psyche. Bonding is an ongoing process that begins in pregnancy and occurs any time you recognize the other person as a being, not an object. It does not have one 'critical period' in humans as it does in animals. If your birth experience was less than optimal, recognize what your feelings and your questions are now, and then seek answers and help in moving through the growth process surrounding this experience. It can help to realize that you were as informed as possible and made the best choices you could at that time. The sooner you can heal and be in the present moment, the sooner you'll really be with your baby, who lives there.

Who Is This 'Intimate Stranger'?

You have known your baby intimately, 'from the inside out,' for nine months. And yet when you look into your newborn's eyes, you realize that she is her own person, and you may have the sense of a very ancient and knowing being who is both familiar and a stranger to you. Who is this child? What will his or her life be like? What an adventure, finding out!

Early in pregnancy, mothers are sometimes given an intimation about the being or name of their child, either through a dream of a child that they later recognize was this actual child, or through a sense of 'knowing' something about this person. This 'annunciation' occurred very dramatically to the Virgin Mary in the Bible, who was able to encounter the angel in full consciousness and to understand his message. I have found in asking mothers what, if anything, they knew about their unborn babies, that there will always be one or two in any group who were either aware of the moment of conception or were aware of a 'being' who wanted to come to them shortly before they became pregnant (fathers are also sometimes aware of this!). König describes this unseen process, of which we might be dimly aware:

> First the being of the child approaches the mother, and through this she finds the child's father. Later, however, the child's angel has a direct meeting with the mother's higher being and entrusts the child to her.... For most mothers this spiritual meeting remains subconscious, but its significance is a lasting one because from this meeting springs the well of the mother's love. This very special love which a mother has for her child, and which transcends all biological powers, is imparted to every woman when she meets her child's angel.[10]

This image seems to me to explain how and why a mother always loves and 'holds the highest picture of her child' and maintains hope, regardless of what the child or adult may do in life, because on some level she knows who he or she really is.

Take a few minutes to think back on anything you knew about your baby before he or she was born. What dreams did you have?

Was there something special about how your baby's name came to you? What did you sense from your baby's movements while inside your womb? It can be helpful to keep a journal of your observations and feelings during pregnancy and throughout your child's first years – it's a great adjunct to the typical 'baby book.'

The Sensitivity of the Newborn

The sensitivity of the newborn at birth was dramatically brought to awareness by Leboyer's work in the 1970s. Medical science had fallen into the belief that babies don't see, feel, or experience very much in the womb, during birth, or as a newborn. Leboyer himself said he had experienced three thousand deliveries before he realized that the newborn's cries were really made in distress.[11] Nowadays it is hard for any thinking and feeling person not to be aware of how vulnerable the senses of a newborn are to sight, sound, temperature, and all the other experiences of the world. Not only have scientists rediscovered that babies see, hear, and respond to so much more than previously thought, but recent studies on the brain have shown the extreme sensitivity of the newborn and infant. Research even indicates that the fetus in the womb is much more aware than was previously thought, a fact that should encourage parents to sing and talk to their unborn babies (but playing Mozart into special speakers laid on their stomachs so their children will get into Harvard is another example of our culture's spiritual materialism).[12]

More than seventy-five years ago, Rudolf Steiner spoke about the completely open senses of a baby and young child. In 1924 Steiner said, 'In the first part of his life ... the child is, so to say, altogether a sense organ. This we have to take very literally. What is the characteristic function of a sense organ? It is receptive to impressions from the environment. If something striking occurs near him – for example, a burst of anger – then the reflection thereof goes right through the child. It will affect even his blood circulation and digestive system.'[13]

A baby does not have the ability to filter out unwanted impressions as adults do when, for example, they read while the television is on. A baby is bombarded by everything in the environment, and its only escape is to go to sleep in order to 'digest' the constant flow of sensations. Steiner states: 'The child needs so much sleep because it is entirely sense-organ. It could not otherwise endure the dazzle and noise of the outer world. Just as the eye must shut itself against the dazzling sunlight, so must this sense-organ, the child – for the child is entirely sense-organ – shut itself off against the world, so must it sleep a great deal. For whenever it is confronted with the world, it has to observe ...'[14] Thus the newborn, coming from the womb to the world, needs special regard for the openness of its senses, not only at birth, but also in the months following.

Stimulating and Protecting Your Baby's Senses

Much has been written today about the importance of stimulating your baby's senses, and maternal deprivation studies in the 1940s of orphanages in Europe, showed that children in institutions who did not receive adequate stimulation from a primary caregiver failed to thrive, showing developmental lags that could not be made up later. In fact, the temporal lobes, which receive input from the senses and regulate emotions, were dramatically less active in institutionalized Romanian orphans who had experienced extreme deprivation in infancy compared to normal children.[15]

However, American popular psychology and business interests have interpreted 'infant stimulation' to mean that you constantly need to be stimulating your baby with bits of coloured plastic and flash cards. Rather than these artificial means, a baby needs the holding, rocking, talking, concern, and love of its mother or other primary caregiver in order to develop normally. More sensible child-development experts remind parents that infant stimulation is not something you need to do separately from caregiving.[16]

You will be providing most of what your baby needs for healthy development if you

1. touch or hold your baby often,
2. talk to him or her,
3. spend time face-to-face, making eye contact, and
4. generally respond quickly to fussiness or crying.

Stimulation of your baby's senses is important for development, but overstimulation can be detrimental. By understanding the sensitivity and needs of the newborn, you will gain confidence that you are providing your baby with the best possible start in life.

The Sense of Touch

Your baby is perhaps most sensitive to touch, the skin being our largest sense organ. The entire birth process is like a massage for the baby, stimulating its skin senses and getting it ready to breathe. The cold air hitting its skin at birth gives the baby its first sense of body definition, of inner and outer. This is in contrast to life in the womb, which is like being immersed in a warm bath.

Your baby's sensitive skin, which has only known water, will now be exposed to all of the elements of ordinary life. No wonder babies are so prone to rashes – it's quite an adjustment. The newborn's skin is so sensitive that you should avoid scrubbing it or using scented baby soaps, powders, and lotions, which can cause allergic reactions. A weekly bath with plain water is probably enough to keep your baby clean and sweet smelling, especially if you are careful to clean the folds of the neck and keep the baby's bottom clean and dry with frequent nappy changes. Advice on such matters as nappy rash, cradle cap, and skin rashes can be found in most books on baby care, including the Steiner-oriented *Guide to Child Health*, listed at the end of this chapter.

One of the best things for your baby is skin-to-skin contact, which is why many mothers like the baby to be put on their bellies immediately after birth, or why fathers sometimes take off their shirts to hold the newborn skin-to-skin. Not only are the tactile sensations reassuring for the newborn, but the smell of your skin and the beating of your heart are also reassuring for your baby. Joseph Chilton Pearce, author of *The Magical Child Matures*, points out that mothers instinctively hold their children more on their left sides, regardless of whether they are right- or left-handed; on the left side, your baby is in touch with your heartbeat, which he or she has heard throughout the pregnancy. Pearce states that it is important to re-establish that 'heart connection' after the birth.[17]

Touch remains important throughout a child's (and an adult's) life, and an increasing body of research from the University of Miami School of Medicine's Touch Research Institute in the US has shown that increased touch can help with immune function, stress, depression, and autism. One study showed that when premature infants were given a gentle 15-minute massage three times a week, they gained weight 47 percent faster, had better motion response, and were released from the hospital six days earlier than preemies who received the standard care of being touched as little as possible.[18]

Compared with other cultures, Americans are touch-deprived. Cross-cultural studies have shown that the United States has one of the lowest rates of casual touch in the world – about two times an hour – compared with Puerto Ricans, who have one of the highest rates, about 180 times an hour. Studies showed that French parents touch their children three times more often than American parents.[19]

It's a pity that so many of the 'givens' of modern child rearing (playpens, baby seats) serve to distance parents and their children and insulate the child from life-giving touch. Among the latest are the plastic baby carriers that the mother can carry from the car to inside the house (or even attach to the stroller) without ever touching the baby. It always amazes me to see a young mother awkwardly bending sideways over the handle of one of these reclining seats as she struggles to carry this heavy, bulky object off to her side. If she had her baby in her arms, she would be much more comfortable, and the baby would benefit from the reassuring warmth and tactile sensations of its mother's arms.

In her excellent book *Untouched*, Mariana Caplan reports that researcher James Prescott documented statistical evidence that the presence or absence of touch is not only the distinguishing factor between a healthy and well-adjusted individual or a violent one, but he also showed how cultural practices regarding touch are responsible for creating either violent or non-violent societies. He apparently developed the means to predict, with 80 percent accuracy, whether a culture would be violent or non-violent simply by looking at whether the infant was carried on the body of its mother or caretaker; when he added in whether or not adolescent sexual activity was permitted or punished, his system was 100 percent accurate.[20]

While babies need to be safely belted into special infant seats in the car, holding and carrying your baby in your arms at other times is better for both of you. But how will you ever get anything done? Here is where investigating the various types of slings and soft front carriers comes to the rescue by leaving your (or your husband's) hands free for other tasks.

However, a word of caution is necessary. The weight of the head and brain and the weakness of the neck place a lot of strain on the central nervous system. In many other cultures, the baby is not held vertically until she can hold her head up by herself. The Central and South American way of wrapping a young baby in a rebozo or shawl is illustrated in *The Incarnating Child*, and several sources for horizontal carriers, which can be adapted for older babies, are listed at the end of this chapter.

Something else to keep in mind about baby carriers is to be careful where you take your baby. With my first child I was eager to prove that giving birth was normal and babies were hardy, so I took my son to discount department stores when he was about a week old. Such places make me zingy, but I figured the baby would sleep through it. Now I would reconsider, understanding more about the openness of the newborn's senses and the special nature of the first six weeks of life.

Returning to the sense of touch, it is helpful to think about what kinds of materials you want to have touching your baby's skin and to choose fabrics that are soft, warming, and pleasurable against the skin. Natural fibers are especially beneficial because they breathe. If some kinds of synthetics make your skin crawl or make you feel like you're in an air-tight container, the effect is magnified for your baby. Not only do cotton, silk, and wool allow air to flow through the fibers, but wool wicks moisture away from the skin and keeps your baby drier than other fabrics. Hospitals have found that premature babies gain weight faster when they are placed on wool sheets, but no one knows why.[21] Steiner would say that natural fibers can actually contribute to the body's vital energy, whereas some synthetics rob the body of energy.

Department stores are increasingly carrying baby clothes made of natural fibers, and numerous natural clothing mail order catalogs exist. Alternatives to paper nappies include 'soakers,' which are worn over cloth nappies in place of rubber pants. Several brands are available in wool fabric, or it is easy to knit or crochet your own soakers. Cloth nappies admit air to lessen nappy rash; a nappy service is as economical and convenient as paper nappies, and it is more ecologically sound.

The Sense of Sight

When babies are first born they seem to have a 'quiet alert' phase for the first thirty to sixty minutes after birth. If you request that your baby not be given any eye prophylaxis until after this time (and then request a substitute for silver nitrate that is less burning to the newborn's eyes), you will find your baby beginning to look at you and respond to your voice, especially if you have talked or sung to your baby before the birth. Newborn's eyes focus best on objects that are about ten inches from their faces, about the distance between a nursing baby and its adoring mother's gaze! Researchers have found that babies respond best to patterns of light and dark resembling the human face. They therefore suggest putting a simple black and white drawing of a human face on the side of your baby's crib at eye level. While this may help parents feel that they are 'doing something' in terms of 'infant stimulation,' there is obviously no substitute for carrying and interacting with your infant and providing the soul contact that comes through the eyes when human beings look at one another.

Mothers all over the world tuck their babies into bed with them at night when they are small, and certainly while they are nursing. The American Academy of Pediatrics recently came out against 'co sleeping' because 50 babies died last year, but they didn't report if either partner had taken alcohol, sleeping medications, or any other drugs that increase drowsiness. Waterbeds obviously are not safe for co-sleeping. The benefits of sleeping with your baby include increased attachment and nighttime security for the baby. And it is certainly easier to nurse a baby in bed than to get up, go to another room and get the baby, and then sit up in a rocking chair and get up yet again to return the baby to his or her bed. Some researchers feel that sleeping in close proximity with your baby helps regulate her breathing and decreases the incidence of Sudden Infant Death

Syndrome (SIDS or Crib Death), which is also decreased if you put your baby to sleep on her back instead of her tummy. It's something you need to decide.

One of the advantages of having a bassinet or hooded basket for your newborn is that it provides a small, enclosed space for naps during the day – and gives you room to stretch out or be with your partner when you want to, without waking the little one. An innovative compromise in the US that allows the best of both worlds is the 'Arm's Reach Bedside Co-Sleeper,' a special three-sided bassinet that attaches to the side of your bed. Your baby is safely tucked in next to you and can still hear your breathing and feel your presence. The lack of a wall between your mattress and the baby's mattress makes it easy to reach your baby for reassuring or for nursing.

Bassinets may be draped with colored silk to filter the light coming to the baby in the early weeks. A combination of blue and pink or rose silk provides an especially soft light, and such pieces are available from several of the mail order catalogs listed at the end of this chapter. And having a special blanket made of natural cotton or silk can help to build up associations with sleep over the months and can help your older baby to settle into sleep when she is tired at night or at naptime. The clothing and the bed, together with the baby's skin, can be thought of as three 'sheaths' that protect the baby in its contact with the outside world.

Is it necessary to take such care with a newborn? Certainly not in the sense of survival. Babies are hardy creatures and can even survive the fluorescent lights and Muzak in a typical US premie nursery. But it is helpful for us to be aware of how completely open to outside influences a baby is. Burton White, in *The First Three Years of Life*, states that the baby in the first six weeks

> is generally unusually sensitive... It is perfectly normal for an infant to startle and cry at any abrupt change in stimulation during her first weeks of life. Such common reactions include a response to sharp nearby noises, or to jolts to the crib or bassinet, or to any rather sudden change in position, particularly when the baby has been inactive. A second, less dramatic indication of sensitivity at this age is the infant's avoidance of bright lights. A Phase I infant [birth to six weeks] will keep his

eyes tightly shut in a brightly lit room or when outside in the sun. In fact, he is much more likely to open his eyes and keep them open in a dimly lit room than in one at an ordinary level of illumination.[22]

So while it isn't 'necessary' to put silk over the baby's bed, it's good to be aware of just how sensitive your newborn is. Keep the room dimly lit and avoid bright lights or sun, so your baby will feel free to open up and explore the world at a level she can manage.

The Sense of Hearing

Just as bright lights cause a baby to 'close down,' loud noises will cause your baby to throw her arms and legs up in the startle reflex and begin to cry. While you'll want to avoid slamming the door or dropping things near your baby, this doesn't mean that you need to tiptoe around the house all the time. Your baby should become used to the natural sounds of your household and will learn to sleep through most of them.

It is good to focus on the quality of the sounds that reach your baby's ears. One measure of quality is loudness; another is harmony and rhythm. One of the most pleasing sounds to your baby is your voice. Not only does she start to recognize your voice and your partner's, but if you hum or sing, she will be especially soothed. Many parents like to make up a little song for their baby that they start singing when pregnant; they have reported that the baby pays attention and is soothed by the song and seems to recognize it, even right after birth. You don't need to be a talented musician to sing to your children – even someone tone deaf can hum! Getting into the habit of singing will help your child's language development and sense for music and rhythm, and it's a delightful way to share together.

The quality of aliveness that comes through the human voice when you sing to your baby is very different from a tape of soothing music for babies, or even a tape of your own singing. There is a nurturing quality in things that come from living sources that disappears when they are transferred to film, record, or tape. Children, especially, have come into this life to be alive and to grow. That which comes directly from a living source connects them with life on earth and the forces of growth, while that which is mechanical is further removed from them. Devices now on the market that simulate the noise of a car going fifty-five miles per hour may drive your baby to sleep, but what an affront to a newborn's senses!

It's obvious that your baby's experience is totally different when you or your partner is singing to her (however ineptly) from when a tape recorder is the source of the sounds. Not only is the experience of a real person's presence missing with recorded music, radio, and television, but also the quality of the sound is different, regardless of the complexity of the sound system. Steiner said that the quality of the sound from mechanical sources had a detrimental effect on the young child, both on the developing sensitivity of the ear and on the entire organism, because everything from each sense affects the entire body.[23] This is not so much the case with a child over the age of seven. Paying attention to the quality of the sounds your baby hears can only be beneficial.

The Sense of Warmth

The sense of warmth is especially important for your baby because her ability to regulate body temperature is not yet fully mature. Also, the newborn's head is so large in proportion to the rest of her body that the potential for heat loss is tremendous. Any outdoor person will tell you, 'If your feet are cold, put on your hat,' because most of the body's heat is lost through the head. Many hospitals in the US are beginning to put stockinette caps on babies in the nurseries, and it is a good idea to keep your baby's head covered throughout the first year. The baby's brain grows as much in the first year as it does throughout the rest of life, and for this process it is good to keep the head warm and protected.

A baby hat not only prevents heat loss, but keeps the fontanelles covered. The fontanelles are the 'soft spots' in the baby's skull. The one toward the back of the head is harder to feel, but the one toward the front can take up to eighteen months to close. During this time the brain and central nervous system are just beneath the fontanelle skin instead of being under the bony layer of the skull. The fontanelles should neither be bulging nor sunken when your baby is at rest (they will bulge when she cries). Many mothers have found that putting a hat on their baby has a calming effect when they are out in the world, for it seems to keep the baby more insulated from outside influences. I personally recommended fitted hats over the stretchy stockinette variety, because stockinette caps fit poorly and tend to always be riding up and need pulling down. This can be irritating to the newborn – perhaps too much like the birth process it has just come through!

The sense of warmth is very important throughout early childhood, for warmth is the vehicle through which the will penetrates the body, as we discussed in the last chapter. You can't judge if a child is warm enough by how you are feeling, or by what a verbal child will tell you. A good guide is whether or not the child's hands and feet are warm, because if an organ isn't warm, the will cannot penetrate it (so the young child who feels cold to the touch will naturally say, 'I'm not cold' since they're not present in the limbs to feel the cold).

Don't let your baby get overheated, but it is important to keep all the organs warm, especially the organs of digestion. This is why formula has to be warmed to body temperature and why traditional remedies for colic often involve warm wraps on the stomach. It is also why babies should always wear a vest or bodysuit (usually in addition to other clothing). Traditional mothers in warm climates always keep their babies covered, to protect them from the heat of the sun and to protect them from drafts. In the US we need to be especially careful when taking the baby into air-conditioned rooms to provide a blanket or clothing to cover the baby's skin and prevent its body warmth from dissipating.

What Can You Expect from Your Newborn?

While we can be open to the transcendent aspects of birth and of this new being, we are also very much interested in the physical aspects. Is the baby all right? Does she have all her fingers and toes? Look at all that hair, or lack thereof! And who is this 'intimate stranger' that you have known for nine months on the inside and now see for the first time?

One of the things you'll notice right away is that your newborn sleeps a lot, which is a blessing for the new mother, who needs to recover her strength and adjust to having a new baby. For decades, pediatricians in America told mothers to make sure their babies slept on their stomachs, for fear they might spit up and choke. However, it was then discovered that babies in most European countries – who were put to sleep on their backs – not only didn't die from choking, but also had a much lower incidence of SIDS or crib death. When the American Academy of Pediatrics launched a campaign to get mothers to make sure babies slept on their backs, the incidence of SIDS decreased here as well.

The special nature of the first six weeks is recognized by contemporary researchers. In *The First Three Years of Life* White states, 'The first four to six weeks of life seem more like a transitional period between very different modes of existence than a time of rapid development.'[24] He is referring to the obvious transition between womb and world, with its differences in breathing, eating, and so forth. We have also seen how this period is a tremendous transition in levels of consciousness for the child. Your baby and you both need for this transition time to be as peaceful and free of demands as possible.

Many cultures intuitively honor the openness of the newborn by setting aside forty days during which the mother and baby are 'confined to quarters' and taken care of by relatives or by women in the community who specialize in postpartum care. Recognizing how much in the 'other world' the baby still is, and how open emotionally the mother is to the creative power of the universe, can be honored by giving yourself time just to be together as a family in the special energy that surrounds birth. Because many young mothers live far away from their extended families, a whole profession of postpartum caregivers has arisen in the US and recently in the UK. These women, often called doulas from the Greek word for servant or slave, provide in-home postpartum support, attending to household tasks such as cooking and cleaning. In addition, such a woman can provide the new mother with advice on baby care and can help the experienced mother by caring for the older children. Practical advice for the postpartum period can be found in my books *Special Delivery* and *Pregnant Feelings*.

Reflex Responses

When your newborn is awake, you will observe many patterns of reflex behavior that will disappear as your baby gets older. At birth your baby has many more reflexes than he will have later in life. Animals, of course, have complex instinctual patterns of behavior that govern their entire lives. The human being is the most helpless of all mammals, and many of the reflex responses present at birth are later replaced by learned behavior and choice. For example, your newborn has a placing and a stepping reflex when the soles of the feet come in contact with a surface. But this disappears and must be replaced by learning to walk as a controlled act.

The grasping reflex is such that the newborn's hands are frequently clenched. However, when her hands are open, she will grasp an object as soon as it touches her palm. Whether she quickly drops it or holds onto it for several minutes, she seems oblivious to it and won't bring it to her mouth, touch it with the other hand, or look at it.

The Moro reflex is also called the startle reflex because your baby will bring up her arms and cry when she is moved suddenly through space or experiences a loud noise or jolt. This reflex worries some parents, but it is completely normal and will disappear within the first few months.

The rooting reflex assures that your baby will turn toward stimulation and start sucking, thus finding the breast and nourishment. Therefore, to prompt a baby to nurse, you should stroke one cheek rather than touch both cheeks as you guide the baby to the breast.

The asymmetrical tonic neck reflex means that when the baby is on its back, the same arm and leg will be extended and the head will look toward the extended arm (the so-called 'fencer's pose'). It also appears with the hand-to-mouth reflex, where the hand and leg are flexed on the face side.

These reflex behaviors will become more efficient and reliable through repeated use and will become coordinated through activities like bringing the fist to the mouth and sucking or gumming it. Such reflexes form the foundation elements of later intelligence and cease to be reflexive as the baby begins to be more 'present' and coordinated.

Control of the Body

Your baby's body is dominated by an inordinately large head and small, weak limbs. This is in marked contrast to the rest of the animal kingdom. I was greatly impressed by the opposite extreme of development with lambs: the lower halves of their legs are so well-developed at birth that they have the same feeling of sturdiness as the adult sheep's.

A baby's head is so developed and heavy that, when on her stomach, she will barely be able to clear the mattress with her nose for a moment or two. It takes several months for a baby to gain full head-neck control, and the head should always be supported when the baby is being lifted or held.

If your baby is on her back, she is incapable of rolling over or moving very far. You will still need a soft bumper placed around the inside of the crib or bassinet, because some babies manage to dig their heels in and thrust their legs out, propelling themselves the entire length of the crib.

Your baby's ability to converge and focus her eyes on small nearby objects is not present at birth and develops gradually over the first two months. Researchers have observed that, as early as the first week, a baby shows a tendency to look towards the eyes of the person holding her. As the windows of the soul, the eyes are perhaps the most 'alive' part of us.

The ability to track a moving object develops around six weeks of age. Before that time your baby won't seem to notice her hands when they move into her line of vision. Looking at her hands leads to mastering their use in reaching for objects and the development of problem-solving behavior.

Can your baby smile, and what does it mean? There is great debate about this in the literature. Many parents report that their infants do smile, and this is illustrated by the day-old baby in Leboyer's *Birth Without Violence*.[25] Social smiling, however, takes longer to develop.

When I was a teenager, I heard people say that babies smiled in their sleep because the angels were whispering to them, and I thought, 'How quaint.' Then a high-school teacher said that babies couldn't really smile and it was just gas pains, and I thought, 'How offensive.' Now I suspect they really are in the angelic spheres when they sleep, but since I can't prove it I have to ask which view is more furthering? Have you ever seen your baby stare right over your head or into the corner of the room with absolute intensity or with a smile? Who is she looking at?

Consider the following from Lark Bergwin-Anderson, a mother in Washington, D.C., who shared the following story in the *Waldorf Kindergarten Association Newsletter*:

> I too was given the gift of an experience through my children which I would like to share. One morning, when I had just finished nursing Daniela, who was just a few months old at the time, she started chattering very animatedly and smiling at the wall across from us. Her attention was riveted in that direction, and she seemed to be carrying on a full-scale 'conversation' with the unadorned, large, white, wooden sliding closet doors. Suddenly I felt bathed in warmth and light from head to toe and had an impression of a host of angels surrounding us. It was a very special moment of love, of overwhelming gratitude to this tiny babe for sharing a glimpse of her special world with me.
>
> I would have thought the experience to be totally unique. However, a few days later, my very articulate and loquacious (just turned) two-year-old, Ileana, was sitting at my side while I nursed Daniela. When Daniela finished, she again looked over toward the closet doors and again began a very animated 'conversation,' smiling incessantly. Ileana looked in the same direction and said, 'Mommy, who is that Lady over there?' I, very hesitantly, said, 'I don't know . . . an angel, maybe?' She answered excitedly, 'Yes, an angel! Hi, Angel!!!' and beamed from head to foot. As did I – to have studied Steiner for so long and then to have reality bear his teachings out, its truth confirmed and articulated by a two-year-old.[26]

What Does Your Baby Need?

Since babies are totally unable to take care of themselves, you need to provide everything, twenty-four hours a day. The main ingredients are love, nourishment, and comfort.

Comfort

It doesn't take long for parents to distinguish their baby's various cries and to recognize the difference between hunger and a cold nappy, for example. If your baby is full and dry and doesn't have an air bubble that will come up, rocking or walking her is often so comforting or pleasurable that it can at least temporarily override discomfort from many sources. Swaddling a baby by wrapping her tightly in a blanket or holding the arm of a disconsolate infant will often be very calming as well. But sometimes you try everything to no avail, and you just need to be there holding the baby without any noticeable success. Keeping calm yourself is of primary importance, because it is almost impossible for a distraught parent to calm a baby. We are too connected emotionally. To the extent that we can be peaceful ourselves and provide a peaceful environment for the newborn, the baby will benefit.

A baby should not be left to 'cry it out.' What this teaches the baby is that the world is an unfriendly place in which he or she doesn't count. Infants in institutions cry less and less during their first year of life, having learned that it usually leads only to exhaustion. Studies have shown that babies whose cries are ordinarily responded to quickly do continue to cry more than institutionally reared infants (thank goodness), but less than babies also raised at home but whose cries are responded to inconsistently.[27] You can't spoil a baby by responding quickly and consistently to its needs!

Love and Bonding

The love and warmth that surround a baby are vital for its healthy development. The mother is in a unique relationship with the newborn, but the love and caring of both parents are like a wonderful cloak that surrounds the baby and counterbalances our questions and uncertainties about how to take care of this infant. By touching your baby frequently and responding promptly to cries as often as you can, you give your baby a feeling of being loved and cared for that is perhaps the most important thing you can do with your infant. It affects the rest of his or her life!

There is a lot of talk today about 'bonding' or 'attachment.'

Immediate and continuous contact between mother and baby is wonderful and should be the norm, not something that is 'allowed' for a few minutes or hours. But please don't feel that all is lost if circumstances prevent it. Human beings are more complex than other animals, and there is no 'critical period' in human bonding, as there is in lower animals. Your baby will not follow the nurse home like a duck might follow a dog, and your baby will love you without any difficulty, because babies are love. (Even children who are physically abused still love the parent.) The real question in bonding is how we, as busy, self-centered adults, are going to make room in our lives twenty-four hours a day for a new and helpless being. Bonding is not something that happens exclusively in the first half-hour after birth. The baby tends to be alert in the first hour after birth and the mother is wide open emotionally and hormonally, so uninterrupted contact during that time is powerful, but bonding starts in pregnancy and continues through the birth experience and through interaction with the baby after it is born. I'm convinced that we are bonded or 'in love' any time we recognize that the other person is a being rather than an object. It's not something that happens or fails to happen once and forever.

I bring this up again because so many mothers feel loss or guilt if they have been separated from their babies immediately after the birth, due to complications. It is natural for the mother to feel loss. She has been totally one with the baby and now they are separated; being together eases that pain of separation and helps to start their relationship on the outside. But the baby isn't suffering irreparable damage if it's being held by dad in the nursery or is sound asleep while mother has stitches.

Love is complex and functions on many levels. Your children will open your hearts, teach you about love and service, and bring into consciousness the blind behaviour that make it possible to do the hurtful things we do to the people we love.

Nourishment

Nourishment includes food, love, and touch. Breastfeeding is, of course, ideal in providing all three – the perfect nourishment for babies, and the opportunity to experience a loving relationship, and the closeness of skin-to-skin contact. Anyone who is pregnant or is having difficulty breastfeeding should contact the La Leche League, whose counselors know how to give practical help and can recommend valuable books on how and why to breastfeed.

Breastfeeding is especially important during the newborn period so that your baby gets colostrum, which stimulates digestive processes and provides passive immunity to certain diseases. Also, breast milk is ideally suited to babies and prevents worry about food allergies or illness from poorly sterilized bottles. Breast milk not only has a different composition from cow's milk and formula products (which keep trying to imitate it), but, by coming from the mother's body, as did the child itself, it has subtle qualities different from milk from soybeans, cows, or goats. Joan Salter, in *Mothering with Soul*, provides an interesting discussion of the physical, soul, and spiritual qualities of breast milk.[28]

Nursing at the breast is the first 'work' that the baby must do, and König suggests that mothers can gain insights into their child's character or temperament by observing their baby's sucking habits. He also discusses how the mother's milk conveys her heart forces, since the breasts are located over the heart area in the human being. He reminds us:

> Yet milk is not material food alone; with it the mother's love passes into the baby's being and this too works powerfully on the newborn child… The mother gives love and comfort and security. Milk gives sustenance and is the gentle call to come down and settle upon the earth. After each feed, the child is one step nearer to its physical existence. Every new day brings further moments of alertness, consciousness and awareness. All of this is due to milk.[29]

Digestion is an all-consuming event for an infant. When your baby is hungry or has an air bubble, nothing else exists. There is only that sensation. Similarly, when your baby rolls back its eyes in ecstasy while at your breast, you know that the satisfaction goes all the way down to its toes.

Ten to twenty percent of all babies have 'colic,' or pain and crying starting in the first few weeks and usually ending by around three months of age. Dealing with a disconsolate baby is very distressing for parents, but the most important thing is to stay calm yourself and not become angry or frustrated. Research on colic is inconclusive, relating it to food allergies, hormonal imbalances, overstimulation, temperament, or immature nervous or gastrointestinal systems. Aletha Solter, in *The Aware Baby*, has found through her own work with a technique called 'co-counseling', that crying is one way we have to process hurt and release stored tension and pain. She feels that being there with the baby while it cries can help it to let go of birth and other trauma. When a baby is not crying from physical discomfort, it sometimes just needs to cry out its tensions. Staying calm yourself and being present in a loving and collected way can help the crying to be healing rather than creating more frustration.[30]

Can You Help Your Baby Develop Specific Skills?

The Importance of the Environment

During the first six weeks, your baby needs gradually to adjust to earthly life and to get her digestive system functioning smoothly. Because she sleeps so much and her perceptual abilities are so limited, any kind of 'enriched environment' will be wasted on the infant. Be skeptical of commercial and media hype regarding the needs of the newborn.

Much of the push to 'stimulate your baby's senses' comes out of a misinterpretation of the studies in European orphanages, as discussed earlier. Babies need the love, the holding, and the connection with a primary caregiver (mother or mother substitute) if they are to take up life fully. They need to be welcomed and held in a peaceful and supportive environment that feeds body and soul, rather than be affronted by buzzers, brightly colored objects, and other stimulation to their senses. Your baby won't even be very interested in the world around her until about two months of age.

If an 'enriched environment' is wasted on your baby, an aesthetic one is not. Creating a feeling of calm in the room (and in the mother) communicates to the baby and helps with sleep, digestion, and peacefulness. Most of the commercial things for babies are expensive and unnecessary. If you do have the luxury of decorating the baby's bedroom, avoid garish wallpaper and cartoon characters. Greens, browns, and grays are also much more 'earthy' than the infant or young child, who is still closely connected to heaven and doesn't yet walk firmly on the ground. The rose-pink-blue environment created by the silks over the crib is especially soothing for babies, and a colour Steiner called 'peach blossom' is especially suited to young children. Looking at the space in which your baby sleeps with attention and reverence adds those qualities to the environment. Adding a little table with fresh flowers, some photos or art reproduction, and some objects from nature like a pretty rock or shell, can remind you of your own still center in the midst of all the demands of caring for a new baby.

Steiner suggested that many paintings by Raphael express higher truths, and he especially recommended that pregnant women contemplate Raphael's *Sistine Madonna*, which is also wonderful to have in a young child's room. Meditating on this picture can reveal many things to the mother about the nature of the eternal feminine and the incarnation process. About this particular painting Steiner says, 'The painting of the Madonna with the child is the symbol of the eternal spirituality in people which comes certainly to the earth from beyond. Yet, this painting, through parted clouds, has everything that can only arise or proceed from the earthly.'[31]

Skill Development

What is your baby doing in the first six weeks? She is getting used to earthly life, and her digestive system is starting to mature. In addition, her brain is undergoing tremendous growth and changes. In the first months of life, it is estimated the number of synapses increases twenty times to more than 1,000 trillion. Experiences determine these new connections, but the experiences should be ones of touching, rocking, and being loved. Brain development involves strengthening those connections that are used and letting those that are not used wither away. The formation of synapses and their pruning occurs at different times in different parts of the brain, which will be discussed in the next chapters.

The main motor skill that your baby develops in the first six weeks is the ability to hold her head off the mattress for longer periods of time and the ability to stare and smile at faces (and face patterns) when they are eight to twelve inches away. These developmental skills don't require any special action on your part. Burton White, in having observed that newborns' heads are almost always turned to the side, whether they are on their backs or stomachs, suggests that if parents want to do anything that they make a 'stabile' instead of the traditional 'mobile' (which hangs over the crib and is useless during the first two months). A stabile doesn't move and is placed at the baby's eye level on the side of the crib. White recommends drawing a human face, because that is what babies respond to best.[32] I personally wouldn't do that because it seems to me like the first of many substitutions for the human being that parents buy into. (Dummies, lullaby bears, stories on tape, and television are others.) But we can thank White's observations for reminding us that babies don't really look overhead until they are about two months old.

Language Development

Because your baby is learning to understand language long before he or she can speak, it is good to get into the habit of speaking intelligently to your baby from the start. Unfortunately many parents don't talk much to their children before they become verbal at around eighteen months of age. Although your baby will be about six months of age before she shows understanding of specific words and commands, talking to your baby not only helps her to develop language skills but also demonstrates your respect for her as a human being.

Dr. Emmi Pikler, the Hungarian pediatrician whose work with child development and orphanages is noted worldwide, emphasizes the importance of treating the baby as a person, as a partner (rather than as an object) in such routine activities as nappy changing and bathing. This involves interacting with your baby, sharing attention and words while you do things together, rather than being distracted and ignoring her, however small she may be.[33]

What Is It Like Being with a Newborn?

Being with a newborn is usually shocking, at least the first time around. Having just given birth, the mother is wide open emotionally and physically. Hormones, starting to breastfeed, interrupted sleep, and roller-coaster emotions put a woman much more in touch with the beauty, vulnerability, and overwhelming aspects of life. Being a new mother or a new father involves a change in being, a stretching of who we are. We need to take on the responsibility and the twenty-four-hour-a-day care of another human being, who (for a while at least) is completely dependent on us.

Most people agree that the first six weeks are the hardest. Even after you recover from the birth itself, you will probably find that the complete lack of rhythm doesn't give you any support. Life gets easier after these first six weeks, so if you can stay in communication with your partner during this transition time and have the sense that you are holding hands as you go under together, you will come back up together as well. Having a first baby is the hardest, because you have to make huge internal changes to become a mother and a father – and everything you're being called on to do is for the first time. It is easier with subsequent children because everything is more familiar. However, a second or third baby can be surprising in the amount of work he or she adds to a system where parents may already feel pressed for time. The key is getting adequate help, so you can relax into what is happening and give up on things that aren't as essential, like cleaning the house yourself. Single mothers, especially, need to try to arrange adequate support in advance.

Being with a baby involves doing a lot of repetitive things (nappy changing, nursing, washing clothes) that can look like nothing because they seem to involve maintenance rather than creative development. So when your husband comes home from work and says, 'What did you do today, dear?' you think about it and burst into tears. I found I could accomplish one thing (one task in the world outside the baby) each day, if I was lucky, during the first two months. For someone who was used to being active and effective, that was a real shock.

How can this period of transition after the birth be made easier for the parents? Detailed suggestions for things to think about and do can be found in my book *Pregnant Feelings*, but the most important thing is to get adequate help. This may mean having a relative come stay with you, hiring someone to come in and straighten up the house, or organizing a circle of friends to drop off a casserole and do a half-hour of what's needed every afternoon during the first week or so.

To the extent you feel that you can just be with your baby, you'll be more at peace. This may involve making sure that all other responsibilities are handled and that all deadlines fall before your due date, or it may mean giving up on cleaning the house for a while. When we finally surfaced about five days after the birth of our first child, every plant in the house was withered, and we were sad!

The first six weeks are a very special time to be together as a family, to just 'be present' with your new baby, adjust to the changes in your life, and regain your strength and bearings. If you can honor the magnitude of the event, arrange for some help and schedule few or no activities, you may find your adjustment much less rocky. Allow yourself to be nourished by the wonderful energy that surrounds a newborn.

The energy of creation that is present at a birth is very powerful and holy. This is true at every birth, but it is more accessible if the energy is acknowledged and protected. Mothers certainly feel it, unless their baby is whisked away and they are completely ignored while the doctor repairs the episiotomy – then the mother may feel let-down and empty rather than filled with excitement and accomplishment. Midwives respect this special time together for the family in the hours immediately following a birth, and I have always been amazed to leave a home where a birth has occurred and find that the world is still the same outside. The energy inside and outside are so different! I sometimes wonder how the postman can be walking down the pavement and the children playing next door. Don't they know what has just happened!?

Because babies are so close to the spiritual world, they call forth love and giving from all sorts of people – some of whom you won't have heard from in years. Learn to receive, to let people do things for you, to say thank you. Use the time to practice doing nothing, to just be centered in the heart or in your breath. If you have other children, you will be especially busy after the birth. See if you can find brief moments to just sit and watch the baby sleeping. Such moments nourish you for the constant demands of mothering. Try to take advantage of the connection to the spirit that your baby has and to which you are still open in the postpartum period. Life will return to a new 'normal' soon enough.

Earlier in this chapter I talked about how most of us forget the life of the spirit when we take on this earthly life. The prophets and the saints are often people for whom the veil of forgetfulness has never come down or for whom it was not very thick. Similarly, some of the great poets seem to remain slightly more in touch with their origins than most of us. William Wordsworth wrote:

> Our birth is but a sleep and a forgetting;
> The Soul that rises with us, our life's Star,
> Hath had elsewhere its setting,
> And cometh from afar:
> Not in entire forgetfulness,
> And not in utter nakedness,
> But trailing clouds of Glory do we come
> From God, who is our home:
> Heaven lies about us in our infancy!

On a young child's birthday in the Steiner/Waldorf preschools we often tell a story about a little angel who wanted to come down to earth and got permission from its big angel to come over the rainbow bridge, after it had a dream about its earthly parents. The little angel finally agrees to leave its wings behind when its big angel assures it that they will be safely kept until his or her return. Then the little angel crosses through the many colors of the beautiful rainbow bridge, while on the earth the seasons change three times. Then it becomes very dark, almost like going to sleep, and when the little angel opens its eyes, there is the loving woman and the man with the kind heart who were in the dream. And the little angel knows it has found its earthly home.

Such an image nourishes a young child by affirming that we know there is more to him or her than just the body. A similar knowledge is reflected in the image of a regal white bird bringing a baby, for such a bird is always a symbol of the spirit, and especially the spirit link between heaven and earth (as when the Holy Spirit descends like a dove, or when a white bird guides Hansel and Gretel through the forest). In speaking of the stork bringing babies, our forebears were not ignorant of where babies came from – even children probably had more exposure to birth through farm life than do our own. Rather, they were giving expression to a sense that the spirit came into earthly life with the birth of a child, something which was perhaps easier for them to perceive but which is still accessible to us. Looking at your baby in this way will not only help to open your heart, but can help you to have patience when the house is a mess and you've been walking the floor for two hours with a fussy four-week-old. Babies do complicate your life, but they also offer tremendous opportunities for growth and development.

Recommended Reading

(Because many of these titles are difficult to find, check first with the mail order book services listed in Appendix A, or see if your local bookstore can order them).

Birth Without Violence by Frederick Leboyer (Knopf). Insights into the newborn's experience and ways to receive him or her.

Conception, Birth and Early Childhood by Norbert Glas (Anthroposophic Press). Written from the author's experience as a doctor working with the insights of Rudolf Steiner.

Eternal Childhood by Karl König (Camphill Books). An outstanding series of essays on conception, pregnancy, birth, and the eternal aspects of childhood by one of the foremost students of Rudolf Steiner, and founder of the Camphill movement.

Gentle Birth Choices by Barbara Harper (Healing Arts Press). A guide to making informed decisions about birthing centers, birth attendants, water birth, home and hospital birth.

A Guide to Child Health by Michaela Glöckler and Wolfgang Goebel (Floris Books). Two Anthroposophic doctors provide advice based on the indications of Rudolf Steiner.

The Incarnating Child by Joan Salter (Hawthorn Press). Excellent book based on the insights of Rudolf Steiner and the author's work at the Gabriel Baby Centre in Australia.

Mothering with Soul by Joan Salter (Hawthorn Press). Discusses aspects of pregnancy, birth, and mothering. Especially interesting chapter on breastfeeding.

Pregnant Feelings by Rahima Baldwin Dancy and Terra Palmarini Richardson (Celestial Arts). A workbook on psychological aspects of pregnancy, birth, and parenting.

Silent Knife by Nancy Wainer Cohen and Lois Estner (Bergin & Garvey). A guide to cesarean prevention and healing from unnecessary cesareans. Also contact the International Cesarean Awareness Network, 1304 Kingsdale Ave., Redondo Beach, CA 90278.

Special Delivery by Rahima Baldwin Dancy (Celestial Arts). A practical guide to pregnancy, birth, and the postpartum period with an emphasis on alternatives and informed choices.

Untouched. The Need for Genuine Affection in an Impersonal World by Mariana Caplan (Hohm Press). A powerful book for healing yourself and raising healthy children.

Resources

The Natural Baby Company, 7835-3 Freedom Ave. NW, N. Canton, OH 44720. Offers free 'Natural Diapering Handbook' and sells baby-care products and toys.

Weleda, Inc., P.O. Box 249, Congers, NY 10920. Natural baby-care soap, powder, oil, and cream.

Natural fiber clothing and bedding are available from:
After the Stork, P.O. Box 44321, Rio Rancho, NM 87174.
Biobottoms, 617-C 2nd St., Petaluma, CA 94852.
Cotton Dreams, 2962 NW 60th St., Ft. Lauderdale, FL 33309.
Garnet Hill, Franconia, NH 05380.
Hanna Anderson, 1010 NW Flanders, Portland, OR 97209.
Mother Hart, 11293 Wingfoot Dr., Boynton Beach, FL 33427.

Horizontal baby carriers are sold by:
California Diversified Manufacturing, 208 Avenida Pelaya, San Clemente, CA 92672.
Co-op America Order Service, 126 Intervale Rd., Burlington, VT 05401.
The Rebozo Way Project, 6063 Ethel Ave., Van Nuys, CA 91401.

Some UK Resources

Doula UK 0871 4333103 www.doula.org.uk Network of home help and support for new parents.

Weleda, Heanor Road, Ilkeston, Derbyshire DE7 8DR 0115 944 8200 www.weleda.co.uk Natural baby care, powder, oils, cream and homeopathic medicines..

Natural clothing, nappies and bedding

Cut 4 Cloth, 4 Fore Street, Constantine, Falmouth TR11 5AB
Tel no. 01326 340956 www.cut4cloth.co.uk

Greenfibres, Totnes TQ9 5ZZ Tel no. 0845 330 3400
www.greenfibres.com

The Natural Baby Company, PO Box 76 Ryde PO33 3XH
Tel no. 01983 810925 www.naturalbabycompany.com

Spirit of Nature, Unit 7 Hannah Way, Gordleton Industrial Park, Lymington S041 8SD Tel no. 08707 259885
www.spiritofnature.co.uk

Treehugger Mums, Tel no. 0845 6443684
www.treehuggermums.co.uk Information on fertility, pregnancy and childbirth, choosing and using cloth nappies.

Yummies, 15 Bond Street, Brighton BN1 1RD
Tel no. 01273 738733 www.yummies.biz

Horizontal baby carriers

Home Grown Baby, 3 Wardles Terrace, Durham City DH1 4EX
Tel no. 0191 386 9390 www.homegrownbaby.co.uk

Baby slings, wraps and carriers as well as organic products to support women through pregnancy, childbirth and the postpartum period.

Breastfeeding and Baby Wearing Company. 33 Greenways Flitwikj, Bedfordshire MK45 1DB Tel no. 01525 750126
www.breastfeedingandbabywearing.co.uk

The Carrying Kind, PO Box 211 Hertford SG13 7ZF
Tel no. 0800 093 1500 www.thecarryingkind.com
Large range of slings and baby carriers.

CHAPTER 3

Growing Down and Waking Up

We think of children as growing up, but we could also say that they 'grow down,' in the sense that they seem to gain control of the body from the head downward. First they gain control of the eyes and the neck, then the torso in rolling over, and finally the limbs in crawling and walking.

At the same time, they are changing from sleepy newborns to alert and lively toddlers who run circles around their parents. This change in consciousness from infancy to three years involves waking up, in the sense that the participatory consciousness of the newborn gradually becomes replaced by a strong sense of self (just try opposing the will of a two-year-old!). Before this strong sense of I can emerge, the child must first develop language, thinking, and memory.

Penetration of the body, which culminates in walking, is a fundamental task of the baby's first year. Talking is a key task of the second year. And thinking and memory are areas of tremendous development in the third year. All these fundamental milestones of the first three years occur by themselves, according to their own timetable. We need only provide love and nourishment, and refrain from doing things that hamper the child's basic pattern of unfolding.

This chapter presents a picture of the tremendous developmental changes occurring in the child during the first three years. The next two chapters suggest many practical things you can do as your child's first teacher that are consonant with healthy and balanced development.

Growing into the Body

Control of the Head

A newborn's head is very large compared to its body, and its limbs are relatively undeveloped appendages, good neither for walking nor eating as they are with other mammals. The image of 'growing down' or penetrating the body also applies to how areas in the brain mature: Developmental neuropsychologist Jane Healy reports that because the development of myelin in the spine proceeds from top to bottom, mouth, eyes, arms, and hands are used adeptly before legs and feet.[1] In the newborn, after the mouth organizes itself around instinctual suckling, the first conscious control begins in the eyes. This is necessary because without a steady visual field, it would not be possible to develop the hand-eye coordination and balance that are necessary for crawling and walking. When a baby is born, her natural focus is about ten inches away – just the distance between a breastfeeding infant and her mother's face. Next the baby learns to follow something with her eyes when it comes into her range of vision, which extends to about twelve inches at two months of age. She may begin to turn her head toward a sound if it comes in one ear more strongly than the other. She begins to be able to hold her head up off the mattress when on her stomach and to turn her head more toward the midline when on her back. But it will be many more months before sufficient head-neck strength will be present for her to sit unassisted.

At three and a half months she can hold her head more centered and look straight up, and her arms and legs are no longer confined to the 'fencer's pose' of the younger infant. She will have the ability to control her head through 180 degrees, but she probably can't turn over before fourteen weeks. When on her stomach, she will be able to hold her head straight up off the mattress for several minutes at a time.

Around three months she will be able to prop herself up on her forearms with full head-neck control. Consonant with our image of 'growing down,' we see that control of the upper arms comes before control of the lower arms, control of the wrists before the fingers, of the legs before the feet.

During the time from six to fourteen weeks, the muscles in your baby's legs are strengthening by kicking out and being held slightly flexed, but there is no real leg control.

Control of the head also manifests in visual ability, which increases rapidly and is nearly completely under control by three-and-a-half months. Once your baby can focus clearly on nearby objects and create a single image of them, she will discover her hands and stare at them – sometimes for five or ten minutes at a time. Between six and fourteen weeks her hands will no longer be held in a fist most of the time, and she will start bringing her hands together and clasping them. Eye and hand convergence is something only primates and humans have, and it is an important step in the development of intelligence.

You will see eye-hand coordination developing as your two- or three-month-old swipes at an object and later brings it to her mouth. This coordination increases with practice and maturation, so that by six months a baby usually has complete control of the use of her hands.

Reaching is an important developmental skill, one of the major ways that children begin to explore the world and build the foundations of intelligence. Your baby will almost always reach for anything that is nearby and will either bring it to her mouth or look at it, sometimes moving it about or taking it from hand to hand.

Control of the Torso

As the months go by, your baby gains increasing control of her body from the head down. Sometime between two and six months she will probably succeed in turning from her back to stomach, followed a few weeks later by being able to turn back the other way. The first time is often a surprise – even to the baby – so be careful not to leave your baby unattended on a changing table or bed where she can flip off ! Even a much younger baby can sometimes unexpectedly succeed in turning from back to stomach through powerful leg thrusts, especially if she is angry.

Further control of the muscles of the torso will result in your baby's being able to sit up unassisted, usually between six and eight months of age. This first achievement of an upright position marks a significant maturing of the muscles. A vertical posture is a uniquely human attribute; it is perhaps a symbol of our unique position between heaven and earth.

Once your baby is adept at turning over in both directions and can sit alone, she will try to bring herself from a lying to a sitting position. This new ability is usually accomplished by around eight months of age.

A baby who can sit up is interested in everything. Her eyes are now more inclined to focus on objects several feet away, but she cannot yet move under her own power. If left on a rug in the middle of a room, she is not able to move her body any distance (exceptions are some babies who learn to propel themselves from place to place by rolling over and over). Coordinated use of the limbs for locomotion will be the next major developmental achievement.

Control of the Legs

All of the movement and kicking your baby does helps to strengthen her legs. Sometime around four months of age she will discover that she has feet, since her eyes had been unable to discern them earlier. But she won't be able to use her legs in a controlled fashion. That changes around eight months of age, when she learns to crawl. Some babies are eager to go and may even be frustrated by their inability to get things they want; others are happy to sit and watch the world go by, and they may first crawl four or five months later than the 'early' ones. The normal range is tremendous. Don't compare your baby with the neighbor's! Insights into later character traits can sometimes be gained by observing how your child learns to crawl and walk. Simply observe and encourage your baby and trust that she is developing according to her own timetable. If you have questions about how your child is developing, seek answers to them rather than worry!

Most children try to move about as soon as they are able. The first stage of crawling occurs when the baby pushes with one foot and reaches with the hand on the same side (officially called 'homolateral crawling, prone position,' but we could also call it 'alligator crawling'). To help the baby achieve locomotion, it is important to have her barefoot on a surface that can provide some traction. The next level of locomotion is cross crawling ('controlateral creeping') with the opposite arm and leg being thrust forward. Babies usually love to exercise their new motor skills and are eager to reach the many things they have been able to see from a distance for several months.

Physical therapists now tell us how important crawling is in later development. The rhythmical pattern of cross crawling is significant, not only for the development of proper physical coordination, but also affects the development of the brain and how a child learns. Some learning and emotional disabilities are related to a lack of crawling or can be helped by sensory integration or other systems of therapy.[2] For this reason, anything that shortens a baby's time spent crawling (baby walkers, leg splints, or braces) should be avoided during this critical period.

Crawling is followed by the baby's ability to pull herself up while holding onto a table or sofa. The ability to walk while holding onto things is followed by increased balance and coordination and the wonderful first steps alone.

Once your baby can crawl, you will find everything changes! Because crawling is such a momentous change for parents and walking is such a momentous accomplishment for babies, I want to discuss parenting the baby up to the age of eight months before going on to discuss walking.

What is Your Baby Like between Six Weeks and Eight Months of Age?

We can say that babies 'grow down and wake up,' for while they are growing and developing physically, they are also becoming more alert and more interested in the world around them. We have seen how they develop physically; let's explore how they behave as they become more 'present' with each passing day.

Your baby will sleep less as the weeks go by and will pay close attention to what is going on around her. Once she discovers her hands, she will use them whenever possible to grasp and explore objects with her eyes and mouth. The tongue and lips are sensitive organs of exploration, and when your baby starts to teethe during this period, counterpressure can sometimes help sore gums. There are many teething rings on the market, some of which can be put in the refrigerator to chill. We especially recommend homeopathic teething pills which are sold in many chemists. Being homeopathic, they present no danger of overdose or side effects. It is not unusual for babies to be fussy while they are teething, or even occasionally to have a fever or runny nose.

By three months your baby will probably be smiling regularly at anyone who gets her attention. Three-month-old babies are delightful to be with, and most of our images of babies from television or advertising are of a three-month-old rather than a newborn. We now have much more of a sense that there is a real person present, someone who seems to respond to us. Indeed, a baby does begin to show more special behavior, such as smiling more with her parents or primary caregivers from the fourth month on. But there is still openness and friendliness to all people at this age.

The baby's sense of self and other is slow to emerge, for the consciousness of a newborn is very diffuse. There is no inner or outer. As we watch the baby slowly distinguish between parents and others, we have the sense that she is more present in her body. It is interesting that you cannot elicit a tickle response from a baby before about fourteen weeks of age. Burton White, author of *The First Three Years of Life,* postulates that tickling depends on the 'ticklee' perceiving that another person is producing the stimulation (you can't tickle yourself). He states, 'The child younger than about fourteen weeks of age is probably not well enough developed socially to have reached whatever awareness of another is necessary to make the tickle functional.'[3]

This is consonant with Steiner's idea of the gradual incarnation of the I and the slowly developing consciousness of the self, which is necessary for any perception of 'other.' Steiner described babies as 'sleeping' in their consciousness, 'dreaming' in their emotions, and most 'awake' in their willing, which manifests in the body. We can see the strength of this willing in the tremendous growth and movement of the body and in the insistence with which a baby demands that its physical needs be met. Try to argue with a crying baby that she's not really hungry, and she ought to be able to wait!

The force of will behind the physical functions of a baby does not respond to reason or consolation – only to physical activity such as eating, sucking, or rocking.

The next step in the differentiation of 'others' is evident in the common phenomenon called stranger anxiety. Sometime in the first year, four out of five babies start reacting with hesitation and fear to anyone who is not in the immediate family. This reaction can start as early as six months, and it is not a sign that anything is wrong.

Aside from becoming wary of people who aren't familiar, most babies enjoy themselves most of the time during the first year. They are basically happy, curious, and growing throughout this time.

Learning to Walk

During the period from eight to sixteen months of age, most children master their physical body and learn to walk. Note that there can be as much as eight months' difference between early and late walkers.

Children learn to walk through practice and through imitation. It has been found in the rare cases where human babies have been reared by animals in the jungles of India that the child never achieves a truly upright posture. There is a strong inner drive in children to stand and to walk, and to be like the people around them. It is something inherent in children and does not require baby gymnastics or other devices to aid its progress. Baby walkers do not lead to early walking; in fact, many physicians now believe that infant walkers may adversely affect muscle development and coordination and lead to a delay in walking.[4] Due to the large number of accidents involving walkers, the Canadian Medical Association has asked the government to ban their sale.[5] Time spent in walkers also takes time away from opportunities to creep and crawl and can affect coordination and balance.

Infant walkers don't seem to lead to increased social and explorative behaviors, as their proponents say; studies have found no difference in these behaviors for infants in or out of walkers. They may give parents some free time, but not without physical and developmental risks to the baby.[6] There is similar concern about baby bouncers (cloth seats suspended by a spring hung over a door sill) by many pediatricians because of potential damage to the baby's bones or joints if they are used on hard floors.[7]

Watching your child learn to walk on her own can sometimes provide insights into character traits, because walking is something the child achieves through her own efforts. Is there a driving will to move, or a great solidity and contentment in sitting? Are falls taken in the child's stride, or are they discouraging? Keep watching and see what your child 'tells' you. All you need to do is be there to encourage and share your child's pride in those first steps.

It is valuable to watch the process of learning to walk for what it can tell us of the child's nature and the incarnation process of the 'I.' Steiner states, 'Walking does not merely mean that the human being ceases to crawl and acquires an upright position. It means that the child attains to the equilibrium of its own organism within the cosmos, learns to control its movements and acquires a free orientation.'[8] He continues,

> And for anyone who is able to observe such a matter in the right way, the most remarkable and most important of life's riddles actually find expression in this activity of learning to walk; a whole universe comes to expression in the manner in which the child progresses from creeping to the upright position, to the placing of the feet, but also in addition to holding the head upright and to the use of arms and legs.[9]

To explain this further, once the baby achieves equilibrium in the upright posture, Steiner observes that the hands and arms are freed to serve the inward life, while the legs serve for bodily movement:

> The liberation of the hands and arms affords the possibility for the soul to find its equilibrium. The function of the legs, the treading, the raising and bending, the harmony between right and left, brings about a relation to what is below us. It has the effect of bringing into the life of body and soul the element of rhythm, of measure, the caesuras of existence. The soul elements which live in the hands and arms become free; this introduces an element of melody, a musical element into the life of the child.[10]

Watching a young child with awareness that more might be going on than meets the eye can make us more open when we are with young children. Even though I can't articulate any great insights I've had, I know that those times of openness and remembrance seem very valuable for me as a spiritual-physical being, for my parenting and for the child.

The Second Year: Mastering Language

A child's first birthday is as much an anniversary for the mother as for the baby. Exactly one year earlier she was going through labour and she remembers vividly what she felt holding her baby for the first time. As dramatic as the changes in the baby were in the first year, they will be equally dramatic in the second. By the time a child is two there is much greater distance from the dreamy dependency of infancy and a much greater sense of who this person is in her own right.

Just as mastering the body and learning to walk were the dominant activities of the first year of your baby's life, so mastering language and learning to talk are the major tasks from age one to two. Language development consists both of comprehension, which develops first, and the ability to speak. Learning to talk, like learning to walk, seems to involve both an innate capacity of the brain and a need to encounter models in the environment. Because language comprehension is so fundamental to all later learning and to good social development, it is valuable to consider it in some detail.

Language Comprehension

I hope you will have been talking to your baby from birth on as if she were a person worthy of respect. This attention and respect not only increase her sense of self-worth and her loving interaction with you, but by using good language rather than baby talk, you are providing a model worthy of imitation.

Recent studies have shown that babies are remarkably perceptive and discerning. Newborns have been shown to suck more frequently in response to hearing their mother's voice, showing that learning/recognition is going on even within the womb. And babies only four days old can distinguish one language from another: French babies sucked much more vigorously when they heard French instead of Russian, and Russian babies did just the opposite.[11]

There are approximately 6,000 languages in the world, and your newborn is equally fluent in all of them! But she quickly learns to distinguish between phonemes (distinct speech sounds) that she hears around her, and between six and ten months grows oblivious to foreign phonemes, while staying attuned to whatever sounds the speakers around her are using. By twelve months, an infant's 'auditory map' in the brain will have been formed. She will be unable to pick out phonemes that she has not heard thousands of times, because no clusters of neurons will have been assigned the job of responding to that sound.

The next step in decoding speech, after recognizing phonemes, is to start recognizing words from the run-together stream of sounds that we register when we hear a language that is foreign to us. Babies start early on to become accustomed to how sounds are used to start syllables in their mother tongue:

> By the time they're seven months old, American babies are well accustomed to hearing r joined with r (as in tram) and c with l (as in clam), but they've been spared combinations like db, gd, kt, ts and ng, all of which occur in other languages. And once they have an ear for syllables, word boundaries become less mysterious. Ten / groaning / deadbeats / are / cleaning / a / train on / blacktop makes acoustic sense in English, even if you don't know the words. Te / ngroanin /gdea / dbea / tsare / cleani / nga / traino / nbla /cktop isn't an option.[12]

Once children start to recognize and play with syllables, they become attuned to metric patterns as well. Peter Jusczyk, a cognitive scientist at Johns Hopkins University, Baltimore, US whose work was cited in the last paragraph, went on to show that between six and ten months, American babies develop a clear bias for words with first-syllable accents (the majority of English words, and virtually all the Daddy-baby-birdie diminutives we use with babies, have the first syllable accented; French words, by contrast, have the accent on the last syllable). His work implies that children less than a year old hear speech not as a blur of sound but as a series of distinct but mostly meaningless words.

The first unmistakable signs of word recognition usually occur around eight months of age. If your husband says, 'Where's Mommy?' while several people are in the room, she will turn toward you when she really knows that word. That depends, of course, on your having referred to yourself as 'Mommy' or 'Mama.' If all your child ever hears is your husband referring to you as 'Jane,' she will also call you by your first name. There is something to be said for having your child refer to the two of you as 'Mommy and Daddy,' 'Mama and Papa,' or some such words, because the sounds of these words are appropriate and easy to learn, and because it expresses relationship (parent and child, family).

One of the best things you can do for your child is to talk to her. Talk to her while you are changing her nappy or giving her a bath. She will usually appreciate the attention and, as a knowing being, will appreciate being treated as a person rather than as an object. And you are helping not only her language development, but also her brain development, as well. And please sing to your child, beginning when you are pregnant and continuing throughout childhood! The melodic quality of language, and the emotions present in a lullaby or a nursery game are very valuable for your baby's development. Comprehension is not the only part of language, although it tends to be overemphasized by our intellectual adult nature. Nonsense rhymes and action verses such as 'To market, to market' become favorites of the toddler and teach the melodic quality of language. This kind of interaction is valuable not only for the developing child, but can also make parenting tasks go more smoothly. For example, getting into the habit of using songs for activities such as washing her hair or going to bed can melt away the resistance of a willful two-year-old. Many other examples are contained in the book *The Singing Day*.[13]

Because so much depends on the development of language, it is important to watch your child for hearing disorders. If your baby is having frequent ear infections, it is advisable to look for allergies or other possible causes of fluid build-up in the ears. Impaired hearing can impede development in many other areas during these critical years of early childhood, so try to find a diagnosis and plan of treatment that you can support.

As your child comes to understand specific words, she will begin following simple instructions, like waving bye-bye or sitting down. Once your child starts to walk, she will frequently be coming to show you things or ask for assistance. Such times, when her attention is clearly directed toward you, are excellent times to talk about what is at hand, and then to act on it. Many parents underestimate what their child can understand at this age. This does not mean to explain everything to a one-year old! It does mean to talk intelligently about what is happening in the present – what the child is seeing and doing. Between the first and third birthdays, language comprehension explodes to the point where most children understand most of the words they will use in ordinary conversation for the rest of their lives!

Being Able to Talk

The ability to produce language proceeds much more slowly than the ability to understand it. While your child will show increasing understanding of words before her first birthday, very few children speak before they are one. The reason for this, according to Steiner, is that language development grows out of movement and the ability to walk. Steiner comments:

> The relation between physical equilibrium (action of the legs) and psychical equilibrium (action of the hands and arms) forms the foundation which enables the child to come into contact with the outer world through the medium of language.
>
> When we observe the formation of sounds and sentences (the rhythm and melody of speech), we can easily see the part played by the upper and lower limbs respectively in their formation. Speech arises from the human being as a whole. The outer, rhythmical element arises from the movement of the legs, the inner thematic element from that of the hands and arms.
>
> When a child walks sturdily and steadily, it has the bodily foundation for a correct syllable-division. This means that in learning to walk the child learns to form its sentences. If it walks

unsteadily, we shall find that it does not observe a proper division of sentences; it drowns its thoughts in a sea of words.

If a child does not properly learn to use its hands and arms harmoniously, its speech will disintegrate. Its voice becomes somewhat harsh. If we cannot get it to feel in its fingers, it will with difficulty develop a true sense for the modulations of speech.

The child should learn to walk before it learns to speak. Speech must have its basis in the equilibrium of movements of the limbs. If it lacks this foundation in the whole being, it becomes a stammering or bleating.[14]

Modern neurolinguistic work supports the relationship between learning to walk and grasp, and learning to speak. With this in mind, we can watch not only how our children learn to walk and the quality of their movements, but we can also observe the quality of their speech as it develops over the years and see if there is any discernible relationship between the two. Certainly both physical and speech therapists, conventional ones and those working out of Steiner's indications for 'curative education,' can see it. In such curative settings, movement and sound are often used separately and in combination to help overcome developmental difficulties.

The Development of Speech

A child's vocabulary increases slowly at first, from an average of three words at twelve months to twenty-two words at eighteen months of age. But around a year and a half, children's language abilities explode, so that most start acquiring new words at the phenomenal rate of one every two hours. By their second birthdays, most children have mastered 1,000 to 2,000 words and have started stringing two words together.[15]

Studies have shown that how much language is in the child's environment makes a huge difference in how much vocabulary she acquires:

The size of a toddler's vocabulary is strongly correlated with how much a mother talks to the child, reports Janellen Huttenlocher of the University of Chicago. At 20 months, children of chatty mothers averaged 131 more words than children of less talkative mothers; at two years, the gap had more than doubled, to 295 words. 'The critical factor is the number of times the child hears different words,' says Huttenlocher. The effect holds for the complexity of sentence structure, too, she finds. Mothers who used complex sentences (those with dependent clauses, such as 'when...' or 'because...') 40 percent of the time had toddlers who did so 35 percent of the time; mothers who used such sentences in only 10 percent of their utterances had children who did so only 5 percent of the time.

However, only 'live' language, not television, produced these vocabulary- and syntax-boosting effects. Why doesn't all the gabbing on TV stimulate language development? Huttenlocher suspects that 'language has to be used in relation to ongoing events, or it's just noise.'[16]

In other words, language needs to come from a living source and be related to events, emotional contexts, and cause-and-effect relationships in a child's life in order for the synapses to register in meaningful ways that the child will remember. So much for educational TV and preschooler's language development!

Developmental rates can vary among children by a year or more, and the majority of late talkers are boys. There is no evidence that late talkers end up less fluent than early talkers and, where there are problems, the pros and cons of early intervention vs. waiting until age five are hotly debated. A study of identical and fraternal twins by Yale University researcher J. Steven Reznick found that language comprehension, rather than actual speech, at ages fourteen months and twenty months was a better indication of how well the twins would do on intelligence tests at twenty-four months. The researchers found that a toddler's surroundings have a greater impact on how many words a child understands, but genetics were a strong influence on how much a child talked. 'Some children are born to be chatty, while others are born to be reticent about sharing their growing vocabulary knowledge,' Reznick said.[17]

However, if your child isn't hearing what is being said or is slow to develop understanding, then you should be concerned and have an evaluation done. Experts list the following 'red flags':

- 0-3 months – Does not turn when you speak or repeat sounds like coos.
- 4-6 months – Does not respond to 'no' or changes in tone of voice, look around for sources of sound like a doorbell, or babble in speechlike sounds such as p, b, and m.
- 7-12 months – Does not recognize words for common items, turn when you call her name, imitate speech sounds, or use sounds other than crying to get your attention.
- 1-2 years – Can't understand difference in meaning ('up' vs. 'down'), follow two requests ('Please pick up the bottle and give it to me'), string together two or three words, or name common objects.
- 3-4 years – Does not answer simple 'who,' 'what,' and 'where' questions. Cannot be understood by people outside the family, use four-word sentences, or pronounce most phonemes correctly. If delays persist until kindergarten, most pediatricians recommend speech therapy.[18]

Dr. Karl König, working with handicapped children and adults, distinguished three levels in speech development, which he called saying, naming, and talking.[19] Saying involves a desire or emotion that comes out as a one-word sentence, like 'Here!' or 'Cookie!' Naming involves learning the names of things and the beginnings of the thought processes that link concepts with perceptions and draw relationships between the general ('dog') and the specific ('Fido'). Talking involves dialogue as we are used to it. As the child experiences the world and the way it is expressed in language, with its inherent logic and grammar, she begins to use whole sentences between ages two and three.

Archetypal Images

While the toddler is learning the names of things, a great deal is happening on the preverbal level in the rapt attention with which the child contemplates each object. For example, while an adult or a school-age child will be most interested in what he or she can do with a ball, a toddler will be most interested in the ball itself – its shape, texture, color, and the fact that it rolls away when it slips out of her hands. Our adult consciousness has lost its connection with what goes on in the dreamy depths of the child's soul, with what is happening behind her dreaming, wondering, or delighted eyes. Daniel Udo de Haes, in his excellent book *The Young Child*, develops a fascinating picture of the unspoken 'soul language' by which simple objects speak to the child of qualities in the spiritual world and the nature of the soul's journey to earth. We can get a taste of Udo de Haes' perception in his description of the fascination young children (and adults) have with water:

> Every human soul is aware, consciously or unconsciously, of a connection with this watery element. Does not each of us long for the clarity which pure water can manifest? Does not every soul feel its own ability to stream and flow in all directions, to wave and to dash, to seethe and toss or to reflect calmly? Ultimately its capacity of rising to the heavens and descending again to earth, is brought to expression by water. The little child experiences all this much more directly and intensely than we do, though less consciously, and it is for this reason that he feels his connection with water and plays with it with such abandon.[20]

In a similar way, Udo de Haes explains children's delight in drawing houses or making houses out of the sofa pillows as arising from a reawakening of something within the child's own soul when it encounters 'houses' on earth. He states, 'Descending to earth, the soul bears within it the task of helping to build the 'house' that it would have to live in during the life that was about to begin; for the task that it was assigned was to help in forming its body. We should therefore not be surprised at the joy with which the child builds a little house, thus symbolically fulfilling the task of building his body.'[21]

In *The Young Child* a very enlivening (and not at all sentimental) picture of the inner life of the young child is developed by Udo de Haes, which I have found valuable to hold as a possibility when I watch a toddler contemplating an object. Jesus said, 'Unless you change and become like little children, you will never enter the kingdom of heaven.' (Matthew 18:3) What is the world like for a little child? This is a question worth holding by anyone who cares for young children. And to the extent that their wonder in the world around them can become real to us as well, the rediscovery of this aspect within ourselves can, without our noticing it, be a help to the young child who is exploring his own world of experiences.

Because of the fascination the young child has with simple objects and the resonance within the soul that such objects awaken, Udo de Haes recommends archetypal toys such as a ball, a bowl, a cup (with sand or water to pour), a little wooden house, a box with a hinged lid, or a small wagon.

The fact that the objects of nature and the simple objects of human life speak to the inner life of the child, reminding him of truths from the spiritual world, is echoed by the seventeenth century English poet Thomas Traherne:

Wonder

How like an Angel came I down!
How Bright are all Things here!
When first among his Works I did appear
O how their Glory did me Crown
The World resembled his Eternitie
In which my Soul did Walk;
And every Thing that I did see,
Did with me talk.

The Emergence of Thinking

Just as walking and talking can be seen as the major tasks of the first and second years of life, so thinking is a major accomplishment of the time from ages two to three. But thinking in its most rudimentary forms can be seen as early as the first year when the baby pushes an obstacle aside in order to grasp an object. Piaget describes this problem-solving behavior, with an element of intentionality, as one of the first signs of intelligence.

This early, practical or sensorimotor intelligence isn't replaced by reflecting on ideas until around the age of two. Prior to that time children tend to use trial-and-error for problem solving. As they turn two, you will increasingly see them pause and think about various alternatives or about the action they are going to do before doing it.

Thinking emerges between ages two and three, after the child has learned to speak. Many people will suppose that one has to think in order to speak, but remember that speech develops as a result of imitation and of feelings. The first words are interjections, and Steiner says, 'When the child says 'Mama' or 'Papa,' it expresses feelings towards Mama and Papa, not any sort of concept or thought. Thinking is first developed from speech.'[22]

According to Steiner, logical thinking develops out of the experience of the logic inherent in the grammar of spoken language (how speech tells us who hit whom, whether it occurred in the past or is going to happen, etc.). Between the ages of two and three years, the child's use of sentences takes off exponentially and includes the rules for tense and for number (plurals). How does a young child learn this? When I read that Steiner said it was an innate gift that the higher hierarchies (i.e., angelic beings) provided before birth, I was at a loss for how to present this. But now researchers agree with Steiner that these abilities are somehow innate. When they talk about the infant's brain being 'hard wired' to seek out – and even invent, if necessary – the grammatical rules in language and the logical thinking that follows, isn't that a materialistic way of saying the same thing? Here is a report from the *Los Angeles Times*:

Babies struggling to turn babble into polished patter use a previously undiscovered instinct for rules to master the building blocks of language, scientists at New York University announced Thursday.

The new insight is persuasive evidence that the ability to think in terms of formulas and rules is not just something that must be learned through school, as some scholars have argued, but is also a fundamental characteristic of every human mind, several language experts said . . .

The research, published today in Science, broadens the understanding of what may be built into every human being at birth, from a rudimentary knowledge of shapes and numbers to a well-stocked intellectual tool kit for learning the complexities of human speech.[23]

Or here's the natural selection view of the same phenomenon:

> ...Three year olds don't talk that way [the way a chimp would with signboards]. The reason, most linguists agree, is that natural selection has outfitted the human brain with software for grammatical analysis. As MIT linguist Noam Chomsky realized more than 30 years ago, the world languages all build sentences from noun phrases ('The big dog') and verb phrases ('ate my homework'). And toddlers who have never heard of grammar identify them effortlessly.[24]

Unless a child has a specific hereditary condition known as Specific Language Impairment, most children are so primed for grammatical rules that they will invent them if necessary, taking whatever rules they find and sharpening and extending them. The author gives the example of hearing adults who take up American Sign Language to share it with their deaf children. Although they tend to make all kinds of grammatical errors, their children still become fluent. But if deaf children are raised without any language, they grow deaf to grammar and are unable to pick it up later, as has been shown in cases where hearing was restored in adulthood.[25] Whether you consider that language is a gift from the hierarchies or from the mechanics who create the wiring in the brain, it must still have models in order to develop. So talk to and with your child a lot!

Most people would guess that we have language because we can think, but it appears more accurate to say that we are able to think because we have language. According to Rudolf Steiner, the ability to think, reason, and problem-solve grows out of language. It is the order in language and the brain's ability to comprehend it that form the basis for later thinking. Here's support for that understanding:

> The *New York Times* reports that research confirms that the tone and quantity of the words an infant hears affect its ability to solve problems, think rationally and reason abstractly. A study at the University of Iowa found that children of parents who are professionals heard an average of 2100 words each hour, while those of working-class parents heard 1200 words and those of parents on welfare, only 600. The parents' tone of voice –

encouraging, scolding, warm or commanding was also noted.

The two-and-a-half-year study showed that the varying input 'had a profound effect on each child's abilities to think conceptually by age 4.' One of the researchers, Dr. Betty Hart, said that the first three years are unique in the lives of humans because infants are so utterly dependent on adults for all their nurture and language.[26]

However exciting it may be to see your child start to show signs of thinking, this doesn't mean you should start providing lengthy explanations of things or reasoning with her. The young child is still centered around the body and the will, and is not governed by thought and reflection. Imitation and example are still the keys for working with a child before the age of seven, as we will see in subsequent chapters.

The Development of Memory

The development of thinking depends on the process of language formation and the maturing of memory. Steiner points out how the development of the child's memory echoes the historical development of humanity. The first type of memory is localized or place memory, which involves recalling something when the child is in the same environment or receives similar sensory cues. For example, she may only visit grandma's house every few months, but she immediately remembers where the toy cupboard and the cookie jar are when she walks in the door. Historically, this kind of early memory is represented by monuments, cairns, monoliths, and other 'markers' that remind people of the events that occurred at that location. This type of memory is very strong in the young child, who cannot pull up memories at will until the age of six. For example, if you ask preschoolers, 'What did you do at school today?' they will typically say, 'Nothing.' But if they get other cues – you start to sing one of the songs or they see or smell something similar – you can get an amazingly detailed rendition of the morning's activities.

The second type of memory that developed historically can be called rhythmical memory, in which history was carried in verse by poets or bards who would recite epic tales to remind people of their heritage. The rhythmical element makes memorization much easier, as with a young child's 'ABC song' or 'One two, buckle my shoe.' With such songs the child can go through the entire sequence, but is unable to start in the middle or remember individual elements without reciting the whole verse from the beginning.

The third kind of memory, picture memory, begins to develop in the third year and involves the child's being able to use images and ideas. Lois Cusick, in the *Waldorf Parenting Handbook*,[27] diagrams the progression in the accompanying illustration.

HEAD-NERVE SYSTEM

Third Year		Picture memory *(images, ideas)*
Second Year	HEART LUNG · RHYTHMIC SYSTEM	Rhythmic memory *(time)*
First Year		Localized memory *(place, space)*

LIMBS-METABOLIC SYSTEM

The Emerging Sense of Self

Your toddler is very different from a baby, not only in her ability to walk and talk, but also in her sense of self. By the time your child is eighteen months old, you will have no doubt that you are dealing with another human being of power.

A baby has what can be called participatory consciousness. There is no separation between self and other. Certainly the individuality is present and can be sensed in an infant, but it seems to surround the baby as the process of incarnation gradually occurs. The young baby participates in all the sense impressions of life without any distance, only gradually distinguishing various sensations, various adults, and the '10,000 things' of the created world.

We have talked about the common occurrence of fear or shyness with strangers that most babies go through around nine months of age, and during the second year you will see other signs of the emerging sense of 'I' and 'not-I.' During the second year, toddlers begin to feel themselves as separate beings, using their own name, starting to be possessive about toys, and starting to resist simple instructions from their parents. What psychologists call negativism is a normal sign in the second half of the second year of life. As the concept 'no' begins to have meaning for them, children will pit their will against that of their parents.

In *The First Three Years of Life*, White writes, 'Why a child has to become ornery and stay that way for a minimum of six or seven months is one of the mysteries that makes the study of early human development so rich and fascinating....The next comparable step seems to occur at puberty and takes the form of adolescent rebellion. We leave it to other researchers to delve further into this fascinating problem.'[28]

Steiner's explanation of such behavior is that the child's 'I' is being experienced more strongly, making him more awake and more centered in the power of his individuality. These times occur at ages two to three, around age nine, and again around age thirteen. Finally, at age twenty-one, the individuality is fully incarnated into earthly life.

The toddler's emerging sense of self is strengthened by the development of memory, which results in the first conscious use of the word 'I.' Indeed, there can be no awareness of oneself without memory. Memory comes from an accumulation of experiences with the 'not-I.' Things that are painful – a knife that cuts, hard cement steps that cause a bump – interrupt the young child's participatory consciousness and separate the world from the self. Memory arises from these and other encounters, increasing the sense of the observer or the experiencer and the thing experienced. This sense of distance or separation is in contrast to the infant's unfocused consciousness, which doesn't distinguish between self and other, which participates completely in whatever sensation is at hand.

The emergence of memory, thinking, and the self go hand in hand, and sometime in the third year you will notice your child first saying 'I' instead of calling herself by her name. Prior to this time she will say 'Susy do it' or 'Susy book,' imitating what she has heard herself called. Saying 'I' can only be done by the person herself, and the earlier ways of talking will disappear.

The age between two and three is an exciting time, one in which your child wholeheartedly says to the world, 'Here am I!' This wonderful step in development can be accompanied by 'self-will' as the child asserts her new-found power of individuality. Having an understanding of the changing consciousness of the child can help us as parents to gain perspective on the forces behind a child's actions, and can help us offer guidance and correction (insisting on 'right action') without our own emotional reactions muddying the waters. Examples of creative ways of coping with negative behavior will be given in Chapter 5.

In Conclusion

Having insights into your child's physical development and the changes in consciousness from birth through age three can help you understand and respond creatively to your child. In the next two chapters we will consider ways in which you can help your child's development during these crucial first three years.

Recommended Reading

(Because many of these titles are difficult to find, check with the mail order book services listed in Appendix A, or see if your local bookstore can order them.)

The First Three Years of Life by Burton L. White (Simon and Schuster). Valuable for his common-sense approach based on many years observing parents and young children. Not at all

Steiner-oriented, but I found it helpful in its descriptions of behavior based on unbiased observation and in his emphasis on balanced development.

The Good Sleep Guide by Angela Henderson (Hawthorn Press).

The Incarnating Child by Joan Salter (Hawthorn Press). Carries through the second birthday (Steiner-orientated). Highly recommended!

Mothering with Soul by Joan Salter (Hawthorn Press).

Sound Sleep by Sarah Woodhouse (Hawthorn Press). Calming and helping your baby or child to sleep.

Waldorf Parenting Handbook by Lois Cusick (Rudolf Steiner College Press). Valuable section on early childhood, as well as a description of the Waldorf (Steiner School) curriculum through adolescence.

The Young Child by Daniel Udo de Haes (Floris Books). Creative living with two- to four-year-olds, with an emphasis on language development and appropriate stories. The author works out of the inspiration and ideas of Steiner.

CHAPTER 4

Helping Your Baby's Development in the First Year

Your baby's rapid physical development in the first year forms the basis for the development of intelligence in the years that follow. In addition, your baby is beginning to develop emotionally and socially, and the lessons about love and trust learned as an infant form a foundation for later emotional health. The nurturing discussed in the chapter on the newborn applies throughout the critical first year of life. Remember that babies who do not have a primary caregiver fail to thrive, and if a baby's cries receive no response, she becomes apathetic and unresponsive.

The work of parenting in the first year may seem mundane, in that it involves tending to the baby's physical needs for food, cleanliness, sleep, and touch. However, there is tremendous value in the care parents provide, for the infant is being shaped by her relationship with parents and the environment. The parents' feelings and interactions have a subtle impact different from that received in even quality daycare. With more and more women putting the baby in full-time childcare at six weeks to return to their careers, we appeal to mothers and fathers to be with their child as much as possible in at least the first year of life! With the possible exception of your baby's grandmother, in your own home, no one can provide the calm environment and loving attention that the mother or father provides. The idea of 'quality time' does not apply to an infant. She needs the constant proximity, the breastfeeding, the carrying, the being in a carrier or on the floor next to you while you do something.

No other mammal is born as helpless as the human being and no other has such potential for development. In many ways a baby is not 'ready' to be born when compared with other mammals, and yet it must be born after nine months' gestation or the head will become too large and calcified to fit through the mother's pelvis. But the baby's needs for being close to the mother's body do not stop at birth; they continue throughout the first year and longer. Most non-industrialized societies practice some form of marsupial mothering, carrying the baby in constant contact with the mother's body up to the age of nine months – almost like a second gestational period. At that time there is a noticeable change, as the baby becomes much more interested in the surrounding world, reaches for table foods, and is able to crawl and then walk on her own.

A different approach from the 'in arms' mothering described above was developed by Dr. Emmi Pikler, one of the leading European doctors who studied and worked with infants. She worked in a children's home in Hungary, and the center for her work in North America is called Resources for Infant Educarers, run by Magda Gerber. Helle Heckmann, who runs a Waldorf daycare center in Denmark, says of Pikler, 'Through her observation of children, she was able to show the importance of confidence and self-reliance as well as the belief in 'being able to,' as fundamental to the child's development into a confident adult. By reinforcing the child's confidence in her physical capabilities, and by respecting each child's individual developmental path, we as caregivers and educators can meet the needs of the young child. Emmi Pickler has given me the courage to work with children in a respectful way.'[1] Heckmann translates that into her approach with infants and describes it as follows:

> There is no doubt that the infant thrives on love. Countless studies of the development of infants have shown that love and care are vital. But caring should not be mistaken for reaction and constant supervision. Show care and affection in situations when it is natural, such as eating and nursing, when it is natural to create a you-and-I situation, when it is natural to nurse, sing, chat, and get to know each other. The rest of the time it is important to leave the infant in peace and quiet to sleep or, when

awake, to get to know herself without constant intervention from her surroundings. Often it is very difficult to show the infant this respect and leave her alone. Constantly satisfying our own need for reassurance and your need to look at your beautiful baby will often influence the infant's ability to be content with herself. Too many disturbances quickly lead to dependence on constant attention from the surroundings, and a vicious cycle of bad habits is created. By giving the infant peace and quiet for the first months of her life, she will get used to her physical life.[2]

Proponents of both attachment parenting and Pikler's more hands-off approach each have numerous arguments on their side. Parents and caregivers in both groups are caring, concerned, and consistent, and – when they are in touch with the being and the real needs of the child – both get good results (i.e., great kids). But when they fall off the tightrope, the former tend to err on the side of 'smother love' or letting the child totally run the circus, while the latter tend to err on the side of rigidity or distance.

Steiner always encouraged people not to accept things by rote or on faith, but to test ideas for themselves. The key, as I see it, is not to follow any 'system' or 'expert' to the sacrifice of the child. Try to inform yourself, and ask, 'what does the child need in this situation for his or her best development?' Use your head, listen to your heart, and make your best decisions based on what you perceive your child needs and what you are able to provide in each situation. And then, if possible, evaluate what happened and grow from what you learned.

While we have spent a great deal of time discussing different approaches to mothering, let's not forget the fathers! The father's ever-expanding relationship with the baby also contributes greatly to the child's growth and development. This relationship can begin during pregnancy, as the father takes time to be in touch with the developing body and being of his child. In experiencing the birth with his wife, he finds his love and connection with this child strengthening dramatically. By sharing the care of the baby and watching it grow, the father's relationship deepens, so that he finds other times and ways to be with the baby, especially when it is being breastfed. As the baby develops and is increasingly able to respond with smiles and play, the relationship of father and child deepens. In addition to the special love and protection a father can provide for his baby and his wife, there are many ways in which he can interact with his baby during the first year. Fathering is of benefit not only to the baby, but also the man, who allows the nurturing aspect of his personality to develop. Mothers enjoy seeing their husbands interact with the baby; in fact, studies have shown that marital satisfaction for women with children is connected with seeing their husbands active as a father.[3]

We will present no recipes for producing a 'super baby.' In fact, what most new parents need is confidence that they themselves are important and can provide the best possible care for their babies. However, based on an increasing knowledge of child development and the gradual nature of the incarnation process, certain principles and activities can be especially helpful for you and your baby.

Physical Development

As we have seen, all babies go through a normal sequence of development that involves assuming control of the body. The differences in developmental rates of individual babies have more to do with timing than with the order in which skills develop. Freedom to move the arms and legs assures that muscles will strengthen and that processes such as language and cognitive development, which are related to physical movement, will unfold appropriately. If you are having serious questions about your baby's development, check with your family doctor or a specialist to reassure yourself that your baby is developing normally. This is especially true if you suspect a hearing problem or if your baby has frequent ear infections. So much of learning depends on good hearing!

Your baby does not need baby exercise courses or other fancy stimulation to develop well. Expensive infant stimulation or home exercise kits are a waste of money and make the false assumption that we know better than the baby which muscles she should move. You can have all the benefits of positive interaction with your baby without spending the money simply by enjoying being with your child and rolling around on the floor together. If you are doing something because it feels good in the moment (massaging your baby or watching him grab at something), then you are interacting positively. But if you are doing it for results (so he'll be serene when he grows up or will walk sooner), then you are out of the present moment and have fallen prey to the media hype that tells us we should help our children to progress faster.

Understanding how your baby develops can help you to have realistic expectations and to provide toys and a physical environment that are developmentally appropriate.

Remember how completely at one with the environment the baby is. During the first six weeks this means providing a very protected atmosphere for the incoming spirit. After around six weeks there is a developmental change, and you may find that your baby has outgrown the silks over the bassinet and is ready for more interaction with the world. Lying outside and experiencing the interplay of light and shadow through the leaves of a tree in the garden will delight a baby if she is warm and not in a draft.

The most important thing that you are doing in the first year is providing a calm and loving environment for your baby, so that she can grow and develop according to her own inner unfolding.

Your baby needs very little to play with in the first few months because her main task is to become accustomed to her body and to develop her muscles (and hence her brain) through natural movements. While your baby is still primarily a horizontal being, you can delight her with a mobile in which the objects are horizontal and thus visible to the baby (remember that what is visible to you is seen as a narrow edge by the baby in the crib). Appropriate toys for a baby who cannot yet sit up include a solidly made crib gym, or other objects suspended across the crib that she can grasp while on her back. While babies seem to enjoy batting at objects on crib gyms, some experts suggest that objects that hang on sticks rather than strings are preferable because they are easier for the baby to catch.

Crib toys should not produce loud noises or flashing lights. It is important for safety to remove hanging crib toys when your baby seems nearly able to pull herself up to a sitting position.

Before a baby can sit up, it is good to have her near you on a blanket on the floor. Babies don't object to being on their backs or on their stomachs instead of sitting. Our culture is visually oriented, and we think that babies always need to be sitting up in molded infant seats when they are awake. Some researchers on developmental learning disabilities feel that babies should not be propped up into a sitting position by infant seats, but should be given the opportunity to achieve the sitting position entirely unaided.[4] It is a question of not jumping ahead of the normal progression of development. You'll also want to carry your baby a lot for closeness and touch. In the last chapter we discussed options for wrapping the baby in a shawl or using a front pack that keeps the baby horizontal until she can sit up by herself. Be sure to care for the head-neck relationship when the baby is in a stroller. Prams and some baby buggies are designed so that babies can lie horizontal until they are able to sit up by themselves. While folding-umbrella buggies are major conveniences for today's mobile mother, they do allow the young baby to flop about, and the babies are facing the wrong way! A baby or toddler would be much more comfortable facing her mother, whom she knows and with whom she feels secure, rather than being exposed to the crowds, dogs, exhaust fumes, and sensory stimulation of our streets. (A few European and American buggies now have the option to face in either direction; they're worth searching for.)

Once your baby can sit up, you'll find she loves to play with small objects, which are important in the development of physical coordination and intelligence. Especially valuable are toys and small objects that can be banged, thrown, or dropped. Think of things you already have that she will find fascinating. (Remember that everything ends up in the mouth, and small pieces that can break off are dangerous. Anything smaller than $1^1/_2$ inches in any dimension could get stuck in a baby's throat.) A wooden spoon, a beautiful shell, a cloth ball, and a small dried gourd can be favorites. Your kitchen is full of wonderful 'toys' – measuring spoons, pots and lids, nesting bowls. The rattle, of which the infant was unaware and which the three-month-old would hold or drop indiscriminately, gradually becomes interesting for its texture and sounds. Several sources of natural toys are listed at the end of this chapter. While there is nothing wrong with chrome and plastic, it seems appropriate to honor the natural connection that young children have with the living world.

The playpen is another invention that doesn't take into account the real developmental needs of the child. Until the baby crawls, playpens are totally useless. A blanket on the floor serves just as well, and a basket for toys can be handy for picking things up when the baby takes a nap. Once the baby starts to crawl, playpens are a real barrier to development.

When Your Baby Starts to Crawl

Development from a parent's point of view seems to go in phases where first everything is all right, then it's fairly difficult, then all is well again, and so on. Joseph Chilton Pearce, in *The Magical Child*, speaks about each developmental step being preceded by a return to the matrix (structure, safety, mother) and then followed by a voyage out into the world to find new experiences and new abilities.[5] This expansion and contraction is like breathing, and it is important for development that times of regression (inwardness, clinging behavior) be understood not as backsliding, but as preparation for the next surge forward toward independence.

This 'regression' often happens just before a baby starts to crawl. You might find yourself carrying around this heavy child much of the time and wondering, 'When will it ever change?' And then suddenly it does, and your baby is off, having mastered the first means of getting around on his own. Parenting changes at this time, because your baby is suddenly into everything. Planning ahead can save you a lot of grief and make this an exciting time in your lives.

Sometime before your baby starts to crawl, you will need to 'babyproof' your home, making it safe for and from the baby. Starting with the kitchen, where your baby will probably spend the most time, make sure that all poisonous and dangerous items are out of reach and put simple toddler locks on cupboards that you don't want the baby to get into. You should also check for unstable objects, such as an ironing board or a potted plant. Breakable items should be put on high shelves or put away for the duration. Putting hooks on the bathroom door and on screen doors is a must. If you have older children, make sure they keep small items out of the baby's reach.

Stairs pose a special risk of falling, but babies love stairs. An invaluable suggestion from White is to place the child guard gate about three steps up instead of at the bottom of your staircase. This gives your baby a place to practice climbing without risk of getting hurt.

Making your home a safe place for the baby is one of the best things you can do to aid your child's development. The objects in your home provide wonderful stimulation for her, and you won't have to say no all the time. It is much better to let your baby roam than to keep her in a playpen, because babies need to crawl, need changing stimulation, and need to be around you. In his observations of families where children developed beautifully, White found that parents had made their homes safe and open to children rather than keeping them caged in playpens, where they rapidly became bored. He states, 'It is my view that to bore a child on a daily basis by the regular use of a playpen for extended periods is a very poor child-rearing practice. The same principle applies to the use of cribs, jump seats, high chairs and other restrictive devices' when they are used to limit a child's movement for long periods every day.[6]

The Development of Intelligence

During the first year of life, your baby's brain weight can actually double. Brain cells, which become stimulated by picking up and relaying messages, develop new dendrite spines, and these neural pathways become myelinated, or insulated to make the pathway that has been created operate more accurately and faster. Your baby is learning constantly through her physical activities. As movements become more coordinated and are repeated hundreds of times each day, your baby learns eye-hand co-ordination and how to grasp something she sees. According to both Piaget and Steiner, these things that seem like the foundation of physical development are also the foundation for later intellectual development.

Between the ages of six and eight months a baby's interests usually change from her own motor skills to the world around her, and memory starts to develop. Interest in dropping, banging, and throwing small objects starts to teach the baby about cause-and-effect and temporal sequence, important foundations for later thinking. For example, the seven-month-old will repeatedly drop a spoon or toy from a high chair and watch where it goes. Toys that involve doing one thing and causing another part to move are also favorites for a child of this age.

Understanding the gradual development of memory is also important when considering the growth of intelligence. Jane Healy concludes from her research in developmental neuropsychology:

> A child's first months lay the groundwork for paying attention, taking in bits of information to each of the senses, and practicing with body movements. During this 'sensorimotor' period, the brain is not ready to deal with much beyond immediate physical experience. Around eight or nine months of age, the prefrontal cortex begins its long march toward maturity, and the child starts to use memory to link past and present experience: 'Oops! Here comes the sitter – time to cry!'[7]

As the prefrontal cortex starts to develop, short-term memory and 'object permanence' start to develop in the baby. Piaget felt that when a young baby drops something, it is completely gone – that there is no memory of it. He created several experiments to determine when short-term memory develops in the child. In one such experiment, a toy was repeatedly hidden under a scarf in full view of a baby, on the baby's right side. The baby would easily remove the scarf and find the toy. Then the same toy was hidden under a scarf on the left side while the baby watched (the first scarf remained on the right side). Babies would typically reach for the object on the right, where they had previously found it, rather than on the left side, where they had just seen it placed. Piaget explains that at first the existence of a small object is tied to the activities that the child has been involved in with that object, rather than to a concept of object permanence.[8] This supports Steiner's contention that the baby experiences the world primarily through movement and its body. Short-term memory gradually increases from seven to eight months of age, so that by the time a toddler is eighteen months old, a desirable object hidden in front of the child one day will immediately be found the next day.

Because babies live very much in the present moment without the same kind of memory as an adult, it is effective simply to remove an object (or remove the baby) when she has some precious object. This is better than saying no, which should be almost unnecessary if you have babyproofed your house.

We've talked about your baby's desire to hold, study, and taste the things she sees. Now she will also become interested in dropping and throwing objects. A baby sitting in her high chair and dropping her spoon for the tenth time is not doing it to annoy you. Rather, she is observing the wonderful phenomenon we call gravity, and playing with the idea of appearance and disappearance (which makes peek-a-boo a favorite game). In this play we can see a metaphor for the coming in and out of existence or manifestation that the baby is exploring by its very being. There is as yet no memory to give an object permanence; mother disappears and reappears as suddenly as the baby itself appeared in the physical world.

Babies around six to eight months of age also love to bang things and explore sounds. Having a cupboard in the kitchen that is the baby's (and putting guard locks on the others) can be a real blessing. While you're busy, your baby can be occupied swinging the door, banging the pot with the wooden spoon, stacking the unbreakable bowls, or rattling the taped container with rice inside.

It is pointless to address a baby's learning ability in an abstract fashion from birth until eight months of age, because all babies go through the normal pattern of development unless they are abused or otherwise disabled. Jane Healy concluded from her study of developmental neuropsychology, 'Your overall goal should be not to 'teach' your baby but to help her discover how to organize experience for herself. . . . Babies come equipped with the 'need to know'; our job is to give them love, acceptance, and the raw material of appropriate stimulation at each level of development. Your own common sense, augmented by current knowledge, is the best guide.'[9]

However, current pressures for early academic achievement and the American maxim that 'faster is better' have clouded the area of common sense when it comes to activities like teaching babies to read. Healy points out that even though babies can be taught to read words with enough condition-response training, they are not reading for meaning and are using a lower part of their brain (simply because the parts of the brain that should be used in reading are not yet developed). She felt this might develop habit patterns that are hard to undo later – see Chapter 12 for further information on reasons not to push academics onto younger and younger children. Let your baby be a baby – play with her through language and movement and enjoy one another!

At this stage it is impossible to separate physical development and the development of intelligence, but one is not predictive of the other. In other words, a child who crawls at six months and walks at eight is not more intelligent or highly developed than a child who crawls at ten months and walks at fourteen. What is important for the development of intelligence is that the motions are gone through; the internal timetable is usually just a question of individual differences within the wide range of normal. Researchers have been unable to find dramatic evidence of poor development in the first year in children who do poorly later, probably because they have not yet developed the deficit.[10] In other words, most parents manage to provide all that is needed for their baby's development in the first year. So relax, enjoy, and put your attention on the spheres that are more open to parental input during the first eight months.

Emotional Development

A baby's sense of well-being depends on having its needs met for love, warmth, touch, and food. Emotional development is based on the love, trust, and touch found in the baby's first relationship with the family.

When you respond promptly to your baby's cries, she learns that the world is a friendly place to live in and that your love and protection surround her. Mothers who follow their instincts know this, and it's nice to find psychologists now stating that you can't spoil a young baby. Unfortunately, however, mothers are still likely to hear grandparents or perhaps even their husbands comment that they are spoiling the baby – or even that it's good for babies to cry. Surrounding your baby with love, warmth, and touch provides a secure foundation for later life that is almost impossible to make up if it has been lacking.

Researchers have observed that babies usually cry only in response to discomfort until around four or five months of age. Then a new kind of intentional behavior can be seen for the first time: crying to bring an adult to pick up and cuddle them. In other words, she has learned, through successfully having her physical needs met, that she can also cry for attention. It is important that she have confidence that an adult, and a pleasant experience, will come when she calls. (Remember that babies in institutions learn that their cries won't bring a response, and so they do not exhibit this new way of getting the attention of adults.) Most professionals would rather see a baby between three and six months cry too much for attention than cry too little and risk inadequate attention during the first few months of life.[10] Beginning to distinguish between the two types of cries is a valuable skill to start developing. Because babies have neither reason nor a sense of time, you can't tell the child to wait or to stop it. Many mothers find this a difficult time in their parenting.

During the months before your baby learns to crawl (perhaps between six and eight months) your baby may become demanding in the sense that she can see everything, wants to experience it, but can't get to it. This driving force for crawling and walking is positive, but it can result in a baby who requires frequent changes of scenery, adult input, or carrying to avoid complaining. Burton White, in his quest to find what creates a pleasant, unspoiled three-year-old, as well as a bright one, has traced the origins of 'spoiling' back to those parents who fall into a pattern of constantly responding to their six- or seven-month-old's cry for attention. 'If you find that you are picking up your child and playing with her seven or eight times an hour for six or seven hours a day, you are probably moving into a pattern that will cause you some grief fairly soon,' White states.[11]

I found this statement interesting because White is a sensible observer, and he must have observed some sort of correlation. While I couldn't figure out how he could mean that you should ignore your baby's call for attention (easier for a father to say than for a mother to do), I pondered this observation for many years. It would seem that if there is a potential problem, it must lie in developing the pattern of a whiny baby who is picked up six or eight times an hour. One of the ways to avoid the pattern is to involve your baby in your life. For example, mothers with one or two other young children don't have this problem as often – they haven't the time. Also, the siblings provide interaction for the baby, so attention needn't always come from the mother.

It seems that White was observing the problems created when the baby became the center of attention instead of an observer of and participant in family life. Ignoring your baby and letting her cry it out is not what is being asked for! Rather, it is to realize that your baby is born into your family and needs to find his or her place there. Mothering is the delicate balance of not letting the baby become the center of the universe to the extent that you are jumping to her every whim, but not ignoring her out of some mistaken philosophy that you will spoil the child. It seems to me that two problems arise. The one we have just discussed seems to be solved by carrying the question, 'How can I be in empathetic connection with my baby and perceive what she needs in this moment?'

The other seems to involve the fact that modern life does not support what young children need and hence leads to problems of babies not being able to observe their mothers doing 'real work' around the house (I discuss this further in the section on work and play in Chapter 7). With the industrial revolution and the move to the cities, labour-saving devices not only changed the nature of home life, but created families in which women were isolated from other members of their families – indeed, from other adults altogether.

Another way to avoid the baby's learning to whine louder and louder to get mother's attention is to have other adults about. Our culture, with its lack of extended family, puts a real strain on the mother. A friend of mine who spent many years in Mexico wanted to practice 'total mothering,' by always carrying her baby in a rebozo or shawl, as most of the Mexican village babies are carried. By the time her son was nine months old, she felt burned out and was beginning to resent never being able to put him down without his fussing. Then she realized she had made a mistake only a foreigner could make. Yes, the babies she had seen were almost always held, carried, and receiving attention, but not always by the mother. Sometimes the aunt had him in the sling, sometimes a cousin or older sibling, other times it was grandma who was tending him while mother sewed or sorted beans nearby. How much you hold and carry your baby can have an effect on him, but it also needs to be balanced with your own needs and emotional well-being.

The larger problem with regard to parenting and the many resulting difficulties has to be: 'How can we overcome our isolation and find or re-create community?' Mothering young children in isolation can be crazy-making – I'm convinced it was never meant to happen. Everyone nods with a certain recognition that 'it takes a village to raise a child.' Two historical forces in American society served to isolate women and their mothering. One was the pioneering spirit to strike out for the last frontier; the other was the migration to the cities. While it was tremendously difficult for pioneer women to be separated from their community of women, life was so hard that children had to be incorporated into the process of helping the family survive, and rural life was at least healthier than conditions in the overcrowded tenements or factories. But with the dominance of city life, the isolation of mothers has continued and intensified as we have become increasingly mobile and tend to live far from any family relatives. If you find yourself home alone with your baby and are not having the time of your life, you need to reach out and find a network of support for yourself. You owe it to your children, your mothering, and yourself. Some suggestions include La Leche League, parent and toddler groups, play groups, or religious groups. Put up signs in the co-op or start talking to other mothers in the park – they're either as isolated as you are, or they've found something worth sharing.

Language Development

As we have discussed in the last chapter, the first year is a critical period for learning the sounds of a language and developing an interest in communicating with others. The baby has been able to hear sounds from the fifth month inside the womb, but most of the sounds come from within the mother's own body or from her internal vibrations as she speaks. Only near the end of pregnancy does the expanded uterus begin to conduct outside sounds with any clarity. Some 'prenatal university' advocates are trying to sell parents taped messages or music with special earphones that attach to the mother's stomach to increase auditory pathways for future language or mathematical development. Just as Steiner says that you wouldn't want to stimulate the developing eye of the baby when it was in the womb, Jane Healy advises that 'until we learn more about this topic it seems sensible to give the fetus a calm, stable start without an atmosphere of overstimulation or pressure. By all means talk and sing to your unborn child as you relax and rock, but reflect carefully before you start 'pushing' any type of learning.' If you're still tempted by the hype associated with these items, she continues:

> Overstimulating parents, however, should think twice about an experiment in which duck embryos were subjected to abnormally intense auditory stimulation (noise); after the ducks were born they failed to learn their mother's call and showed other signs of abnormal attention and development. When you are tempted to turn up the stereo, remind yourself that 'augmented sensory experience' is probably not good for human babies either.[12]

Infants show preferences for their mother's voice and start trying to understand and remember speech sounds soon after birth. Nothing can substitute for the love and attention you give your baby when you talk to her. She will turn toward the sound of your voice, and she is always interested in your face! By talking to your baby when you change her, for example, you are providing loving stimulation and a model for language development. At around four months your baby will turn and smile when you say her name. This is a stage called pre-language comprehension, because any name will work equally well – but it is an exciting time. By eight months she will probably be responding to a few specific words, which usually include some variation of Mother, Daddy, baby, and bye-bye if English is your primary language in the home.

Babies prefer sounds that are high pitched, and respond especially well to the voice when it is rhythmical and melodic – hence the use of lullabies with babies throughout all cultures. But nursery rhymes and songs are also enjoyable to do with your baby when she is awake and alert. *In The Laughing Baby: Remembering Nursery Rhymes and Reasons*,[13] Anne Scott not only shares songs and rhymes from around the world, but also combines the traditions of age-old cultures with current research regarding infant development, showing that such instinctive behavior has its justification in scientific fact. If you can't remember songs or rhymes from your own childhood, perhaps books such as this one can help us regain the intuition that produced these ancient pastimes.

Any time you hum or sing to your baby, you are doing her a wonderful service. Some parents worry that they 'aren't musical,' but everyone can hum, and songs can be extremely simple, involving only a few words and one or two notes. A simple musical instrument called a children's harp or lyre is very soothing at nap or bedtime and can also help parents bring the musical element to their young children. The harp is tuned in a special way that is called pentatonic, so that anything you play sounds angelic – there are no wrong notes. Sources for the children's harp are listed at the end of this chapter, and music is discussed more in Chapter 10.

Toys for the First Year

American companies spent $2 billion on advertising to children in 1998, 20 times more than in 1988. Despite what Madison Avenue would like you to believe, your baby will develop quite healthily without your buying any toys in the first year. Helle Heckmann says, 'The infant has himself, and it is by observing himself and his limbs that the infant develops. That is why the infant should not be offered any toys.'[14] However, every baby is going to have toys, so what principles can guide our selections?

At the Center for Parent Education in Newton, Massachusetts, Burton White and Michael Meyerhoff did extensive observations and reviews of toys on the market to see which ones children play with, whether they are developmentally appropriate, and whether they are labeled for the proper age group. They found that even products of good quality are often labeled for the wrong age child, and they warn parents about the hard sell and the oversell, which pressure you to believe that terribly expensive items are necessary. If you are going to buy toys from your local toy shop, White and Meyerhoff's findings can be a help.[15]

In this chapter I have already discussed some toys you can make or buy for the baby, including a mobile, crib gym, and rattle. Items from nature and from your kitchen are also favorites. Toys that show simple mechanisms through moveable parts are especially good for the child discovering cause and effect (around seven months). For example, toys that involve turning a crank to make a windmill go around or pulling a stick to make the woodsmen chop their wood are fun for children to manipulate. Similarly, anything with hinges is a welcome toy: boxes with hinged lids, cupboard doors, or books with stiff pages (don't expect much interest in pictures or stories until after eighteen months).

Balls of all sizes and varieties are favorites of toddlers. Felted wool balls are ideal for inside play because of their softness. Ping pong balls can be chased all over the room and a large beach ball can be carried, chased, thrown, or kicked.

Even very young children love water play, and objects for floating or pouring can also make bath time more enjoyable.

What your baby needs is a balance of playing with objects, moving to develop physical skills, and interacting with people. Interaction can come through the daily care you give your baby – through breastfeeding and, later, spoon feedings, changing, and bathing. Just make sure that you are attentive and aware of your baby as a human being during these times, rather than treating her as an object or a chore that has to be accomplished. Talking and singing to your baby can lead into playing games as she becomes a little older. Babies love to play peek-a-boo after they are about six months old, delighting in the appearance and disappearance of themselves and the world. Simple movement games like 'pat-a-cake' or 'so big' also delight a one-year-old.

Recommended Toys and Equipment

- A rocking chair
- A children's harp or lyre
- An infant car seat (birth to nine months); a child car seat (nine months on)
- A cloth sling for carrying young babies; a sling or backpack for older babies

- A pram and, later, a stroller or push chair for outdoor walks
- A stainless steel mirror (especially around four months of age)
- A crib gym (from six weeks until the baby is sitting)
- A stair gate placed on the third stair to allow for safe climbing practice, or you can construct three steps and a platform.
- A baby food grinder to fix foods from your table (no need to give solid food before six months – and your food is fresh and salt- and sugar-free, unlike processed baby foods)
- A large box or basket to keep toys in (when he's asleep and you want the house to look tidy)
- Several balls of various sizes, including a cloth or felt ball for the younger child; avoid foam balls, which can easily be pulled apart and eaten
- Pots and pans (six to twelve months)
- Containers with lids; hinged boxes (seven to fifteen months)
- A box or basket with about a dozen safe objects (large wooden thread spools, a large shell, pieces of driftwood, a pretty rock)
- Books with stiff pages
- Low four-wheeled toys that can be straddled (once your baby is walking)
- Water toys

Of Questionable Value

- Dummies – Perhaps nursing, or your finger, would work as well? Some babies do need to suck more than they need to eat, and a dummy can be soothing during the first year of life, but its danger is that it replaces human interaction. Toddlers and older children who have a dummy pinned to their clothing often have it stuck in their mouths just to keep them quiet. And in the late 1990s there was quite a stir about plastic dummies containing a chemical that caused cancer in animals. Although the Food and Drug Administration, (FDA), in the US refused to recall the products, the companies involved voluntarily removed the chemical from the products – but after how many years of infants sucking on them?
- Props for bottles – Propping a bottle means that your baby is losing the love and attention that accompanies breastfeeding or

bottle feeding. Letting a baby fall asleep with a bottle in his mouth can result in serious tooth decay, because the juice or milk sits in the mouth and the sugars encourage bacterial growth and 'bottle mouth syndrome.'

- Baby bouncer – This gets the baby vertical before she can stand, and the force of jumping can have a negative impact on the leg bones.
- Baby walker – Although babies love the mobility, it makes them vertical before they can stand and takes time away from crawling; it is also implicated in many accidents in the home.
- Playpen – This is not worth the expense for the rare moments you need your baby to be confined. Better to babyproof your home!
- Swimming classes – Although these were formerly in vogue, many mothers reported negative experiences and no real gains.
- Baby gymnastics – Your baby knows best how to move to develop! Gymnastics can be all right as an excuse to meet other mothers if it's nondirected, but it tends to be too stimulating and can place your baby or toddler at risk.

Some Things To Do

- Value touching, carrying, skin-to-skin contact.
- Talk to your baby; focus on her as a person when you're caring for her.
- Hum and sing to your baby.
- Value contact with nature: your baby will love to see the interplay of light and shadow when under a tree; toddlers love sand and water play, indoors or out; avoid over-exposure to bright sun.
- Nursery rhymes and movement games, including peek-a-boo, pat-a-cake, this little pig, hickory dickory, and where's baby?

Recommended Reading

Various Styles of Mothering

The Continuum Concept by Jean Leidloff (Arkana). The classic discussion of attachment parenting.

Juno Magazine – natural approach to family life. PO Box 592, East Grinstead, West Sussex RH19 3AQ www.junomagazine.com

The Laughing Baby by Anne Scott (Celestial Arts). Nursery rhymes from around the world.

The Lullaby Treasury by Mathile Polee and Petra Rosenberg (Floris Books). Cradle songs from around the world.

The Mother Magazine www.themothermagazine.co.uk

Mothering, PO Box 1690, Santa Fe, NM 876504; US parenting magazine with six issues of great reading each year.

Mothering and Fathering by Tine Thevenin (Avery). Discusses the gender differences in parenting – both in society and in the home.

Resources for Infant Educarers (RIE), 1550 Murray Circle, Los Angeles, CA 90026. Books, videos, training opportunities, and other information are available on the approach of Emmi Pickler.

The Singing Day by Candy Verney (Hawthorn Press).

Your Child at Play: Birth to One Year by Marilyn Segal (Newmarket Press). A practical book with numerous photos.

Things to Do with Your Baby

Sources for toys

For valuable reviews of conventional toys on the market, see *The First Three Years of Life* by Burton L. White or inquire about the review of toys he has prepared for the Center for Parent Education, 55 Chapel Street, Newton, MA 02160.

For toys for babies made from wood, wool, cotton, and other natural materials, write:
US

The Natural Baby Catalog, 7835-3 Freedom Ave. NW, N. Canton, OH 44720. www.storc.yahoo.com

The Playstore, 508 University Ave., Palo Alto, CA 94301.
   www.playstoretoys.com
(See a more complete list at the end of Chapter 7.)

UK

Myriad Natural Toys, Ringwood, Hampshire.
   Tel no. 01725 517085 www.myriadonline.co.uk

For children's harps, write:
US

Choroi, P.O. Box 684544, Austin, TX 78768.

Harps of Lorien, Raphael Weisman, P.O. Box 77, Questa,
   NM 87556.

Rose Lyre Workshop, P.O. Box 538, Claverack, NY 12513.

Song of the Sea, Ed and Anne Damm, 47 West St., Bar Harbor,
   ME 04609.

UK

Myriad Natural Toys (as above)

Herga Music, 4 High Street, Wealdstone, Harrow, Middlesex
   Tel no. 020 8861 1590 www.hergamusic.co.uk

CHAPTER 5

Helping Your Toddler's Development

Encouraging Balanced Development

Between the ages of one and two, your toddler is improving physical mastery of her body and also developing facility with language. With the development of language, you will start to see your child use ideas and images in her mind rather than physical actions to solve problems. This growth of thinking and memory interact with her behavior, so that a two-year-old is a highly complex social being. This aspect of development is marked by the emergence of individuality and personal power, the growing sense of 'I.'

The main task of parents as first teachers during the time from twelve to twenty-four months is to encourage a balanced development. Physical development involves practicing new motor skills; emotional development centers around her relationship with her mother, father, or other primary caretakers; intellectual development comes primarily through exploring the world around her.

Your toddler's natural inquisitiveness is best met by letting it unfold naturally in a babyproofed home, free from restraints. Much of her time will be spent exploring objects and mastering skills (such as taking things apart, stacking them up and knocking them down). Hinged doors, stairs, and climbing up on a chair to look out the window are favorite activities. The toilet bowl is a favorite source of play, so be sure to keep the bathroom inaccessible. Outdoor play is encouraged since there are so many things to explore. Children in this age range love to swing and to play in the sandbox.

Because everything she explores still goes into her mouth and will be swallowed if possible, make sure that toxic items are stored out of reach in locked cupboards (toddlers love to climb). We wonder how children can swallow petrol or cleaning fluid, but their curiosity is stronger than bad tastes or smells, and children may swallow just about anything. Take time to re-check your home for safety when your child is between one and two years of age!

In terms of social development, a child in the second year will be focused primarily on her parents, not going very long without checking back in with them for nurturing, advice, assistance, or just making sure they are there. By being available when your child wants you and letting him explore without you, you are teaching your child both independence and security. And your encouragement and interaction when she brings you something to look at fosters her natural curiosity, showing that you value both inquisitiveness and learning.

Positive social interaction among two-year-olds is not very common – they usually lack the social skills to play together. The only advantage of a play group at this age is the social interaction it provides the mothers. The children, in fact, will need to be closely supervised to make sure they remain harmonious. Play will be more side-by-side than interactive.

In terms of interest in practicing motor skills, you will find that your baby from the age of fourteen months is able not only to walk, but also to climb. Running will also start to develop. Your eighteen-month-old will also probably like toys that she can straddle and 'walk' along. The ability to operate a tricycle usually isn't present until after the age of two, and such toys are best delayed until the child is older.

The best way to keep a balance in these areas of exploration, movement, and social interaction is to provide an environment where the child can explore by herself (with adult awareness of safety but not always with adult interaction). This will usually be your home, made safe and provided with a few simple toys in addition to common household items.

'Aids to Learning'

Because of the natural impulse to want to provide the best opportunities for their children, many parents are turning to classes to help their eighteen-month-old learn to swim, read, become a gymnast, or whatever. Classes to teach infants to swim were very popular several years ago and have since drawn a great deal of criticism. Most mothers' experiences were that early gains were lost, and their children's experiences were often heart-wrenching. Trust yourself, and don't do anything you don't feel good about. Putting your child into a frightening situation is not worthwhile. No classes are necessary for optimal or even enhanced development. If you do go to any kind of group, make sure that you stay with your child, that the activity is appropriate for her age, and that the environment is not overwhelming on a sensory level. As mentioned before, a baby gymnastics class can be fun as a social experience for mothers with 'cabin fever', but such classes can push children beyond their developmental stage. The toddler knows best which muscles to exercise to develop optimally. An excellent summary of reasons parents want their children to be in classes and why it is better to avoid them is contained in *Miseducation: Preschoolers at Risk*, by David Elkind.[1] Even a play group is probably not very appropriate for a child of this age, but a mother's support group, in which one or two mothers take turns watching the children while the others meet together to talk can be a tremendous support. (They can also meet at night while dad watches the children!) Many Steiner/Waldorf schools have parent and child groups, as do many churches and service organizations.

Similarly, any kind of emphasis on intellectual development that takes time away from physical movement can lead to imbalance. There's a saying, 'Don't push the river.' Your baby is developing according to his or her own inner clock. Tampering with the mechanism by trying to speed up one area can lead to problems in other areas.

Parents wonder if their child will be missing out if she doesn't watch *Sesame Street* or other TV programmes designed to promote early language skills. However, children learn how to use 'before' and 'after' in their speech perfectly well from hearing you speak –

they don't need Grover to give a lesson on it! In fact, one study showed that only language from living sources, not television, produced vocabulary and syntax-boosting effects.[2] Burton White corroborates this by saying, 'Rest assured that if he never sees a single television program he can still learn language through you in an absolutely magnificent manner.'[3] Before the age of two, children who are exposed to television don't really watch the screen for more than a few seconds at a time. The medium is totally inappropriate for the toddler, who needs to be moving and actively exploring. Up until now, young children have fortunately been unable to sit long enough to watch the screen; if they did so with older siblings, it was more in an imitative and social way than through paying attention to what was on. Unfortunately, television producers have now studied what attracts toddlers and have begun programming designed to capture their attention. After the success of Barney among the preschool crowd, the Teletubbies were designed specifically to appeal to toddlers. Toys R Us was even selling a video designed for infants under twelve months of age, called *Early Images*. It combines 'pictures and sounds attractive to infants in twenty-seven vignettes that are designed to stimulate their sensory abilities.' For a detailed discussion of how the two-dimensional, flickering sensory stimulation from television is not what a young child needs, see Chapter 13. In the meantime, it would be best for your baby if you moved your television into another room where adults and older children could watch it, without the images and sounds cluttering the environment of your baby or toddler.

As your child's first teacher, you have primary responsibility for him in the first years of life. One of the most important things you can do is to pay attention to all that surrounds your child. This includes the food, clothing, images, toys, sunshine, sand, and water. It also includes the less tangible 'nourishment' that comes from your warmth and love and the emotions that surround your child. To help your toddler develop, work on yourself, which means cultivating patience and firmness and getting rid of blame and guilt when you are not the ideal parent. No one is, but it is the striving and the effort to grow inwardly that speaks most strongly to children, who are so involved with physical and emotional growth. Our children come to see our faults and forgive us; our orientation toward inner growth through parenting fosters change within ourselves and is a great gift to our children.

Understanding your child's development, you will be less likely to do things that impede it (such as boring him by restraining him in a car seat, playpen or high chair for hours every day). You will also avoid unrealistic expectations of your child, such as expecting her to remember that certain things aren't allowed or trying to reason with her. Remember the principles of imitation and movement in correcting her actions! This will make you better able to provide the correction and guidance that are needed, and to avoid the emotional annoyance that can lead to telling your child she is 'bad' for exploring things you want her to stay out of.

Dealing with Negative Behavior

One of the challenges of living with the child from eighteen to thirty-six months is dealing with the 'negativism' that he manifests. If you can recognize your child's emerging sense of self and power as something positive, you won't fall into the trap of thinking that you have done something wrong ('If only we hadn't moved...' or 'He must be selfish because I have a short temper'). You can take the adult and parental viewpoint of enjoying your child's development while providing the guidance he needs.

Most first children are over-indulged, whether from love, insecurity, or mistaken ideals. With a second or third child, there just isn't the time to indulge her every whim, and life has to become more rhythmical and orderly, or mother won't survive. With my first child, I fell into the philosophical pit of not wanting to be authoritarian, and chaos reigned until I realized that I could (and should) insist on right behavior. This needs to be done with calmness rather than anger, but with absolute certainty that the child can and will learn what is expected. It is appropriate that parents be guardians and guides (less charged words than authorities) and help children in the process of becoming pleasant as well as bright three-year-olds! Your children unconsciously trust you to know more about becoming adults than they do. Because their ego is not yet fully incarnated, you must provide the ego for them (that is, the source of wisdom and responsibility that holds them and keeps them from getting 'out of themselves'), just as an effective teacher does for an entire class in school.

In observing families where parents had already produced 'outstanding children,' White found that 'the effective parents we have studied have always been loving but firm with their children from early infancy on. The principal problem that average families run into in this area is allowing the child to infringe on their own rights too much.'[4] This means, for example, that you set up your house so that the child has maximum freedom and requires a minimum of no's, and then you are firm about what is not allowed. It is wonderful for your child to be curious, but he doesn't have to play with your makeup, which can be met with a stern no, removing the child from the scene, and then putting the makeup in a less accessible place. There is no need to punish the child, because a toddler is unable to understand what he has done or to remember the next time.

Preventing your child from running your home becomes more of an issue when he starts to assert himself by saying no to you. Sometimes you can get around the almost reflexive negativism of a two-year-old by starting to do the very thing that just evoked a verbal no (for example, you hand the child a toy as you put one in the basket yourself). Because children are so imitative, their bodies often can't resist moving with you.

Young children tend to be very verbal, and parents often fall into the trap of relating to them on a rational level. Asking your two-year-old, 'Do you want to…' invites a negative answer from a child of this age. Instead, positive and neutral statements such as, 'It's time to brush teeth for bed' can be very effective, when combined with the absolute certainty that there is no other choice and it is impossible to argue with time. Adding a bit of fantasy, movement, or song while going upstairs can also engage a child and circumvent negativity.

Keeping things the same as much as possible can also avoid problems with this child. Many two-year-olds hate change and fall apart during transitions between activities. Everything has to be a certain way or pandemonium breaks loose. This doesn't mean you need to give in each time or put up with whiny behavior, but understanding this aged child's attachment to order can help you avoid problems. It is a phase that will ease off in intensity as your child matures. You'll no doubt find he's not attached to order as an adolescent!

One mother I know lights a candle while she sings a song, and then lets the child blow out the match, which is an exciting incentive to get the child to go into the bedroom. Then they go into the bathroom to put on pajamas and brush teeth. The mother has turned off the bedroom light, so when they return, they have to tiptoe and be very quiet as they enter the softly lighted room and lie down together for songs and playing the children's harp.

However, sometimes your child will just be negative, and she may astonish you with the force of her refusal. When this happens, you can still physically move the child to the required place, leaving her there a few moments, or sitting and holding her if that seems appropriate. You could ask yourself if there is anything going on – is she overtired, possibly coming down with a cold? – or there may be no apparent explanation. Sometimes one or two minutes of your leaving the room will calm a child right down (what's the point when no one's watching?); other times singing a song or starting a favorite fingerplay can bring the child into a better mood. Regardless of what works, you then need to lovingly and firmly follow through by insisting on the action that caused the problem. What doesn't work is becoming angry, hitting or belittling the child, or giving in and letting her have her way.

One of the most effective ways of handling negative behavior is removing the child from the area of activity. With a young child, this requires going with her and staying with her until she is ready to return. For example, fussiness and throwing food at dinner can be quickly handled by taking her down the hall, telling her that when she is a happy clown the two of you can go back, and then standing there like a stone until she comes around. It usually takes about one to three minutes, because it's very boring being out of the action with a deadpan mother or father who won't interact until you're ready to do what is expected. This is infinitely more effective than the usual scenario of ignoring the child (trying to talk around her), objecting, threatening, and finally losing one's temper, which results in tears and a big scene. If it is absolutely clear that inappropriate behavior can't be present at mealtime, the learning curve is very short.

If temper tantrums occur, removing the child is probably the best technique. Parents are always physically stronger than a child under two, and the child first trying a tantrum is almost always asking for limits to be set. Calmly but firmly carry the child out with the absolute conviction that such behavior is not allowed. Tell the child simply that he must stop screaming, banging his head, or whatever he was doing. After the child has settled down (five to ten minutes?), then bring him back to the situation. If the tantrum recurs, you need to repeat the procedure. Perseverance furthers! Don't hold it against the child, feeling that he ought to be better or is just doing it to annoy you; but don't ignore it or give in either. You are the adult, and you can insist on right behavior while keeping your own temper.

Knowing you can correct behavior helps you to maintain your patience and keeps you from allowing a child to walk all over you and then resenting it. Correction always occurs in the present moment, where the child lives. You can't expect your two-year-old to 'remember' not to do that again, which is why punishment will not work. If you have an especially willful child, you may need to set the limits again and again during this period, but persistence pays off. Setting firm and consistent limits throughout the second year will usually prevent temper tantrums after the child turns two. Temper tantrums and the Terrible Twos are common, but not inevitable. White encourages parents to teach the child that he is terribly important, that his needs and interests are special, but that he is no more important than any other person in the world, especially his parents.[5] If a child moves into the third year without it having been made clear who runs the home and whether you really mean it when you forbid something, you are in for trouble. More detailed discussion of discipline and the importance of rhythm in home life can be found in Chapter 11.

Encouraging the Development of Language and Understanding

Because we cannot really be certain what the child experiences when she contemplates an object, it is best to leave the toddler in peace until there is a natural break in her activities, or she comes to you with something. Because of our lack of awareness and our desire to take advantage of teaching situations, we are constantly interrupting children to tell them the names of things when they are happily engrossed in an object. Instead, we should observe them and let them explore the world. Daniel Udo de Haes, in *The Young Child*,[6] makes the valuable suggestion that you do your teaching when you give the child an object, not when he or she is playing with it. For example, you might say, 'Water … water,' when you give your daughter a bowl full of water and some measuring cups to play with, perhaps even picking up some of the water in your hand while you say the words. Then let her play by herself. Similarly, if she has discovered something fascinating in the yard, don't rush over to teach her about it. Wait until she wants you and then be there to comment on what she has found ('Bug. What a big bug!').

If we are conscious of the 'silent language' of objects, then we can let our human language interact with it harmoniously. For example, after the child hears the wind rustling in the trees we might say 'rustling', letting the child hear in these sounds something of what the rustling tree has first spoken to him. In this way it is possible for the child to experience through our words an inner connection between the language of things and the human language.[7]

With the toddler it is best not to speak about things, but to let the things speak for themselves whenever possible. In other words, there is nothing harmful, and even something beneficial, in letting the doll say, 'Good morning!' to the child or in personifying or animating objects and letting them speak for themselves. For the young child, all the world is alive, everything does speak; the time to be able to distinguish reality from imagination lies in the future and will come naturally. As adults we tend to offer far too many intellectual explanations to our young children, having forgotten how to experience the world in movement and in pictures. If the personification of objects is done in a natural and responsible manner, it can strengthen an inward listening in the child.[8]

Around the second half of the second year, your child will become more interested in the pictures in books than with turning the pages. Several sources of good books for young children are listed at the end of Chapter 7. There is a value in bringing before the child a picture of what she has experienced in nature. Just as an artist can help us to see something, so a picture book can help the child to recognize that others share her visions and experiences. With this in mind, pictures of everyday objects, far from being trivial, have great value in bringing before the child the most fundamental aspects of life on earth, and have the recognition value of mirroring the child's own experience. In this sense, a picture of baby's cup might be more valuable than an elephant, which the child won't yet have experienced! Thus pictures of the simplest objects, with no story thread, are best for the child before the age of three.

Because the child is trying to experience the world and gain a picture of life as it is, it is helpful to put before her appropriate and true pictures of life, rather than caricatures of a rabbit wearing clothes or cartoon depictions of characters. The young child does not have the sophistication to laugh at cartoon renditions of absurd events, which imply that the observer, like the artist, is placing himself over and against it in judgment and laughter. A picture book has value for the toddler when he finds in it a portrayal, created by adults with dedication and respect, of everything that has resonated in his inner being.[9]

Very few good books for toddlers exist, but if we understand the value of sharing the same book over and over (even several times in the same day), then very few are needed! It is beneficial to read only one book at a sitting because each book has its own atmosphere, and mixing them can clutter the child's soul, especially at bedtime. Similarly, too many pictures give the child no time to digest them, and destroy the quiet intimacy that belongs with each picture. Children may bring another book and always want more, but being clear that one story is enough will not only help your child to live fully with those images, but will help convey the value of the individual experience, in contrast to always having more of something.

It is also very valuable for your child if you draw your own picture book for her, preferably with her watching. Most adults think they can't draw, usually as a result of their own experiences in childhood. But the child is not concerned with our artistic ability. Rather, the magical quality appears when our attempts, which she invests with her own imagination, call forth her own inner recognition-experiences. By so doing, we show the child that her quest for the earthly world is understood.[10]

Another source of books for toddlers is to use a storybook whose pictures meet these criteria, but omit the story content. Simply comment in simple language something like, 'There is Mother Hen with all of her chicks. Peep. Peep. Peep.' Then when we turn the page (or the child does) we can let him look at the picture for a while before adding our simple words. At first the child may turn the pages at random. Later he will want you to read or tell the story with the same words each time and will be nourished by their familiarity. As the years go by, stories can gradually be made more complicated, or you can begin conversations about a story, so that a good picture book can last from toddlerhood throughout the preschool years.

The Beginnings of Imaginative Play

A young child's earliest play involves movement for the pure joy of it. Running, jumping, whirling, and standing on tiptoe are enjoyable in themselves. The imaginative element will start to enter in when your son or daughter hops like a bunny or rides a stick horse. In the second year you may have glimpses of imaginative play as your child begins to pretend she is eating or drinking or talking on the phone. Through imagination, the child is able to unite herself with the world at the same time that memory and thinking are separating her from it. Fantasy and play are like complementary opposites to memory and thinking. The creative power of imaginative play continues to develop throughout early childhood, blossoming between ages three and six.

For the young toddler, pretending first begins as imitation and is carried out as actions rather than words, like pretending to drink something from a real or imaginary cup. As children approach the age of two, their growing facility with language enables their pretending to be more conversational and interactive. Simple toys further your child's imagination. For example, having a toy plate leads to talking about what is on it. This soon develops into preparing food, which can be easily done as a chair is turned into a stovetop with an oven underneath.

A toy telephone also leads to conversational play, but your hand can do just as well. Many times, messages delivered this way can make the next set of activities into a game:

Mother (with hand to ear): Ring. Ring. Heather, your phone is ringing.
Heather: Hello.
Mother: This is Mommy. I need to buy some eggs. Get your shoes on and you can come to the shop with me.
Heather: Okay!
Mother: Bye.

A bit of fantasy goes a long way in circumventing your child's negative reaction. For example, holding a face cloth like a puppet who talks to the child may soon convince him to rub noses with this talking friend. Or suggesting that all the little mice pick up the crumbs (scraps of paper) will immediately result in a 'little mouse' helping you to clean up the mess.

Providing a Rich Environment for Your Toddler

You don't have to spend a lot of money on fancy toys to provide a rich environment for your toddler. Making accessible the items in your home, plus a few free or inexpensive items, such as a ball and a cardboard box, will provide your child with hours of valuable exploration. Your toddler will want to touch and explore everything in your home, seeing what it feels like, if she can carry, empty, or fill it, and whether it comes apart. The toddler age requires constant supervision, because your daughter can hurt herself or other things the minute you turn your back. It's a time when you'll need to start teaching discrimination: it's all right to play with her toy telephone, but not the real one; she can play with the large necklace in her drawer, but not go into your jewelry box. It's understandable that it takes time for toddlers to learn the difference!

One valuable suggestion is to provide lots of things that your child can touch and explore – for example a cupboard in the kitchen with a pot, wooden spoon, flour sifter, and metal coffee percolator; a drawer in the family room that is hers – filled with old envelopes, a magazine, and other things that you change periodically as the child loses interest in them. Remembering how much your child likes to imitate, you will find that adult objects are probably more fascinating than many toys designed for children. By providing alternatives to the items you wish to protect, you can give your child areas where he can explore without having to be told 'no' all the time.

One valuable thing you will be teaching your child during this time is how to touch and how to care for things. Because your child is such an imitator, always demonstrate the behavior you want and make positive statements such as, 'Touch the kitty gently,' rather than 'Don't hurt the kitty.' Or 'Here, sniff the pretty flower,' rather than 'Don't crush the flower!' You will also need to start teaching the lessons of 'Sharp!' and 'Hot!' by modeling the behavior of taking your hand or your child's away from the object in question.

Toddlers are delightful if you can view their being into everything as their way of exploring the world, of experiencing new sights and touch, of emptying, filling, exploring gravity, using their muscles. They have no sense of adult order or goal-directed behavior. If you want Joey to clean up, start putting the toys in the basket with him. He's glad to help, but he's equally glad to dump them all out again if you walk away from him. When you find yourself being annoyed, take a minute to enter into a toddler's world, and you will realize that he isn't doing it to annoy you. Quite the contrary, he's probably doing it out of pure 'doingness' and is quite oblivious to you. You can (and must) correct and teach him what is and is not acceptable, but you needn't be annoyed when you do it. If you want to get your toddler to do a specific action, the key is to model the behavior you want, while he or she watches and/or does it with you.

Even though it is necessary to know where toddlers are at all times, it's good to provide them with time and space to explore the world while you appear not to be looking. Independence is fostered by not always interrupting them, but being accessible when they come to you for assistance or to share a discovery.

Besides loving to explore, your toddler loves simply to move for the joy of movement. She will delight in running, jumping, climbing, pushing, carrying. All of these activities help in the development of the large muscles and express the young child's nature: to be in movement. Aside from deciding which furniture it's all right to climb on and jump off, you can provide your child with a low balance beam made from placing a wide board over a couple of low concrete blocks. If the bridge you have made is too challenging for your one-year-old, place it next to a wall; raise it as she becomes more skillful.

Toys that help with the development of large muscles include the very popular indoor wooden slide and ladder with crawling space underneath. Four-wheel straddle toys that are low to the ground are also favorites of toddlers. A push cart or doll carriage is also a good toy. Make sure it is sturdy enough to take the child's weight.

Toddlers love to be outside, and a sandbox (covered to keep cats away) and paddling pool provide long periods of enjoyment. Again, make sure that you have inspected your garden and have a locked gate or other means to keep the child away from the street. Most children love to swing, so a sturdy swing is good from age one on. Toys for sand and water play are also valuable inside when the weather is bad.

Many of the toys listed in the preceding chapter will still interest a toddler. As a guide for buying toys, always take into consideration safety and durability – a toddler will still pull things apart and put them in her mouth. As she becomes more adroit at manipulating objects, stacking boxes or nesting dolls are very popular. Wooden toys with moving parts are especially recommended for young children by Rudolf Steiner, who stated, 'What a healthy toy it is, for example, which represents, by moveable wooden figures, two smiths facing each other and hammering on an anvil. Such things can still be bought in country districts. Excellent also are the picture-books where the figures can be set in motion by pulling threads from below, so that the child himself can transform the dead picture into a representation of living action.'[11] The ability to have an effect on something and to transform it through movement suits the young child's nature.

Your child loves to stack things, so we suggest making a set of blocks by cutting the trunk and large branches of a tree into blocks of various sizes and shapes. (See photo with Chapter 7.) Unlike the geometrically perfect blocks you buy in stores, these irregularly shaped blocks will be used throughout the preschool years for much more than stacking. Their unfinished quality lets the child use his imagination with them; they can easily become people, cans of cat food, or baby bottles; flat pieces from a trunk can be used as plates or cakes. Your child's imagination will be endless. But your toddler will be most interested in stacking them up and knocking them down.

When purchasing toys, consider not only their safety, but also their aesthetic qualities. Are they beautiful? How do they feel to the touch? What kind of picture of the world do they put before the child? Darth Vader figures or chartreuse ponies with platinum hair are caricatures of reality that simply are not beautiful or true representations of the human being or the world. Everything the young child takes in makes a profound impression on him. The effect of toys and the power of imitation was strikingly illustrated by a photo that appeared in *American Baby* a number of years back. This prize-winning photo showed a six-month-old baby next to a Cabbage Patch doll; the baby was copying exactly the inane expression on the doll's face. Such imitation is completely unconscious and would have been missed if the photographer hadn't been there. Such a photo captures in black and white how deeply sense impressions penetrate the child and are manifested through the physical organs.

In another remarkable case described by Professor of Child Therapy Alfred Nitschke, a ten-month-old baby girl was admitted to the hospital with extreme lethargy. She was unable to sit up, being doubled over in a jack-knife position; she had a listless expression and a blank gaze. No one had been able to diagnose the problem. Finally one doctor was inspired to notice that the child looked exactly like her constant companion, a floppy stuffed rabbit that was long-limbed and droopy with large, fixed eyes. The doctor brought a new toy that was friendly looking and had a well-defined shape. The child soon became attached to the new toy, and within a few days had begun to improve in her posture, appetite, and mood without any other treatment.[12] In contemplating stuffed toys or dolls for your children, you might remember these examples.

Especially for the young child, the simpler and more archetypal a thing is, the more possibilities it holds for the child. Steiner states:

> As the muscles of the hand grow firm and strong in performing the work for which they are fitted, so the brain and other organs of the physical body of man are guided into the right lines of development if they receive the right impressions from their environment. An example will best illustrate this point.
>
> You can make a doll for a child by folding up an old napkin, making two corners into legs, the other two corners into arms, a knot for the head, and painting eyes, nose and mouth with blots of ink. Or else you can buy the child what they call a 'pretty' doll, with real hair and painted cheeks.... If the child has before him the folded napkin, he has to fill in from his own imagination all that is needed to make it real and human. The brain unfolds as the muscles of the hand unfold, when they do the work for which they are fitted. Give the child the so-called pretty doll, and the brain has nothing to do.[13]

Because the young child is not fully conscious of its own body, what it is most aware of in itself and others is the head. Thus a knot doll with a large head is quite recognizable and satisfactory for the young child. For a very young child, you can change the basic doll into a 'baby' by stuffing the bottom like a blanket or pillow, instead of making a body and legs from the two bottom corners.[14]

Toys and Equipment

Check the list at the end of the last chapter. Many of the toys will still be enjoyed by your toddler.

- Low four-wheeled toy that can be straddled
- Push toys; push cart or doll carriage (sturdy enough to lean on)
- Wooden slide and climbing toy
- Wooden blocks cut from various diameters of a tree
- Wading pool, low container for water play outdoors, water and bath toys

- Sandbox and sand toys
- Outdoor swing
- Toy telephone
- Simple first doll of natural materials
- Balls of various sizes, especially an inflatable beach ball
- Wooden toys that have moving parts (pecking chickens, two men with hammers)
- Wooden nesting dolls
- Simple picture books with stiff pages
- Books with parts that move
- Large empty cardboard boxes to play in
- Crayons (age two on); especially good are block crayons, as described in Chapter 9

Some Things To Do

- Let your toddler start 'helping' with things you do (loading the dishwasher, stirring the cake, putting things in the dustbin, sweeping, folding clothes, watering the plants); it will take you longer, but it is true quality time.
- Help your child experience nature through walks, parks, feeding the ducks.
- Set up a 'nature table' at home with things you find on your walks (a pretty shell, a plant). Change the colours of the cloth and the themes to match the seasons.
- Your toddler loves to be lifted up to the ceiling and be like an airplane on your extended legs while you lie on your back; a friend said she liked the ocean so much because it was the only thing big enough to toss her around the way her father did when she was little.
- Simple hiding games are fun; you and your child can take turns hiding under a blanket (we always played 'lump in the bed' while trying to make it); hiding objects in your pocket is also fun for toddlers, who love to find them. Chase, catch, and hug is a favorite game, too.
- Use a song or a bit of fantasy for daily activities like brushing teeth or getting dressed. Several excellent verses can be found in *The Singing Day*.[15] I made up a little tune for when I wanted my

daughter to lie down in the bathtub and get her hair wet: 'Mermaid, mermaid, swimming in the water. Mermaid, mermaid, see my little mermaid.'

- Continue singing to your child! Include action rhymes whenever you can.

Recommended Reading

Playing with Toddlers

Children at Play: Preparation for Life by Heidi Britz-Crecelius (Inner Traditions). Will help you understand how the child experiences the world through play. Draws from Steiner's insights.

The Genius of Play by Sally Jenkinson (Hawthorn Press). A classic on the importance of play.

The Laughing Baby by Anne Scott (Celestial Arts). Nursery rhymes and songs for children.

The Parent and Child Group Handbook by Dot Male (Hawthorn Press). A Steiner/Waldorf approach

The Singing Day by Candy Verney (Hawthorn Press).

Toymaking with Children by Freya Jaffke (Floris Books). Directions for making knot dolls and other toys for young children.

The Well Balanced Child by Sally Goddard Blythe (Hawthorn Press). Clearly explains the need for a 'whole body' approach to learning in the early years.

The Young Child: Creative Living with Two to Four Year Olds by Daniel Udo de Haes (Floris Books). Provides many insights into the world of the young child, with numerous suggestions on things to do; Steiner-oriented.

Your Child at Play: One to Two Years by Marilyn Segal and Don Adcock (Newmarket Press). A practical book with many photos.

Sources for Creative Toys

See the list at the end of Chapter 7.

CHAPTER 6

Parenting Issues of the First Three Years

Why Does Parenting Take So Much Energy?

It takes a tremendous amount of energy to mother a baby or young child. Even preschool, nursery and kindergarten teachers find that they must get enough sleep to replenish the kind of energy young children seem to demand. Your best intentions about parenting will be ineffectual when you are too tired or irritable. The first thing to do to assure a happy and healthy baby is for the mother to be happy and healthy. This means to be sure you are eating well and taking vitamin supplements for at least as long as you are breastfeeding. Interrupted sleep, especially in the first few months, can compound fatigue and the adjustment to new parenting. Babies are nourished by your love and care just as they are nourished by physical food. The reason that parenting young children takes so much energy is that the life forces of the mother and baby are interconnected throughout the first three years. Young children are surrounded by and consume what Steiner calls etheric or life energy from their parents, caregivers, and teachers. (We might call it vitality or life force.) Mothering is deceptive, because sometimes it seems as if you're accomplishing so little – why should you be so tired? However, caring for young children draws on your vital energy, and you need to replenish your own vital forces in order to continue to feel good in your mothering.

Three things that can really help to replenish this energy are:

sleep, artistic activity, and meditation. Try to make sure that you get enough sleep – schedule a nap when the baby naps. Maintain a quiet time every afternoon for your child when he or she stops napping – as much for yourself as for the child. I know that when I taught preschool, being in bed by ten was an essential part of my preparation. Otherwise I couldn't stand the noise and couldn't keep my emotions on an even keel.

Artistic activity involves the same vital or creative forces that your baby is using, but it replenishes rather than depletes them. Playing a musical instrument, drawing, sculpting, painting, all can help mothers to have more energy. Writing down your thoughts, experiences, and insights can also be helpful. The regularity of doing something like taking a walk each day can also be of great help in keeping you balanced and replenishing your energy. Contact with nature can also help us feel refreshed.

Meditation can be as simple as setting aside five minutes before you go to bed to center yourself in your breathing or concentrate on a single thought. Returning to your own center through meditation or prayer not only helps to replenish your energy but can also help you maintain equanimity in the midst of all the stresses of parenting. If you don't have any regular practices, Rudolf Steiner suggested many simple but powerful exercises in his book *Knowledge of Higher Worlds*.[1]

In addition to setting aside time for meditation, set aside time for yourself alone, out of the house when needed. Even an hour or two can help you in your mothering. Most women in nuclear families live isolated from other adults. You can really get 'cabin fever' with only a toddler to talk to day after day!

The father can play a very important role in helping the mother to maintain her vitality. With a child under the age of three, this involves actively supporting her mothering emotionally and financially, so that she is encouraged and strengthened in being with the children. I hate to risk sounding traditional by speaking of men as 'providers and protectors,' but there is some validity to that image when both partners are applying it with consciousness. However, this does not preclude men's developing their own nurturing side so they can assume co-responsibility for the children, rather than depending on the mother to rise to the occasion (a crying baby, a nappy that needs changing, a squabble between siblings). Single parenting, with or without a husband in the home, is not an easy task.

The Importance of Rhythm

Most of the parents who are my age were brought up on a bottle every four hours (and not a half-hour sooner), no matter how hard we protested. In reaction to this sacrifice of the individual to the clock or the book, many women breastfeeding today nurse their babies whenever they are hungry or fussy. Demand feeding takes as its model primitive cultures where the baby is carried in a sling next to the mother's body and can nurse any time it wants, which usually involves nursing frequently for short periods. Many mothers who take their babies to bed with them find this same pattern of frequent nursing continuing throughout the night as well.

Most everyone today agrees that a young baby's needs should be met as they arise, and mothers feel confident in trusting their instincts to respond with love and the breast to their babies. But when does this change? At six weeks, six months, two years, or later?

I would like to propose an alternative to the polarity of feeding on demand versus feeding according to a schedule: working toward establishing rhythm, which will change as the baby grows. The idea of rhythm fits in very well with Evelyn Thoman's metaphor of parenting as dancing in her book *Born Dancing*.[2]

One of the tasks of the growing child and one of the functions of parenting is to bring the child into rhythm. Consider how arhythmical a newborn's breathing is. Sometimes she takes short gasps, other times she holds her breath – it's quite startling if you really listen to your newborn breathe. Babies' heart rates are also much faster than adults'. As the child matures, the breathing and the heart rate gradually become coordinated and then assume the adult ratio of one breath for each four beats of the heart.

Part of what makes the first six weeks of caring for a new baby so hard is that the baby seems to have no pattern to its eating and sleeping – at least nothing you can depend on. Rhythm gradually does emerge from chaos, and life becomes easier as rhythm provides a framework that can support you in your other activities. This lack of framework can be very disorienting, as when a person retires or a career woman quits work when pregnant and finds she can barely get out of bed in the morning because life has become so unstructured. However, even when rhythm emerges, it will be different for a breastfed baby than for a bottle-fed baby, because of the difference in the type of protein and the amount of liquid the baby takes in at any given feeding – breastfed babies eat more often!

Working toward rhythm does not mean slavishly 'going by the clock' or letting your baby 'cry it out.' It does mean being aware of rhythms as they emerge and change, honoring and encouraging them. This is especially valuable in dealing with naps and sleep and avoiding sleep problems. At first your baby requires sustenance during the night; it's a physiological fact. But after the baby's stomach and digestive system can get enough nourishment to last for an extended period, waking and feeding are for other purposes: simply from habit, to be comforted by your presence, or to play.

If you were to get up, turn on the lights, feed and talk to your baby, he or she might start wanting to be awake and playing at that time every night. Some babies can even get day and night reversed, sleeping most of the day and wanting to be active at night. Nursing mothers are usually able to avoid these pitfalls by somnolently tucking the baby into bed with them and barely waking up while nursing.[3]

You need to decide your style of mothering and what is right for you and your family. As long as you are happy nursing your baby at night, there is no need to change. But when you grow tired of being awakened at night – and your older baby could be sleeping longer – it is possible to change his habit pattern. You need to gather your intention to stop nursing the baby when he awakes at night. When he cries, you can go in and say, 'I love you, but this is time to sleep.' You might hold and rock him, or just pat his back and then go out. It isn't easy to hear him cry, but stay connected and go back in after three minutes and pat him, saying, 'I'm sorry you're upset, but it is time to sleep,' keeping your voice and actions very drowsy. You go out for a longer time and repeat as necessary. The child soon learns that food will not be forthcoming, but also doesn't feel abandoned, because of your love and concern. With no possibility of food or play, he will soon start sleeping longer without waking up. My own experience is that it generally takes three days or nights to change a pattern, but it can also take a week or longer.

There are so many schools of thought on what babies need and how to parent; I encourage you to trust your own heart and to be as aware as possible of your baby's needs and of what you are really feeling. If you're content nursing your baby all night, it's wonderful. But if you feel as though you'd appreciate uninterrupted sleep at night and are starting to resent the cry in the night or the constant nuzzling against your body, you should realize that it's all right and easy to change your child's behavior if it's done with love and awareness. Bringing the child into rhythm when the time is right is part of life in all cultures. Only you can decide when that time is for your baby, for you, and your family.

What About Weaning?

Breastfeeding is the best start you can possibly give your baby, and you should continue as long as it feels good to both mother and baby. Any amount of nursing is better than no nursing at all. If you are considering weaning in the first month, chances are that you are having difficulties; it should be pleasurable for both you and your baby. Call La Leche League or a lactation consultant and get the help you need. Often doctors give the wrong advice, which is less likely to happen with women who are knowledgeable and trained to help nursing mothers. If you encounter special situations, such as going back to work or illness, the League or lactation consultants also can provide the support you need to successfully breastfeed in these circumstances.

As you have probably figured out, I am not into authorities telling women what to do with their bodies. When women listened to doctors, they didn't breastfeed at all, which was clearly wrong advice. Then American doctors recommended breastfeeding for six months, and now the American Academy of Pediatrics has extended the time to twelve months. The information and impulses from our formula-pushing culture need to be balanced by the information on natural mothering and extended breastfeeding provided by organizations such as La Leche League. However, their emphasis on 'child-led weaning' needs to be balanced by information that it really needs to be 'nursing-couple-led weaning' – both your emotions and the baby's emotions and needs count. It really is all right to stop offering your baby or toddler the breast when it comes to that time. Weaning, like death, is part of the 'shadow side' of life. It involves the ending of one phase and the moving on to another. Try to become aware of your own needs, comforts, fears, and questions. (Breastfeeding is so pleasurable, why would I ever want to stop? It's so wonderful to be touched and needed like this – do I really want my child to become more independent? How will I show my love for my toddler in the next phase?). Being aware of your own emotional undercurrents can help you be more aware of your baby's real needs and more alert to the subtle cues that she is giving you. You may even find that there are spiritual realities that make weaning at nine or twelve months a natural event.

People working out of Steiner's indications have observed that when the child achieves uprightness and walks (between nine and twelve months), it is freeing itself and asserting its individuality; they have felt that achieving similar freedom in the area of nutrition is appropriate at this same time, as well. Certainly the baby is able to eat and even reach for table foods at this age. One of the tasks of the first seven years is for the child to assert its individuality by overcoming or remolding the forces of heredity; because these forces are particularly strong in the milk, prolonged nursing of toddlers is viewed with alarm.[4] Readers may be surprised, amused, or annoyed by the rigidity of some of the books by Anthroposophical doctors who prescribe weaning at the 'traditional time of 40 weeks' (nine months). Since these same doctors were arguing for weaning at six months in earlier editions, one has to try to distinguish between cultural influences and spiritual truths; and it can be valuable to ask ourselves if there is an observable truth behind what anthroposophical writers are noticing about the toddler's changing consciousness and needs in today's world. In her newest book, Joan Salter describes how many women connected with the Gabriel Baby Centre in Australia have felt that weaning at nine months was too early, so they are starting to wean around nine months and finishing by twelve.[5] The fact that she felt it necessary to justify this by using esoteric numerology to show how the nine is transformed into the twelve left me somewhat bemused, however.

Once the baby is able to eat table foods (around nine months) the nature of breastfeeding changes to fulfilling a need that is more emotional than nutritive. La Leche League speaks of baby-led weaning, pointing out that some babies really do wean themselves and others don't (they might be three or four years old). The League and *The Continuum Concept* by Jean Leidloff point out how common it is in less technologically developed cultures for children to be nursed two or three years or longer.

The development of individual consciousness, which is so advanced in the West, presents a fundamental dilemma. On the one hand, our extreme individuality has brought us to alienation, anxiety, competition, and denial of the spirit. On the other, we can't escape it just because we can read about other cultures, whose group consciousness may not necessarily be appropriate for us in the world in which we live. However, something new clearly is needed, or we're going to destroy ourselves. Steiner's answer is that our individuality is appropriate, but we must now go on to include a reintegration of spirit and matter from our modern vantage point. We have to start where we are.

While some mothers are content to take their cues from other cultures in nursing their toddler or even older child, I have encountered many mothers who are 'suffering through' nursing after a year or longer, anxiously waiting for their baby to wean herself. I've even had mothers with nursing four-year-olds come to me for advice on weaning, terrified of the scenes and 'trauma to the child' that they are convinced weaning is going to produce. And there were several mothers at the Birth Center where I worked who didn't want to stop nursing their toddlers during pregnancy, but found that once the new baby was born, they felt completely exhausted and overwhelmed. Yet they still didn't feel free to wean the older child. My feeling is that perhaps, in these cases, we should take our lesson from the cats, bears, and most other mammals who are more into self-preservation and preservation of the young than that. There is no way I can believe that an older child's sucking need is being well served by a resentful mother. Babies and older siblings register and take in emotions just as deeply as actions. Breastfeeding is like making love – nothing is gained in suffering through it (and, in fact, your baby is much more sensitive and aware of what is going on than some 'he' might have been!).

Regardless of how long you breastfeed (or bottle feed) your baby, the question remains about when to start introducing solid foods. In our culture, pediatricians used to want you to introduce solid foods at three months (or earlier), either because your baby was not growing enough or (in my case) because he was too fat! The trend now is more toward waiting until six months. La Leche League has good advice about how and when to introduce foods, and if there is a history of allergy in your family, giving nothing but breast milk for the first year can help prevent sensitization to food and other allergies. There is no need to supplement iron for breastfed babies; they don't become anemic in the first year from a breast milk diet.

Steiner gave many indications about nutrition that vary quite a bit from information commonly available today. Interested readers can refer to *When a Child Is Born* by W. zur Linden[6] or *A Guide to Child Health* by M. Glöckler and W. Goebel.[7] One interesting thing I have gleaned is that what children eat before the age of three is what they acquire a taste for, and I have seen this to be true many times. For example, we gave our youngest daughter almost no red meat before the age of three, following Steiner's indications that red meat is very dense and inappropriate for young children. Even though we aren't vegetarians, she still won't eat most meat and prefers tofu. A friend brought up her child without any sugar or sweets before the age of three. Then she allowed sweets when the child entered preschool. It was interesting to observe that the girl really had little taste for the cupcakes and other treats at birthday parties. This seemed to go beyond a desire to please her mother's wish that she partake moderately of these foods.

Crying Babies

Since babies can't verbalize what is happening with them, they cry for a wide variety of reasons. We are taught to see if they are wet or hungry. If not, we as a culture try to hush them up or ignore them. As we have seen, it is important to respond to a crying baby, not leave her to 'cry it out.'

The next time you hear a baby cry, see what feelings and associations it brings up in you. And take some time to think about how you respond to your baby's cues; are you more concerned with your own or the child's discomfort? Many valuable exercises to help parents understand their own feelings about crying, sleep, food, and so forth can be found in 'Exercises in Self-Awareness for New Parents' by Aletha Jauch Solter.[8] Her book *The Aware Baby* also offers much good advice about crying babies.[9]

Having a 'colicky' or high-needs infant can be a real strain on parents. Many things can be tried – looking for food allergies, burping the baby frequently, putting warmth or pressure on the tummy, giving weak camomile tea – but there doesn't seem to be any statistical correlation between causes and cures for colic. Limiting stimulation and trying to create a calm environment should certainly be the place to start. Above all, try to remain calm yourself, because it is impossible to calm a baby if you are tense and annoyed (remember how imitative they are on the physical level!). Also remember that you are not responsible for your child's personality or temperament. Sometimes the best you can do is just be there for the infant, lovingly holding her and letting her cry. Crying can be a great release if done in the arms of someone who loves you.

Vimala Schneider, author and founder of the International Association of Infant Massage Instructors, writes:

Forcing babies to 'cry it out,' hushing babies' cries by stopping up their mouths, and letting babies cry 'cathartically' can all be excuses for not taking the time to listen to what they have to say. There is no quick fix. A good parent – a good culture – must go through the sometimes difficult process of responding to babies' cues individually, with compassion and with common sense.[10]

One father describes his trying to become more intuitively aware of what his daughter's cries mean:

In the evening, after we put Tara to bed, she sometimes wakes up after about an hour or so. At this point, she starts to cry, and we do not respond immediately, because we want her to learn to go back to sleep... The decision whether to get up or not is a function of the nature of the crying. There's a kind of crying that is whimpering, where it's clear she is still asleep, and a kind of cry that is screeching, and it's obvious she is awake and distressed. However, there are some in-between cries, where it's hard to tell how she's feeling.

I found myself trying the following technique. Rather than listening with my ear or with my mind, I have started to try and listen first with my heart. I try and let the crying go to my heart and then, with my mind, examine how my heart is feeling and responding. Is she in distress? Does she need comforting? Or is she just complaining, feeling uncomfortable? The distinction is important, in that Wendy and I want her to feel completely trusting of our presence, but we also want her to experience, in small increments, taking care of herself. I do not believe in having her cry herself to sleep, as some parents recommend at this point, where she really screams for long periods of time and exhausts herself. Rather, I suspect the process can be much more incremental and evolutionary, like the changing of the tides. Each night there are small changes that over time build up into a major shift. In my case, the learning for me here is in trying to respond first at an intuitive, feeling level and then consulting that feeling. This is a process I have been exploring for a while, but this feels like a new dimension of it.[11]

Some parents sleep with their baby in bed and respond with breastfeeding – barely even waking up. Others find that there comes a time when they want more space at night and then must get up to respond to their older baby or toddler.

Once again, there are no simple formulas for the right or wrong way to parent your child. You need to feel your own way through the easy and difficult times.

What About Going Back to Work?

With 55 percent of new mothers in the US returning to the labour force in 1995 within 12 months of giving birth, daycare for children under three has become a reality of American life. It has become so much a part of our society that even the Waldorf Early Childhood Association has turned its attention to the years from birth to three. The number of Waldorf daycare homes is increasing, and the question is being asked, 'What does appropriate care in a daycare center look like?' Their conclusion seems to be to take the home as the model, as much as possible. Nøkken, a Waldorf-based program for children in Copenhagen, Denmark, has around 25 children from age one (or when they can walk) until they are ready for first grade at age seven. All ages are together as a large, healthy family, except when the younger children have snack and nap. Joan Almon, president of the Waldorf Early Childhood Association of North America, commented after visiting Nøkken:

> Prior to my visit, I had been very concerned that those raised in childcare centers would have a hard time nurturing their own children when they grew up. Within most childcare centers, children are stratified by age, so a three-year-old does not see an infant being cared for. There is little opportunity to learn about such things through imitation. That Nøkken was able to overcome this problem made a deep impression on me…
>
> As I watched the children at Nøkken play being mothers, I was struck by the thought that where it was once a village that raised a child, more and more there now need to be such life-filled centers to provide the nurture children need…
>
> A number of Waldorf early-childhood teachers in the United States and elsewhere are exploring ways to meet these needs of children. An imaginative picture is developing of a multi-age center that includes mixed age groups from infancy to age six, as well as children up to age twelve who come for care before and after school. It's possible also to develop activities for adolescents, to include the elderly as foster grandparents, or to offer courses for the elderly, for pregnant parents, and more. In such life centers, young children can feel embedded as they once did in their own homes that were part of an extended family or village. It is hoped that within a few years a number of such centers will exist. There is a growing commitment for such work within the Waldorf early-childhood movement, which now numbers over 1200 programs in fifty countries.[12]

Until such idealistic centers are to be found in every community, parents are left to ponder the findings of the 1995 'Cost, Quality and Outcomes Study' which considered a random sample of 401 full-day childcare centers in Los Angeles, central Colorado, Connecticut, and central North Carolina: fewer than 25 percent delivered high-quality care; more than 11 percent were substandard; and most centers fell somewhere in between. In following up on the children four years later, at the end of second grade, researchers found that children from daycare classes with good teaching practices had significantly better language and math skills than those from mediocre centers. And children who had close relationships with their caregivers were found to have fewer behavior problems and better social skills as well as higher academic scores than their less fortunate peers.[13]

A seven-year study released by the National Institutes of Health in the US has been used to reassure parents that young children in the care of others while their parents work generally suffer no disadvantage in cognitive or linguistic development. But many of the reports in the popular press overlooked the fact that 'the federally funded study, which so far has tracked more than 1300 children from birth to three years of age, concluded that when a child spends long hours in 'nonmaternal' care, the quality of interaction between the child and its mother is slightly eroded. The more hours a child spends in day care, the study showed, the more negative and less sensitive a mother was toward the child in situations observed by researchers. At two and three years old, a child cared for by others also was less affectionate toward his mother in proportion to the amount of day care the child received. Collectively, these measures of mother-child interaction are considered strong predictors of a child's sense of security in her mother and in turn, of her overall emotional well-being. Researchers called the link between a child's hours in care and poor mother-child interaction weak but statistically significant.'[14]

While it is clearly out of step with the times to say the following (like asking for books on birth in the feminist book shop in the early 1970s), I nevertheless have to take the risk and say, 'If you can possibly stay home with your baby for the first year, please do so. In fact, it is better to stay home for the first three years!' Among the early childhood 'experts,' only T. Berry Brazelton, called America's favorite pediatrician, has swallowed hard enough to write a book about putting your child in daycare. In his popular book *Working and Caring*,[15] he discusses what mothers need to consider in looking for daycare for a baby or a young child, the emotions involved in going back to work, the concern about the primary caretaker replacing you in the child's affections, the increased number of illnesses and need for antibiotics, and so forth. If that list sounds negative, my bias may be showing through. Burton White, on the other hand, became very unpopular when he said it makes a difference in development if mothers stay home with their children younger than three. But he decided to stick by his guns and to say it again in the revised edition of *The First Three Years of Life* (1986):

> I stated then (1979), and I will state again now, that full-time substitute care for babies under three years of age, and especially for those only a few months of age, does not seem to be in the best interest of babies.[16]

Based on his years of observation and research, White concludes:

> Simply stated, I firmly believe that most children get a better start in life when, during the majority of their waking hours of their first three years, they are cared for by their parents or other nuclear family members, not by any form of substitute care.[17]

The reasons for this are many, including the uniqueness of the parent-child bond that is forming in the first two years. No caregiver can match the enthusiasm and excitement of parents over a baby's accomplishments such as sitting up and walking. Such reactions reinforce the parents' commitment and love and contribute to the child's developing sense of self-worth and security. In addition, the parents are best able to be there to satisfy a toddler's curiosity with all the things she discovers. While studies have shown that ideal substitute care situations do no measurable harm to children, all situations are not ideal, and no studies show substitute care as being better than any but the most abusive family.

Steiner explains the uniqueness of the mother-child relationship, which White observed in the first three years. Steiner observed that the etheric or vital energy of the baby is connected with and protected by the mother's vital energy, which surrounds it like a sheath, just as the physical body was protected before birth by the physical body of the mother that surrounded it. Just as the child's physical body is freed at birth, the child's etheric body is gradually 'born' over the first seven years, with an important freeing from the mother occurring around the age of three. This change is quite dramatic if you are alert for it – suddenly your child is much more independent, much more able to be away from you comfortably and more able to participate in group activities. This is why Waldorf preschools prefer to accept children around age three and a half, after they have gone through this freeing from the mother.

According to Steiner, the baby in the first year is still totally connected to the mother's vital (etheric) energy and nurtured by it. This seems to explain the psychic connection or heightened awareness that exists between mothers and their babies. We experienced a dramatic example of this connection when we lived with a woman and her nine-month-old daughter. The mother had weaned her baby to go into the hospital and have a benign but growing lump removed from her breast. During the surgery it was discovered that she actually had advanced breast cancer. Within twenty-four hours the baby came down with pneumonia, and we were dealing with recovery from surgery, the shock of cancer, and a seriously ill infant. It was as if the supports for the child had been pulled out from under her while her mother was in shock. Full-time daycare is not as great a separation as that for an infant, but it is still a shock for the baby and can cause what Steiner calls a 'tearing of the etheric sheath' surrounding the baby. As a Waldorf preschool teacher in a community where most mothers stayed home with their children or only worked part-time (Ann Arbor, Michigan), I observed that the children who had been in daycare since the age of six weeks stood out quite noticeably. They tended to be sick more often and more used to antibiotics because their parents couldn't stay home for recuperation time; they were less childlike, having dealt with the stress of other adults and groups for many years. David Elkind, in his books *The Hurried Child* and *Miseducation*, speaks of the high level of anxiety with which our children live, and how we push them to grow up and cope with things that should be beyond their years.[18]

If there is any way you can stay at home at least during the first year, it is of tremendous value for your baby and can be rewarding for you as well. Your baby only begins life once and will grow up so quickly! But there is not a lot of support for mothers to stay home. Leaves of absence are usually too short, careers won't wait for many women who are in their late thirties when they decide to have children, and today's lifestyles often demand two incomes. But if it is your heart's desire, work something out and find the support you need. In the UK, the *Mother* magazine and *Juno* magazine are real supports for women who value what they do with their children. *Of Cradles and Careers* by Kaye Lowman (from La Leche League) is also helpful. If you are going to stay home, find supportive friends, or find ways of working at home or working part-time. Further resources are listed at the end of Chapter 1.

If you decide to return to work before your child is a year old, what kind of daycare is best? Through his work with young children, White found that the best type of substitute care is individual care in your own home; fortunately, the number of agencies handling nannies and *au pair* programs is increasing rapidly. Second best is individual care in another person's home. Next is home-based family daycare, followed by nonprofit centre-based care. Last is profit-oriented centre-based care, which in the US is often done as a franchise and pays little over minimum wage.[19]

Obviously, finding quality childcare is one of the major dilemmas facing parents today. If you need to find a home or a facility for your child, take the time to really check out several of them. How your child is cared for all day does matter.

Is There a Difference Between Fathering and Mothering?

If the mother is going to return to work, having the father or grandmother take care of the baby at home is probably the first choice, because they can be excellent mother substitutes. But is there a difference between the mother's connection with the baby and the father's? In *Pregnant Feelings* I wrote something about 'the obvious statement that mothering is different from fathering.' My co author objected vehemently, despite my assurances that I didn't mean men couldn't change nappies or father their babies instead of babysitting while mother was out. I finally had to change it to 'the controversial statement that mothering is different from fathering.' I wish I had had the excellent book *Mothering and Fathering. The Gender Differences in Child Rearing* by Tine Thevenin to send to her!

Fathers, adoptive parents, and other relatives can all learn the art of mothering if they want to, or if they must take on the responsibility. (Otherwise they will tend to sleep through the night or not maintain awareness of the child at each moment because 'mother' is somehow still doing it.) But there is a difference that the mother experiences physically through breastfeeding and hormonal changes, which is that intangible connection Steiner explains as the interweaving of their life forces in the first three years. Especially during the first year, one of the most valuable things a father can do, in my opinion, is to support the mother in her mothering – financially, emotionally, and by sharing in the increased workload in the home. He may also be fathering older children as his relationship with this new baby unfolds. It's a busy time!

Ideals and values in parenting need to be discussed ahead of time and re-evaluated as the realities of having a new baby become known. An *American Baby* magazine readers' poll found the majority of mothers still have primary responsibility for 11 of 13 baby-care activities and household chores (laundry, cooking, feeding baby during the night, washing dishes, house cleaning, grocery shopping, bathing and dressing baby, changing nappies, caring for baby when sick, making child-care arrangements, and taking the baby to the doctor). The majority of fathers share primary responsibility for only one of the thirteen: providing income. And only one of the activities was equally shared: playing with the baby.[20] If a father-to-be thinks he's being wonderfully supportive by working overtime to meet the increased financial demands and she's feeling emotionally abandoned by never seeing him, everyone's best intentions won't lead to harmony. *Pregnant Feelings* contains many exercises to help couples communicate about parenting issues, clarify values, and work together.[21]

What About Immunizations?

If you are seeing a pediatrician or visiting a well-baby clinic, immunizations will become an issue during the first year of your child's life, since most clinics and pediatricians want to start them at two months of age. There is much controversy today about immunization; in the US the pharmaceutical companies have halted production of some vaccines because of the number of lawsuits from parents who claim their children have been damaged.

In the UK and mainland Europe, doctors who work with the indications of Rudolf Steiner, in addition to being fully licensed and recognized medical doctors, compromise and do immunize against the more severe illnesses, such as polio and tetanus. But they refuse to immunize children before the age of one because of the shock to the child's physical and vital energy that introducing those illnesses into the body entails. They feel that a child who is not yet walking is unlikely to injure himself outdoors where tetanus germs grow on rusty nails or in manure. However, some unimmunized children under the age of one do get whooping cough, so you need to decide whether you can make the commitment of spending one month or longer at home nursing a very sick child. The issue of immunization will be discussed again in greater detail in Chapter 13.

Do the Toddler's Senses Still Need Protecting?

Obviously you're not going to be taking the same care to put silks over the bed with a ten-month-old that you might with a one-week-old! The baby is much more 'here' and is quickly adapting to earthly life. But is it still beneficial to maintain an awareness of the quality of the baby's sensory experiences? The answer is yes, not just in infancy, but throughout the early childhood years. Continue to pay attention to the quality of sights and sounds your child experiences. Clothing and toys from living sources feel good to the touch and help introduce your child to the world of nature. Synthetics, those wonderful creations of the human mind, can be introduced when the child is older.

It is especially important to continue to keep the baby warmly dressed (but not overheated!) and protected from the sun. The explanations given in the chapter on the newborn still apply to the baby throughout the first year. It is also important to keep toddlers and preschoolers warmly dressed, especially remembering to keep little girls' legs warm when they are wearing dresses.

The environment continues to be tremendously important to the young child. This includes the emotional as well as the physical surroundings. The best way to help a baby develop in the first three years is to provide warmth and love to meet her physical and emotional needs, and then to work on oneself. Is it possible to work toward always treating your child with respect, talking to your baby, not blaming him for being fussy, or accusing your toddler of emptying the waste paper basket just to annoy you? You'll find yourself having inner emotional reactions that you know aren't appropriate to your child's intentions or level of control. It's all right for you to feel the things you feel (all mothers get frustrated, get 'cabin fever', even hate their children on occasion), but it's important not to express it around the child. Find other ways of releasing the energy and regaining your perspective. Can you see and dismantle your reactions, or take your frustrations out in chopping wood or jumping up and down in the bathroom rather than in front of the baby? No one is perfect, and the path of parenting is one of growth.

Remember the keys of sleep, artistic creativity, and meditation. Arrange for time by yourself, when you can center, read or write, or do nothing. Once the baby has established certain rhythms, use one naptime for yourself instead of for the housecleaning (you can always clean with the baby in a carrier or sitting and watching you). Don't make impossible demands on yourself, realizing that you are doing a tremendous amount in providing the best possible beginning for your baby. Raising a young child demands a tremendous amount of just 'being there.' This seems also to be true of adolescence, for a friend who had four teenage sons reported that being with teenagers was very much like being with toddlers: they need to know you are there, and want you to 'hang out' with them or talk about things in which you really have no adult interest. My friend found that she had to cut back her midwifery practice and be home more when her sons became teenagers, just as she had done when they were little.

What Makes Children So Different from One Another?

Parents who have an 'easy' child are often silently critical of other parents and think, 'If they only would do what I did.' Then when their next one comes along and is totally different and a real handful, they are amazed by how different children can be with the same parents. There's nothing like children to keep us humble! Similarly, a mother with a 'difficult' child may feel like a failure until she has another child who is sweetness and light.

What we need is perspective on how different children can be, and why. For one thing, they are unique individuals even if they share the same genetic pool. In addition, each person has a characteristic way of being and interacting with the world. T. Berry Brazelton, pediatrician and author of *Infants and Toddlers: Differences in Development*, states, 'Just as adults have different personalities, so do babies, and these personalities are distinctive almost from birth.' He develops the idea of three basic personalities in infants – quiet, average, and active – and each is quite normal.[22]

Rudolf Steiner recognized four basic 'temperaments' or groups of traits. While everyone is a mixture of several of the temperaments, one tends to dominate. By gaining insight into your child's and your own temperament, you can understand how people can be so different, and will be able to try different ways of parenting and teaching children with different temperaments.

The first type of person Steiner described is one who has an abundance of energy and likes to do things. As adults they are quick to see the future and want to manifest things. Such children are very powerful, with tremendous force of will and action. They tend to dominate in play, using images of power such as eagles, tornadoes, or bears. Their emotions tend to be hard to control (especially anger, aggression, and annoyance), and they become frustrated if not given enough opportunity to engage their abilities. They can be overbearing, but they also have positive leadership abilities and can be characterized as the 'movers and shakers' who make things happen. They tend to be compactly and powerfully built, and walk with their heels dug into the ground. Well-known examples of this choleric or fiery temperament would be Napoleon or Teddy Roosevelt.

Contrast that child with one who is dreamy and likes to sit. Sometimes movement seems like too much effort for this type of child. These children are very concerned with the comfort of their bodies, and their favorite part of the day is often snack time. When they interact with other children, they usually have a harmonizing effect; often they are content to just sit and watch. These children are very comforted by routine and rhythm; they are hard to get started, but they are equally hard to change. Transitions and any kind of changes are hard for these children, and they can have as many temper tantrums as the choleric child. Such a child will become engrossed in anything he starts and will keep at something like a painting until the paper has a hole in it! Such a phlegmatic temperament is related to the element of water, with its rhythmical wave action that goes on and on without tiring.

A third type of temperament appears in the child who is almost always bright and happy. He or she is usually very cheerful, with tears changing to laughter as quickly as they appear. This child seems to barely touch the ground, and in fact can be observed to walk on the toes much of the time. These children can be very easy to parent; the difficulty in the elementary grades is in getting them to finish their work. Their interest is so ephemeral that they're like butterflies flitting from one thing to the next. They are quick and observant and enthusiastically rush into things, but tend to lack follow-through. They are so aware of sense impressions that they are easily distracted by each new thing. This sanguine temperament is related to the quality of air, which is light and always changing.

To round out our description of the temperaments, picture a child who is often very inward, more involved in his or her own emotional world than in external action. This kind of child is not so easy to spot in early childhood, because most young children seem to be happy much of the time. But as they grow older, such children seem to take everything personally, carrying a great deal of personal suffering (because someone doesn't like him, or because one child didn't give her a valentine). Crying at his or her birthday party is often typical of this child. The positive side of this temperament is a very compassionate and caring nature, but the negative side is extreme sensitivity, being more caught up in their own reactions than what is actually happening. They tend to live in the past, to contemplate their thoughts, memories, and emotional reactions. This melancholic temperament is related to the element of the earth, offering resistance to what is happening; but like geode stones with shining crystals inside, such people have a rich inner life of thoughts and feelings.

Knowledge of the temperaments can help us find ways of teaching and disciplining that meet the child's real needs. For example, recognizing that the choleric is centered in the ego (while the phlegmatic is centered in the body) will help you to realize that the choleric can't help being egocentric, oblivious to the effects of his actions on others when characteristically behaving like a little king or queen. The task of bringing balance can then replace one's first reaction of anger or frustration in dealing with such a child. Similarly, understanding the melancholic can help lessen one's annoyance or despair when dealing with a child who whines and complains all the time.

Knowledge of the temperaments is an invaluable tool for parents and teachers because it can increase our understanding and compassion for someone who is different from ourselves. A person's temperament changes from childhood to adulthood in characteristic ways, and anyone interested in this fascinating area is encouraged to read *The Four Temperaments* by Rudolf Steiner.[23]

Toilet Training

Teaching a child to use the toilet is like teaching her to read: when the child is ready, she will learn it. No person with normal faculties gets to age twenty-one without being able to read or be toilet trained. The major cause of 'failure' is starting too young. Expecting a child before the age of two to have bladder control is unfair. Sitting him on the potty at the same time each day doesn't encourage him to know when he has to go.

Although potty training continues to be the most anxiety-ridden experience of their child's early years, parents are becoming increasingly relaxed about it. A 1962 study by Barry Brazelton, M.D., published in Pediatrics, found that about 90 percent of kids were out of nappies by age two and a half. A study published in

1998 in *Pediatrics* found only 22 percent are trained by that age. And almost half of boys weren't trained by age three.[24]

Most child development experts advocate child-oriented toilet learning. Brazelton is even promoting the new size 6 Pampers, which were introduced at the end of 1998 for children weighing over thirty-five pounds, larger than today's average three-year-old. Brazelton apparently felt so strongly that the pressures to train early were resurfacing, that he approached Pampers with the idea of the size 6 nappy. In the same article cited above, he said, 'I think it has to do with the pressure to get them trained by age three for preschool and pressures with day care. Can't we let up on them?'

Experts cite a number of factors for the change to later toilet training and the surprising popularity of the size 6 Pampers and Huggies: the advent of comfy, leak-proof disposable nappies that give children no inclination to train; our hectic lives; the Brazelton-led impulse to listen to kids more rather than dictating their development; and the fact that so many toddlers are so big for their age.[25]

Second children usually toilet train themselves much more easily than first children because they have a sibling to imitate, and because parents are much more relaxed about it. Remembering how imitative children are, let toddlers see how it's done, and provide a little potty around the age of two. Many children feel insecure sitting on the big toilet, so a potty chair is very helpful. Making it a special present and praising children each time they use it will reinforce their new behavior. Patience and a cheerful, 'Too bad, maybe next time you can run faster,' will soon lead to effective training.

Separation Anxiety

There has been a lot written in recent years on mother-child attachment, or bonding, and what can happen when this breaks down through prolonged separation, as in the cases of premature or ill newborns. However, we also need to realize that under normal circumstances the mother and child are going through a separation process. They start out as one, contained within one body, united physically and psychically. Instead of trying to create a bond at birth, the question arises, 'How can the separation of birth not be so painful or prolonged that the mother disconnects from the child?' The obvious answer is through mother and child remaining together. Increased contact helps to bridge the separation, to establish a new relationship rather than leaving the mother feeling let down and isolated by the passing of the old one.

This separation process of mother and child goes on throughout life as the individuality of the child asserts itself more and more. The mother must constantly let go of her image of the child and their relationship as it has been, so the child can more fully be itself and a new relationship can be born.

We have talked about the nine-month-old's common anxiety about people outside the family, and the child's pattern of going away from and coming back to the matrix or source of security. However, separation is also painful for the mother, as anyone knows who has left her baby for the first time. The full breasts, the psychic connection, the concern with how the baby is taking it, the worry that no one can possibly care for this child as well as she does, all pull at a mother's heart strings. The same is true the first time the child goes to school, has her first date, drives the car alone.

We want to protect our children, but we need to realize that they are not extensions of ourselves. Your child is in fact a unique individual who has chosen you to be his or her parents. The individuation process needs to be allowed to occur in order for the child to grow up in a healthy way. In fact, a failure of individuation can cause as great a problem as neglect.

We need to recognize a child as a unique individual from the beginning and do everything we can to avoid putting hindrances in the way of her realizing her full potential and destiny in life. How does this translate into action? For one thing, it means being watchful, but not overly protective. (What if the mother of Sir Edmond Hillary, who first successfully climbed Mt. Everest, hadn't let him climb the stairs as a toddler?) Perhaps it means letting it be all right for your child to climb a tree or climb to the top of the swing set at the park; maybe in another culture she would have become a high-wire artist in the circus! After three trips to the emergency room, you might suggest another activity, but chances are your child will do fine if she undertakes it at all (children are fairly self-regulating if allowed to be so).

Another way of putting it is, 'How can we be as relaxed about our first child as we would be about our fourth?' Naturally, we can't be, because everything is so new. But the 'benign neglect' and the interaction with siblings that a younger child receives are beneficial compared to the over-indulgence and propulsion into adult activity that first and only children tend to receive. As parents, we need always to keep our toddlers in our psychic awareness, but we don't always need to be interacting with them. Raising a child who can play alone, who is self-motivating and not always needing adult input is a real blessing. We need to hold our children in our love and awareness, provide a rich and safe environment for them to explore by themselves, and be there when they come back to 'touch base.' This may happen every few minutes at first, or every few hours as they become older.

One of the reasons raising children used to be simpler was that parents were doing work that involved movement – washing the clothes by hand, making butter, working in the fields. Toddlers played nearby or were watched by an older sibling or relative, and began to imitate and help as soon as they were able. The idea of a thirty-seven-year-old professional being home all day with nothing but a baby to put her energy into is a uniquely modern situation. Our children do need us for the heart connection, but they don't need constant adult input and intellectual stimulation. Allowing children to be children today means recognizing their need to be in movement, their need to imitate actions, and their need for creative play, which is the work of childhood. These topics will be discussed in greater detail in the next chapter.

Cabin Fever

Raising a child is a full-time task. Someone has to be attending to your child all the time. You as parents have a unique relationship with this person and should value both the time and effort necessary to take care of a toddler. But one person doesn't have to do it all the time: you can trade off, engage grandma, have a babysitter or mother's helper, work out trades with a friend who has a young child. Do whatever you need to maintain your own composure and ability to mother. But don't undervalue mothering, or accept the comfortable illusion that 'quality time' makes up for the constant demands of the toddler to be in relationship with you as he or she goes out to explore the world. If you must return to work full time, try to choose an environment for your child that is as much like a home as possible. Having someone come into your home or having your child be part of another mother's 'family' by choosing a woman with similar values who is caring for one or two other children in her own home are perhaps the best solutions. Large groups and institutional care (despite the fact that the ratio of adults to children is usually one to two or one to three) is more stressful to a toddler than situations that provide less stimulation and are less likely to overwhelm the child.

Because of the lack of value placed on mothering and the isolation and frustration that first-time mothers often feel, many would rather work to pay childcare than stay home with their children. If you find yourself dying to get away from your children, try exploring some of the reasons and possible solutions. Here are some things to consider.

1.   *Is your child especially clingy?*

Could you change the environment and make more interesting things accessible to your child, encouraging his exploration of the world? Can you change your expectations of your child, relaxing and recognizing that 'This too shall pass'? Decide to spend three days devoted to nothing but 'being there' and observing, without resentment and without trying to get twenty-five other things done. Perhaps your child will start to branch out as he feels the solid base of your calm support. As your child approaches three, having more children around is often easier than having only one. Can you trade days of childcare with a friend, thus making your time with the children more intentional and giving you time away?

2.   *Do you find yourself involved in constant conflict with your child?*

List the times of day and the activities that lead to conflict. What could you do to change each situation (lay out clothes the night before, get up fifteen minutes earlier, have more ritual and rhythm at bedtime, change your reactions)? What attitudes and expectations do you have? If you are a single parent, can you enlist someone else to observe the two of you and give you some much-needed perspective? If you have a partner, what does he perceive about what is going on? What does he feel about it? Is he supporting you and correcting the child, or ignoring the situation? Do you get louder to try to get a reaction from him?

3.   Do you miss intellectual stimulation or adult companionship?

Can you find a mother's support group or join a play group? Can you go to the park once a week with a friend who also has a toddler? Satisfied mothers of young children seem to be much more social than someone like me who types all day and tries to meet deadlines. They are often going to visit a friend with children or having them over. Sitting in the park or visiting are not luxuries we have at every stage of life. Can you come to appreciate them?

Are you in good relationship with your husband? Do you have evenings free? If taking care of the children goes on until 11:00 PM, see Chapter 11 on rhythm and discipline in home life. What is happening sexually between you?

Would learning more about early childhood help make your task seem more worthwhile and help engage your mind? Would a new activity, such as getting out to an art class, satisfy your need? Taking some time away can often improve your state of mind and your mothering. A friend, who was a mother of five young children and lived by the airport, got her pilot's license after the birth of her sixth child because within five minutes she could be hundreds of feet above all the dirty nappies and toys on the floor. In a similar vein, I took a course to become a travel agent when my children were two and a half years and six months. I see it now as one of the main things that kept me sane during a very difficult time. It provided intellectual stimulation two afternoons a week and was pure fantasy fulfillment. (I never became a travel agent!)

4.   Do you feel at a loss for things to do with your child?

One friend expressed her frustration by saying, 'But I find doing puzzles so boring!' In general, we need to enjoy our children rather than be concerned about playing with them. By this I mean that we need to have a positive attitude and provide them with things to do, not always do the same things they are doing. Think of ways to involve your toddler in the things you do, rather than trying to get them done more quickly without her. Children love to 'help' do the things adults are doing. Provide things for your child to do and be happy keeping a watchful eye. In the next chapter we will talk more about toys and creative play. Invite children over once your child is older than two and a half and let them play with each other. (It requires supervision and judicious adult input, but lets the child be in his element rather than constantly requiring adult input to play.)

If you are still feeling dissatisfied, see if you can discern why and discuss it with your partner or a friend. You don't have to settle for 'getting through it' rather than enjoying parenting and being with your children. New knowledge and perspective, establishing rhythm and discipline, and understanding how children learn and play can all help you to enjoy the adventure of parenting. It isn't always easy, but it's always worthwhile and rewarding.

Recommended Reading

Being a Parent – Parentline Plus (Hawthorn Press). Helpful book to be used on its own or as a workbook for the Parentline Plus course.

Beyond the Rainbow Bridge by Barbara J. Patterson and Pamela Bradley (Michaelmas Press). A Steiner-oriented guide to nurturing our children from birth to seven, with an excellent section on creating balance.

The First Three Years of Life by Burton White (Prentice Hall). White's common-sense approach is based on the observations of hundreds of families in their own homes.

The Four Temperaments by Rudolf Steiner, published in the book *Rhythms of Learning* (Anthroposophic Press). An introduction to the study of temperaments, which is a great help in parenting.

The Incarnating Child by Joan Salter (Hawthorn Press). Addresses parenting in the first two years from the standpoint of Steiner's indications and the author's wide experience at the Gabriel Baby Centre in Australia.

Juno Magazine PO Box 592, East Grinstead, RH19 3AQ
www.junomagazine.com

Lifeways by Gudrun Davy and Bons Voors (Hawthorn Press). Issues
of family life growing out of discussions by a women's group
working with Steiner's insights.

Miseducation: Preschoolers at Risk by David Elkind (Knopf).
Discusses the various styles of parenting and provides support
for letting children be children.

The Mother Magazine – support and ideas for mothers.
www.themothermagazine.co.uk

Mothering, P.O. Box 1690, Santa Fe, NM 87504. US magazine
offering great support for women concerned with issues of
mothering; six times per year.

Mothering and Fathering by Tine Thevenin (Avery). Explores the
gender differences in parenting and the value of both. Provides
valuable perspectives if you find yourself constantly at odds with
your husband or pediatrician on parenting issues.

Mothering with Soul by Joan Salter (Hawthorn Press).

Parenting for a Healthy Future by Dotty T. Coplen (Hawthorn
Press). Understanding parenting from both a practical and
holistic spiritual perspective.

Pregnant Feelings by Rahima Baldwin Dancy and Terra Palmarini
Richardson. The last three chapters help couples explore their
attitudes toward parenting.

Chapter 7

The Development of Fantasy and Creative Play

Three Stages of Play

Play Arising from the Body

While your child is first mastering new body skills, most play consists in pure movement without the element of fantasy. A young child loves to run, jump, walk on tiptoe, climb, turn around, or roll on the ground. Like a lamb in springtime or a young colt, your child delights in movement for the sheer joy of it. And such movement is an important part of muscle growth and the acquiring of motor skills. If left unhindered, your child knows best what movements she needs to develop in a healthy way – there is no need for special baby gymnastics.

Anyone who has ever followed a toddler around knows that she is constantly in movement and expends a tremendous amount of energy! Where does this driving force for movement come from? The energy comes from the process of metabolism, manifested through the movement of the limbs. The metabolic/will/limb system is one of three major systems in Steiner's way of looking at the human being; the other two are the nerve/sense/head system and the heart/lung/middle rhythmic system. These three systems all interpenetrate, and all are active and growing throughout childhood. But Steiner recognized that at different ages one or another system may be dominant. Not only is one system growing most actively, but it also has a major influence on how the child experiences the world and on how she learns. The metabolic/will/limb system predominates in the child under the age of seven; the middle system dominates during the elementary school years; and the head/nerve system is predominant beginning in adolescence.

0-7 years	Metabolic/limb system	Willing/Movement/Imitation
7-14 years	Heart/lung/rhythmic system	Feeling/Imagination
14-21 years	Nerve/sense/head system	Thinking/Analysis

Understanding this shift in emphasis as the child grows can help parents and educators meet the real needs of the developing child.

The metabolic/limb system can be called the vital pole because it is the center of vitality – the center for the anabolic processes of assimilating food and turning it into new physical substance. The growth processes are enormously powerful in a young child, whose life and growth forces are so strong that wounds heal almost immediately. Contrast this with elderly people, whose life forces are declining, and whose wounds and broken bones mend only with great difficulty.

The movements of a baby and toddler can be seen as an expression of the movement of the energy that is active within the growth and inner processes of her body. The baby kicks her feet in the air and watches the movement; she moves her hands and follows the movement with her eyes. At first her movements lack intentionality and control. Then she loves to drop things, and to fling everything out of her crib, taking joy in the development of her own power. For the infant, the mere moving of her limbs is play enough at first, and a manifestation of the happy unfolding of her powers.

In Childhood: A Study of the Growing Soul, Caroline von Heydebrand discusses how the first games of childhood are bound up with the body and have a hidden interplay with organic activities, with the swing of the breath, the rhythmic flow of the circulating fluids, and the forming and excreting of substances. 'The small child piles up his blocks so as to be able to tumble them down again. This is more important to him at first than to build a house or a tower. He feels the same satisfaction in construction and destruction when playing with blocks as he does in anabolic and catabolic processes of his organism when they are healthy.'[1]

Similarly, when a two-year-old scribbles with a large crayon on a piece of paper, you will see spiral, circular movements punctuated by up-and-down movements. The child is expressing the dynamic of his inner being, not trying to make a representational drawing. This aspect of children's art will be discussed more in Chapter 9.

Play Arising from Imagination and Imitation

The time when a little child first begins to feel her movements no longer as expressions of energy but as intentional activities within the sphere of her imaginative games varies with every child, but usually first becomes apparent to the observer between the ages of two and three. The first kinds of play you are likely to see are your child's pretending to eat and drink or talk on the telephone. This type of pretend play comes through the imitation of things the child has done or seen the people around her do. Thus if your child sees you picking up potatoes or balls of yarn and putting them in a basket, she will be happy to copy you and put pine cones or spools in her own basket. Then she will dump them out again, for a child's play has no utilitarian purpose; there is nothing she is trying to accomplish. Your three-year-old may imitate your sweeping by using her own little broom, but she will be completely involved in the gestures of sweeping and unconcerned about picking up any dust.

Without discriminating, a young child takes in everything in her physical and emotional environment. These impressions, which are taken in by the child without filtering or screening, find their expression in play. A child will imitate not only the activity, but also the 'soul mood' or emotions present when an action was performed. Thus if your daughter observes a worker hammering a nail with great anger, she will copy the movement and the anger; or, if you straighten up the room with annoyance, you will see your annoyance in the way she handles her toys. We must pay attention both to the quality of our emotions when we are around young children and to the quality of our movements. Once I was throwing together a cake in a great hurry. I told my four-year-old she could help, but I was going so fast I wasn't paying much attention to her. Suddenly I noticed something was wrong. 'What's the matter?' I asked. 'You're stirring it too fast!' she said through her tears. And she was right – my movements were an affront to her. I apologized and slowed down!

The progression of play from movement to imaginative play can be seen in a young child's relationship to a rocking horse. At first there is no concept of horse, there is just the joy of rhythmical movement. The idea of being a fast rider and 'going somewhere' might come next; later the horse will be incorporated into a five-year-old's elaborate scenarios of being a cowboy or taking care of horses or using one to get away from wolves that are chasing him.

The age between three and five years has been called the age of fantasy because all of the intensity that went into learning to stand, walk, speak, and begin to think now finds its expression in imaginative play, which becomes a story without end. Beginning with the sheer joy of movement, your daughter becomes a bunny hopping or a kitty wanting some milk as the imaginative element is added. Then she begins to transform objects from one thing to another in a stream-of-consciousness flow of associations suggested by the objects themselves and her interactions with them. For example, a piece of wood may serve as an iron if your child has seen you ironing, then it can become a rolling pin and the clothes, dough for biscuits. The rolling pin now changes to a carton of milk to go with the biscuits, and a tea party is under way. If you're lucky, you'll be invited.

This kind of play is similar to dreams in the way one object and situation can flow into another, but it represents a high-level use of the child's creative fantasy. Play is the work of the child from age three on, the way by which she unites herself with the world and tries on all of the activities and roles she sees.

Intentional Pretending

When your child is around four-and-a-half or five, you will see a new element enter and begin to dominate her play. This new element is intentionality, and manifests as 'let's pretend.' Play now tends to be much more socially oriented – a group phenomenon in which as much time can be spent in planning 'you be the mother and I'll be the sister and you be the dog' as in playing out the actual scene. Now play begins to arise more from within the child herself, and she is beginning to make a picture or mental image of what she wants to do.

The child now not only manipulates objects and concepts by having one thing turn into another, she also has the self-awareness to plan ahead in pretending to be someone else. By being the mother, the knight, the carpenter, or the baker, she is assimilating the world as she experiences it and 'living into' the adult world. This is the age when children love bits of cloth and simple costumes to enact little stories. Or they will use dolls and table puppets to put on plays that they make up. Their powers of fantasy and intentionality are also clearly revealed when they model with coloured beeswax or clay, paint with watercolours, or colour with crayons.

Experiencing the World Through Play

Creative play is the way in which children get to know the world, and it has been called the work of early childhood. 'There is nothing that human beings do, know, think, hope and fear that has not been attempted, experienced, practised or at least anticipated in children's play.' This opening sentence from *Children at Play* by Heidi Britz-Crecelius[2] is developed further as she explains the various 'worlds' the child experiences through play.

The World of Space, Time, and the Cosmos

The tiny baby plays unconsciously with his hands and feet. Von Heydebrand states, 'He stretches out to the moon or to the sunlight dancing on the ceiling, not only because he cannot yet estimate distances, but because in the dim dawning of consciousness he has a closer relation to distant spaces than the fully conscious, grown-up person.'[3] But he soon learns that, while the wooden ring can be caught hold of, the brightly shining moon cannot. His first attempts at grasping objects thus become an adventure in learning about near and far, attainable and unattainable. The infant's first movements in learning to grasp objects put him in relationship to space and time and all the laws of nature. Gravity is delightful when it causes the spoon to disappear over the edge of the high chair, but not so when the baby rolls off the edge of the bed!

The child learns much more about space as he learns to move through it, delighting in the play of running, jumping, climbing, and flinging himself onto a pillow or beanbag chair.

The young child is still closely related to the cosmos and delights in play that involves the sun, moon, and stars and their rhythmical movements in the cosmos. Such play includes the image of the circle in all its forms favored by young children: balls, bubbles, balloons, circle games. The ball, a perfect sphere, is a likeness of the earth, the sun, and the 'heavenly sphere' that seems to surround the earth. Soap bubbles are delicate balls that float away on the child's own breath. And watching a balloon floating up to heaven can fill a child with delight or great sadness, depending on his temperament. A form of the circle game also echoes the unified world personified by the sphere; some circle games even involve the planets, such as 'Sally Go Round the Sun':

> Sally go round the sun,
> Sally go round the moon,
> Sally go round the chimney tops
> On a Saturday afternoon.

The World of Nature

It is through play that children come to know the natural world of animals and plants, and the ancient elements of earth, air, fire, and water. With what delight young children play in all types of water, from the bathtub to a mud puddle, as well as water in its winter forms of ice and snow. The element of earth is often first contacted in the form of sand, but clay and stones are also wonderful to play with. And the experience of soil in indoor and outdoor gardening conveys so much more than the commonly used American word dirt. Earth and water mix to form mud, marshes, and stream beds – how lucky are children who live by a small stream!

Air can be played in with kites, flags, pinwheels, windmills, tissue-paper parachutes, and leaves or any light thing tied to a string. Fire is more difficult for children to experience in our age of central heating and refuse pickup. But the joys of a campfire are well known, and Britz-Crecelius states that when a fire is built often enough with adults, the prohibition of lighting fires without an adult will be easier to enforce.[4]

Getting out of the sandbox and actually digging in the earth puts a child immediately into contact with a myriad of life forms; many worms, centipedes, and tiny spiders can be discovered. Similarly, teeming life is discovered when the child turns over a stone by the river or sinks down into tall grass. In a country setting, intimate encounters between children and animals and plants occur without our help; in the cities we may have to help arrange for such encounters so our children do not remain strangers to nature for the whole of their lives. Climbing trees, picking fruit and flowers, sowing seeds and watching them sprout, are all important experiences for a child.

Nature is all around us, even in the city. If you can't exercise your powers of observation on a Sunday walk in the local park, you won't experience anything by the sea or in the mountains. 'One who cannot see a woodpecker or a squirrel here, need not think he will see a starfish or a marmot there.'[5] Contact with nature is renewing for adults, but its importance for children should not be underestimated. Children are especially nourished by contact with the world of living things because their own life forces are so strong. Child psychologist Bruno Bettelheim reminds us, '...the child's thinking remains animistic until the age of puberty. His parents and teachers tell him that things cannot feel and act; and as much as he may pretend to believe this to please these adults, or not to be ridiculed, deep down the child knows better.'[6]

Young children feel a natural kinship with baby animals, taking them into their hearts as comrades and companions. Visiting a farm in springtime can be a lovely experience, and even 'petting barns' at the zoo can give children a bit of an opportunity to touch animals. If a family does not have any pets, Britz-Crecelius suggests that you could at least find a caterpillar or cocoon and share with your child in its amazing transformation.

It is also important to think about what kinds of animal toys the child has. Realistic stuffed toys are not as beneficial as quite primitive ones that merely suggest the form and movement of the animal. A young child does not see the animal as the grown-up sees it, and von Heydebrand states, 'It is not good for the tiny creature who is striving to become 'man' in the best sense of the word to have to live with animals made in 'realistic imitation' of Nature, looking at them as though they were prototypes of his own supple, yielding being.'[7] This is perhaps most visible with stuffed monkeys, which are almost like caricatures of human beings, but the effect can be very strong with other characters, such as the floppy stuffed bunny that the lethargic child seemed to be imitating (described in Chapter 5).

This idea may sound quite strange, since we live in a culture in which stuffed animals, plush toys, and cartoon characters are an integral part of childhood. It certainly doesn't mean that a healthy child will be ruined by having a stuffed dog or bear! But it is helpful to realize that the young child is trying to get to know the world as it is and lacks the sophistication and humor that most characterizations involve. When animals are taken out of their normal postures, dressed up in clothes, and made to imitate people, the image of the human being is also being brought down to a lower level. Respect for our unique position in relation to the rest of the animal kingdom is worth fostering in a culture that tends to reduce the human being to animal or mechanistic levels.

The Human World

Through play the child interacts first with his parents and those in his immediate family. He can very soon start to help the adults in their work, washing the car, or putting away the silverware. Because much of the interesting housework and handiwork that children used to grow into through play is now done by machines, it is all the more important to let children participate in what you are doing whenever possible.

Through observing and helping in the home, the child will start to reflect what he knows in his play. If he is given toys that allow imaginative play, you will see everything your child takes in reflected in his play. Through the taking on of different roles, your child not only tries on what he sees of the adult world, but he can also work through certain difficulties and emotions in the present (as in playing 'baby' when a new sibling is expected or has recently been born).

Children don't usually play with each other until the imaginative element starts to dominate. Prior to that time they play next to each other, each two-year-old engrossed in her own activity or immediately wanting whatever she sees the other child pick up. This characteristic of two-year-olds is a result of the power of imitation. Naturally, she is interested in whatever she sees the other child has, and wants to do the same things.

However, once children start to play imaginatively, their pretend situations can easily involve other children, and they will begin to want someone to play with when only adults are around. This is the age where two compatible children are infinitely easier to take care of than one! As they grow, play continues to be an area in which children learn social skills and are able to experience their own influence within the context of their peers.

The Special Role of Dolls

Through play the child familiarizes himself with the world and assimilates it, making it his own. His senses become sharpened, he is better able to control the instrument of his body and he becomes better able to relate to nature and his fellow human beings. Play with dolls is of special importance because it is one of the ways through which the child can externalize his own inner being. 'Through the doll the child finds its own self,' Britz-Crecelius states, offering in *Children at Play* many examples of how involved children can become with a favorite doll, so that adults have to be very careful not to commit a *faux pas* of denying the reality of such a doll.[8] Parents must treat these attachments with respect and stay alert to which dolls are 'living' for the child, for it can change with time and circumstances. The favorite doll can become like an alter ego for the child, invested with a bit of the child's own emerging sense of self.

Because a doll plays many varied and complex roles, according to the circumstances, it is easy to understand that the more indistinct and undefined a doll's expression, the less trouble it will cause the imagination of the child. If the doll has a fixed character, it will most often be assigned a specific role in play; it is less useful as a second I than a soft doll with eyes but no mouth, which can easily be happy, sad, or angry.

Constant invisible companions are used in much the same way, and Britz-Crecelius states, 'The disappearance of an invisible companion, the discarding of a doll, are important steps on the path of the child to itself. If, however, one removes them forcibly and before the child is ready, then one makes it unsure of itself.'[9]

Dolls also give children an opportunity to imitate and work out the ways in which parents treat them. For girls, play with dolls is mainly a mother-and-child game, while boys' play with dolls is rarely that. Boys are also less likely to dress and undress their dolls, so they don't need removable clothes and wardrobes as girls' dolls do. However, boys between two and six have a need as great as girls for a doll that can represent a second I, a being the child clasps in his arms when he is beyond himself in order to come to himself again. Many people in our culture are shy of giving dolls to boys, or want to make sure they are 'macho images' such as He-Man or GI Joe. However, our sons need both to be allowed to be children and to exhibit nurturing behavior just as much as our daughters!

Most psychologists also support boys being encouraged to play with dolls. Bruno Bettelheim states, 'If parents feel relaxed about their son's playing with dolls, they will provide him with valuable opportunities for enriching his play life. For them to do so, it is not sufficient that they simply refrain from disparaging such play. Because of the still prevalent attitude that doll play is only for girls, both parents need to have a positive feeling about a boy's doll play if he is to be able to take full advantage of it.'[10]

We need to put our attention into the quality of the dolls our children have. Not only their expression is important, but the quality of the material as well. Is the doll cold and hard, or soft and huggable? Is the hair platinum and grotesquely matted after a week's play? A soft cloth doll with yarn hair and a neutral expression provides the child with a companion who can change as she does. 'Walk, talk, cry, laugh, eat, drink, wet itself, blush, get a temperature, get brown in the sun – any rag doll, any nice, simple doll can do that in the hands of a child. The mechanical creatures on the toy market can do it much less well, and provoke every older or younger brother into opening them up to have a look – and rightly so! Because these are not dolls, but machines, whose mechanics leave no room for the little bit of the child's soul that seeks to enclose itself there.'[11] Even eyes that close are very mechanical, as evidenced by a little girl who said of her doll with its wooden head: 'My Tommy doesn't always need to go to sleep straight away, he can also like awake sometimes.'[12]

The beautiful doll and the anatomically correct doll are a hindrance to the inner development of the child. Not only do they leave nothing for the child's imagination to supply, but they provide more than the young child can hold in awareness. Young children are mostly aware of the head, as evidenced by their drawings. (This will be discussed more in Chapter 9.) Giving a child a doll with breasts is projecting her out of her childhood into the teenage world. Barbie is a multi-million dollar enterprise, and encouraging our young children to indulge in her designer jeans and convertible supports values that impoverish the world of the young child.

The Importance of Play

Noted psychologist Bruno Bettelheim defines a young child's play as activities characterized by freedom from all but personally imposed rules (which are changed at will), by free-wheeling fantasy involvement and by the absence of any goals outside of the activity itself.[13] Not only is play important for the healthy creative and emotional growth of a child, but it also forms the best foundation for later intellectual growth. Bettelheim states:

> Play teaches the child, without his being aware of it, the habits most needed for intellectual growth, such as stick-to-itiveness, which is so important in all learning. Perseverance is easily acquired around enjoyable activities such as chosen play. But if it has not become a habit through what is enjoyable, it is not likely to become one through an endeavor like schoolwork.[14]

Kindergarten, as first conceived by Friedrich Froebel in the 19th century, was a place where child would play, as if in a garden.

However, during most of the period in which kindergartens have existed, they have been pre-schools.[15] This unfortunate trend toward replacing creative play with academic work has accelerated since the 1950s. Instead of being allowed to play, children are made to fill in workbooks or are given computers to 'play with,' which overlook the fact that play needs to involve movement and 'the absence of any goals outside of the activity itself.' Similarly, objects that can be played with in only one 'right' way are useful only for teaching concepts, rather than allowing the child's fantasy to roam freely. The imaginative play of the young child, in which objects transform from one thing into another, is an ideal foundation for the symbol manipulation involved in later reading. We shouldn't skip the stage of concrete, although fanciful, manipulation of objects in free play by going directly into reading, writing, and math. The years from three to six provide a lifelong foundation for creativity that should not be undervalued or foreshortened.

Just as it is important not to skip steps like crawling in physical development, so the age of fantasy should be honored as a valuable part of normal development. Play allows for the development of a wide range of experience, so that what is first grasped through action can later be learned anew through thought. Thus, when the adolescent studies the laws of levers and mechanics, he will have had the experience of shifting further forward or back on the seesaw, depending on the size of his friend; or the study of trajectories will have had its foundation in throwing balls or skipping stones.

The imaginative play of early childhood changes as the child matures to reflect the child's growing interests. She may form a detectives' club around ten years old, when Nancy Drew, *Swallows and Amazons* or the Hardy Boys adventures are often read. Physical development and imitation will continue to inform the changing content of children's play as they become older. Children from time immemorial have reached the world of adults by a staircase of games. Each step is made up of the games of a particular age group, and each step is important. Children will advance from their natural levels of play only when they are ready. For example, a girl who, although younger than her classmates, is top in her class academically, may still prefer to play with the children from the year below her in the holidays.

Many factors work against free play today: the emphasis on early academics, the passive quality of watching television and films, the seductive attraction of video games, the difficulty in connecting with nature, and the need for constant supervision in urban environments. The fact that adults are so busy and most mothers work at least part time outside the home leaves adults with little creative energy to put into children's play, or leaves the child in structured daycare from 8:00 AM until 5:30 PM. The abundance of toys based on television and film characters (and therefore with fixed personalities) also leaves little room for creative imagination in play.

Before I became involved in Steiner/Waldorf education, my own children were constantly asking what they should do or wanting me to entertain them or take them somewhere. When our friends came to visit from Mexico, their bilingual daughter – who had been raised in a small village with no television – would suddenly bring everything to life. She would organize everyone into a circus or put on a show for the adults; suddenly all the children were playing and having a great time with no adult input. I looked back on my own childhood and could remember doing similar things with my best friend: pretending we owned ranches, with bikes for horses and huge ponderosa pine cones for dogs; or making forts in the rocks down at the creek; or playing 'office' with a dozen little characters who lived around our desks; or making pipe-cleaner dolls when we were seven years old and spending the next two months at home making orange-crate houses and furniture for them.

Clearly my children had somehow lost the ability to play. While I was able to diagnose the problem, I was at a loss to know what to do about it. Then I discovered the Waldorf schools and ways in which parents can help their children to play creatively, which I want to share with you. The improvement in their children's play at home was an often-heard observation at the first parents' meeting when I taught kindergarten at the Rudolf Steiner School. If we understand the elements of creative play, we can help our children not miss out on this important part of early childhood.

Ways to Encourage Your Child's Creative Play

Creating an Inviting Environment

Most children today are like descendants of the old woman in the shoe and 'have so many toys, they don't know what to do.' The spoils of Christmases and birthdays past are most often stuffed onto shelves or thrown together in a toy box or basket, so it is frequently more fun to dump everything out, rather than imaginatively to play with particular toys. Helle Heckmann, who runs a Waldorf daycare center in Denmark, describes this cross-cultural phenomenon: 'The abundance of the children's room must be every parent's or child's worst nightmare. 'I'm bored.' 'I've got nothing to play with' – even though the shelves are full to the brim. Dust-collectors, a useless mess. Where is the love for the teddy bear, the doll, the car? The present which was given in love and did not drown in abundance is hard to find. The child does not need the toys – the toy factories need the child.'[16]

So I invite you to consider your child's bedroom and/or the play room and contemplate which items don't seem to contribute to imaginative play or are never used in play. The weeding out can be done openly or covertly. Some parents have enlisted enthusiasm for the project by saying to the child, 'You have so many things. Let's sort through the ones you don't play with any more and give them to the Goodwill, so other children whose parents don't have the money to buy them any toys will be able to have some of yours.' Other items can simply disappear into a box for a few weeks, to be brought back if they are missed – or passed on if they are not. One mother told me she sets aside a box of 'extra' toys as a 'rainy day box,' which she can go to at times when her child really seems ready for new input.

You might also consider your children's toys from the point of view of aesthetics. More than seventy years ago Steiner railed against giving children 'beautiful dolls' instead of natural ones. But what about all of the grotesque and bizarre toys that today's children play with, which intentionally try to embody 'the dark forces?' Does beauty matter? Young children are looking to know the real world, and to maintain the inner conviction that it is good, true, and beautiful (a deep inner conviction that needs to remain in their unconscious to be drawn upon as teenagers. Such wellsprings are necessary if teens are to have any kind of idealism and ability to seek solutions to the problems and evil in the world instead of succumbing to nihilism and despair). Dr. Gilbert Childs, a noted British educator, writes that it is as if we in society are actually surrounding our children with ugliness as a principle.[17] It's something to consider.

Once you've done an appraisal of your children's toys and you can begin to see the floor and the shelves, you'll be much more aware of the individual toys. Then you can think about how to arrange them, because the way in which you display a child's toys determines to a large extent whether or not your child will play with them. Remember that much of play is suggested by the objects themselves as they spark associations in the child's imagination. When toys are piled together in a toy box or basket, they aren't inviting to your child, and you'll never have the possibility of your child's playing quietly by himself after waking up, allowing you to get another twenty minutes of sleep.

There are other advantages to creating order in your child's play space by making sure that everything has a 'home.' Having a place for everything can provide the child with a feeling that there is order in the larger scheme of things. And it is through play that a child develops habits for work. Helping your child use things and put them away not only teaches good habits in present time, but can be of help in the later development of thought processes. Dr. Gilbert Childs writes, 'Such tidiness in practical affairs will assist the order of thought processes, so laying the foundations for clear thinking in adult years. Children learn to 'think with their hands,' and doing repetitious activities that are allied to household and human tasks in life strengthens their will-power.'[18] While it may seem like extra work to clean up with your child at the end of each day, arranging toys invitingly on shelves will encourage your child to be self-motivating in his play. Arranging little scenes on tables or shelves will also invite the child to 'live into' the scene and start to play with it.

Another aid to your child's play is having activity areas, if your home or apartment is large enough. For example, a play kitchen area with a child-sized table and chairs and some kind of toy stove and dishes will provide hours of imitative play. Community Playthings makes wonderful wooden kitchen appliances and other toys for children. You can write for their brochure using the address at the end of the chapter. But it is also possible to make a simple stove-sink combination by finding or building a wooden box, then cutting a hole into which you put a metal bowl for a sink, and painting burners on it. Hinged doors and shelves inside for cupboard and oven are all the better, but not necessary.

Most of the play dishes, pots, and pans sold in toy shops last a few weeks or months before they are broken or dented beyond recognition. Adult items are sturdier and can usually be picked up inexpensively at second-hand shops – wooden bowls, small pots, silverware, saucers, and pitchers, for instance. Wooden fruit can be found at many shops, and a jigsaw can be used to cut pieces of bread from a scrap of plywood.

Another area of great enjoyment is a workbench with a real vice, small hammer, saw, and nails. Children enjoy the activities of hammering and sawing, and they can also make toys such as boats or cars. An old tree stump that can be kept indoors for pounding nails is a great way to engage children's excess energy.

A doll corner is a special place where the dolls can be put to bed each night and greeted in the morning. Cradles, baskets lined with cloth, a small high chair, and a drawer for dolls' clothes all add to the play in this area. The kitchen or dining room table can serve as an area for painting, colouring, and crafts; these activities will be discussed more in Chapter 9.

When you set up activity areas, remember that your child will most often want to play fairly close to where you spend most of your time. A play area in a dining room or family room is often used more frequently than a bedroom that is upstairs and far away from the main activities of the family.

An invaluable aid to play are clothes stands. These wooden structures can be made in a variety of ways, as long as they are both sturdy and light enough for the child to move himself. They are about three feet high and can have sheets and other lengths of cloth draped over them to form houses, caves, and other enclosed play spaces. Simple wooden horses made from timber and metal braces work quite well, or trestles requiring more carpentry skill can be seen in various toy catalogs or the book *Toymaking with Children* listed at the end of this chapter.

Along with sheets and long lengths of cloth, you will want to keep a box of coloured pieces of cloth of various sizes from one to two yards. These will be used for table cloths, baby blankets, rivers, and to define a space when a child wants to create an action scene for a doll or puppet play.

Costumes

A few simple costumes can greatly enhance your child's play. Children love to play 'dress up' for the sheer joy of putting on and taking off fancy clothes; they also love to transform themselves into characters who can then act out roles in imaginative play – especially if several siblings or friends play together.

Having a few special hooks for capes and a shelf for hats can make costumes easily accessible and suggestive of creative play. Again, don't make a lot of things at once – give your child a chance to play with and relish each new thing. Try making something as it fits in with your child's play, or engage in a little imaginative play with your child the first time he puts on something new that you have provided. Your interacting with the characters suggested by the costumes will go a long way toward their being used in the future. Here are some suggestions for things you can easily make.

Hats
- Make a crown out of stiff paper; cover with aluminum foil.
- Make a crown by sewing the ends of some fancy braids to a few inches of one-inch-wide elastic to make a circle that will fit your child's head.
- Make a couple of squares of thin material, like chiffon, that can be worn as veils held on by the braid crowns.
- Cut two kitty ears out of coloured felt; sew onto bias tape or ribbon; they'll stick up when worn; also works for dogs, bunnies (with paper between two layers to stiffen the ears).
- Collect hats from second-hand shops: dress-up, sailor, farmer, train engineer.

Capes
- Take a length of material, turn under one-inch casing, put elastic through and sew the ends together for the neck; hem; add braid or other decoration if desired.
- Make a cape with a hood by closing one end and putting casing for the elastic down about ten inches. Sew the ends of the elastic to the edges of the cape and add ties.

Clothes
- Capes with elastic around the top are also worn as skirts; or make a simple skirt with elastic to match a cape. Add braid and a crown to delight any princess!
- Make a tunic by cutting a head hole in a piece of cloth about eighteen inches wide; sew a tie to the center back. A must for knights, bears, cowboys, anything your child wants to be.
- Save and collect dress-up clothes: velvets, blouses, jackets, etc.

Accessories
- Go through your own home, grandma's attic, charity shops, or jumble sales for aprons, gloves, silver shoes, and so forth.

Toys for Imaginative Play

The less formed and more archetypal a toy is, the more possibilities it leaves for the child's imagination. In *Love of Seven Dolls* by Paul Gallico, the little girl is taking leave of the seven dolls she loves so much. The doll 'Monsieur Nicholas,' who repairs and makes toys, gives her the following present: '… and Monsieur Nicholas gave her an oddly turned piece of wood that has not one but many shapes.

"'For your first-born,' he says. 'It is a toy I have made for him that is not any, yet is still all toys, for in his imagination, when he plays with it, it will be whatever he sees in it, or wishes it to be.'"[19]

Shapes and forms from nature have that possibility: gnarled knots from trees, pieces of bark, small pieces of branches, or 1-inch rounds from a tree trunk. This is where a large box or basket filled with 'blocks' made from a tree trunk and branches will be used for much more than stacking and knocking down.

Baskets of natural objects can also be used in many ways by

children. Rocks, shells, pine cones, chestnuts, or walnuts, if made available in small baskets or other containers, will appear as part of the scenery, pieces of food, small animals, or whatever is needed in the moment's play.

It is easy to make several stand-up dolls with which your child can act out various scenes in play. These simple dolls/puppets have cylindrical bodies and no arms or legs. Instructions are available in *Toymaking with Children* and *The Children's Year*. Try making a mother, father, old man, old woman, king, queen, baker, or boy and girl. The list is as long as your imagination.

In addition to the stand-up dolls or puppets just described, you will want to have dolls of various kinds. Instructions for making more complex soft or knitted dolls can be found in the books just mentioned. You can buy the dolls ready-made through mail order catalogs, or many of these companies also sell kits for making your own. The time and love you invest into your child's doll makes it extra special for him or her.

Doll accessories can by made by picking up baskets for cribs at discount or second-hand shops and lining them with cloth, which you can also use to make a matching pillow and blanket. While the dolls themselves are wonderful, it is the 'aliveness' that the child (and you) invest in them that makes them 'come to life' and have meaning for the child (if you don't know *The Velveteen Rabbit*, it's a must!).

If you like to play with shapes, you can make animals by sculpting coloured wool fleece with a needle and thread. For example, a simple bird can be made by tying a knot in a length of coloured wool for the head and inserting another piece crosswise for wings. Attach a string to it and hang it in a window or tie it on a stick for a very successful bird.

Another possibility for sculpting animals is to make them from knitted squares of various colours. Instructions for knitting animals and dwarves are available in the books listed at the end of this chapter.

The magical art of creating forms through folds and knots is made easy to follow through the book *Hanky Panky*, which even comes complete with a large white handkerchief for making into a bunny or mouse.

Outdoor Play

In addition to a sandbox, swing, and slide, one of the best outdoor toys for three- and four-year-olds is a climbing dome. Such a dome is just the right height for these children and will be used for climbing, hanging, sitting on, and playing rocket ship.

Another well-used toy will be a balancing board (not yet as narrow as a balance beam). By attaching cross pieces to the underside of both ends, the board can be laid securely across horizontal bars of the climbing frame, be secured across two chairs of equal height or be used in many other ways.

If you can make a small 'hill' in your yard, it will be a constant delight for a young child to climb, run down, march up, sit on, and sled down if you have snow. Also, make use of any natural landscape you have to encourage little secret spots behind the hedge, construct simple tree houses together, and otherwise make your yard accessible to your children.

Trips to the park will be enjoyable for the large climbing and play equipment that is there, but also try to schedule walks with your child down country roads or through a wooded area. And be sure to walk at the child's pace, allowing ample time for exploration and discovery. I was always amazed at what an eye my daughter had for teeny tiny little things: flowers, bugs, bits of coloured paper.

Don't be afraid of the elements. While most people with children buy appropriate clothing for outdoor play in the snow, few people let their children play in the rain. Waterproof rubber boots and a good rain coat can give your child lots of pleasure stomping through the puddles or playing in the mud. Similarly, be sure to go out when it's windy, letting your child be blown by the wind and fly kites or a large maple leaf attached to a string.

The children in Nøkken, the Waldorf-based childcare center in Denmark, are outside for several hours every day, in all kinds of weather. 'There's no such thing as bad weather,' director Helle Heckmann asserts, 'only bad clothing.' She and her assistants walk with the twenty-four children each day to a nearby park. She describes how Karoline and Johanne, both one-year-olds, have started stroking a tree together and laughing, continuing undisturbed in this experience for about an hour. And how two older children are making dinner with the mud. She writes:

> What makes it so important that Sarah and Magnus can sit in a puddle underneath a tree in which the wind is blowing, and in deep concentration cook dinner? What do they shape when they shape the mud-balls? To me, it is definitely themselves – their inner organs. Mud, soil, sand, and water do not have definite shapes; they have the ability to constantly change. This is exactly what the 3- to 4-year-olds need as an identification with the surrounding world. Getting dirty is a sign of health.
>
> The four elements, earth, water, air and fire, are the basic elements which children are nourished by and from which they grow. No shaped toys – be they wood or plastic – can compete with these materials. The seriousness with which the children play, the deep concentration speaks for itself, and shows how important this 'playing' is. Nobody needs to fight about anything – there is plenty of mud for everybody.[20]

When I've done workshops on early childhood, I've asked participants to introduce themselves and then share an early childhood memory. The overwhelming majority of people remember something to do with nature. Often it's just lying in a field and watching the clouds. Try to let your child experience nature and the seasons of the year. You'll probably find it refreshing and energizing yourself!

Encouraging Play by Modeling Meaningful Activity

We have discussed the powerful imitative powers of the young child and his need to re-enact his experiences of the world around him through play. One of the reasons that children can't play is that they don't very often see the adults around them engaged in meaningful activity. Why is this? There are two main reasons. The first is that frequently the adult is spending all her time relating directly to the child. Barbara Dewey, a Waldorf teacher and consultant, describes it as follows:

> As I observe these parents, I see that they are devoted parents who have read everything they can possibly read about parenting

and are trying desperately to apply ALL of it! They are usually mothers who have given up a meaningful career to stay at home and raise their children, and they feel a need to raise children FULL TIME in order to justify their being home with them. They carry their child around a good portion of the time and interact with the child every waking minute…

In an article in *Mothering*, Winter 1994, Jean Leidloff, author of *The Continuum Concept*, writes of the mis-interpretation of her work. What she says is right in line with what Steiner says about the young child. In her book she recommends keeping babies in physical contact all day and night until they crawl, as is done in the Yequana culture, where the parent or caregiver may occasionally play with the child, but most of the time pays attention to something else, not the baby. She says in her article, 'Being played with, talked to, or admired all day deprives the babe of this in-arms spectator phase that would feel right to him. Unable to say what he needs, he will act out his discontentment.'

This is the attention-getting behavior parents interpret as needing more attention when in reality, the child just wants the parent to take charge of adult life, because the child needs to see a life in order to imitate it![21]

So what's a mother to do? The other part of the problem is that most of the 'work' we do around the house these days more often involves pushing a button than rhythmically moving. The dishes need washing? We push the button on the dishwasher. The clothes need washing? We push the button on the washing machine. The floor is dirty? We push the button on the hoover and jab here and there instead of rhythmically sweeping the floor. Because young children are so caught up in the will forces and are so involved in movement, they discount all these activities as meaningless. It's almost as if they're not sure we're alive unless we're moving. (This could explain why both your young child and your dog insist on banging on your newspaper or inserting themselves between you and the paper you are trying to read: first, they want to make sure you're still alive, because you aren't moving; and they also can feel that your peripheral attention has left and gone somewhere else, and it's really lonely without you!)

Because rhythmical activity speaks so strongly to children, it is helpful to bring conscious gestures into our household tasks, such as folding clothes, sweeping floors, and washing the windows, car, or floor. The children will watch, join in to help, or simply take it all in as they go about their work of playing. As busy parents, we need to realize the value of the things we do in the home and do them as conscious activities around the young child – this could involve something as simple as peeling an apple for the child down on her little table instead of up on the counter, sitting and mending with needle and thread, or embroidering a placemat or cloth napkin for her.

Are you beginning to get a feeling for what I'm saying? It sounds like we're back at the same old stuff – housework – but there are two differences. One is we're doing these activities with awareness of how we move, with awareness of their beneficial effect on the young child, and with caring. The other is that we might be doing things we wouldn't ordinarily do, like sweeping, washing place mats on a scrubbing board, ironing, grinding grain with a hand mill, baking, cleaning cupboards, repairing a toy, sanding wood, and so forth. It may sound 'quaint,' but let me assure you that it beats having a whiny two-year-old or plugging another kid video into the VCR to get her out of your hair. It's kind of like the Zen saying of 'Before enlightenment, chopping wood and carrying water. After enlightenment, chopping wood and carrying water.' By becoming conscious of our own activities, by regulating our daily lives in a harmonious, rhythmical way – by valuing what we do around our children – we are shaping their will forces, and helping their physical bodies to develop in as healthy a way as possible. In return, our children give us the gift of slowing down, of becoming aware of our movements and our emotions, and of appreciating the uniqueness of each moment.

Barbara Dewey concludes:

In less materialistic cultures and in our grandparents' day, parents had to work most of the time on procuring the basics. In those cultures the child naturally got to see those activities. As modern parents, we need to go back to that way of thinking. In so doing, we will get in touch with ourselves, the sources of our food, clothing, and shelter and perhaps discover an old art or craft form which really inspires us. When you give your child the gift of being home with her, she gives you the gift of a life of your own pursuits, the wonders of which you wouldn't have dreamed in your wildest dreams! Accept that gift and 'Get a life!'[22]

In Conclusion

The primary reason so many parents today find it difficult to be with young children is because modern life doesn't provide what young children need. The Steiner/Waldorf mixed-age preschool group typically has six, twelve, twenty or even more children from three to six years of age actively playing and doing things together in an environment of harmony and calm. The Waldorf teacher models her classroom and activities on the healthy home. You, the parents, have such a home, or at least the possibility of creating one. Creating such an environment comes through understanding the real needs and the developmental stages of young children. Once you understand the importance of creating rhythm in the life of the child and then provide appropriate opportunities for his or her creative play and imaginative/artistic development, you'll find that your child is much happier and easier to live with. And nurturing children in this way also nurtures the caregiver, whether teacher or parent.

More than seventy years ago, Rudolf Steiner observed:

Generally speaking, education has followed in the footsteps of our modern civilization which has gradually become more and more materialistic. A symptom of this is the frequent use of mechanical methods in preference to organic methods, and this just during the early years of childhood up to the change of teeth, which is the most impressionable and important time of life. We must not lose sight of the fact that up to the second dentition the child lives by imitation. The serious side of life, with all its demands in daily work, is re-enacted in deep earnestness by the child in its play. The difference between a child's play and an adult's work is that an adult's contribution to society is governed by a sense of purpose and has to fit into outer demands, whereas the child wants to be active simply out of an inborn and natural impulse. Play activity streams outward from within. Adult work takes the opposite direction, namely, inwards from the periphery...

But because, through lack of knowledge of the human being, the key to childhood has been lost, all kinds of artificial play activities for children of kindergarten age have been intellectually contrived by adults... There is no need for the nursery class staff to go from one child to the next to show each one what it has to do. The child does not yet want to follow given instructions. All it wants to do is to copy what the adult is doing.[23]

Recommended Reading

Children at Play: Preparation for Life by Heidi Britz-Crecelius (Floris Books). Describes how the child comes to know the world through play. Excellent.

The Children's Year by Stephanie Cooper, et al. (Hawthorn Press). Directions for soft dolls, knitted animals, and many other toys to make with children.

Earthwise by Carol Petrash (Floris Books). Simple environmental activities for young children.

Earth, Water, Fire, Air by Walter Kraul (Floris Books). Play for explorations in the four elements.

A First Book of Knitting by Bonnie Gosse & Jill Allerton (Wynstones). Simple instructions and handwork patterns for you or your child (grades 1-3). A real delight.

Free to Learn by Lynne Oldfield (Hawthorn Press).

The Genius of Play by Sally Jenkinson (Hawthorn Press).

Hanky Panky by Elizabeth Burns. A delightful little book (complete with white handkerchief) on the playful art of making magical characters with knots and folds. Order from the author at 4060 Whitworth Rd., Gustine, CA 95322.

Making Dolls by Sunnhild Reinckens (Floris Books). Richly illustrated instructions for making several types of soft Waldorf dolls.

Making Waldorf Dolls by Maricristin Sealey (Hawthorn Press). A Waldorf Doll-making handbook.

Sock Doll Workshop by Crandall-Frasier (Lark Books). Instructions for making 30 different sock dolls.

Toymaking with Children by Freya Jaffke (Floris Books) Instructions for making dolls, knitted animals, wooden trestles, and many more soft and hard toys found in the Waldorf kindergartens.

Work and Play in Early Childhood by Freya Jaffke (Floris Books). Discusses the pillars of rhythm and repetition, example and imitation. Beautiful pictures from Waldorf kindergartens.

Waldorf in the Home www.waldorfinthehome.org Website full of ideas, resources, courses and links (US focus).

Toys

Pass these wonderful catalogs on to grandparents, aunts, and uncles. They'll be delighted not to have to go to Toys R Us!

US

Camphill Products, Camphill Rd., Copake, NY 12516.

A Child's Dream, PO Box 1499, Boulder, CO 80306. www.achildsdream.com

The Natural Baby Catalog, 7835-3 Freedom Ave. NW, N. Canton, OH 44720. www.store.yahoo.com

Nova Natural, 817 Chestnut Ridge Rd., Spring Valley, NY 10977. www.novanatural.com

The Playstore, 508 University Ave., Palo Alto, CA 94301. www.playstoretoys.com

UK

Myriad Natural Toys, Ringwood, Hampshire
    Tel no. 01725 517085 www.myriadonline.co.uk

Community Playthings LLC, Robertsbridge,
    East Sussex TN32 5DR Tel no. 0800 387 531
    www.communityplaythings.co.uk High quality children's furniture and toys

Lessons in Play, Orchard Cottage, 9 Meareway, Glastonbury, Somerset BA6 9TY Tel no. 0845 458 7529
    www.lessonsinplay.co.uk. Natural toys and play silks.

Supplies for Making Dolls and Puppets

US
Mercurius, 7426 Sunset Ave., #C, Fair Oaks, CA 95628. Wool and
   wool-blend felt squares for stand-up puppets. Cotton knit for
   dolls' bodies.
Sureway Trading Enterprises, 826 Pine Ave., Suites 5 & 6, Niagara
   Falls, NY 14301. Very inexpensive white silk.

UK
Dainty Supplies Ltd, Unit 35, Phoenix Road, Crowther Industrial
   Estate, Washington NE38 0AD Tel no. 0191 416886
Mercurius, PO Box 1379, Swindon SN1 3SN
   Tel no. 01793 431480   Stockists to UK Steiner Schools.
My Favourite Things, 53 Salisbury Road, Redland, Bristol BS6 7AS
   Tel no. 0117 924 3577 Carded sheep's wool, stockinette and
   other doll making supplies.
Myriad, Ringwood, Hampshire. Tel no. 01725 517085
   www.myriadonline.co.uk

CHAPTER 8

Nourishing Your Child's Imagination

The Importance and Development of Imagination

Creativity in the young child manifests in imagination or fantasy, which we see most clearly in a child's free play. The child can easily transform herself from a carpenter to a mother to a fire engine driver, all within the course of an hour's play; similarly, we have seen how the child's active imagination can transform objects from one thing to another and create scenes and dramas with small toys and characters. Play enlivens fantasy and fantasy kindles and diversifies play. As the child becomes older, this creative imagination develops into the formation of images. This same ability later transforms into creative thinking. Developmental psychologists have stated, 'The development of imagery in the thinking processes of children is an important part of child development, related to play patterns, to creativity, and to adult achievements.'[1]

According to Rudolf Steiner, the life forces that aid in the growth of the physical body 'spill over,' or are freed for imagination when they are not needed for physical growth and transformation. We see this for the first time between ages two and three, when the body has developed enough for the child to start using imagination in creative free play. Once the physical work of the first seven years is over (as manifested by the eruption of the second teeth) this energy is freed further and transforms into 'poetic, artistic fantasy.'[2] Thus between the ages of seven and fourteen, subjects are taught in the Waldorf schools in ways that appeal to this artistic, imaginative sphere in which children live. The final transformation of this growth energy is into intellect. At around age fourteen the child's forces are still further freed for abstract intellectual analysis. Steiner explains, 'Although it is highly necessary, in view of the nature of our modern civilization, that a person should be fully awake in later life, the child must be allowed to remain as long as possible in the peaceful, dream-like condition of pictorial imagination in which his early years are passed. For if we allow his organism to grow strong in this way, he will in later life develop the intellectuality needed in the world today.'[3]

The role of imagination or the ability to think in images is recognized as an important component in creative thinking. Albert Einstein said he discovered the theory of relativity by picturing himself riding on a ray of light. He said that words did not play a role in his thought.[4] In the well-known story of Elias Howe, inventor of the sewing machine, his dream of being attacked by natives holding spears with holes near the tips enabled him to complete his invention by putting the hole near the point of the sewing machine needle. Along with inventors, artists and musicians often work by trying to give expression to what they have seen or heard in their minds.

The faculty of imagination develops simultaneously as memory develops. In the third year, the child begins to develop memory and ideas through the separation of himself from the world in consciousness. As the 'I' comes to experience itself as separate from the world, there is someone present to remember things. At the same time, the child is able to unite his increasingly conscious self with the world through his will in play, and fantasy soon follows. The two simultaneous developmental processes can be diagrammed as follows:

knowledge	will
▼	▼
separation of self and world in consciousness	union of self and world play
▼	▼
memory/ideas	play/fantasy

Researcher Dr. Karen Olness asks, 'If, indeed, spontaneous play leads to images which are valuable from a creative and coping point of view, how can the quality of spontaneous play be cultivated and retained?'[5]

From the preceding chapter we have seen some of the things that encourage imaginative play:

- Appreciate play and how it develops in the first six years.
- Allowing time for free play. Do not interrupt your child all the time. Observe more, intervene less.
- Provide areas of activities, with things arranged in a way that invites the child's involvement.
- Provide simple toys that require the child to complete them with his or her imagination.
- Provide plenty of contact with the world of nature and opportunities to play with sand, soil, water, air, etc.
- Provide examples of real work for imitation; as children see and help adults transform things through work, this will become transformed into their play.

To this list we can add three more things:

- Provide artistic activities that allow the child to express freely what lives inside him (these will be discussed in the next chapter).
- Provide nourishing images from stories the child hears.
- Limit the images the child receives from television, computer games, videos, and films.

The Difference Between Auditory and Visual Images

Images a child hears actively engage his own imaginative or picture-making processes. A good storyteller knows that she is weaving a cloak of magic around the listeners as she describes the characters and the unfolding action. Once I overheard my eleven-year-old say to her friend, 'I like to read books without pictures best, because then I can picture them any way I want to.' Perhaps this is one of the reasons why film renditions of books we have read are never quite as satisfying as the originals.

Images we make of things we have read or heard are easy to transform in our imaginations or daydreams because we have already given them life by creating them with our mind's eye. Images we see, however, have a tremendous sticking power and are very difficult to change because they come to us already completed. Who can think of the Seven Dwarves without seeing Happy, Sleepy, Doc and the entire retinue as Disney portrayed them? I was surprised when my two older children talked to each other about cartoons they had seen five years earlier, before we had got rid of the television set. But then I realized that I could still call up images from television programs seen when I was a child. Television and films don't have as strong an effect on adults as they do on children. For me, seeing E.T. was sort of like eating cotton candy – it didn't make too deep an impression on me. So I was amazed when a year later my children still remembered Elliot's brother's name! Not only do images from television and the movies make a deep impression on the young child, who is all sense organ, but their power means that these images will be repeated in play as the child tries to digest and assimilate what he has taken in. Even an older child (and many an adult!) will continually talk about a film right after having seen it as he attempts to digest it.

Because the images from television and films are so powerful and change so quickly, children often do not understand the story line, and are left imitating the rapid movements and the elements that make the strongest impression: chasing, shooting, crashing, and so on. Also, because children are kept passive while watching television, they have all the more need to race about when they are finished. Young children's natural state is movement.

Images from television always reminded me of those automatic reflex responses that bypass the brain, like pulling back your finger from a hot stove before realizing what has happened. In a similar way, images from television and films seem to bypass the child himself and come out again in frenzied movement, without the child having transformed them into his own unfolding story. As a preschool and kindergarten teacher, I observed a dramatic difference in the quality of play of children who did not watch television. Their inside play was much more imaginative and more likely to have a story line, compared to the running around and catching one another that was dominant with the other children. When a child arrived at preschool with a Batman T-shirt, the play immediately turned into chasing one another. I then asked the parents not to send their children in clothing with insignias so their imaginative play could find a little space in which to grow and flower.

Some parents are afraid that if they don't let their children watch television they will be seen as social misfits. On the contrary, they are often welcomed (as I enjoyed my Mexican friend's daughter who brought such a creative element into my children's play). After being involved with Waldorf education for a couple of years, a neighbor said to me, 'We love to have Faith over. She's so creative. Last time she came over...' Needless to say, I was pleased.

Children who do not watch television will still play games with their friends involving TV or film characters, whose nature they can easily pick up from the plastic figures. But when everyone was playing characters from *Star Wars*, for example, the internal process of play was very different in the child who had not seen the film. The imagination was more active and original in the child who was not relating to the fixed visual images from the screen.

The Importance of Oral Language and Storytelling

In his book *A Is for Ox*, Professor Barry Sanders develops the thesis that true literacy, and the ability to reflect upon one's self and one's actions, which it encourages, can only be based upon a firm foundation of oral language. His book provides a fascinating and cogent argument why, as he states, 'The teaching of literacy has to be founded on a curriculum of song, dance, play, and joking, coupled with improvisation and recitation. Students need to hear stories, either made up by the teacher or read out loud. They need to make them up themselves or try to retell them in their own words. Teachers need to provide continual instruction in the oral arts – from primary school, through the upper grades, and on into college.'[6] He also shows that this continuing emphasis on the spoken word in schools needs to be built upon the oral foundation provided by the parents in the home, through conversation, singing, nursery rhymes, and stories.

It is significant that Sanders mentions lullabies and nursery rhymes, which are valuable for the rhythmical qualities of language in which they bathe the child. Some are built on tongue-twisters or riddles, delighting a child by their playful sounds and associations. Others introduce the child to the concepts, values, and traditions of our normal waking consciousness.

While some nursery rhymes help the child make the transition into waking consciousness, others present a series of interesting but fantastic pictures which have the quality of images we might encounter in dreams. Take, for example, 'Sing a Song of Sixpence.' Eileen Hutchins, in 'The Value of Fairy Tales and Nursery Rhymes,' gives indications of some of the possible inner meanings behind such a verse.

> In many rhymes and tales the soul powers of thinking, feeling and willing appear as beings. Thinking has an active and masculine quality and so is represented as the father or the king. Feeling is more inward and womanly in character, while willing, the power which is the least developed and controlled, resembles the child. Birds can represent the flight of time. Thus in this rhyme we find the four and twenty hours of the night and day hidden from sight within the round of time until the moment when they become the present and reveal their secrets. With our thinking we ponder over the accumulated wisdom of the past like the king in his counting house. With our feeling we enjoy the gifts of the present, which like the honey appear before us without any special labour on our part. With our willing, like the maid, we are active in the outer world. But as our deeds are never really complete and our will during earthly life cannot entirely fulfill itself, something has to be carried over into the future. This is expressed in the picture of the bird who flies away with the nose. Nursery rhymes cast their strange spell because children feel in their hearts that they are true.[7]

Not as much work has been done on the inner meaning of nursery rhymes compared to intercultural studies of fairy tales. Robert Carter, in *The Tao and Mother Goose*, takes a basically Jungian approach to understanding nursery rhymes and concludes:

It has been pointed out that nursery rhymes constitute a mythology of infancy and early childhood; and that, like dreams, they offer an irrational sequence of images which have 'a certain hidden coherence.' It has been claimed that the rhymes may contain archetypal imagery drawn from the collective unconscious, and that they thereby serve the psychic needs of early childhood, just as fairy tales serve the needs of middle childhood, and myth serves in the culture where it thrives. But this is a very broad definition of the functions of nursery rhyme. And of the 200 or so rhymes we associate with Mother Goose, certainly not all can be said to contain profound and hidden messages for the unconscious mind of the child. But we can accurately describe the rhymes as an initiatory body of literature for the very young.[8]

In addition to nursery rhymes, three-year-olds especially love stories that are built on repeating phrases such as 'This Is the House That Jack Built' or 'Little Tuppens,' with its story of what the mother hen must ask of each animal so that the oak tree will give her an acorn cup for some water for little Tuppens who is coughing. A help in memorizing such stories is to visualize the sequence of events (i.e., see all of the characters in a chain) and to repeat it over and over – rhythm and repetition make memorization simpler. Other simple repetitious tales with which you probably are familiar include 'The Three Billy Goats Gruff,' 'The Little Red Hen,' and 'The Little Gingerbread Boy.'

To encourage the transition from nursery rhymes to stories, parents are always encouraged to read to their children, so the children will be exposed to books and to reading. Having parents who read and older siblings who have successfully learned to read increase a child's eagerness to do the same. However, there is also a great deal of value in telling stories to your children. Not only do the children gain listening skills, they also appreciate the fact that you are doing something creative with them. When you tell a story, you weave a magic web in which the listeners become engrossed, and there is nothing between you and the children to distract your attention or theirs. By telling a story rather than reading it, you are also free to note the effect the story might be having on the child.

With two- and barely three-year-olds, your stories can be simple descriptions of the world that your child knows. For example, if your child likes to feed the ducks in the park, you might make up something like:

Mrs. Duck called her five baby ducklings to follow her into the water. Across the river they swam, because they saw Jimmy and his mother had come with a bag of bread crumbs. Jimmy threw some of the bread into the water, and 'splash' went all the ducks as they snapped up the bread. Jimmy laughed to see how hungry they were. When all the bread was gone, Mrs. Duck and her ducklings swam away and Jimmy and his mother went over to play on the swings.

Everyday events are great adventures for a toddler, and he loves to live through them again and again in his imagination. It is important to describe things in a natural way, letting your words bring to mind what the child has experienced. Introducing ideas from fairy tales, such as an 'enchanted stream' or a 'poison well,' would only confuse a young child who is still taking in the direct experience of the water itself. Telling simple stories from everyday life in a slow, deliberate way with a musical tone of voice will delight a two-year-old. A lot of what your two-year-old appreciates is the special time with you and the soothing quality of your voice, which can bring up images or create a mood of security or fun with its rhythms and rhymes.

Children who are three years and older love to hear stories from your own childhood. 'When I was a little girl my mother worked at an olive cannery where they had great big barrels where the olives floated in salty water to make them taste good to eat. And there among the barrels my mother found a little gray kitten... Well, what do you think we named her?' These stories, which have their basis in your own experiences, can also stimulate your imagination, so that you start telling a whole made-up series of stories about the adventures of the kitten named 'Olive.' Imagination isn't just for kids!

In stories for young children, although the animals might be personified (like Mrs. Duck), it is best if they are still true to their natures and their lives in the natural world, which the child is coming to know and love. Cartoon characters represent an adult level of sophistication that goes beyond the world of early childhood.

Children also love to hear stories about themselves, especially about when they were a baby (now that they are so grown up!). They like to hear about things they said and did, the time they went to grandma's house, and so on.

When is your child old enough for stories? Obviously it takes a certain maturity of language development for a child to listen to a story. Until that time children are still totally immersed in experiencing the things themselves. Take your cues from your child, and start with very short stories as described above, gradually working through longer ones with repetition, and then into simple fairy tales.

The Inner Meaning of Fairy Tales

When the child is about four years old, you will find he will be fascinated by fairy tales, told or read. A simple story like 'Sweet Porridge' from Grimm's collection will delight even a three-year-old. They enjoy hearing of the little pot, so full of abundance, which overflows until stopped by the right phrase. At this age the children themselves have a sense of life's eternal abundance, which one child expressed when her mother told her that she did not have enough time to take her out to play: 'But Mother, I have lots of time. I'll give you some.'[9] Then a simple story such as 'The Star Child' can later be followed by longer ones such as 'Goldilocks' and 'The Hungry Cat.' Some fairy tales are so rich and complex that they can nourish children up to the age of eight or even nine.

Bruno Bettelheim, who became interested in the psychological value of fairy tales through his work at the University of Chicago's residential treatment center for severely emotionally disturbed children, wrote the award-winning book on the value of fairy tales entitled *The Uses of Enchantment*. He says that 'when children are exposed to children's literature, fairy tales consistently have the greatest appeal.'[10]

Most parents today are unfamiliar with real fairy tales as

literature, having grown up with only the cartoon or Disney versions or the stories 'as retold by' someone who took great liberties with them. Such renditions are of questionable value, and I found that reading the English or Germanic tales in their original, unedited versions was an entirely different experience. As I became open to their possible inner meanings and read them with new eyes, I found a great wealth in their images.

Fairy tales have gone in and out of fashion over the centuries. During the age of rationalism, they were dismissed as nonsense and were a dying oral tradition when the Grimm brothers and others made their collections by visiting village storytellers in the late 1800s. The title of their well-known collection of stories in German is called *Kinder und Hausmärchen* (Children's and Household Tales), which indicates their original nature as tales or 'little reports' that were commonly repeated in the home and told to children. The tales rarely had to do with fairies, but they did seem to talk about a world different from our everyday one, yet somehow strongly connected to our inner life.

Today there is renewed interest in fairy tales through the work of psychologists such as Carl Jung and Bruno Bettelheim, and by writers such as Rudolf Steiner and Kornei Chukovsky, whose important book on language and stories in early childhood, *From Two to Five*, is now available in English.[11] Jung speaks of fairy tales as projections of the collective unconscious in trying to explain their cross-cultural similarities. Rudolf Steiner states that fairy tales are like 'readings' or reports from the childhood of humanity, a time when people participated in a dreamlike, experiential consciousness that radiated feeling and was filled with images. This preceded the development of our scientifically critical, observant, awake consciousness that is filled with ideas.[12] Both Jung and Steiner agree that all of the characters in a fairy tale are elements within each individual person, aspects of our own selves and our destinies here on earth. Prince and princess, animus and anima, spirit and soul, all are metaphors for our own striving to achieve a sense of union (marriage) of the parts of ourselves.

Miriam Whitfield, in her valuable booklet *Fairy Stories... Why, When, How*[13] gives excellent examples of ways of interpreting fairy tales. For example, many stories echo our process of incarnation and subsequent return to a state of union with God. This we see in tales that begin with a king, queen, or princess – someone who owned much, who is in possession of cosmic wisdom, i.e., the human being before leaving Paradise, before incarnating on earth, one who is still in union with God.

> Then, from this state of cosmic wealth, the hero is often plunged into great misfortune and trials. He or she is tested to his utmost endurance and has to rely on his own inner powers. These powers are often brought to him by some helpful being. It may be an old woman in the woods (wisdom from the past); it may be an animal who has been helped by the hero's kindness and wishes to repay by some magic gift (heart forces). All the while, witches and sorcerers, wild animals and mighty giants are trying to waylay his quest, but with endurance and courage he wins through.[14]

She also gives examples of how fairy tales can echo the evolution of humanity through the gradual rise of individual consciousness in which we live today.

> The king stories take us back to our own – and humanity's – distant past. The nobleman, the merchant, the craftsman are characters much closer to our present era. The tailor cuts up cloth and fits it to your size. He can be thought of as the modern mind which uses its analytical powers to assess a situation. The 'little tailor' (because although we think ourselves very clever, we are only at the beginning of the development of our conscious forces) often has to outwit the giant. Well, the giants are those great archetypal nature forces which are part of humanity. They are in the unconscious and – if not awakened and recognized and tamed – tend to overwhelm us. Are not jealousy, hatred, sloth or greed, giants who tend to overwhelm us? And don't we need all of the cunning and smartness of the [clever] little tailor to overcome them?[15]

If we read and ponder a fairy tale such as 'Hansel and Gretel' with these thoughts in mind, a deeper pattern emerges so that the story can be seen as a parable of our life's journey from the home of our 'heavenly father' to the earth. The earth can be seen as our stepmother, in the sense that the material world presents trials and difficulties for the spirit who has had to leave its original home. The children, who can be seen as representing spirit and soul, are at first guided in the forest by a white bird, that messenger of the spiritual world we have encountered before. But Hansel and Gretel lose their way and are distracted by many temptations to the senses, culminating in the candy house which, like the body, poses the danger of becoming a prison to our higher nature, just as the witch imprisons Hansel.

Once Hansel and Gretel overcome the witch, they are able to take the jewels, the fruits of earthly life, with which they fill their pockets. On their return to their father's house, they are again guided by a white bird, a duck who can take them across the water. In this homecoming, the stepmother is gone and the children are joyously welcomed into the state of union they have achieved.

The richness of the story in its original version cannot be done justice by a short description such as this, but perhaps such a summary can encourage you to read and ponder the fairy tales with a new openness to their inner possibilities.

To the extent that we as adults can 'live into' the inner richness of a fairy tale, we and our children will be the more nourished by it. We would never want to give explanations to a child or ask him to explain, 'Why did Goldilocks go into the house? How do you think she felt when she woke up and saw the three bears?' Fairy tales should not be reduced to intellectual or emotional levels. They do not need any explaining or rationalizing to be appreciated by the child. Just as humanity has passed through various stages of consciousness, so children are passing through these same stages. For this reason, they live with the fairy tale images and are warmed and fulfilled by them again and again. When we tell a fairy tale with an inner understanding and appreciation of its deeper meaning, it is as if the young child feels, 'Ah! You understand, too!'

The Role of the Feminine in Fairy Tales

Feminists and others have decried the passive image of women in many fairy tales, such as the distressed maiden waiting to be rescued or the sleeping beauty singing 'Some day my prince will come' and longing for the man to awaken her to wholeness and 'happy-ever-aftering.' While psychological and spiritual interpretations of the tales can reassure us that we each contain all of the characters within us, the images function on many levels simultaneously. Many parents feel that it matters which images we put before our sons and daughters and try to bring a wide variety of tales to their children. Nearly a dozen stories that present women in strong roles have been gathered under the title *The Maid of the North* (see listing at the end of this chapter).

Linda Pritzker, a Jungian psychotherapist and Waldorf parent, has made a valuable contribution to the discussion of gender in fairy tales in her book *The Princess Who Wept Pearls – The Feminine Journey in Fairy Tales*. In addition to emphasizing the need for each of us to work toward balancing masculine and feminine qualities in our own lives, she discusses the need for feminine qualities to be portrayed in strong images, not just for female characters to develop their masculine qualities. Pritzker explains, 'In my research, I came upon many 'feminist' fairy tales that had the main characters performing masculine activities and displaying the masculine qualities I have listed. The only difference was that these actions were usually being done by girls and women… Where were the fairy tales that showed a different kind of journey? Where were the feminine journeys? Where were the stories that elevated feminine values, strengths and qualities? What about power-with, and power-within, shown as valuable strengths? In choosing stories for this book, I looked for ones in which the hera (the original feminine term for 'hero') was female, the other strong characters were female, and the journey itself was feminine in its character – no dragon-killing.'[16] Her book is a valuable resource for all parents by bringing together eight traditional stories that celebrate the feminine journey in fairy tales.

The Question of Cruelty and Evil in Fairy Tales

Many parents today also question the violence in fairy tales, and certainly a Hollywood rendition of a story can scare a young child and give him nightmares. However, when fairy tales are told in a melodic voice, without emotional dramatization, the moral pattern of the fairy tale emerges. In the journal *Ethics in Education*, Diana Hughes states that fairy tales speak directly to the natural morality in the child and to his or her sense of moral order in the world. When the good wins and the evil is punished, a child is visibly satisfied.[17] The cruelty of having the witch dance to death in red-hot shoes or the wolf drown from the weight of the stones in its belly does not upset children, because there is a certain rightness to the fact that evil is naturally the cause of its own undoing and is overcome. Through the adventures and triumphs of the main character and as a report that evil is always self-consuming, fairy tales are usually a source of reassurance and comfort to a child. A more subtle theme in several stories is that when one recognizes the potential for evil, it loses its potency. For example, once Rumpelstiltskin and his equivalent Tom-Tit-Tot have been correctly named, they lose their power and their temper.[18]

Bettelheim states, 'It is not the fact that virtue wins out at the end which promotes morality, but that the hero is most attractive to the child, who identifies with the hero in all struggles.'[19] There is not a fairy tale known that doesn't end with successful growth and resolution by the hero or heroine.

Steiner recognized that the world of the fairy tale and the world of the young child are essentially the same. Both worlds share moral absolutes, mobility of imagination, and limitless possibilities for transformation.[20] Bettelheim states that fairy tales can often help children resolve fears and build feelings of competence.[21] Neil Postman, in *The Disappearance of Childhood*, praises Bettelheim's demonstration that the importance of fairy tales 'lies in their capacity to reveal the existence of evil in a form that permits children to integrate it without trauma.'[22]

If you have trouble with a fairy tale or its images, skip that one and choose another, but don't change parts of it as you go along. The 'true' fairy tales are artistic wholes in which actions and descriptions are very precise. They should be told as accurately as possible, without emotional dramatization. The report of the witch locking up Hansel and later getting pushed into the oven by Gretel will not frighten a child if you are not in conflict about the story!

Sharing Fairy Tales with Young Children

It is important that you be comfortable with a fairy tale and at least open to and appreciative of its deeper meaning. If a particular story pushes your buttons, don't share that one with your children. Rather, choose a fairy tale that speaks to you, one you can meditate on and try to penetrate to its mood and inner meanings. You can gain a familiarity with various approaches to the interpretation of fairy tales by reading some of the books listed at the end of this chapter, but ultimately you will need to let the fairy tale speak to you directly. Try reading it to yourself every night before you go to bed. By taking it into your sleep, you will gradually gain insight into it.

Choose an anthology of fairy tales that is as close to the original as possible (not 'as retold by…'). A complete edition of *Grimm's Fairy Tales* can be purchased very economically and has more than two hundred stories suitable for all ages; sources for non-European tales are listed at the end of this chapter. Jacob's *English Fairy Tales* are appropriate for children around age seven; the French and Russian fairy tales tend to be suitable for even older children.

Whether you are reading or telling a fairy tale, repeat the same one over and over for your child. Children love repetition, and this gives them time to really live into the images and revel in their familiarity. In the Waldorf kindergarten, I would tell the same story every day for two or three weeks. Sometimes it could have gone on longer, but I got bored, not the children! Whenever you are sharing a story with a child under the age of seven, it is best to leave out emotional dramatization. This is very different from how librarians are taught storytelling, but their method is more appropriate for the school-aged child, with his developing inner emotional life. The young child lives more in the cadence and rhythm of the language, and in fact can become frightened or develop nightmares if too much emotion is put into the rendition of a story. However, if you tell or read the stories in a melodic voice, as if you were reporting what you were seeing, the young child will take everything in and be able to digest it and be nourished by it.

In addition to reading stories to your child at bedtime, you might want to memorize and tell a story for a group of children at a birthday party or as a special treat. Weaving the storyteller's web is different from reading the same story – it involves more of your creative effort and has a different effect on the children. Memorizing and telling stories is not as difficult as it might seem – and it's never as hard as it is the first time. To memorize a story, read it out loud several times. Then visualize the scenes where the action takes place. 'First they are by the well. Then after the frog gives back her golden ball, they are in the castle eating dinner. Then they move to the bedroom. Finally Faithful Henry comes and takes them away in the coach.' Now as you read and practice retelling each part of the story, picture it unfolding in front of you. Do this when you tell it to the child. It is not necessary to memorize a story verbatim, although I have found that memorizing the first few sentences can help me find my way into a story.

Whenever possible, incorporate hand gestures into the story, keeping them always the same so they will help the child come to know the story. Udo de Haes writes, 'When we consider the child to be ready for fairy-tales, our storytelling must address the whole human-being and not merely the head. We are then not expecting the child to discover the story purely through the words but are guiding him along a living experience which leads to the meaning of the fairy-tale. We should relate with the facial expressions and gestures called forth by the story itself, in a manner that is free of sentimentality and 'realism,' for it is through these [expressions and gestures] that the tale can become alive for the child.'[23]

One way to match fairy tales to the age of the child is to look at their degree of complexity. In almost every fairy tale there is either a problem that must be solved or a confrontation with evil. The milder the problem, the more appropriate the tale for younger children, and conversely, the greater the evil, the more appropriate the tale is for older children.[24]

Similarly, there are often several trials of varying complexity. In 'The Three Little Pigs,' the pig is too smart for the wolf three times before he finally overcomes the wolf. The tasks are not really very ominous and are met with a fair amount of humor, making this tale well-loved by most four-year-olds. In contrast, the sister in 'The Seven Ravens' must journey to the sun, the moon, and the stars in order to free her brothers; this is a tale for five- and six-year-olds. Even more complex tales, such as 'East of the Sun and West of the Moon,' are appropriate for school-age children.

The following list is adapted from Joan Almon's 'Choosing Fairy Tales for Different Ages.'[25] She reminds readers that you will have to make your own decisions based on a particular group of children or an individual child. Book references are contained in parentheses – see the end of this chapter for useful references. ('Grimm, 103' refers to #103 in the anthology of Grimm's tales.)

1. *Simple or sequential stories (three-year-olds):*
- Sweet Porridge (Grimm, 103)
- Goldilocks and the Three Bears (Voland)
- Little Tuppens (Voland)
- Little Louse and Little Flea (Spindrift)
- The Turnip (Russian)
- The Mitten (Russian)
- Little Madam (Spindrift)
- The Gingerbread Man
- The Johnny Cake (English)
- The Hungry Cat (Norwegian, Plays for Puppets)

2. *Slightly more complex stories, but cheerful without too much struggle (fours and young fives):*
- Billy Goats Gruff (Norwegian, Voland)
- Three Little Pigs (English)
- The Wolf and the Seven Kids (Grimm, 5)
- The Pancake Mill
- Mashenka and the Bear (Russian, Plays for Puppets)
- The Shoemaker and the Elves (Grimm, 39)

3. *More challenge and more detail; although obstacles are encountered, they do not weigh too heavily on the soul of the individual (five- and six-year-olds):*
- Star Money (Grimm, 153)
- The Frog Prince (Grimm, 1)

- Mother Holle (Grimm, 24)
- Little Red Cap (Grimm, 26)
- The Bremen Town Musicians (Grimm, 27)
- The Golden Goose (Grimm, 64)
- Spindle, Shuttle, and Needle (Grimm, 188)
- The Hut in the Forest (Grimm, 169)
- The Queen Bee (Grimm, 62)
- The Snow Maiden (Russian, Plays for Puppets)
- The Seven Ravens (Grimm, 25)
- Snow White and Rose Red (Grimm, 161)
- Little Briar Rose ('Sleeping Beauty') (Grimm, 50)
- The Donkey (Grimm, 55)
- Rumpelstiltskin (Grimm, 55)
- Snow White and the Seven Dwarves (Grimm, 53)
- Hansel and Gretel (Grimm, 15)

4. *Tales in which characters have personal experiences of suffering or sorrow (six-year-olds in the kindergarten or first-graders, to match their sense of departure from the heart of early childhood):*
- Jorinda and Joringel (Grimm, 69)
- Brother and Sister (Grimm, 11)
- Cinderella (Grimm, 21)
- Rapunzel (Grimm, 12)

Almon points out that if a fairy tale is widely known in the society, children are often ready for it at an earlier age. Also, if the storyteller particularly loves a fairy tale, she can often tell it successfully to younger children. With children of mixed ages (such as three- to six-year-olds in a Waldorf mixed-age kindergarten or home-schooling situation), stories will still be successful if they are appropriate for only some of the children (the rest will listen as if carried by these other children). Udo de Haes points out that you needn't worry about toddlers in a family hearing stories that are being read to an older brother or sister. In such cases, the toddler will be most interested in the closeness of sitting with the mother and listening to the cadences of her voice and will not pay the same kind of attention as the child to whom the story is addressed.[26]

Sharing Stories from Other Cultures

Steven Spitalny, a Waldorf kindergarten teacher in California, reminds us that Rudolf Steiner stated, 'The most important thing is to establish an education through which human beings learn once again how to live with one another' (lecture given in Stuttgart, October 13, 1922, published in *The Younger Generation*). The universal truths of fairy tales are clothed in the languages and cultures in which they have arisen. Because the world surrounding us is growing ever more diverse, perhaps sharing stories can help heal the legacy of racism and nationalism for our children by providing a taste of different cultures and the regions of the earth from which they come. By so doing, perhaps they will become a little less 'other.' But remember, in keeping with the dream consciousness of the young child, that the goal is not to turn the story into a 'teaching moment' about other cultures, but to provide a 'soul taste' of universal truths.[27]

For parents from other cultures, parents with children adopted from other cultures, and parents wanting to expose their children to the richness of other cultures, various anthologies are listed at the end of this chapter. You will need to evaluate the individual stories, however, because many of them are fables or legends/folk tales rather than fairy tales. In trying to distinguish the different types of stories, keep in mind that fairy tales speak of the development of an individual human soul, and the characters are aspects of each of us; fables exaggerate human characteristics and tendencies in animal form in order to dramatize a moral lesson; and legends speak of the (often exaggerated) exploits of a 'real' human being. The anthologies listed can serve as valuable resources well into the grades, because many of the animal fables are best suited to the seven- and eight-year-olds, and folk tales speak most strongly to even older children.

The Healing Power of Puppet Plays

When stories and fairy tales are translated into cartoons or films, they lose their evocative quality and are often too powerful or too inane for young children. But when the stories are acted out in front of the children, using stand-up puppets or silk marionettes, the experiences can have a very calming and healing effect on the children.

Such puppet shows for young children can be easily produced by spreading some coloured silk or cotton cloth on a table or on the rug and using the stand-up dolls/puppets described in the preceding chapter. Scenery is built up by assembling pieces of bark, cloth, pine cones, shells, stones, unspun wool, and similar materials to suggest the various areas of forest, home, castle – whatever the story needs. The scene is covered by a thin chiffon or gauze cloth that is carefully removed as if lifting a veil, revealing the scene in all its wonders. Then you simply tell the story while you move the puppets. You can have someone help by reading the story or playing a children's harp if you have a play group or preschool or birthday party.

Bronja Zahlingen, who was a Waldorf early-childhood teacher for more than fifty years, as well as being a master puppeteer, wrote:

It is also important for the right development and activity of the child's senses that he can watch such a play take place in actual space – length, breadth and depth; otherwise his sense organs are easily stupefied and made passive. Pictures of action which appear to be moving on a flat screen, brought about artificially by technical skills, confuse the young child's eye, his sense of direction and movement, and often even his mind.

If the child can see the stories unfold step by step, grow and change in the simple but beautiful way described, the pictures can be taken right into the stream of his life forces, without creating hard and fixed impressions.… The simplicity and transparency of our table plays call forth the child's powers of imagination, and he is right in the midst of all that takes place. Through this, the creative power for his own play as well as for his own movement and language development are stimulated. In this way the child can also be helped to become a person of independence and creative activity in later life.[28]

The young children won't be bothered by seeing you move the puppets, because they are so interested in what is happening. And the image of an adult making things happen is an image of security for a young child.

You can also easily make flowing silk marionettes, like the ones in the photo at the beginning of this chapter. They are moved by three strings on your fingers without any sticks to introduce jerky movements. The silk marionettes are made like the knot dolls described in Chapter 7, with the addition of small stones sewn into the hands to give them weight and strings sewn onto the hands and head. Detailed instructions are given in *Toymaking with Children* by Freya Jaffke. Again, the performing adult is visible, giving the child a sense of the world being guided and directed from above. You move the puppets as you tell the story, or you can have someone sit by the side and play the children's harp and then read the story while the puppets move through the scenes spread out with cloths on the table or floor.

Recommended Reading

Anthologies of Stories from Various Cultures

Arabian Fairy Tales by Amina Shah.

The Brocaded Slipper and Other Vietnamese Tales by Lynette Dyer Vuong (Harper Collins, ISBN 0-201-08088-5).

Celebrating Christmas Together by Estelle Bryer and Janni Nicol (Hawthorn Press)

Christmas Stories Together by Estelle Bryer and Janni Nicol (Hawthorn Press)

The Complete Grimm's Fairy Tales, (Routledge, London). More than 200 stories from which to pick and choose.

The Day It Snowed Tortillas – Tales from Spanish New Mexico, retold by Joe Hayes (Santa Fe: A Mariposa Book, 1992).

East of the Sun and West of the Moon by George Dasent (Dover). Scandinavian tales.

English Fairy Tales by Flora Annie Steel (Wordsworth Editions Ltd)

English Fairy Tales by Joseph Jacobs (Dover).

Favorite Russian Fairy Tales by Arthur Ransome (Dover).

Indian Fairy Tales by Joseph Jacobs (Dover).

Irish Fairy Tales by Philip Smith (Dover).

Japanese Fairy Tales, compiled by Yei Theodora Ozabi.

Japanese Fairy Tales, by Phillip Smith (Dover).

Keepers of the Earth by Michael J. Caduto and Joseph Bruchac (Golden CO: Fulcrum Inc., ISBN 0-55591-027-0).

The Maid of the North – Feminist Folk Tales from Around the World by Ethel Johnston Phelps (Holt, Rinehart & Co.).

Misoso, Once Upon a Time Tales from Africa, by Aardema (Random House).

North American Indian Tales by W. T. Larned (Dover).

The Oxford Treasury of Fairy Tales by Geraldine McCaughrean (Oxford University Press)

The People Could Fly, American Black Folktales told by Virginia Hamilton (Knopf, ISBN 0-394-86925-7).

The Princess Who Wept Pearls – The Feminine Journey in Fairy Tales by Linda Pritzker. Available from Rudolf Steiner College Book Store, 9200 Fair Oaks Blvd., Fair Oaks, CA 95628.

Pueblo Stories and Storyteller, by Mark Bahti (Tucson, AZ: Treasure Chest Publications, ISBN 0-918080-16-9).

The Red Fairy Book, The Blue Fairy Book etc. by Andrew Lang (Dover).

Russian Fairy Tales, Aleksandr Afanas'Ev (Pantheon).

Spring, Summer, Autumn, Winter and Spindrift. Stories and songs gathered by British Steiner/Waldorf kindergarten teachers (available from Wynstones Press).

Yiddish Folktales by Weinreich and Wolf.

About Nursery Rhymes and Fairy Tales

A Is for Ox – Violence, Electronic Media, and the Silencing of the Written Word by Barry Sanders (Pantheon). A fascinating analysis of the importance of the oral tradition in developing a sense of self, and the crises facing youth and society today.

From Two to Five by Kornei Chukovsky (University of California Press, 1963).

The Interpretation of Fairy Tales by Rudolf Steiner (Anthroposophic Press).

The Laughing Baby. Remembering Nursery Rhymes and Reasons by Anne Scott (Bergin & Garvey).

Lifeways by Gudrun Davy and Bons Voors (Hawthorn Press). Contains two chapters on the inner meaning of fairy tales.

The Poetry and Meaning of Fairy Tales by Rudolf Steiner (Mercury Press).

Storytelling with Children by Nancy Mellon (Hawthorn Press).

The Tao and Mother Goose by Robert Carter (Theosophical Publishing House, 306 W. Geneva Rd., Wheaton, IL 60187).

The Uses of Enchantment – The Meaning and Importance of Fairy Tales by Bruno Bettelheim (Knopf).

The Wisdom of Fairy Tales by Rudolf Meyer (Floris Books). Interpretations working out of the indications of Rudolf Steiner.

Puppets and Puppet Plays

Plays for Puppets and Marionettes compiled by Bronja Zahlingen (Rudolf Steiner College Book Store, US).

Toymaking with Children by Freya Jaffke (Floris Books).

TV and Childhood

Set Free Childhood by Martin Large (Hawthorn Press).

Poems and Verses

The Winding Road compiled by Matthew Barton (Hawthorn Press). A family treasury of poems and verses.

CHAPTER 9

Developing Your Child's Artistic Ability

The Experience of Colour

Children have natural artistic ability that can easily go undeveloped or become stifled by inappropriate activities; this often results in frustration and beliefs such as, 'I can't draw.' Helping your child's artistic ability to unfold is a great gift you can give him – not that a child will necessarily grow up to be an artist, but that he will maintain a living relationship with colour, that he will be able to appreciate the play of light and shadow with a sensitive eye, and that he will feel confident about expressing himself through some artistic medium and find enjoyment in the process.

The world of colour is directly related to the way we feel. Colours affect our attitude to life and our moods, which are then expressed in colours. Even our speech reflects this relationship – 'green with envy,' 'feeling blue,' 'livid with rage,' 'seeing red,' 'rose-coloured spectacles,' 'jaundiced view.' You could say that the very substance of the soul is colour. Colour is to the spiritual life what food, air, and water are to the physical life. As these nourish our bodies, so colour nourishes the soul and spirit.

The world of nature is bathed in colour. Colour comes and goes seasonally, and indeed each day with the coming and going of the light. Just as sunrise and sunset express their own moods through colour, so the mood of spring, with its cold earth and moist air, is very different from the mood of autumn, with its warm earth and cool dry air.[1]

Children love colours and unite with the colours that flow toward them from their surroundings. Children's feelings are also strongly affected by colours, so that one colour may produce a feeling of well-being, while another calls up a feeling of discomfort. Because children are so much more receptive than adults, their experience of colour is all the more intense.

In the first seven years the young child takes in everything with her total being; body, soul, and spirit are still united. The young child is completely open to experiences of colour in her environment, and for this reason we need to create environments that reflect her sensitivity to good artistic qualities – colours, forms, wall decorations, sounds, and toys. This achieves a deeper effect than 'art education' offered in a few spare hours.

The psychological effects of colour on people are now being recognized and are beginning to be put into practice in such places as hospitals and mental institutions. When we consider the psychological effects of colour on children, Steiner says that the complementary colour must be taken into account up to the age of nine:

> A 'nervous,' that is to say excitable child, should be treated differently as regards the environment from one who is quiet and lethargic. Everything comes into consideration, from the colour of the room and the various objects that are generally around the child, to the colour of the clothes in which he is dressed.... An excitable child should be surrounded by and dressed in red and reddish-yellow colours, whereas for a lethargic child one should have recourse to the blue or blueish-green shades of colour. For the important thing is the complementary colour, which is created within the child. In the case of red it is green, and in the case of blue, orange-yellow.[2]

I saw this phenomenon in my kindergarten when each day the largest, rowdiest boy would immediately head for the costume rack and put on a red satin shirt. When he had it on, he was somehow more settled within himself. The explanation that the complementary colour works more directly on the young child was one I was unaware of until I read about it in Steiner's writings. As adults we experience the phenomenon only briefly if we stare at a bright red circle and see a green circle when we look away. According to Steiner, the inner experience of the complementary colour is stronger for the young child than the experience of the external colour; only in the course of time does he come to experience colours as a grown-up does.

Ordinarily we think of colours as attributes of objects. But to the inward vision of the soul, the essential natures of colours can be revealed. Goethe's *Theory of Colour* forms a basis for much of Steiner's writing on colour.[3] Steiner states:

> Goethe draws our attention to the feelings which the colours arouse in us. He points out the challenging nature of red, and his teaching is as much concerned with what the soul feels when it beholds red, as with what the eye sees. Likewise he mentions the stillness and contemplativeness which the soul feels in the presence of blue. We can present the colours to children in such a way that they will spontaneously experience the shades of feelings engendered by the colours, and will naturally feel the colours' inner life.[4]

Therefore parents and teachers are advised to let the child live and work in the world of colour as soon as possible, immersing himself in the feelings it engenders. Brunhild Müller, in *Painting with Children*, states, 'Not only do children perceive the colour but at the same time they sense its quality, they feel in themselves its intrinsic nature, and they are conscious of the non-material essential being of such colour. This consciousness is lost as the child grows older, and by the time children go to school they experience colours as attributes of objects (the blue ball, the red roof and so on).'[5]

Therefore it is appropriate to expose the young child to activities such as painting and crayoning when they emphasize the experience of colour and are not approached as 'lessons' in which the child has to imitate the adult or achieve an end-product or finished form. Such experiences of art are valuable for the young child as pure colour experiences. Such experiences can also lead to abilities that can be transformed throughout the child's life.

Watercolour Painting with Young Children

One of the best experiences of colour for the young child comes through painting with watercolours on wet paper. Colours are in their own true element in water. Their waving, shimmering, and streaming nature is manifest the moment they lose their heavy and earthy hardness. Rauld Russell, who wrote *How to Do Wet-on-Wet Watercolor Painting and Teach it to Children*, explains: 'A wet paper surface lends flowing movement to color. Color in a thin sea of water can move, mingle, change, lighten and darken, just like feelings and emotions. To fix all the richness of inner life, all the potentiality, into a rigid form with hard boundaries (as one would do in 'dry' painting) can evoke 'hardened' images of life. The application of wet-on-wet most truly corresponds to the soft, unfinished, still growing nature of the child.'[6]

No one paints like kindergarten-aged children, because they are totally unself-conscious. If you are not familiar with children's paintings done in this wet-on-wet technique, two inexpensive books with colour illustrations of such paintings are *Painting with Children* by Brunhild Müller and *Echoes of a Dream* by Susan Smith, both listed at the end of this chapter. You can easily do this kind of painting with your child, and the results are beautiful.

Supplies

The thought of going into an art supply shop may be overwhelming to you, but you only need three tubes of colour! In Waldorf preschools we only use the primary colours red, yellow, and blue with the young children, allowing the infinite number of other colours they form to appear on the paper under the child's excited eye. Russell reminds us that, 'Because watercolor painting reaches into the deep psycho-biological processes that affect a child's growth, for a very young child you will want to choose a bright medium golden yellow, a cobalt or ultramarine blue, and a rose-crimson red. The purity of the color is essential...' He recommends Stockmar, Grumbacher, Winsor Newton, or other artist's grade watercolours. (Inexpensive acrylics will not work.)[7]

It is also worthwhile to invest in some good-quality paper such as Grumbacher or Aquabee all-purpose paper or Strathmore 80- to 90- lb. painting paper. Less expensive paper will not bring out the luminous quality and intensity of the colours and will shred into paper-towel consistency before your child finishes a painting. Large sheets of paper are expensive but can be cut into four pieces, and you and your child only need to paint one picture each session. This kind of painting is special — it's not like covering as many sheets of typing paper as possible with paints from a box.

While you are at the art shop, buy yourself and your child a large flat brush (at least three-quarter-inch wide) rather than a pointed brush. The flat brushes give more of an experience of colour and discourage outlining.

Things You Will Need from Home Include:

- A set of three baby-food-sized jars for each painter.
- Pint-sized jars for premixing and storing colours (you may need to store them in the refrigerator if they spoil easily).
- Similar jars for rinsing brushes between colours (the advantage of jars over cans is that they don't rust, and the child can see the changing colour of the water as he paints – fully as interesting as the painting itself).
- Because the paintings need to be kept horizontal to dry, a wooden or masonite board (16' x 20' x 1/4') is handy for painting on and drying.
- A clean sponge used only to wipe off the wet paper before starting.
- A sponge or cloth for each painter to wipe her brush on.
- Smocks or painting shirts.

Preparation

Children love to help with the preparations for painting. Putting on your smock and getting out the materials will almost always produce a willing helper.

- Prepare the paper by cutting it to size (a two-year-old will need a smaller piece than a five-year-old). In the Waldorf early-childhood programs we always round off the corners of the paper because the rounded form is more suitable for the young child than the square geometric form. The rounded form also frees the children from painting around the outline of the paper, which many will do with a square sheet.

- Put the individual sheets in water to soak. A sink will do; a plastic tray is helpful if you have lots of children painting.
- Squeeze some colour from the tube into your mixing jar and add water to dilute it to a light-syrup consistency. You'll need more colour with yellow than you will with blue. Then put a small amount of this pre-mixed colour (one-half inch) in each painting jar so it won't be wasted if it becomes muddied or spilled. You can store the extra and refill the small jars as needed.
- Let your child help put the painting boards down and fill the water jars. Arrange the three paint jars on each board and give a dampened sponge to each painter to wipe her brush on. Keeping the brushes until everything else is ready will prevent premature enthusiasm from carrying everyone away.
- Now put a sheet of paper on the board and wipe it off with the sponge that is reserved for this job. If the paper is too wet, the colours will float away and dry into puddles. But don't wipe it too dry, either!

Starting to Paint

The first time you use these techniques with a young child, you can just mix up one colour. Then, over the first several sessions, the child will experience what yellow, blue, and red have to tell him when each is used all by itself.

You will want to demonstrate for your child how to wipe the brush dry on the edge of the jar and on the sponge before it is dipped into the colour so that later on greater control can be achieved.

When you introduce two colours, demonstrate how the paint brush needs to be rinsed before changing colours. I often said something like, 'Peter Paintbrush needs to take a bath and wash his hair before he puts on his new clothes. And he needs to dry his hair on the sponge first to see if it is clean.' We would look at the sponge to see if it was clean, and if so, Peter would go into the next colour. Wiping the rinsed brush on the sponge both tests for cleanness and removes excess water. That simple technique is all you need to teach during painting – you don't need lessons or themes – but don't expect young children to remember always to rinse their brushes. Simply let the child experience the colours as they unfold in his painting. Because young children are so imitative, it is best for you to do a similar kind of colour painting without trying to bring form or meaning to it. Let your child lead you, rather than producing an adult painting with meaning. When you start working with two colours, your child will be delighted to discover what happens when yellow plays with blue, for example, The children's experiences with colour are alive and active when they paint in this way, so they will have had a living experience rather than an intellectual idea that 'yellow and blue make green.' Not having had the experience of such things myself as a child, I can recall being ten years old and trying to remember whether yellow and blue made green or blue and green made yellow. Children who paint in this way never have that intellectual dilemma!

You can introduce yellow and blue, yellow and red, and red and blue before you put out all three colours at once. You won't need more than the three primary colours until your child is in grade school. For suggestions on how this approach to painting can evolve with older children, see *How to Do Wet-on-Wet Watercolor Painting and Teach it to Children* or *Painting with Children*, listed at the end of this chapter. From a foundation of having experienced the colours, older children are gradually able to bring forms out of the colours, rather than trying to paint forms based on outlines like a colouring book.

Children's Experience of Painting

Three-year-olds are often satisfied with a single colour, and they are finished painting only when their colour jar is empty. If a three-year-old is given two or three colours at the start, he will probably paint the colours over the top of, rather than next to, one another, and a muddy surface will result. But if you begin with a single colour and only gradually add the second and the third, your child will soon learn to paint by laying the colours next to one another.

Four- and five-year-old children paint with the colours next to each other on the paper, and will happily share their discoveries of the new colours or the forms that have appeared on their paper. Five- and six-year-olds will approach painting with more of a plan, just as they now approach free play with an idea of what they want to do. Before they dip their brushes into the first colour, they often have an image of a definite colour they want to use or an object such as a tree, rainbow, or heart they want to paint. The watercolours and damp paper make it difficult to paint solid outlines, which is good for the further development of the child's fantasy forces. Many times when the children add a new colour to the already started form, they will have a new sense-association that will interact with the fantasy. These older children will gladly tell you or another child something about their picture – which colour they especially like or what content they discover in the painted picture.

Be receptive to any comments your child makes, but refrain from asking, 'What is it?' or 'What does it mean?' The child has had a colour experience that may or may not arrive at any completed forms. Also, it is better to praise the beauty of the colours or the nature of their interaction rather than the artist. This postpones self-consciousness and the element of judgment.

A child who is precocious or 'overly awake' can be helped by the fluid qualities of painting. Von Heydebrand states, 'Colour surfaces or waves of colour flowing into each other, not strengthening or crystallizing into too hardened forms, bring the over-precocious child or too clever child back into the right condition of the more dreamy atmosphere of childhood.'[8]

Having already put up favorite paintings on the refrigerator or walls, you will soon have a wonderful, growing stack that you can use for other purposes: as birthday invitations, place cards, gift wrappings, crowns, book covers, or origami figures. Even those paintings that don't appear very interesting often have areas where the colours flow beautifully and that can be cut into wondrous things.

Metamorphosis in Later Stages of Life

In addition to the wonderful present-time activity of painting, there are other benefits. When a child finds the colours in this way true to his own inner experience and being and then finds them again in nature, he will look at them with more sensitivity to the interplay of light and colour. Even if it is not his destiny to become an artist, he will have a greater understanding and appreciation of the world, having been awakened to reverence.

There are other benefits, less directly related to the artistic experience, but of great value in a person's life. These qualities in later life that were unconsciously influenced by the young child's experience of painting are discussed by Freya Jaffke in her article 'About Painting and Human Development Through Art.'[9] For example, painting includes such processes as being careful, paying attention, waiting, following the course of the work, experiencing the laws of colour mixing, and applying colour in various strengths.

> All of these activities give ever-renewed stimulus to the gradually awakening soul of the child, helping him to grasp his physical body and make his sense organization and his limbs ever more responsive. One who at an early age has learned to pay attention to the strength or delicacy of colour and to gradations in applying it, will later find it easier to apply the same soul capacities in social situations, for example in self-assertion and in acquiescence or in the ability to hold conversations in which he brings forth his own arguments and is yet receptive to the responses of his partner. In a similar way, the adult process of logical thinking is helped by the inner order in the sequence of the steps of painting.[10]

As Jaffke points out, 'sequencing' is best learned by the young child through doing, not by talking about what we did first, second, and last.

Jaffke concludes by saying, 'Naturally, the child is not conscious of this. He does not reflect on what he is doing, but lives intensively in the activities. In this way he has experiences at deep levels which can wait there to be grasped by him consciously in later stages of life and to find expression in an ability to lead his own life. These effects reveal the true human justification for artistic endeavors in the preschool. Art is not an aesthetic add-on to 'real life,' but as an exercise of continual striving it can become the foundation of a truly human mastery of life.'[11]

Colouring with Crayons

Understanding Children's Drawings

A child often starts drawing before the age of two, either enthusiastically or tentatively grasping the pencil or crayon for the first time. But once he joyously discovers the potential involved, he will be delighted to colour frequently and on any surface that presents itself ! At whatever age within the first seven years that the child starts drawing, he will begin at the two-year-old scribbling stage. If the child is already past that age, he will go through all the earlier stages in rapid succession, and stop at the motif corresponding to his own development. What are the stages and motifs you can watch for in your child's drawings? It will strengthen your appreciation for the being of your child when you observe her development as reflected in her drawings.

The following information is taken from the excellent book *Understanding Children's Drawings* by Michaela Strauss,[12] based on a lifetime of observation by Hanns Strauss, who left behind a collection of more than six thousand young children's drawings that he had assembled and annotated.

Children's drawings can be roughly divided into three stages, similar to those found in their play and their painting. In the first phase, before age three, the child creates purely out of the movement that carries her. The process of creation arises in a dreamy way, out of the rhythms and movements coming from within her own body, so if you ask a very young child about her drawing, she will usually be unable to explain the content to you.

In the second phase, between ages three and five, the child lets the arising picture take hold of her imagination. While she draws she will tell you about the picture as it unfolds in front of her.

After the fifth year, the child often approaches colouring with a definite idea or picture in mind, 'I am going to draw my dog, Blacky, chasing a rabbit.'

Within each phase, certain motifs predominate, and the new ones don't appear until the child has reached the next developmental stage. For example, two types of movements dominate the drawings of children under three. These are a spiral movement and a perpendicular or vertical movement. At first the movements are very large, even larger than the paper, which barely seems to contain them. Strauss observed that until the age of three, spirals are always drawn from outward to inward, only gradually forming a center that reflects the child's growing realization of self between ages two and three. The flash of ego consciousness is documented by the ability to draw the form of the circle which, even if the child says 'I' earlier on, rarely appears in drawings before the third year. It is also interesting to note that monkeys are quite good at drawing like young children – certainly their jumping and swinging give them an inward propensity toward movement and they have the interest and dexterity to use a crayon or brush – but they are unable to make a connected circle out of the spiral movements they have in common with the child under three.[13]

Strauss suggests that the spiral movements in 'scribbling' are echoes of the movements of the cosmos and of the flowing rhythms of the fluids within the young child's own body. Similarly, she suggests that the vertical element that appears along with the spiral one is an expression of the child's own recent experience of standing upright.

At the same time a child is able to form a circle, he will probably be seen to make a crossed horizontal and vertical line for the first time. Soon the cross will be drawn inside the circle, and circles will also be drawn that have a dot inside them. Both cases reflect the child's first experiences of inner and outer in his increasing consciousness during the third year.

After the third year, the circle and crossed lines are fused into a unity, and they appear in the most diverse variations until the fifth year and beyond. However, changes continue to occur during this time. The point and the cross, having crystallized as 'I' symbols, begin to transform and to radiate from the center outward. At first the radiating lines will stop at the edge of the circle, then reach out like feelers beyond the edge of the circle.

As the child continues to develop, trees and people are frequently drawn. Strauss shows how the forms of a tree and a human being are the same for a young child and represent his own changing awareness of his body. First the focus is on the head, with a trunk extending down from it (a floating tree or 'pillar person'). It is not until the child is older that the legs become divided and firmly planted on the ground. Around the age of four the child's focal point shifts from the head to the trunk, and a ladder pattern emerges in children's drawings, like the branches of a tree or the branching of the spinal column and the ribs. Drawings now for the first time have left-right orientation around an axis of symmetry, like the body around the backbone.

Children at this age also draw people with arms coming off from the head or huge fingers, reflecting their increasing connection with the world: reaching out and getting into everything. The feet take the longest time to be developed in drawings and are thick and heavy, becoming rooted to the ground. The child draws the human being, not as we see it, but as he experiences his own self and body. The inner life processes, not the external form, are the determining factors.[14]

The house is another theme through which the child represents her changing relationship between self and world. Drawings of a very young child often show a circle or 'head person' inside a larger circle, like the child in the cosmos or the baby in the womb. As the close unity between self and world gives way to separate individuality, the spherical 'cosmic' house becomes more square in form and anchored near the bottom of the paper. In the third year, the form of the square or box appears for the first time surrounding the person. The narrowing down in the perception of cosmic realms through the acquiring of selfhood – the process of becoming an 'I' – resembles an encapsulating of the soul. A child may draw a person looking out of the house, and the connections between inner world and outer world can be seen in the doors, windows, and chimneys that now begin to appear.

Colour as a new means of expression is added to the drawing of lines in the middle phase, ages three to five. Before the third year the child tends to use colour mostly to emphasize the line. But toward the fourth year a new element appears, drawing colour for its own sake. Strauss writes, 'Touched by the nature of colour, the soul of the child becomes creative. When the world of feeling comes into drawing, the world of colour comes into it too.'[15] Before the child uses colour for drawing objects, he uses it in drawings to cover a surface, exploring the qualities of colours by filling in areas in a dramatic and more symmetrical 'checkerboard' fashion. It is just at this age that block crayons (see next section) enable the child to cover large surfaces and increase his colour experience.

Around the age of five children will start making illustrative drawings and wish to represent objects and scenes from life or stories. These narrative-illustrative drawings will start to wrestle with the elements of space and changing perspective; the profile of the face appears for the first time. The triangle also appears for the first time and can become the focus of multicoloured geometrical designs that kindergarten children love to make.

When primary-school-age children draw a tree and house, the forms look more as we have come to expect them to look. But close observation of such drawings can also reveal interesting things about the inner life of the older child. One very dreamy boy never drew his people touching the ground, even as late as second grade. And a kindergarten boy in my class drew a sad figure between two houses. He said that one was a house and one was a fire station, but from the interview with his mother I knew that his parents were divorcing and he was spending time with both his mother and father – a sad little boy feeling himself on the road between two homes.

The relationship of children's art to their developing consciousness parallels the developing consciousness of humanity as expressed in primitive art and its evolution over the centuries. Just as the first babbling of a baby is unconnected with particular racial or national characteristics, this first picture writing is also universally human. In this early period of the first seven years the language of symbols is the same the world over. Both Strauss's book and *The Incarnating Child* provide many illustrations of children's drawings, which can become another pathway to increase your understanding of the changing consciousness of the young child.

Colouring with Block Crayons

Using block rather than stick crayons enables your child to cover an entire page with colour with very little effort. By using the flat edges rather than the corners of the block crayons, bands of colour rather than outlines are made. Within these broad bands of colour, forms spring and grow naturally. The yellow streams down and outward; the red is concentrated and strong; the blue gently curves and surrounds. Into these gestures of colour spring forms, without demanding precision and intricacy.

When you make a picture in front of a young child, every breath, every thought, every peaceful, careful stroke you make feeds and instructs the child. A picture you carefully and lovingly make for your child is a gift on many levels. It need not be great art! If at night you make a picture for your child from her own experience of the day's activities, with what wonder your child will wake up to this gift, just as the 'Rhyme Elves' often left a little poem and drawing of important events for Sylvia in the *Seven-Year-Old Wonder-Book*.[16] Such pictures can be kept in a special collection, perhaps in a special box or drawer.

You'll find your own appreciation of colour and artistic ability increasing as you colour and paint with your child. All children have innate artistic ability. If they are given watercolours rather than marking pens, if they can colour on blank sheets of paper instead of 'keeping within the lines,' this ability is more likely to remain alive and accessible to them throughout their lives.

The block crayons used in Waldorf Schools are made of sweet-smelling beeswax rather than paraffin and can be purchased through several mail order catalogs.

Modeling with Beeswax

Another artistic activity your child will enjoy is modeling with coloured beeswax. Beeswax has several advantages over clay – it smells nice, isn't messy, can be used over and over, and involves warmth. The child must take a bit of coloured beeswax and warm it with his hands, with both his hands and the beeswax becoming warm in the process. Clay, on the other hand, is cold earth and tends to rob the body of warmth; for this reason, clay is often used with children over nine and beeswax with younger children. With very young children or in cold weather, the beeswax may be too hard for the child to soften; then it can be warmed a bit by your own efforts or by setting it next to a heater to give the child a head start on softening it.

Coloured beeswax as used in the Waldorf schools is available from Stockmar and makes a wonderful birthday present or holiday gift. To use it, warm a piece in your hands while your child does the same.

This is a good time to tell a little story. Then start to make something. As with the other artistic activities, let your child make whatever comes to him without instruction. For preschool children, art is an expression of their inner experience, and it is inappropriate to try to make it conform to ideas imposed from the outside. Remembering the principle of imitation, do your beeswax modeling along with your child. I always found that by finishing last I was able to see the children's creations without them wanting to make what I had made, or wanting me to make the same thing for them! Very young children will simply enjoy the texture of beeswax, pinching and stretching it. As a fantasy element enters in, they will tell you what it is they have made (even though there may be no resemblance that you can discern). As they turn four and five they can become quite skilled and creative in what they make, and the figures can be placed on a little log in a special place to be played with or to wait until next time they are warmed and transformed into something else.

Making Things with Your Children

Making things with your child or letting him imitate things he has seen you make are artistic activities that encourage creativity, dexterity, and aesthetic judgment. Because the preschool children often saw me sewing, they loved to work from their own sewing basket, and a couple of them made dolls that were much more creative than mine because they lacked the conscious element of how a doll 'should' look. If you find yourself starting to make dolls and toys suggested in this book, set up a sewing basket for your child. Imitating real work is one of a child's greatest delights.

Similarly, the children loved to embroider, at first using large needles with yarn on burlap placed in embroidery hoops. We were able to make designs on placemats, bookmarks, and 'nature bags,' which we used for gathering treasures on walks. The older children were able to use embroidery thread and sharp needles, and soon learned how to handle safely the sharp scissors for making dolls.

You and your child can also make things out of bark, branches, and slices of logs – boats to sail, bird feeders, or doll furniture from wood and spools. The act of creation through the transformation of materials is one of the fundamentally human acts. Actually making something is so much more satisfying for children than cutting out shapes or fitting square pegs into round holes. Many wonderful ideas for craft projects can be found in the books listed at the end of this chapter.

Freeing Your Own Inner Artist

One of the added benefits of doing these artistic activities with your children is that you can reclaim and nourish your own inner innate creative ability, which was probably squelched through lack of use or beliefs such as, 'I'm not good enough' or 'I can't paint.' One of the most exciting things about the Waldorf teacher training or growing along with your child can be the rehabilitation of your own childhood and artistic ability.

Most of us, unless we had a Steiner/Waldorf education, have probably managed to internalize the criticisms that our creative efforts received from those around us and have stopped having any kind of artistic or other creative expression (writing, dancing, singing, and so forth). If you are interested in not letting your children have all the fun and want to unlock your own inner creativity, I highly recommend the approach outlined in *The Artist's Way: A Spiritual Path to Higher Creativity* by Julia Cameron. She gives practical exercises and encouragement for attitude adjustments (which she calls 'spiritual chiropractic') that can help harried mothers and blocked artists alike to reclaim their essential creativity.

Taking a little time for yourself can not only change your life, but also provide you with the creative and nurturing forces that you need for your parenting. Cameron states, 'A lot of times people think that art is decadent – they say, 'but what about all the starving people?' I say, if you are emotionally and creatively starved yourself, you don't have the sense of abundance necessary to be as helpful as you might be to others. If you are filling your own well, if you are caring for your own spirit, then you are able to effectively help others.' The creative path goes well beyond creating art and into every moment of life itself.[17]

Recommended Reading

About Drawing and Painting

Analyzing Children's Art by Rhoda Kellogg (Mayfield).

Echoes of a Dream by Susan Smith. Available from the Waldorf School Association of London, 7 Beaufort St., London, Ontario, Canada N6G 1A5 or Rudolf Steiner College Book Store.

How to Do Wet-on-Wet Watercolor Painting and Teach it to Children by Rauld Russell. Available from the author at The Iris, 1820 Stock Slough Road, Coos Bay, OR 97420.

Painting with Children by Brunhild Müller (Floris Books).

Understanding Children's Drawings by Michaela Strauss (Rudolf Steiner Press).

Craft Ideas to Do with Children

All Year Round by Ann Druitt, Christine Fynes-Clinton and Marije Rowling (Hawthorn Press). Craft ideas for the different seasonal festivals.

The Children's Year by Stephanie Cooper, Christine Fynes-Clinton and Marije Rowling (Hawthorn Press).

The Christmas Craft Book by Thomas Berger (Floris Books).

Crafts throughout the Year by Thomas Berger et al (Floris Books).

Earthwise. Simple Environmental Activities for Young Children by Carol Petrash (Floris Books).

The Easter Craft Book by Thomas Berger (Floris Books).

Echoes of a Dream by Susan Smith (see above).

Feltcraft by Petra Berger (Floris Books).

Felting by Hand by Anne Einset Vickrey (Craft Works Publishing).

Festivals, Family and Food by Diana Carey and Judy Large (Hawthorn Press).

A First Book of Knitting by Bonnie Gosse and Jill Allerton (Wynstones). Simple instructions and handwork patterns for you or your child (grades 1-3). A real delight.

The Harvest Craft Book by Thomas Berger (Floris Books).

Making Flower Children by Sybille Adolphi (Floris Books).

Toymaking with Children by Freya Jaffke (Celestial Arts).

Sources for Watercolours, Beeswax Crayons, and Beeswax for Modeling

US
Home Again, 1825 N 183rd St., Seattle, WA 98133
Mercurius, 7426 Sunset Ave., #C, Fair Oaks, CA 95628

UK
Mercurius, PO Box 1379, Swindon SN1 3SN
    Tel no. 01793 431480
Myriad, Ringwood, Hampshire Tel no. 01725 517085
    www.myriadonline.co.uk

Nourishing Your Own Creativity

The Artist's Way by Julia Cameron with Mark Bryan (Tarcher/Putnam). A spiritual path of higher creativity with plenty of practical exercises to explore your inner landscape and free your creativity in all fields.

The Vein of Gold by Julia Cameron (Tarcher/Putnam). A journey to your creative heart.

CHAPTER 10

Your Child's Musical Ability

Make a Joyful Noise

Children love sounds. They love to make them – with their own voices, by banging a spoon on a cooking pot, by blowing into a wooden flute. And they love to hear sounds, because sounds give them exciting news about the inner structure of an object. They unconsciously absorb the sound that manifests the nature of the object when it is touched, knocked, or dropped. The baby with a rattle is expressing its nature to be in movement, but it is also listening to the sounds its movements produce that stop when it stops moving.

Movement is interwoven with sound for the young child. Neurologists have found that a child who is unable to make certain movements is unable to make certain sounds. The young child is naturally in movement. The child's movement often remains free-flowing until school age if it has not been repressed by the environment. The movement forms itself into long and short rhythms, but doesn't manifest what we call beat (regular emphasis every so many counts) until the child turns nine. Around the age of nine, the child enters a new relationship with the world and is able to feel and understand triads and scales.[1]

Speaking of the inner musical nature of the young child, Rudolf

Steiner states, 'We shall then notice that it is man's nature, up to a point, to be born a 'musician'... It is a fact that the individual is born into the world with the desire to bring his own body into a musical rhythm, into a musical relationship with the world, and this inner musical capacity is most active in children in their third and fourth year.'[2]

Music and Cognitive Development

Seeing to your child's musical and movement activities in the preschool years might or might not make him a great musician in later life (that depends on musical talent and destiny), but it can lay the foundation for healthy development, which has ramifications in all spheres of life. Parents today are being bombarded with reports of the so-called 'Mozart effect,' which has got so out-of-control in the US that new parents in many hospitals are being sent home with a CD of classical music to play for their babies in order to make them smarter (courtesy of the National Academy of Recording Arts and Science Foundation and the maker of Enfamil baby formula, and paid for by the state legislatures in Georgia and Tennessee; Florida has even mandated that state-run daycare facilities play such music every day). What did the studies really show?

The 'Mozart effect' described the results of a 1993 study by Dr. Gordon Shaw, a physicist at the University of California at Irvine and Dr. Frances Rauscher, a psychologist presently at the University of Wisconsin at Oshkosh. In the study, college students who listened to ten minutes of Mozart's *Sonata in D Major for Two Pianos* scored eight or nine points higher on a spatial-temporal test than when they had ten minutes of silence or listened to relaxation tapes. Spatial-temporal reasoning is a key to the higher brain function required in mathematics, physics, and engineering. (It should be noted, however, that the added ability was lost after 1 hour, and studies by other researchers have been unable to duplicate the results).

The Mozart experiment actually began in 1990, when Dr. Shaw's research team discovered that the brain in a sense made its own music. The researchers made computer-generated models of neural firing patterns (electrical brain activity). When the research team fed these various brain patterns through a synthesizer, they heard recognizable but different styles of music. 'Some sounded like Baroque music, some like Eastern music, others like folk music. In other words, the communicating neurons (nerve cells) 'play' music.'[3] This made the researchers question whether or not music itself might encourage those neurons to communicate.

Drs. Rauscher and Shaw devised a study with preschoolers to see how musical training might affect their brain development. In their study, reported in the February 1997 journal *Neurological Research*, 111 three- and four-year-olds were randomly divided into four groups. One group received daily singing lessons and two 15-minute private piano lessons per week at school. A piano also was made available if the children wished to practice on their own. A second group received only the group singing lessons. Members of the third group received two 15-minute private computer lessons each week, while those in the fourth group received no lessons at all. At the beginning of the study, all of the students scored at the national norm on the tests. At the end of six months, those who received piano lessons scored an average of 34 percent higher on the tests of spatial-temporal ability, while those in the other three groups showed no improvement on any of the tests. The study was unable to follow the children into various public schools to see if the effect was lasting, but other studies with classically trained musicians have shown permanent physical changes in the brain compared to men who had not had extensive musical training.

The study discussed above showed that giving piano lessons to preschoolers significantly increased their ability to perform the types of reasoning required for excellence in science and maths, while lessons on using a computer keyboard provided no similar benefit. As a Waldorf educator, I would want to make sure that whatever was done was developmentally appropriate and presented in a way that used the appropriate part of the brain, and not a lower part, as may be the case when babies are taught to 'read' by memorizing flash cards. Given the dreamy state of consciousness of the young child, the piano lessons would need to involve a lot of fun, not reading music or the pressure to be singled out and to 'perform.' But this study can demonstrate to parents that if they're debating investing in a computer versus buying an instrument and paying for music lessons, the active involvement with music is more valuable in terms of brain development.

Brain activity is similar for musical skills, mathematics, and spatial reasoning. Both music and mathematics activate parts of the brain in or near the cortex. There is a definitive relationship between mathematics and musical skills. The crucial window of development, as with language, is from birth to about the age of ten. So what should parents do, that is still developmentally appropriate, to ensure optimal enjoyment of music as well as optimal brain development?

Singing with Your Child

One of the simplest and best musical things you can do with your child is to sing. This can begin prenatally and continue through lullabies and special songs that you make up for your baby. After you sing or say a nursery rhyme with your child, listen and see if your baby responds. Katherine Barr Norling, director of a parent-child resource center and school in Boston in the US, writes, 'I love singing, even to an 8-month-old, then stopping. Often, even such a young baby will respond by babbling back. One way to experience sound is to talk to your child. But don't stop there. Take that break and listen; allow him to answer in some way. There is so much children can learn even prior to speaking.'[4]

Once your child becomes verbal, she will love to sing with you, the more so if you add gestures and movements to match the words. Singing involves the breath and the middle heart/lung sphere, whose development is emphasized between the ages of three and five. Its proper development forms the basis for later health and balanced overall development. Rudolf Steiner said, 'You will be fostering all this if you give the child plenty of singing. You must have a feeling that the child is a musical instrument while he is singing.... Every child is a musical instrument and inwardly feels a kind of well-being in the sound.'[5]

Julius Knierim, a music specialist working out of the indications of Rudolf Steiner, observed that children before the age of nine mostly sing much higher when by themselves than the pitch of music they have heard in their environment. They will also sing faster than an adult's rhythmic sense would dictate. Much of their singing is not yet rhythmically 'correct' because their pulse/breathing ratio has not yet settled at the 4:1 ratio that characterizes an adult's; and their voices are still light, nonresonant, hovering, and silvery. Children lack the complexity of adult experience and feel completely satisfied and fulfilled with simple melodies, whereas an adult would feel something was lacking and might long for more complicated harmonies and rhythms.[6]

It is difficult to simplify enough for the young child. Even a song with one note can be completely satisfying. Here is one that I made up while looking out the window. It can have hand movements like falling rain and a circle formed by the arms for a puddle.

See the rain-drops fal-ling down! Mak-ing pud-dles on the ground.

When in doubt, choose the note A above Middle C. The qualities of this note are associated with the sun and are especially suitable for early childhood, according to Steiner. Here's a song that goes up and down from the A.

I can run in the sun. I can fly in the sky!

If you take off running and flying, your child will delightedly be there with you.

You can also make up songs to go with activities around the house, such as stirring or sewing. Songs can also ease transitions such as cleaning up the toys or going upstairs to nap. Waldorf teacher Mary Lynn Channer shares this transition song for nap time:

May I ride piggy -back, piggy-back, piggy-back?

May I ride piggy -back? And then I'll take my nap.

When you are telling fairy tales, remember how simply key phrases can become a song, like the following from Briar Rose ('Sleeping Beauty').

Mirror, mirror on the wall: Who's the fairest of them all?

Many favorite folk songs and holiday songs that are part of our culture become 'old friends' for your child when they come around each year with the cycle of the seasons. Some traditional songs contain the same kind of folk wisdom we found in the nursery rhymes. For example, 'Rock-a-bye-baby,' according to Eileen Hutchins, 'tells of the child cradled in the mother's womb and surrounded by the world of spirit (for spirit literally means breath or wind). But the time of birth draws near and child and cradle (or caul) are cast out into the world.'[7]

Singing with your child is one of the joys of parenting. If you can't remember songs from your own childhood, several excellent anthologies are listed at the end of this chapter.

Movement Games and Fingerplays

As an adult who hadn't moved for a few decades, I found putting movements to songs and verses not my strong suit as a new early-childhood teacher. I could remember 'I'm a Little Teapot' from when I was three years old, but that was about all. But I decided to continue inwardly to understand the gesture of various activities (the movements that express the essential nature of an activity). Gradually the children taught me, and I began to understand more and more. Now I can do appropriate preschool movements to any song or verse, but I certainly felt awkward and self-conscious when I started! Seeing how imitative young children are and how much it is part of their nature to move along with the words helped me rediscover this childlike part of myself.

Start with fingerplays and movement verses from your own childhood; perhaps you remember 'The Wheels on the Bus' or 'Six Little Ducks' or 'Where Is Thumbkin?' The interaction with your child, the engaging of the faculties of imitation, and the musical elements all unite in this kind of play that has delighted children for centuries and that has great value for their development. Steiner points out how fingerplays and other tasks which develop dexterity in the fingers, such as knitting, help with brain development and later facility in clear thought.[8]

Circle games are also an ancient part of early childhood that delight young children. Modern ones like 'Motorboat, motorboat, go so slow... Motorboat, motorboat, go so fast... Motorboat, motorboat, step on the gas!' are fun for their quality of changing speed and movement, but they lack the musical element. Older circle games such as 'Ring Around the Roses' and 'Sally Go Round the Sun' provide a picture in movement and song of the child's incarnating process. Jane Winslow Eliot, in her book on circle games, writes:

Watch when a child falls on the ground. The shrieks are out of proportion to the damage done. It is because the little one has been shocked out of an enveloping cloud into a sudden realization of the solidity of earth. The soul resents this. When you ritualize this happening in the garment of a game such as the lovely Ring Around the Roses, you lead the child lovingly, gently down to earth and she begins to enjoy the fun of it. Bit by bit the children don't mind staying.[9]

Ring games are joyful, sociable, simple, and yet they have all of the solemnity of a ritual in the way they are repeated over and over. Circle games contain rhythms that affect the beat of the children's pulses; they sometimes incorporate the ability to do tasks without self-consciousness, as in washing the clothes or brushing one's hair in 'Here We Go 'Round the Mulberry Bush'; others deal with the interplay between the individual and the group, as in 'The Farmer in the Dell' (which is a game that can be too strong for three-year-olds, who don't yet like being singled out and standing alone at the end). A child who does not want to be chosen should never be forced, for games that single out individual characters are too self-conscious for the very young child. The five-year-old, on the other hand, loves to be the Farmer or the Cheese and to be caught in the games 'London Bridge' or 'Oranges and Lemons.' Younger children will enjoy these games if they can participate as part of the circle without being singled out before they are ready.

Steiner comments about the value of rhythmical games for young children:

> For early childhood it is important to realize the value of children's songs as a means of education. They must make a pretty and rhythmical impression on the senses; the beauty of sound is to be valued more than the meaning of words. The more vivid the impression made on the ear, the better. Dancing movements in musical rhythm have a powerful influence in building up the physical organs and this should likewise not be undervalued.[10]

Pentatonic Music and the 'Mood of the Fifth'

The pentatonic scale has five notes instead of the seven we are used to in our normal diatonic scales. For example, a pentatonic scale built around A would have the notes D, E, G, A, B with no half steps (so the notes C and F are not included). If you look closely at children's songs and folk songs, you will see that many are written with this simpler scale that does not include the notes C or F.

Pentatonic music has the characteristic that it can go on and on without having an ending note that gives it a feeling of being finished (provided the song doesn't end on D, which changes the key from D pentatonic to G major). According to Steiner, these types of songs that are not grounded by a resolving note at the end are very appropriate for the young child, who is not yet 'firmly on the ground.' Such music encourages the young child to stay in a dreamy state, so the greatest amount of energy is available for the healthy forming of the physical body. If this is done in early childhood, then the child can later wake up intellectual capacities while still maintaining a strong contact with wonder, beauty, and creativity. In the Waldorf schools, pentatonic songs are used until third grade, when the children have developed an inner emotional life that makes the major and minor scales more suitable for them.

The pentatonic scale was once used by most of humanity; the Greek scale was pentatonic, and it was used in Europe up to the Middle Ages. The Chinese scale is pentatonic, as was the ancient Egyptian. The quality of consciousness of ancient cultures was close to that of the young child – less earth-bound, still on the threshold of two worlds. Pentatonic music and 'music in the mood of the fifth'[11] can have a healing influence on the young child by not rushing the child into fully incarnated earth-bound consciousness and experience.

A kinderharp (children's harp or lyre, pictured at the beginning of this chapter) is a small hand-held harp that can be tuned to the pentatonic scale, which enables anyone to play beautiful music on it; all the notes sound harmonious together and the quality of the sound is ideal for the young child. Such instruments, without sounding boxes, give a very pure experience of each note, without harmonic overtones. This simple, pure experience of the tones is ideal for young children and is recommended by Steiner over more complex instruments like the piano.

Kinderharps are lovely instruments for naptime and bedtime. Their music is very 'angelic,' and can really help to calm a child and lull him or her to sleep. As children get older, they also like to pick out tunes on the kinderharp. Such instruments are used in Waldorf early childhood programs for the children to play (very carefully) and for the teacher to play at circle time, or at naptime in afternoon programs.

Kinderharps can be purchased from the addresses listed at the end of this chapter. In addition, Choroi makes other pentatonic instruments, such as a recorder made out of pear wood, and a klangspiel (xylophone or glockenspiel). Percussion instruments are not generally recommended for young children because a beat that is too strong can drive children too deeply into their physical bodies. This is in opposition to the fluid molding of their inner organs that occurs during the first seven years. Rock music has an especially strong beat and should be avoided for the young child.

I hope I've built a fairly convincing case for the benefits of simple, live music for the young child. We must remind ourselves again and again that the young child is 'all sense organ' and monitor our children's environment for the quality of the sounds that surround and permeate them. In addition to being oblivious to the real nature of the young child, one of the unfortunate characteristics of our culture is to substitute non-living or mechanistic actions for living interactions. Thus, instead of letting our babies sleep where they can sense our presence, we put on a tape of a heart beat. Instead of holding and rocking them to sleep, we are told to turn on a machine that simulates a car going 55 miles per hour or the noise of a clothes dryer. Instead of reading to them and then letting them lie quietly until they fall asleep, we pop the professional rendering of a story into the tape player and beat a hasty retreat. Or instead of singing with our children and letting them help in what we are doing or play quietly near us while we work, we put on one of their CDs, tapes, or videos to make them become passive and free us from them. Even though you may think that someone singing children's songs is doing a much better job than you could possibly do and is providing a better experience for your child, he or she would not agree. Your child would always vote for you, because it is the 'aliveness' that provides the real nourishment.

What About Music and Dance Lessons?

Young children are naturally musical. Steiner describes it: 'The musical element which lives in the human being from birth onwards and which expresses itself particularly in the child's third and fourth years in a gift for dancing, is essentially an element of will, potent with life... If people had the right agility, they would dance with little children, they would somehow join in the movement of all children. It is a fact that the individual is born into the world with the desire to bring his own body into musical rhythm, into musical relation with the world, and this inner musical capacity is most active in children in their third and fourth years.[12]

Is it, therefore, best to start music and dance lessons at a young age? Unfortunately, most teachers of young children don't understand the principles of imitation and the importance of play and fantasy. They teach cognitively and put pressure on the child to learn a lesson or to do it right. Such a direct approach is far too self-conscious and can be stressful for the young child. While children need play that incorporates dance and music, most lessons are designed for older children, even though they may indicate that they are for four- or five-year-olds.

Elkind, in *Miseducation: Preschoolers at Risk*, develops a strong case that any kind of lessons place preschoolers at risk with no real gain.[13] Waldorf teachers would agree that most lessons are inappropriate for the young child. If you do consider any kind of lessons for your nursery or kindergarten-age child – swimming, gymnastics, modern dance, sports – be sure to observe the classes before you decide whether or not to enroll your child. Does the instructor teach from imitation? Are the things that are asked and done clothed in fantasy? Or is there instruction appropriate for a much older child? Does your child really feel comfortable being away from you? Would the classes be enjoyable or stressful for your child? Would classes be taking away time from play or just being at home (especially important for children who are in programs all day because their parents work). Don't sacrifice the present level of your child's development for some future achievement. If it isn't fun, it is better left undone at this age!

Steiner made two recommendations that aren't going to win him any points with parents today. He recommended that children avoid ballet and football. In ballet the fixed and artificial positions are foreign to the fluid and changing nature of the growing child. And ballet affects the same kind of vital energy involved in growth and reproduction, as evidenced by the high rate of menstrual irregularities in professional ballerinas. The discipline and fixed positions of ballet are very different from the rhythmical movement which Steiner recommends for 'dancing with children.'

In football the exclusive use of the feet and the head in hitting the ball puts undue emphasis on the extremities at a time when the primary-school child is centered in the middle sphere, the heart/lung area. With professional and elite amateur football players, studies of the long-term effects are just being undertaken after neurologist Barry Jordan recently found that Dutch pro football forwards and defensive players (those most likely to 'head' the ball) were more likely to have subtle problems in everything from memory to visual perception than were mid-fielders and goalies. They also had more concussions. Jordan also found with professional boxers that those who carried a specific gene linked to early-onset Alzheimer's disease were more likely to suffer cognitive impairment, and he will be checking to see if the same is true with football players.[14] While your child won't experience the same kind of battering that professional football players endure, one can't totally discount Steiner's observation that such use of the head is not healthy for the growing child.

Returning from the football fields to the realm of music, unless your child is a musical genius who clearly needs a tutor at age three, there are many reasons to wait until primary school before beginning music instruction. Unfortunately, most people who work with preschool children don't know how to teach from imitation and start by teaching how to read music. Even the idea of having to learn a lesson through imitation is too direct an approach for a young child. While the Suzuki method does work through the principle of imitation, the emphasis on tape-recorded music is not consonant with the young child's need to hear live music and simple tunes. Performing at young ages introduces pressure and self-consciousness into the dream-like world of early childhood. In the Steiner/Waldorf schools children often don't present anything before an audience until they start class work, when they share their poems, plays, songs, and recorder music with one another and the parents at school assemblies.

Playing the wooden recorder is begun in Class 1 in Steiner/ Waldorf schools, but the children learn strictly through imitating their teacher. Reading music isn't introduced until third year, when the child has reached a certain level of maturity and eye-hand coordination and is ready for the full range of musical experience, progressing to stringed instruments in third grade.

Everyone wants his child to develop according to his full potential. But an understanding of the inner development of the child leads to the realization that certain subjects and certain skills are most beneficial when introduced at the age that corresponds to the child's inner ripeness for them. 'Do more sooner' is a symptom of our spiritual materialism that can lead to skipping steps and hastening a child's development in one sphere without realizing the possible ramifications in another. These comments are not meant to provide a list of 'Thou shalt nots,' but to encourage you to trust your own knowledge, combined with your heart sense, to form an intuitive perception of what is best for your child. If parents do this, they won't subject their children to the Super Baby syndrome at the expense of the important years of early childhood.

Recommended Reading

Fingerplays, Nursery Rhymes, and Circle Games

The Eentsy Weentsy Spider – Finger Plays and Action Rhymes by Joanna Cole and Stephanie Calmenson (Harper Trophy).
Finger Plays for Nursery and Kindergarten by Emilie Poulson (Outlet).
The Laughing Baby – Remembering Nursery Rhymes and Reasons by Anne Scott (Greenwood Press).
Let Us Form a Ring (Waldorf Early Childhood Association – WECAN). www.waldorfearlychildhood.com
The Real Mother Goose (Scholastic).
Sing-Song – A Nursery Rhyme Book by Christina Rossetti (Dover).
This Little Puffin compiled by Elizabeth Matterson (Penguin).

Waldorf-Inspired

Clump-a-Dump and Snickle-Snack by Johanne Russ. Pentatonic children's songs from Mercury Press.
Gateways and other volumes by Margret Meyerkort. Six booklets of songs and stories collected from the Waldorf Kindergarten teachers in Great Britain. Available from Wynstones Press.

Giving Love, Bringing Joy – Gesture Games and Lullabies in the Mood of the Fifth by Wilma Ellersiek (Waldorf Early Childhood Association – WECAN).

Quintenlieder. Introduction to the Mood of the Fifth by Julius Knierim. From Rudolf Steiner College.

The Singing Day by Candy Verney (Hawthorn Press).

Other Selections

American Folksongs for Children by Ruth Crawford Seeger (Doubleday).

Jabulani! by Carol Shepherd and Bobbie Stormont (Hawthorn Press). Ideas for creating music.

The Lullaby Treasury – Cradle Songs from Around the World by Mathilde Polee and Petra Rosenberg (Floris Books).

Pentatonic Instruments

US

Pentatonic Instruments (kinderharps, recorders) Choroi, P.O. Box 684544, Austin, TX 78768.

Harps of Lorien, Raphael Weisman, P.O. Box 77, Questa, NM 87556.

UK

Herga, Suppliers of Choroi instruments, 4 High Street, Wealdstone, Harrow, Middlessex HA3 7AA Tel no. 01208 8611590

Myriad, Ringwood, Hampshire Tel no. 01725 517085
www.myriadonline.co.uk

CHAPTER 11

Rhythm and Discipline in Home Life

Discipline with the Young Child

The Question of Discipline

The very fact that the issue of discipline is a question to parents is symptomatic of our times. Many parents know more of what they don't want to do regarding the discipline of their children than what to do, or what the results of their approach will be. We need to discuss with one another questions about creative discipline and ways to raise children – but not in front of the children! It is important for couples to discuss their ideas about bringing up children and how they feel about the ways their own parents raised them. Children deserve the security of feeling that mom and dad are united and know what they are doing, otherwise they quickly learn how to get around one parent by going to the other.

Many parents don't want to be authoritarian, and they question whether they should insist that their child obey. Studies have shown that among authoritarian, authoritative, and permissive parents, the children whose parents are authoritative do best. That means effectively and consistently setting limits for the child. Parents have a natural authority with their children because the parents are adults, so children naturally look to them as knowing more about the world than they do. Children 'come to earth' only gradually, so the adult must provide the ego force for the child that will direct his emotions; they must make decisions based on a mature viewpoint, rather than on the child's own likes and dislikes. This is also true for the teacher, who must 'hold' the class with the strength of his or her own being, or be overrun by a group of children who know that the teacher can't manage them.

It is necessary and appropriate to correct children's behavior – to insist on what I have come to call *right action*. But you can't expect young children to remember what they're supposed to do the next time! It is necessary to repeat right action over and over again with emotional equanimity. Understanding that we need to correct actions in the present moment without any hope of the young child's remembering it the next time can help us to keep our own tempers and to model the right behavior over and over again. Firmness permeated by love provides the child with the kind of guidance he needs to grow from baby to adult.

Discipline means more than correcting undesirable behavior. It also means guiding the child to develop in a healthy way physically, emotionally, and mentally. We guide the baby largely by nurturing his physical body; we lead the toddler by ordering the rhythm of her day; as the child becomes older we take her by the hand and try to be an example ourselves. Once the child reaches school age, he is guided most by stories and the spoken word.[1] How to guide a child depends on his age, personality, and the nature of the parent-child relationship. Even within the same family, differences due to temperament and age mean that all children do not have to be treated in the same way – only fairly.

It is impossible to speak about disciplining a baby in the sense of correcting or making her do the right thing, because the baby's will is both so strong and so unintentional. A baby doesn't do things in relation to us and can't change her behavior because we want her to, or insist upon it. This can strengthen the patience and develop the nurturing capacities of new parents, or it can result in extreme frustration. According to a nationwide study by Dr. Jacy Showers of the Shaken Baby Syndrome Prevention Plus Program in the US, 37 percent of parents and other caregivers were unaware that shaking babies is dangerous (it can cause blindness, developmental delays, and permanent brain damage; and it is fatal in approximately one in four cases). Taking care of an infant is not easy, and newborns cry an average of one to four hours a day. Anyone can experience transient anger toward a crying baby, but if the impulse to shake or hit is strong and recurrent, find local help or start by calling an agency such as the National Child Abuse Hotline.

The tremendous will forces of an infant are not conscious or under the child's control. According to Steiner, will begins as instinct in a baby, and gradually changes over the years into urge, then desire, then motive. Urge is still strongly connected to the body (biological urges). Such urges will further metamorphose into desire when the emotional element enters around the age of two or three. At this stage parents often think they can start discussing with their children what the children do and don't like, what they want to do, or why they did a certain thing. However, children of this age have not yet developed the faculty for motives; only an awakened self has a motive for doing something. A three-year-old is incapable of acting with reflection, so we are asking something of which the child is incapable, although the articulate ones will start giving us all kinds of creative answers! Steiner states that you might be able to appeal to reason in a child in adolescence, but not before. When you constantly reason with a young child to have her do what you want, you end up with a five-year-old who has learned through imitation to do the same with you, all of the time.

Imitation and Example

Instead of getting angry or reasoning with your child, keep in mind the principles of example and imitation with the child under the age of eight. If you want to teach a certain behavior to your child, one of the best ways is to actually do it in front of (or with) him. This demands that we as adults get up and actually do something, rather than giving the child orders or directions. For example, instead of correcting the child by saying, 'Don't eat with your fingers,' pick up your spoon and very purposefully go through the motions yourself while saying, 'We eat with our spoon.' Or instead of saying, 'Go clean up your toys,' we need to go with the child and do it together while we might say, 'It's time to put your toys away.'

Movement combined with the smallest amount of fantasy or good humor can go a long way toward getting the child to do what you want. For example, with cleaning up, you can ask the truck driver to steer the truck to its garage or get the cowboy to ride the stick horse over to the stable. Another example is to join in the children's fantasy, rather than interrupting it. So if the children are involved in play, ask the train drivers to move the train out of the walkway while you start moving the chairs with them instead of breaking their fantasy by telling them to move out of the way. Similarly, if you want to have tiny bits of paper cleaned up from your newly vacuumed floor, call on all the little mice to bring the grains of corn to you while you start putting bits into your hand. Your helpers will have the job done in minutes!

What about things you've told a child a hundred times? For example, you've told five-year-old Ryan at least that many times, 'Don't slam the door!' but to no avail. Try gathering your intention, meeting him at the door and saying, 'We close the door quietly,' while you move his hand through the motion of gently closing the door. That will probably do it. If not, a second time is probably all that is necessary. Movement and stating what it is you want to have happen communicate with children in a way they can understand.

Whenever possible, state the positive: 'Pet the kitty gently,' while you show how to do it, rather than shrieking, 'Don't hurt the kitty!' Sentences with 'don't' will communicate your displeasure, but the brain often doesn't process every word, so the message may in fact register as, '... hurt ... kitty!' It's a lot more effective to be saying, '... gentle ... kitty,' instead.

Not Expecting Results

It isn't until 6 or 7 years old that a child is ready to respond consistently to authority that is expressed only through the spoken word without being accompanied by actions. With the preschool-age child, you need to correct and demonstrate the right behavior again and again, but you can't expect children to remember it. Their memories simply aren't that mature yet. There will be slow improvement over time, but the 'learning' that does occur takes place through gradual maturation and the repetition of actions that form habit patterns. For example, early in the year at our Waldorf preschool, several children couldn't sit calmly during snack time. 'We sit with our feet in front of us,' we repeated again and again as we reseated the child or showed our own straight way of sitting. After several months the children were older and able to sit calmly during snack time, and the lesson had been repeated so many times that it had begun to penetrate the body. Gradually the child who couldn't stay in his chair could calmly eat and wait for 'Red Bird' to come and choose who would blow out the candle, signifying everyone could go and play. But it took a month or two of constant repetition.

Only around the age of five does the child have enough memory and distance on the world to begin to remember what he should and should not do. I saw this stage with a little boy in the preschool who was corrected nearly every day for rough behavior toward the other children. We tried everything! As he approached five he started to remember after he hit someone that he wasn't supposed to do that, and he began to feel regret both for the action and the consequences that would follow. But it took even more maturity for him to be able to start remembering before he struck out; because of his temperament it was more difficult for him to get control of his emotions than for many children. It was a real effort and a test of patience to work with him and to constantly insist on the right behavior that took him so long to be able to master.

Steiner describes the change in a child around age five: 'Previously, unable to understand what it ought or ought not to do, it could only imitate, but now, little by little, it begins to listen to and to believe in what its elders say. Only towards the fifth year is it possible to awaken in a child the sense of what is right or wrong. We will educate the child rightly only if we realize that during the first seven-year period – that is up to the change of teeth – the child lives by imitation, and that only gradually will it develop imagination and memory as well as a first belief in what grown-ups say.'[2]

Steiner gives another example of a young couple who were distraught because their young child was 'stealing' money from a jar in the cupboard. Steiner explained that the child was only imitating having seen the mother take money from the jar. He explained that only after the age of five can the child begin to have concepts of right and wrong sufficient to support or avoid the idea of stealing. Prior to that time the child is acting out of imitation.[3]

When You Say 'No!'

Despite moving with your child and stating things positively, there will be times when you need to say no and your child needs to know that you mean it. Elizabeth Grunelius, the first Waldorf kindergarten teacher, said that she found only three reasons for having to say no to a child:

1. When what he wishes to do would be harmful to himself – for instance, to go out on a cold day without a coat.
2. When what he wishes to do would be harmful to others – for instance, to make a noise when the baby is sleeping.
3. When what he wishes to do would result in real damage – for instance, to use his crayons on the wall.[4]

Even in these instances it isn't necessary to start out with a head-on confrontation and battle of the wills. In the first case, you simply help the child put his coat on; in the second, you could suggest that he can play quietly inside or go outside and play; and in the third case you give him a piece of paper and try to switch his activity into more appropriate channels.

Deciding when something will be harmful to a child requires judgment, and the more you can fine-tune your judgment, the better for your child. If we can support our children in getting their own experiences without excessively saying no and without interrupting them, they will learn a great deal about the world and about their own abilities. Climbing trees is an example. Yes, there is a certain amount of danger, but if I hadn't let my daughter climb trees I never would have known that she really should have been born into a circus family that performs high-wire acts. She would climb up fifty feet and sit and play her wooden recorder! Once when she was four she got stuck up in a tree and my husband was away, so I had to get a neighbor to climb up our forty-foot ladder to help her (not for me, thanks!). The neighbors were hysterical and kept calling up to her, 'Don't be afraid!' I had to explain that she wasn't afraid, just stuck! She did fall once, but it only slowed her down for a few hours.

It is important before you say no to a child that you be sure what the child intends and sure of your answer. Sometimes it is good to pause for a moment and decide, because if you change your mind when you realize how intent on a thing your child is, you can confuse him and encourage a habit of pleading until you change your mind. Keeping discipline simple and consistent is important so that your child knows you mean what you say, and that your word is followed immediately by action.

Negative Emotions

Many parents ignore their child's negative behavior until they either give in or lose their temper. For example, a lady with a baby and a two-year-old in one shopping cart and groceries in the other was ignoring the crazy behavior of her two-year-old, who became more and more annoying, trying to get a reaction. By the time we were both at the checkout stand, he was in a full-blown fit. Although she was still able to calmly ignore it, we need to recognize that it is frustrating to children to be allowed to get crazier and crazier as they keep 'upping the ante.' There were a lot of calm but effective things she could have done along the way, like stopping the cart and saying it doesn't move unless he's sitting down; singing to him; engaging him by saying she'd let him get the pineapple juice, putting five things in the cart on the way to the pineapple juice, then letting him stand up and pick it off the shelf; asking him to watch in the produce section and tell her when he saw the carrots. Children don't have to be crazy or drive us crazy, but they do require creative interaction.

However, no one is all sweetness and light in correcting her child. Sometimes a sharp no is called for and a child who continues to raise a fuss can be removed from the action until he is ready to do what is needed (play nicely, take turns or whatever is at issue). Usually three minutes is about all it takes for a child to get himself back together and be ready to try again. Remember that you need to move with the young child, not give orders. So you go out, away from the action, along with the young child and state that just as soon as he is ready to return (and have a 'happy face' at dinner or take turns with his brother), he can go back. Then you stand there absolutely stone faced, so it's really boring to be out in the hall with mom while everyone else is having a good time. If a child is really 'out of himself,' it may take longer or repeated episodes of 'time out' before he is ready. Getting him interested in something that is going on can also help him to reintegrate into social activity if he was having a particularly difficult time.

With negative behavior, such as biting or hitting, again it is best to emphasize the positive actions. 'We need to be gentle with our friends.' 'We need to share the toy.' If possible, put energy into the child who has been wronged rather than putting your attention into the offender. Obviously, spanking or hitting the child is providing a model of the thing you are trying to get him to stop doing. It gives a really mixed message, because our actions speak to a young child much more powerfully than our words.

Many parents talk to their children about the emotions they are experiencing and encourage them to express their frustration by screaming and yelling instead of hitting. Many parents who went through personal growth work or psychotherapy don't want their children to be 'repressed.' However, emotions for the child under the age of seven lack the complexity that they have for an adolescent. Usually tears or being afraid will quickly pass. They may require hugs or distraction in the moment, but we don't need to dwell on the upset, talk about it, practice having other emotions or all of the things that make emotions far too conscious for a young child. Children whose parents do these kinds of emotional exercises with them usually become very aware and very verbal at a young age. They easily learn to play the verbal games and come up with the answers the parents want – after all, it's a major way of relating with the parent. But the young child's emotions are much more present-time oriented and are much easier to deal with if allowed to pass without a great deal of comment – while right action is being insisted on. Remember the young child is centered in the will, in movement and doing.

Because children are so imitative, we need to monitor our own emotions and actions when disciplining them, for our actions speak louder than our words. How can we keep our own tempers when we might like to throttle our children, or at a minimum yell uncontrollably at them? Understanding that we need to correct actions in the present moment without any expectation that the young child will remember it the next time can help us keep our own tempers and model the right behavior over and over again. One of the keys to discipline involves bringing one's own consciousness and objectivity to the incident – talking in a quiet voice, sticking by what you say, repeating it if necessary, and, whenever possible, actually moving with the young child.

Too many parents are silent until they overreact from a string of annoyances that have been building and smoldering. In consequence, the child is running circles around the parent and making life miserable, while the parent is feeling overwhelmed or angry much of the time. If this is happening to you, get some help. You and your child deserve it! Find a friend you can talk to, or a family counselor who can provide a more objective viewpoint, or attend parenting classes. You need some new knowledge and new perspectives, as well as ways of defusing your own emotions. This is especially true if you come out of a family situation in which you were abused emotionally or physically as a child. If you are so enraged you don't know what to do or find yourself hitting your child, seek help from a professional or call a parenting hot line to track down the kind of help you need, whether it is individual counseling or group classes or sessions. Your child is providing you with the opportunity to fix what is broken – before it becomes broken in him or her as well.

Living with young children is both demanding and rewarding. It requires attention to create a harmonious life, and there is often very little time for other activities (this is where extended family or support systems are a must). Children are young only once. They will soon be away at school and there will be much more time for one's own activities. Understanding the nature of the young child can help you to raise a happy and well-behaved child, as well as a bright one, and can help you to have fun and find satisfaction in it while you continue in your own growth.

Rhythm and Discipline in Home Life

Some of the suggestions just given can be helpful when problems arise, but the real key is creating an environment in which problems don't arise. The Steiner/Waldorf nursery or kindergarten looks effortless; it looks as if the teacher isn't doing very much. Up to twenty children play harmoniously and move from one activity to the next throughout the morning without the teacher having to stop to solve major problems or interruptions. While it may look easy, a great deal of preparation has gone into creating an environment that fits the children and planning a rhythmical series of activities that allow freedom of movement within a structure that holds and supports the children. The rhythms of the day and the week help with the transitions from one activity to the next, so that a short song or similar sign from the teacher is all that the children need to move on to the next activity.

Attention to rhythm and the environment can work similar wonders in home life, helping to avoid most discipline problems and direct confrontations with your child. Because the young child is so centered in the body and in imitation, rhythm is one of the most important keys to discipline. It both guides the child's life by creating good habits and helps avoid arguments and problems. So much of discipline for young children involves self-discipline on the part of the adults: keeping regular rhythms in the home life, working on your own patience and emotional responses, being there when your child needs interaction. (For example, playing with your child first can free up an entire twenty minutes to read the paper, whereas telling him you'll do it in ten minutes can results in all kinds of emotional disasters.) Grunelius states:

> Much of a child's happiness depends on our success in conducting the daily life with and around him with a minimum amount of friction. Every time we may feel like stepping in with advice or an order or a correction, we might well pause for a moment to do two things: firstly, to ask ourselves whether our interference at this particular instant is really necessary; and secondly, to find out what the child is actually trying to do.[5]

The Need for Rhythm in Daily Life

We are surrounded by rhythm in nature: the alternation of day and night, the phases of the moon, the cycle of the seasons, the ebb and flow of the tides. Our bodies are permeated by rhythm, in the beating of our hearts, the breathing of our lungs, women's cycles of fertility, and the circadian rhythms of our metabolism. But as modern human beings, we have also established a life that is removed from the rhythms of nature. Through electric lighting we can work well into the night; we can shop at twenty-four-hour supermarkets; we can fly strawberries to Minnesota in January. Through technology we can live outside of most of the rhythms of nature. As a result, we have often become unaware of the messages and rhythms of our bodies and have forgotten the importance of rhythm in daily life. Steiner describes it as follows:

> Rhythm holds sway in the whole of nature, up to the level of man [sic]. Then, and only then is there a change. The rhythm which through the course of the year holds sway in the forces of growth, of propagation and so forth, ceases when we come to man. For man is to have his roots in freedom; and the more civilized he is, the more does this rhythm decline. As the light disappears at Christmas time, so has rhythm apparently departed from the life of man. Chaos prevails. But man must give birth again to rhythm out of his innermost being, his own initiative.[6]

The baby, who has been surrounded by the mother's heartbeat and rocked by her breathing in the womb, emerges into earthly life and must find its new rhythms, gradually developing from the fast and irregular heartbeat and breathing of the newborn to the rhythm of one breath to each four heartbeats of the adult.

A regular lifestyle, like the pattern of life in the womb, offers a stable environment during the rapid growth and changes in rhythm of the body during childhood. Children provided with this regular life feel confident about their world and are not concerned by uncertainty about when the next thing will happen. Rhythm in home life can also help to calm a nervous or difficult child by turning the child's life into a series of events in which he participates, and from which he gains a new sense of security. Regular mealtimes and regular nap- and bedtimes help to start orienting the child to a natural feeling for the passing of time. They go a long way toward preventing discipline problems, because bedtimes become something that happen as regularly as the sky turning dark – there is no one to argue with or complain to each night.

Elizabeth Grunelius summarizes, 'The rhythm then becomes a habit, is accepted as self-evident and will eliminate many difficulties, struggles and arguments about eating and going to bed... Regularity should prevail in as many of the child's daily activities as possible. It is the key to establishing good habits for life.'[7]

Grunelius gives an example of how supportive rhythm is for young children and how much they learn through it. She tells about taking care of a two-year-old child whom she bathed each day in the same way – first soaping her hands, then her arms, then her neck, and so on. When she took care of the child again after several weeks, the child spontaneously asked, 'May I wash myself?' and proceeded carefully and happily through the whole sequence exactly as it had been done so many times before. The child was extremely satisfied with herself![8] This example amazed me, because it never occurred to me to wash a child in a regular fashion, thus providing the child with something it would then be possible to learn.

Andrea Gambardella, a Steiner/Waldorf teacher working in the US, explains, 'With the young child and the elementary-school student this requirement for an outer structure continues to be vital to growth and emotional well-being. Learning that there is a 'time for all things' is a life's lesson. Now is the time for you to play and do as you will, now for a meal, now for homework, now to prepare for bed.'[9]

Rhythm is also a blessing for parents, because it enables the daily activity of life to flow more smoothly, require less energy, and become a platform that supports the family, its activities, and interactions. Many mothers don't discover the secrets of rhythm until they have two or more children, and suddenly there isn't enough time not to be organized! Regular meals prevent constant feeding and cleaning up or overhungry and whiny children; regular bedtimes suddenly free the evening for adult conversation and life again as a couple. The benefits are many, and yet it is sometimes difficult to create rhythm in family life – it requires an inner discipline of its own! Creating rhythm in one's life doesn't mean to be rigid and dogmatic. There is still plenty of room for special activities and surprises (and sometimes the piper to pay the next day when the child has missed a needed nap or had a late, exciting evening – but it's worth it!). But freedom is not without form, and one is truly free when not hampered by a disorganized life. The rhythmic structure imposed on a young child and permeated with the parents' love is a discipline in the most positive sense of the word. And as your children become older, they will transform this outer structure into an inner self-discipline that will be invaluable for homework and getting other jobs done. Putting attention into these areas can help the quality of life for both you and your children from the time they are toddlers until they leave home.

A Word of Caution

Before reading the following practical suggestions, remind yourself that I'm not suggesting you have to do all these things to be a good mother! Rather, by mentioning so many things in so many areas, I hope that you will be sparked to consider adding even one rhythmical element to even one area of your child's life. Most women are too busy to have every part of the day be a wonderful time for their children. In my house, breakfasts were efficient, without frills; there was no way, during the school year, that I was going to put special place settings on the table! So I put my attention into bedtimes. But for someone else, early mornings might be a real time for their family to be together, especially if evenings are shortened by dad working late.

Once they come to appreciate the value of rhythm, some women feel guilty because they don't provide a rhythmical home life, or they reject the whole idea out of annoyance. My suggestion is that you consider just one area after reading this chapter. You might want to focus on an area that is going the least smoothly in your life. It might be naptime, or it might be dinner, or it might be getting the children out the door in the morning. Whatever the area, think about what happens now, and how you could make things go more smoothly by applying some of the suggestions or by inventing some of your own. Having a regular rhythm, adding a bit of ritual like a song or verse, and avoiding too many choices can transform a hectic part of family life into an activity or transition that flows smoothly. Discuss your ideas with your partner, agree on a new series of actions for an activity, and then start doing them with the children. You'll be amazed by the results!

Mealtimes

Eating together is a major part of family life and can be a valuable cohesive force in bringing people together. However, attention needs to be put into mealtimes, so they don't turn into times of tension or chaos or disappear because everyone has grabbed something to eat on the run.

When do meals occur? Who is present? There are no right or wrong answers when you look at rhythms and family life. You need to look at the configuration and needs of your family members and decide what works for you. The important thing is to bring your consciousness to seeing your situation and working toward what feels best. We know a family where the father and three-year-old had breakfast together on weekdays before he went to work, while the mother got some extra sleep. It was a special time for the two of them that they really cherished. Similarly, work schedules will probably determine what time dinner happens and whether your children will need to eat earlier. Whatever you work out for your family, having meals at a regular time (and regular snacks for the children as needed) is helpful for creating rhythm in family life.

Now look at the setting. Do you have a table around which a family can gather? Any little touches you add to meals, like a candle or fresh flowers, can help make meals a special time for the family. I found, in the summertime, that by setting the breakfast table the night before, even I felt nourished and cared for by waking up to a table that was inviting. And family members, who tended to get up and eat at different times during the summer, all felt 'held' by the family, even though no one else might be at the table with them.

Next, consider the atmosphere. Are mealtimes relaxed and

conducive to digestion? Small children especially need to eat in calm surroundings, without television and radio. (The six o'clock news is enough to give anyone indigestion through the graphic reports of murders and other atrocities.) Similarly, the adults should be careful not to be negative about people or to dwell on disappointments of the day. Children take everything in and are unable to disconnect emotions from their body's functioning.

Conversation at meals changes with the arrival of children. It becomes impossible to conduct adult conversation in the same way, and children need to be accepted as conversationalists. Mealtime then becomes a time for listening, sharing, and balancing conversations so that each child can bring something of himself or herself to the family's time together. The essay on 'Family Meals' in *Lifeways*[10] carries many ideas for harmonious meals with growing children.

Beginning the meal with a spoken or sung blessing encourages feelings of thankfulness and assures that everyone starts together. Young children are especially nourished by whatever ritual you develop around your family's mealtimes. But you need to bring feelings of gratitude, not empty words said in haste! If you don't have any graces from your religious background, here are two that give a feeling for the connectedness of life and gratitude for our sustenance:

> Before the flour, the mill,
> Before the mill, the grain,
> Before the grain, the sun and rain,
> The beauty of God's will.
>
> *(Unknown)*

> Earth, who gives to us this food,
> Sun, who makes it ripe and good,
> Dear Sun, dear Earth, by you we live,
> Our loving thanks to you we give.
>
> *(Christian Morgenstern)*

It is important for children to be grateful for their food and for the efforts of the cook in preparing it. Such an attitude will be fostered by the care we take in preparing and serving the food. This is another area where working on our own gratitude and appreciation for the gift of life will communicate most strongly with our children. How you handle a child and foods he doesn't like requires some creative thinking. You will need to set your own table rules about what can be said about food and what needs to be eaten before a child can leave the table or have dessert.

Certain behavior can be insisted on, so meals can be a calm and harmonious experience for everyone. If a young child who is whiny or who throws a fit is immediately taken out by a stern adult as described earlier, he will probably change his behavior within three minutes. No one wants to be away from the action!

Do your dinners have a formal ending, just drift off, or degenerate rapidly? Having children ask to be excused at the end of a meal is not an old-fashioned formality, but a useful way to keep track of who's finished and can set boundaries that a child is either sitting at the table or has left the room. While some families prefer that everyone stays at the table until a song or short verse is said to end the meal, we preferred that our children were excused when they were finished. This gave them a short time to run around (outside of the dining-room) and provided us with a chance to sit back and talk as a couple for a few minutes before calling everyone back to do their jobs of clearing the table, loading the dishwasher, washing the pots and pans, and so forth.

Mealtimes provide one of the earliest opportunities for 'family chores,' which can occur on a regular basis. While each child can take his or her plate to the kitchen, jobs which benefit the whole family can be rotated among the children, such as setting the table, clearing, wiping the counters, and so forth. Even the youngest child can have his or her special task in contributing to the 'family meal.'

Mealtimes change as your children grow older. They are different with toddlers, teenagers, or mixtures of a wide range of ages. But gathering around the table for meals and participating in the family's evolving rituals can be an important part of your family's life.

Nutrition

While it is important for parents to be aware of nutrition, it is just as well to leave young children unaware of the intricacies of vitamins and minimum daily requirements. When a child is really allergic to something like milk or peanuts, he needs to be able to tell people so he won't inadvertently eat those things. But analysis of ingredients or search for refined sugars makes preschoolers pick apart and analyze everything on the table, rather than feeling that what they are being served is good. Allergic becomes a synonym for 'I don't like,' and any kind of common snack becomes impossible because Billy doesn't eat dairy and Jane doesn't eat wheat and Joey is allergic to peanuts and Mary can't have anything with sugar in it.

Trusting that what you give your child is good for him is most important for the child; excessive consciousness among three- and four-year-olds is only divisive. One time, two kindergarten boys at the lunch table noticed that one had a huge lunch with a big thermos of milk, two white-bread sandwiches, potato chips, and fruit roll-up, while the other had carob soy milk, a whole-wheat sandwich with tofu and sprouts, a piece of fruit, and a granola bar. These children, starting to be self-aware and aware of the world around them, noticed the discrepancy. One said to the teacher, 'My mother says that milk is good for you and helps your bones and teeth.'

The other said, 'My mom says that milk gives you mucus!'

'Who's right?' they asked together.

The kindergarten teacher wisely replied, 'Your mother is right.' And both boys were satisfied.

We found our preschool children had become so picky nutritionally that any kind of common snack was impossible. The social element of eating together was tentative at best!

Children instinctively feel that the world is whole and good and that whatever their mother gives them is good for them. It isn't necessary to tell your child more than is minimally necessary for health or for philosophical distinctions like vegetarianism. What you do will be more important than long explanations. 'Our family doesn't eat meat' is usually enough for a child to know, and your telling friends and teachers will help keep the child from having to make choices. With something like trying to avoid sugar, if you feed your child wisely at home and tell grandma that you wish she would put away the candy jar before visits, then you may decide the little bit your child eats at a birthday party or a friend's house may not be worth all of the intellectual and emotional investment required to tell the child he can't have things. These are issues you have to discuss with each other as parents, and decisions you will have to make based on your medical and philosophical convictions. I can only tell you as a preschool teacher that the awareness and misinformation children have about nutrition these days reflects an increased consciousness of the metabolic sphere that wreaks havoc with the unitive worldview of the young child.

Nap or Quiet Times

Young children need restful or quiet times during the day as a means of being restored for play. Like the rhythm of breathing, the child's activities alternate between active play, in which the full body is in motion, and quiet times for a snack or a story. Focusing attention on something close at hand, such as making something, colouring or modeling with beeswax, brings the child into himself and balances active play in which he is totally in movement.

Many children today sleep very little and seem ready to give up afternoon naps at an early age. However, the afternoon nap is of great benefit for a child in 'digesting' the impressions of the day, and it provides a welcome time for parents as well. The time can be used for sleep or just as a quiet time in which the child has to stay on his bed or in his room. If the rhythm of a daily rest is maintained, the child will learn that this is a time to be by himself and not to call on mother. All the kindergarten and nursery children who stay afternoons in our Waldorf program lie down on cots; then a story is read or told, and the kinderharp is played. Many of the five-year-olds do in fact fall asleep, even when they wouldn't ordinarily nap at home. And the others rest while playing silently with a favorite doll. Again, the same song is used each time to start and end naptime – and the ending is especially welcome because 'Red Bird' (a felt bird on a stick) comes and wakes the children or lets them get up to play.

Recognizing the value of a quiet time for preschool children is the first step in instituting one. An hour in the afternoon without the children can also be a valuable time for a mother to center and refresh her energies by resting or doing something she wants to do. If your child is not used to a quiet time and you want to start having one, think it through first. What time will work for you? What are the parameters of acceptable behavior? You can tell the child that he doesn't have to sleep, he just has to stay on his bed, for example. What kinds of dolls or toys will you make accessible to him, if any? What needs to be done in preparation? Going to the toilet, washing hands, putting shoes neatly under the chair? Will you sing or tell a story? A kinderharp is wonderful for calming a child and helping him go off to sleep. If you want to sit with your child until he falls asleep, look and act very sleepy yourself – eyelids heavy, not talking or answering questions, letting sleep ooze from your pores. Putting your hand on a child's head or back can also be very calming. Sleep or rest time is a valuable part of your child's day, through kindergarten age. If you don't have such a time, you will probably find that your child comes home from a half day and just wants to sit or play alone for a while after lunch anyway. The children have been so active in a group during the morning that a more inward time is a needed balance.

Bedtime

What is bedtime like at your house? Does the evening have a rhythm to it, ending in going to bed at a regular time and according to a regular set of activities? A regular bedtime preceded by a set ritual can help calm your child and prevent arguments. It can also help him to learn to do more and more of the activities involved in getting ready for bed by himself as he becomes older. It can also help him to feel more secure when you have a babysitter if the sitter is taught to do things in the same order.

How a child enters sleep is important for refreshing the spirit as well as the body. Falling asleep and waking are portals to the spiritual world, the world of dreams and inspirations. How we and our children enter sleep and wake up can affect the quality of both sleeping and waking life. With a young child, the entire time after dinner is often focused on leading toward bedtime. Quiet play can be followed by straightening up the room, then by a bath when necessary or washing up, brushing teeth, and putting on pajamas. Talking slowly or singing softly can help set a quiet mood for bedtime. Lighting a candle in the room and then whispering as you enter with the child who is ready for bed can help create a mood of calmness and sharing. A few songs, a story, a verse, or prayer that unites the child's soul with the divine can help a child to drift peacefully into sleep. You might play some music on the kinderharp if you have one. If you have used a candle, you'll want to blow it out before leaving the room, but its warm, soft light can be very calming during songs and story. If your child has difficulty going to sleep, many more suggestions can be found in the essay 'Sleeping and Waking' in *Lifeways*.[11]

Children love consciousness and cling to it, and thus will stay up to the point of becoming overtired. They really can't be depended on to go to bed when they need to! When I first enrolled in the teacher training program at the Waldorf Institute, my children were in kindergarten and school and were going to bed at 8:30. One of the instructors talked about sleep and suggested that my children could easily be going to bed at 7:30. I thought, 'Not my kids! Eight-thirty is hard enough!' But I decided to try his suggestion to see if it would work. To my utter surprise, the children went to bed an hour earlier without a fuss and slept an hour longer at night, even though they hadn't seemed to be tired on the old schedule. I was dumbfounded! I have had similar experiences, suggesting that preschool parents start their child for bed at 7:30 instead of putting him to bed at 11:00. To their surprise it took less than three days for the child to get into the new rhythm, so that one boy even told his babysitter that it was time for bed in the early evening.

If your child goes to bed early, will he wake up at the crack of dawn? You will have to try it and see. A preschool child who wakes up bright and smiling with the sun can't understand why adults want her to go back to sleep! But most children will not wake up so early, and they can be taught to put on a dressing gown and slippers, if it is cold, and to play in their room (often with something that has been set out after they have gone to sleep) if you need to sleep a little longer.

Mornings

The transition out of sleep is also an important time, and putting attention into this time of day can help both adults and children. How do you wake up? Many mothers have found that getting up a half-hour before the rest of the family gives them a quiet, centered time in the morning that affects their whole day. Or if they don't get up early, they arrange as many things as possible the night before: what clothes each child will wear, jackets or snowsuits and mittens if needed, bags for school, lunches, the breakfast table, and whatever else is needed. The biggest problem with mornings is being rushed, which makes children move even more slowly and puts everyone in a bad mood.

Assuming you wake your child, how do you do it? Margret Meyerkort reminds us, 'It is important for both children and adults that the experience of the night-consciousness be allowed to stay more or less actively for a while just below the level of the day-consciousness. For here rest the hints, understandings, reassurances and sense of the spiritual world. Therefore the alarm-clock needs to be kept well away from the young child, for it is such a cold, stern and literally shocking awakener. After such an awakening, the child could be disgruntled for hours afterwards. Instead the parent can hum a melody or sing a seasonal or morning song.'[12] Holding a young child up to the window to see the light of the new day is also a nice way to start the morning.

Because a child is still in a kind of night-consciousness after awakening, he often can't cope with any kind of questions for the first ten or fifteen minutes. He simply doesn't have the day-consciousness to come up with the answer, so try to avoid questions and choices. Make your choices together the night before, about what to wear and so forth, so that morning doesn't have to become a battleground of the wills.

Once your child is fully awake, do the events of getting ready for the day have a particular order? Remember that doing things in an orderly way gives a child something to learn and makes it much more likely that your eight-year-old will remember to brush her teeth and hair before taking off for school, or won't forget it even though it is Saturday. Think about your mornings: getting dressed, eating breakfast, brushing teeth, brushing hair; what about making the bed (together at first)?

Greeting the day is something that children love to do with a verse or a song. If you don't know any, here are two suggestions:

> Morning has come.
> Night is away.
> Rise with the sun
> And welcome the day!
>
> *(Elisabeth Lebret)*

> Good morning, dear earth; Good morning, dear sun!
> Good morning dear stones and flowers every one!
> Good morning dear busy bees and birds in the trees!
> Good morning to you and good morning to me!
>
> *(Unknown)*

Here is a verse given by Rudolf Steiner that can easily have hand gestures added as you point to your eyes, your heart, make a circle like the sun, and put your head on your hands in a resting gesture.

> With my own eyes
> I see the world,
> The lovely world of God.
> My heart must give thanks
> That I may live
> In this, God's world,
> That I may wake
> In the brightness of day,
> And may rest at night
> In the blessing of God.[13]

Helping your young child achieve a sense for the rhythm of the week is more easily accomplished if special activities regularly occur on a specific day. If you tend to go to the park once a week, going every Tuesday will give your child a sense of this activity as a punctuation mark for the week; it will also help you to organize your other activities. If you paint with your child, you could do it every Monday, adding another rhythmically recurring event to your child's life.

In former times work was done according to the days of the week as expressed in this traditional verse:

> Wash on Monday
> Iron on Tuesday
> Mend on Wednesday
> Churn on Thursday
> Clean on Friday
> Bake on Saturday
> Rest on Sunday

This kind of rhythm is still observed in the American Amish communities and, rather than being boring, creates for them a pattern in the chaos of having so much to do in daily life. While most of us no longer live according to such rhythms of work, if we appreciate their value for the young child we can do certain activities on set days, or shop together on a certain day, so the child starts to feel at home in the week and its recurring nature.

Within the pattern of the week, something needs to be said about the Sabbath, which used to be a very special day in which no work or play occurred during the observance of religious practices. If your family doesn't go to church, temple, or mosque, Sunday (or Saturday or Friday) may have lost its sense of a day for inwardness, for communion with God, oneself, nature, or the family. Think about what your family does on this day. With or without going to church, would it be nourishing to do something regularly, like having a special breakfast, getting out into nature, having spiritual study for adults with Bible stories told to the children? What would be meaningful for your family?

The days of the week all have qualities, colours, grains, activities, and planets associated with them. For example, Tuesday is associated with Mars (which is still reflected in *mardi* in French and *martes* in Spanish). Since Mars is the God of war in the Greek pantheon, the theme could be considered strength and energy, and activities could involve heavy chores, grinding, sports, and so forth. The Waldorf *Living Home Kindergarten* (Home Schooling Program in the US) discusses the various qualities in greater detail, for anyone who is interested in learning more (see resources listed at the end of this chapter).

The Rhythm of the Year

As we live through the changing cycle of the seasons, we can gain an appreciation for nature and the rhythm of the year through the analogy of breathing. In the summer it is as if the earth breathes out, creating the myriad forms and colours of summer foliage and the feeling of being right out there in the stratosphere when you lie on your back and look into a summer sky. Winter, on the other hand, is like an in-breath; the cold brings a contracted quality, and much of life becomes dormant and sleeps in burrows or as seeds in the earth.

We can also experience the year through the waxing and waning of the light in the sun's cycle and recognize how we echo within ourselves the changes occurring in nature. As the days grow cooler in the autumn, they become shorter and darkness increases. As life draws inward with the waning light, it is necessary that we strengthen our inner life of thought and resolve. It is common to find that you think more clearly on a crisp autumn day, or that you can finish a project much more easily during the winter months than during the summer.

When the winter solstice is reached in late December, the light begins to gain strength again. The increasing strength of the sun in springtime warms the earth and awakens the sleeping trees and flowers, so that life springs forth again in all its glory. At the summer solstice in June (also called Midsummer), the sun is at its strongest, and the leaves and fruits soak up the warmth of its rays, ready to give back their summer experience of the sun in the richness of harvest and the flaming autumn colours of the trees.

Many of the major religions acknowledge and incorporate our experience of the year into the celebrations of their festivals. Thus in the autumn, with the decline of outer light, we have the need to kindle our own inner light and resolve to transform the unredeemed qualities in our own souls, manifested through the image of St.

Michael and the dragon (September 29 is Michaelmas). In the autumn many countries have festivals that bring together this juxtaposition of outer darkness and fire or inner light: the bonfires of Guy Fawkes Day in Great Britain (November 5); Halloween jack-o-lanterns in Europe and the US; the traditional lantern walks in Germany on St. Martin's Day (November 11); or the Santa Lucia festival of lights in Scandinavia (December 13), in which the youngest daughter wears a crown of burning candles and brings special cakes to her family members for breakfast.

In Judaism, Hanukkah is a Festival of Lights that occurs at the time of greatest darkness in December. In Christianity, the four candles of the Advent wreath prepare the way for the 'Light of the World,' whose birth is celebrated just at the turning point of the year in relation to the sun.

Similarly, the image of the resurrection of Christ is echoed in nature through the rebirth of the world each spring. To complete our cycle of the major festivals of the calendar, we need to mention St. John's (June 24 or Midsummer),which has traditionally been celebrated in European countries with bonfires at this time of the sun's greatest strength.

Celebrating Festivals and the Course of the Year

Many people today feel a need for festivals and meaningful celebrations or rituals in their lives. If they have turned away from the religious upbringing of their childhood, they are nonetheless seeking new ways of celebrating meaningful events in their lives (such as marriages), or finding new ways to approach the meaning of Christmas despite all the commercialism that surrounds it today. The celebration of festivals is not only important in individuals' lives, but it is important socially and for the possibility it provides us to step out of 'ordinary time' and be connected with something more abiding. Steiner felt that renewed awareness in the celebration of festivals could form a valuable link between the earthly and divine worlds.

Whatever your heritage, I encourage you to look forward toward the festivals of the year within your religion and find ways to celebrate them that are meaningful to you and can nourish your children. Because I came from a Christian background, my greatest familiarity was with the Christian festivals; but I learned a great deal through the Jewish, Buddhist, and Moslem parents of my students, who brought some of the festivals to their children in a living way and have shared their efforts with our classes. *Celebrating the Festivals with Children*[14] and several other books listed at the end of this chapter can provide helpful backgrounds on the inner meaning of the Christian festivals and ways to celebrate them.

Festivals, Family and Food[15] gives numerous stories, recipes and craft ideas for celebrating the major and lesser-known festivals of the year with children. Remember that, with young children, the preparation for the festival is as important as the celebration itself – the baking, making of special presents, decorating, and singing of special songs year after year. Be sure to include your children in all of the preparation activities! In trying to convey the inner spiritual realities of a festival to a young child, remember that what you do speaks more loudly than what you say. The care you put into making a present teaches more about giving than a lecture on divine love. In bringing festivals to a young child, tell the story in simple images she can follow. Then the story, like the one of King Hamen and Mordecai accompanied by noise-makers and the Hammentaschen cookies, will be a wonderful celebration for the young child. An example related to Easter comes through a story from the Waldorf kindergartens in Britain about a caterpillar who wanted to be like a flower and worship the sun.[16] Mother Earth told him that there was a way of transformation, but it was almost like dying and being born again in a new form. The brave caterpillar becoming a flower that can fly is an image of the resurrection, in which nature mirrors the miracle of the resurrection of Christ and our own potential for inner transformation.

Christmas is a festival that young children relate to naturally because Jesus as a baby is very near to them. The celebration of Advent with children makes a time of inner preparation more visible both to them and to us. The Advent calendar, with its magic windows, and the Advent wreath that can be lighted each night as a story is told, can help keep the inner side of Christmas from getting lost in the flurry of activity.

In addition to whatever religious festivals you celebrate with your children, you can enrich your own and your children's lives by observing the passing of the seasons. Seasonal songs, foods prepared in special ways, and seasonal activities all help us to raise our awareness of the changes in nature that surround us. *Festivals, Family and Food, The Children's Year* and *All Year Round* suggest a wealth of things to do with your children, and the Living Home Kindergarten program comes in four volumes corresponding to the four seasons.

You can bring a bit of nature into your home through a seasonal table, a place where you can keep special things, like the shells collected at the beach during the summer or a special birthday card from grandma. The colours of the cloth on this little table can be changed with the seasons, just as the objects on it change to reflect the changes in nature.

Birthdays

Children's birthdays are special festivals that parents can either find delightful or a real strain. In planning celebrations for children, remember the simpler, the better. Try to avoid sensory overload. If you don't actively enjoy a place, the chances are your child shouldn't be there either. It is unfortunate that so many parties for young children now occur in pizza or ice-cream parlors with blaring music, nauseating clowns, or 'singing' mechanical characters and video games.

Many suggestions for delightful birthday celebrations at home can be found in *Festivals, Family and Food* and *The Birthday Book*. With a group of children you can do some movement games, or try decorating 'treasure bags' and taking a walk in the woods, or making a 'fairy garden' out of moss on a paper plate that is decorated with acorns and a pretty stone that the child finds.

A birthday celebration, even just within the family, is a way of saying, 'We're glad you were born!' Ways of letting the child be special that day can include having a special drawing or crown at her place at breakfast, letting her choose what will be cooked for dinner, or whatever you devise. Think of traditions you might want to start: making a card for your child for each year that includes several photos of that year – riding a tricycle, getting a new kitty, going on a trip. Such cards can become things that will be saved and treasured when the child is older.

For the young child, a birthday story that tells of her coming down to earth over the 'rainbow bridge' is fitting, because the young child is still very connected to the spiritual world. Birthdays provide us with an opportunity to note the passage of time, which seems to go by so quickly when we see how our children grow and change in the course of a year. Birthdays, holidays, the changing seasons, all provide a familiarity and rhythm that can nourish us as well as our children. On a daily basis, a rhythmical lifestyle is one of the greatest gifts we can provide the young child.

Recommended Reading

Rhythm and Family Life

Beyond the Rainbow Bridge by Barbara Patterson and Pamela Bradley (Michaelmas Press).

Lifeways – Working with Family Questions by Gudrun Davy and Bons Voors, Eds. (Hawthorn Press).

More Lifeways – Finding Support and Inspiration in Family Life by Patti Smith & Signe Schaefer, Eds. (Hawthorn Press).

Prayers for Parents and Children by Rudolf Steiner (Rudolf Steiner Press).

Punishment in Self-Education and the Education of the Child by Erich Gabert (purchase from Rudolf Steiner College).

Serving Fire – Rhythms and Rituals of the Hearth by Anne Scott (Celestial Arts).

Seven Times the Sun – Guiding Your Child Through the Rhythms of the Day by Shea Darian (Gideon Press).

The Singing Day by Candy Verney (Hawthorn Press).

Sing Through the Day by the Society of Brothers (The Plough Publishing).

The Spiritual Tasks of the Homemaker by Manfred Schmidt-Brabant (Temple Lodge).

Festivals and Seasons of the Year

All Year Round by Ann Druitt, Christine Fynes-Clinton and Marije Rowling (Hawthorn Press). Craft ideas for the different seasonal festivals.

The Birthday Book by Ann Druitt, Christine Fynes-Clinton and Marije Rowling (Hawthorn Press).

Celebrating Irish Festivals by Ruth Marshall (Hawthorn Press).

The Cycle of the Year as Breathing Process of the Earth by Rudolf Steiner (Anthroposophic Press).

The Festivals and Their Meaning by Rudolf Steiner (Rudolf Steiner Press).

Festivals, Family and Food by Diana Carey and Judy Large (Hawthorn Press).

Festivals Together by Sue Fitzjohn, Minda Weston and Judy Large (Hawthorn Press).

The First Jewish Catalog by Richard Siegel, et al (The Jewish Publication Society of America).

The Islamic Year by Noorah Al-Gailani and Chris Smith (Hawthorn Press).

The Nature Corner by Leeuwen and Moeskops (Floris Books).

Sing Through the Seasons by the Society of Brothers (The Plough Publishing).

Work and Play in Early Childhood by Freya Jaffke (Floris Books).

For seasonal songs, see list at the end of Chapter 10.

Waldorf Kindergarten Home Schooling Curriculum in the US

The Living Home Kindergarten (Waldorf home schooling programs in 4 volumes, *In Autumn*, *Winter*, *Spring*, and *Summer*, plus monthly consultation with a Waldorf teacher). Valuable throughout the early childhood years. Contact Live Education!, P.O. Box 306, Aptos, CA 95001. (408/457-4243). www.live-education.com

CHAPTER 12

Cognitive Development and Early Childhood Education

Parents naturally want to give their child the best start in life and do everything they can to ensure their intellectual development. In earlier chapters we have indicated that the best thing you can do for your baby's cognitive development, once she starts to crawl, is to childproof your home and let her explore freely while she is near you. The baby needs to move and to explore, and the objects in your home provide better stimulation than many expensive educational toys.

Once your child becomes verbal and begins to ask endless questions, there is a tendency to start providing rational and scientific answers. In *Miseducation*, Elkind points out that we must constantly remember that young children's verbal skills far outpace their conceptual knowledge. Because children's questions sound so mature and sophisticated, we are tempted to answer them at a level of abstraction far beyond their level of comprehension. Children are really asking about the purpose of things, not about how they work.[1] For example, when your four-year-old asks, 'Why does the sun shine?' he is quite satisfied by the answer, 'To make the plants grow and keep us healthy.' He doesn't need an answer about burning gases and ultraviolet rays, which introduce concepts he has no way of understanding.

Grunelius agrees that concepts are products of the mind at a more advanced age level, while images or additional observation will lead the child to arrive at his own answer. She gives the following example:

Coming home from the beach, a six-year-old may ask, 'Why are there waves in the ocean?' Instead of explaining, we may say, 'Come, let me show you,' fill the wash-basin with water and blow on it. The child will see the waves, repeat blowing on the water several times and get what is for him a more perfect answer than any explanation could furnish.

Speaking about the child's reaction to the ocean, he will notice that the sea at times rises higher and at other times recedes, and ask about it. To answer him by telling him the influence of the moon is not to answer a child at all, who is not ripe to comprehend any more than the rhythmic sequence of the up-and-down movement of the water.

We answer him with complete accuracy, however, if we let him hold his own hand over his breast so as to feel his inbreathing and outbreathing, and then tell him how the rise and fall of the sea resembles that breathing movement in his own body.[2]

Academic vs. Play-Based Approaches

In the US like the UK there is tremendous pressure to teach reading, writing, and maths to children at an increasingly early age. It is therefore useful to look at the US experience, as it highlights the dangers and consequences of early academic education. First however, it is helpful to clarify the distinctions between American and UK early years educational systems. In the UK children enter reception class in Primary schools at an average of $4^{1}/_{2}$ years of age. Formal learning and Foundation Key Stage 1 starts when children are 5-5$^{1}/_{2}$ years old. In America children attend Pre-school nurseries until 4 years old and then go to Kindergarten (K) for one year between 5 and 6 years of age.(Kindergarten is traditionally half-day education, 5 days a week. While kindergarten used to be 'play based', with only rudimentary introduction of reading and writing, government-mandated curricula are increasingly determining what teachers must cover each day.) Elementary school starts when the child is 6-7 years old. The first year is referred to as Grade 1 and this is when formal reading and writing begins. This age for starting formal education in the US is therefore broadly similar to mainstream Europe and schools in the Steiner/Waldorf movement, but up to a whole year later than in UK schools. There is no National Curriculum or Foundation Stage legislation as in the UK, although individual states, like Connecticut or Arizona, can create their own early years standards and curricula.

In the US most publicly funded Kindergartens are now doing what was once a first grade school program, while nursery-age children have taken on tasks previously meant for older children. As the publicly funded pre- Kindergarten programs increase, the academic pressure on three and four year olds increases as well. 'Today we're asking kids to meet higher standards in K through to 12 grade', says American Federation of Teachers president Sandra Feldman, in justification of this downward shift into the preschool. 'But if we don't prepare them earlier, then they're not going to meet them'.

However, the fact that reading problems have increased and that test scores have failed to improve has only led to even greater pressure for kindergarten teachers to pound the alphabet and the numbers into young heads, and to teach with an eye toward standardized curricula and the standardized tests that determine a school's standing and funding. For example, the state of Georgia's universal pre-kindergarten curriculum includes language, literacy and math concepts. Although kindergarten teachers across the nation are increasingly unhappy, they feel powerless in relation to the school boards and state legislators who keep mandating what they teach.

In US private preschools and kindergartens, there has also been tremendous pressure from parents to ensure that their children are successfully taught academic subjects early. The drive is to help ensure their children's success in school and give them an 'edge up' on other children. In the 1980s parents who were professionals in their late 30s fueled this push toward early academics by utilizing baby flash cards, classes, and academically-oriented preschools to help get their children into the 'best' private elementary schools. However, the damaging effect of the 'Super Baby Syndrome' was pointed out by pediatricians and by authors such as David Elkind in his book *The Hurried Child*. In February 1987 Newsweek reported: 'Now the pendulum may be swinging away from 'hothousing,' as the academic preschool phenomenon has come to be known. After years of internal debate, the early-childhood establishment has rallied against formal instruction of very young children on the grounds that it can lead to educational 'burnout' and a sense of failure.'[3]

However, the rejection of early academics spoken of in 1987 did not really manifest because of the digital revolution. Parents suddenly became worried that if their three-year-old wasn't 'computer literate,' he or she would be locked out of the future. And computer-based educational programs promised that computer instruction was the tool that had been missing for teaching preschool children how to read and do maths. Parents began buying software for their toddlers, and preschools were pressured to include computer instruction.

The whole question of both the value and the misuse of computers in education has been explored in depth by developmental neuropsychologist Jane Healy in her book *Failure to Connect*. Through reviewing hundreds of studies in the literature, trying out hundreds of computer programs, and visiting hundreds of schools, Healy concluded that there is no advantage – and there may even be disadvantages – for children under the age of seven in using computers at all. With elementary-school-aged children, she gives excellent guidelines for assessing and buying programs that really teach, and for paying attention to physiological factors, such as how much screen time the child is putting in, the amount of glare, his posture, and so forth. Her book is a 'must read' for all parents and educators today.

Why Not Introduce Academics Early?

Both Maria Montessori and Rudolf Steiner recognized that the young child should not be taught cognitive work directly. Montessori said that the child should be taught through the body, hence the wealth of special equipment (not called toys) in a Montessori program, for teaching such concepts as geometric shapes, weights, and so forth. Steiner went even further and said that concepts shouldn't be taught at all to children before the change of teeth, which normally happens between 6 and 7 years old. He placed the emphasis on creative play, imagination, imitation, movement games and fingerplays, crafts and artistic activities, until the physical body is more developed and the energy needed for its intense early growth is freed for forming mental pictures and memory work.

In noting the tremendous changes that occur naturally around the age of seven, Steiner gave indications of the problems that could arise by introducing early cognitive learning to children. While it is possible to speed up development in certain areas with some children, tampering with nature's timetable can result in negative effects in other areas. Whenever you call directly on the intellect and memory of the young child, you are using energy that is needed for physical development during the first seven years. The same forces that are active in the physical development of the young child are used later for intellectual activity. Attention to this factor in development during the early years can form the foundation for health and vitality throughout life. Obviously the child is learning a tremendous amount and developing cognitively during these years. Steiner simply means not to address the intellect directly, but to encourage the child's learning through direct life experiences and imitation. He explains:

> In the human embryo the eyes are protected and the external physical sunlight must not work upon their development. In the same sense external education must not endeavour to effect a training or influence the moulding of the memory, before the change of teeth. If we, however, simply give it nourishment and do not try as yet to develop it by external measure, we shall see how the memory unfolds in this period, freely and of its own accord.[4]

Some children can be taught to read before they are five years old; some babies can even be conditioned to recognize flash cards. But through her research on brain development, Jane Healy reminds us that reading and writing are built on language ability – the power to listen carefully, understand what others are saying and to express ideas effectively. In *Your Child's Growing Mind*, she concludes:

> Even babies can be conditioned to associate two stimuli that are presented repeatedly, but this learning lacks real meaning for the child and may use inappropriate parts of the cortex instead of

those best suited for the job. In fact, forced learning of any type may result in the use of lower systems, since the higher ones which should do the work have not yet developed. The 'habit' of using inferior brain areas for higher-level tasks (such as reading) and of receiving instruction rather than creating patterns of meaning causes big trouble later on.[5]

   ...Yes, even babies can be trained to recognize words. Babies, however, cannot read, tapping into a vast personal store house of language and knowledge that takes years to build. Most preschoolers, likewise, can be trained through a stimulus-response type of teaching. The human brain can be trained to do almost anything, if the task is simplified enough and one is willing to devote the necessary time and energy. Yet the brain power – and possibly the neural connections – are stolen from the foundation of real intelligence. Reading becomes a low-level skill, and there is a danger that it will remain at the level where it was learned and practiced.[6]

Healy points out that truly gifted early readers are insatiable in their desire to learn to read. They don't have to be taught, and they make instinctive connections with thought and language. In contrast to these children, who usually learn without lessons from adults or older siblings reading to them, she states that 'reading problems can be created by forced early instruction. Many authorities believe that age seven is the right time to begin formally teaching reading. Studies in different countries have shown that when five- and seven-year-olds are taught by the same methods, the seven-year-olds learn far more quickly and happily than do the fives, who are more likely to develop reading difficulties.'[7]

   The practice of having four- and five-year-olds fill out worksheets and copy lessons is also decried by most educators and developmental psychologists. Healy states: 'Children under the age of six should not be expected to copy sentences. Meaningful copying requires brain maturation to integrate two or three modalities (looking, feeling, moving and sometimes even hearing a word). Little ones can copy at a rote level, but they're probably not using the circuits which will connect with meaning. Let it wait. Children of this age should not be sitting at desks doing academic tasks. Get their busy brains out doing and learning, not practicing low-level skills.'[8]

Piaget, Steiner, and others have pointed out that children go through various stages in their development and thinking. The latest brain research has actually shown that the brain goes through a developmental and differentiating process. Healy, through her extensive research in brain development, concluded that, 'The immature human brain neither needs nor profits from attempts to 'jumpstart' it. The fact that the phrase is being successfully used to sell technology [educational software] for toddlers illustrates our ignorance of early childhood development.'[9]

In addition to skipping stages or utilizing lower levels of the brain to accomplish learning tasks, early academics can take an emotional toll as well. According to Healy, 'Studies show that four-, five-, and six-year-olds in heavily 'academic' classes tend to become less creative and more anxious – without gaining significant advantages over their peers. Youngsters in well-structured 'play'-oriented schools develop more positive attitudes toward learning, along with better ultimate skill development.'[10] Another study of young children looked at creativity along with academic gains. It showed significant reductions in creativity after even moderate use of a popular reading software system.[11]

The Value of Preschool

Today in the US virtually all children attend kindergarten around the age of five, and 63 percent of all parents say they plan to start sending their child to some sort of pre-school by the age of four. This is more than four times the 1965 rate, and it will probably become greater as an increasing number of school systems and government-funded programs become available for younger and younger children. Well-off families can usually afford private preschools, and the poor are eligible for Head Start (although not enough places are available to meet the need). Middle class families are just starting to see state aid: thirty-nine states pay for at least one kind of pre-kindergarten program, according to a 1997 report by the Families and Work Institute.

The problem, however, is that enrichment programs not only become the social norm, but then they also become required by law. When Georgia Governor Zell Miller first proposed the idea of publicly funding pre-kindergarten facilities in 1992, his plan was denied as 'state-sponsored babysitting.' Now Georgia's universal pre-kindergartens serve 61,000 children – and Miller now advocates mandatory enrollment. New York is currently funding pre-kindergarten programs, chosen mainly by lottery, and has pledged universal access by 2003. Unfortunately, no one is supporting, let alone funding, at-home mothering.

In the US nearly a quarter of families with children under three live in poverty. And the trend toward early institutionalization of children is increasing as welfare reform values mothers' joining the working poor over staying at home with their young children. With 56 percent of the mothers of children under four in the work force at least part-time in 1997, most children today have some kind of daycare or preschool experience. Burton White suggests that the pressure to fund public preschool is actually the result of the lack of quality daycare – public or private – since 'there is no mandate in the law for child care and there is a mandate for education.'[12]

Even mothers who don't need to work like the social and learning experiences a part-time preschool program provides for their child, and the free mornings can give them needed time away from children or time alone with a new baby.

Long-range studies, like the one at High Scope Educational Research Foundation in Ypsilanti, Michigan, have shown an advantage in attending play-based preschool for children from low socio-economic backgrounds. Following 123 poor black youths with low IQs from the age of three or four up through age nineteen, this study compared the group who attended the preschool program at Perry Elementary School and had home visits from trained staff, with a group who received no preschool education at all. Those who attended preschool went on to spend less time in special-education classes, have higher attendance rates, and graduate from high school in greater numbers; fewer received public assistance, were arrested, or became pregnant before age nineteen.[13]

However, 'for children from emotionally and financially stable homes, the advantages of preschool are less evident. While many experts believe that the early years are an enormously fertile time for teaching little children… some think that they learn best at their own pace at home. 'School for four-year-olds is indefensible on educational grounds,' says Burton White, author of *The First Three Years of Life.*'[14]

The experiences of life provided in a nursery or kindergarten can often be provided as well at home as in a formal program. There is no need to seek out preschool if you and your child are doing well at home; there is also no need to avoid it or feel guilty if your child is eager to play with other children and welcomes the activities a guided program can provide. This is as true for families in the UK as it is in the US.

Evaluating Early Childhood Settings

In the US and Europe there are many early childhood settings which are play-based rather than academically based. Some of the most successful of these are the Steiner/Waldorf programs. In America they are known under the term Waldorf (after the name of the first Steiner school founded in Stuttgart in 1919), whilst in Europe and many other countries the term *Steiner* is used, as in Steiner Kindergarten.. For the purposes of this discussion the term Waldorf will be used unless the broader worldwide educational movement as a whole is implied, in which case the term Steiner/Waldorf will be used.

It has now been shown that play-based programs are on the leading edge of brain development and are the best preparation for academic work when the child is ready at 6-7 years of age. This, for example, is what happened in Germany, as reported by Joan Almon, president of the Waldorf Early Childhood Association of North America:

> There is a growing body of research that supports the position of Waldorf schools that children should remain in a play-oriented preschool until the age of six. The clearest example of such research which has come to our attention is a major study undertaken in Germany comparing 100 public school classes for five-year-olds. Fifty of them had only play in their program and

the other 50 had academics and play together. The children entered first grade when they were six, and the study surveyed their progress until they were 10. The first year there was little difference to be seen. By the time the children were 10, however, those who had been allowed to play when they were five surpassed their schoolmates in every area measured. One can imagine how startling these results were to the state educators. They considered the results so conclusive that within months they had converted all of the academic programs back into play programs. They also recognized the advantage of mixed-age kindergartens in which, through play, the children help one another to grow and learn.'[15]

Wherever you live, if you find an Early Years setting in which you are interested, you need to arrange a visit to talk to the director and see what the children are doing. Talk to the director about her background, philosophy and the type of program that is offered. Meet the teachers and inquire about staff turnover. Arrange to visit and observe the surroundings and what the children are doing. Above all, make sure there is a rich oral language tradition (stories, songs, games) and that ample time is allowed for play that is self-directed and serves no other motive than the child's own.

You will also want to consider the hours of the program. If you are working full time, you will probably be looking for a full-day program. If you are able to stay home with your child, you will probably want to consider a gentle transition. For young children who are used to being at home, attending two-or three-day half-days is often the best way to start. Take your cues from your child and find a setting that balances your needs and his.

These are some things to consider when choosing daycare, pre-school nursery or kindergarten for your child.

- Is there a rhythm to the day, providing a structure within which there is time for large movement as well as guided activities?
- Is there an appreciation of the importance of imaginative play, and toys to support it?
- Do the children play outside every day? What equipment is available?

- What is the teacher's background, training, philosophy, experience in teaching and/or in mothering?
- What does the teacher hope the children will learn? Early reading, deskwork, and workbooks don't match the young child's needs.
- Are there artistic activities – painting, colouring, crafts?
- What role does music play in the program? Is it all from tapes and records, or are there singing and movement games?
- Do the children watch television or play with computers? High tech is best avoided with young children.
- How many children are there? How many teachers? Does it feel calm or hectic?
- What is the environment like? Is it safe? Is it beautiful? Warm?
- Does the teacher love the children?

Steiner/Waldorf Early Childhood Settings

Steiner/Waldorf early childhood settings provide a nurturing environment based on an understanding of the young child's special developmental needs before the age of seven. Sometimes they have separate nursery and kindergarten classes, but more often there are mixed-age kindergartens with children from three to six years old in one group. The Steiner/Waldorf program is modeled after a good home environment. The mixed-age kindergarten has the advantage of being even more like a large family; the older children provide a model for the younger ones and help them, while the little ones bring a softer element to the five- and six-year-olds. And as they stay in the kindergarten for two or three years, those who were younger get to experience being the bigger children for the new ones.

Over the last twenty years, interest in Steiner/Waldorf education in North America, Europe and other countries around the world has exploded, with many new preschools and kindergartens being founded each year. Since the pressures of today's world often make it impossible for a child to stay at home, such nursery schools are a necessity. Often they have the added task of healing the effects on the young child of our increasingly technologically geared world. Many early childhood programs are associated with existing Steiner/Waldorf schools, while others are separate early childhood centers that later may grow into schools. An increasing number of schools and centers are also offering parent-child groups and day care. Steiner/Waldorf Organisations and websites with information about Early Childhood settings and schools are listed at the end of the chapter.

Steiner/Waldorf early years settings are run in a similar way all over the world and embrace many different cultures and religious beliefs. Therefore the description which follows of a 'typical day' in a US Waldorf early childhood program can serve as a more detailed guide of what you can generally expect to find in any country. What follows may also be a useful guide for what to look for, even if there is not a Steiner/Waldorf early years setting in your area. The understanding of the young child and the activities suggested by this education can be incorporated into home life or into existing day care or preschool programs. Or, a reader may become so inspired that he or she will want to find out more about trainings to become a Steiner/Waldorf early childhood teacher.

The Activities

Let's take a look at a child's day as it might occur in a US Waldorf kindergarten setting for three to six-year-olds, remembering that Steiner/Waldorf early years settings all over the world will have many similarities. A morning typically consists of creative play, an artistic activity, a story, singing games and finger plays, snack and outside play.

Creative Play:
As the children arrive, they hang up their sweaters, say hello to the teacher, and happily become engrossed in their favorite play. We might see several boys and girls in the home area, cooking and playing with the dolls. Nearby, three children are moving blanket stands to make a house covered with a sheet. Another child has put on kitty ears and is mewing at their door. Another boy arrives, puts on a cape, and crawls under the table with two standup dolls. Two other boys have taken their backpacks off the hook and are being scuba divers. One child sits next to the teacher, who is cutting fruit for snacks, and helps her. As more children arrive, the room

becomes filled with the sounds of their play. Two children have become engrossed at the workbench. Now several children are sliding down and jumping off the wooden indoor slide. Two children have put embroidery hoops over their heads for dog collars and tied on yarn to be taken for a walk by their owner. The transformations are endless as the children's play unfolds over forty-five minutes to an hour.

The room could seem chaotic to a casual observer as the children experience the world through their inner-directed play. The teacher and her assistant watch attentively and help as needed by tying on a costume or helping two children take turns with a contested object. They are happy to be brought things as part of the children's imaginative play and will interact with them, but they don't get down and play with the children or interrupt them except as necessary for safety or to resolve conflicts that the children don't work out themselves. The teacher remains aware of everyone in the room while she is busy preparing the snack or sewing a new toy for the children. In this way the children not only see a model of creative work, but her activity can also be transformed by them in their play.

Story Time:

A song tells the children it is time to put all the toys away, and the little gnome comes out of his house to see what good workers they are. When everything is in its place, another song brings the children to morning circle.

Through verse and song the children greet one another and the day and then listen attentively as the teacher begins to tell a story. She has already been telling the same fairy tale for a week and a half, and some of the children join in with the hand movements it contains.

Snack Time:

After story it is time to wash hands and set the table for snack. The children eagerly help to put around the napkins and placemats. Today there is fruit salad, which the teacher and her helpers have been making during free play. Another day there might be hot cereal, wholegrain crackers, or bread the children have baked. The children sing a song of thanks for the food, and then talk with one another while they eat. When they are finished, they sing, 'Red Bird,

Red Bird, who will you choose today?' and eagerly wait for the red felt bird suspended from a stick to visit the nests they make with their hands and to nibble at the crumbs. He chooses a lucky child at each table to blow out the candle and then dismisses the children one by one to go and play.

Artistic Activity:
After the tables are wiped, preparation is made for the day's activity. With this group, Monday is painting day, Tuesday is beeswax, Wednesday is baking, Thursday is crafts, and Friday is colouring. Today is crafts, and the teacher brings out pine cones and feathers to make birds. Several of the children immediately come over and watch her place small pieces of beeswax in the sides and stick feathers into it for wings. Another piece of beeswax forms the beak. The children quickly copy. Then the teacher helps them tie on a piece of string so they can fly the birds around. While they are working, the teacher sings a song about a little bird.

The children who are finished fly their birds and some start to play being birds. Other children want their turn, and finally the teacher calls over the last two little boys, who are engrossed in their play, by asking what colour feathers they like for their birds.

The project materials are put away, and when it is time for games, the birds all fly to their 'nests' in the children's backpacks.

Movement Circle:
The teacher now begins to sing, 'Sally Go Round the Sun' while she takes two children's hands. Soon a circle has been formed, and the children play circle games interspersed with fingerplays and verses with accompanying movements. The circle varies in tempo and loudness, with active games alternating with slow movements or fingerplays. Movement circle ends with a goodbye song, and the children get ready to go outside.

Outside Play:
The children play outside for about half an hour and are picked up by their parents at noon. They play on the swings, slide, and climbing dome. There is also a sandbox and a large horse made out of logs and branches. The children's play area is like a garden and

feels enclosed by foliage. Sometimes the children go for a walk with their teacher to the park or the woods during outside time.

Within the rhythm of the day, which holds the children, the specific activities and stories change according to the seasons of the year. This includes collecting things for the seasonal table, baking seasonal foods, making things for the festivals, and outdoor activities such as making leaf crowns or planting spring bulbs. Much of the teacher's preparation relates to the rhythm of the year and the children's experience of it. This is reflected in the daily activities, the changing decorations in the room, and the special events she plans – such as a field trip to pick apples in the autumn, an Advent garden in December, or a trip to see newborn lambs in spring.

With a mixed-age group, activities take place on many levels simultaneously, as with a craft project in which the older children can do all of it themselves while the younger ones require help from the teacher. Stories from various levels are told with mixed-age classes. Kindergartners love hearing again the story of 'The Three Little Pigs' while younger children will be carried along by the group when a story for older children is being told.

Direct intellectual teaching does not take place in a Steiner/Waldorf nursery or kindergarten. There are no exercises in reading readiness or doing pages from math workbooks. Nor are shapes and weights manipulated to learn concepts such as 'triangle' or 'heavy and light.' The child is allowed to take in the world through his senses and to participate in it through movement, making things, and play. It is recognized that one of the tasks of early childhood is the healthy mastering of body skills; fingerplays and movement games help to develop coordination and contribute to the formation of speech. They also can form the basis for later mathematical learning by matching rhythmical counting with body movements, forming a valuable foundation in the body for number and rhythm. Similarly, the transformation of one object into another in creative play provides a concrete basis for the more abstract manipulation of symbols involved in reading. Developmental steps are not skipped or hurried. Rather, there is a confidence in the unfolding of the young child according to the patterns of nature and the stamp of the child's own individuality.

Many times children who can already write the alphabet, or even read, enter a Steiner/Waldorf early childhood program. However, the children are not provided time to practice such skills. Because their days are so full of creative play, stories, puppet shows, crafts, and artistic activity, they are fully engaged and often do not even notice that they aren't reading or doing mathematics in kindergarten. And the rich experience they receive can serve as a balancing force for the early intellectual development they have experienced.

The Setting

Because the environment is so important for the young child, a great deal of care is put into creating a room that is nourishing and inviting to the children. When it is possible to build according to Steiner's indications for architecture, the buildings produced really feel as if they embrace and surround the children with their curves, cubby holes, and play areas. However, since it is usually necessary to adapt an existing building for a kindergarten, lights and right angles are often softened by hanging coloured cotton gauze or silk in the corners and in front of light fixtures. I once used a parachute to cover a ceiling in a public school building and create a feeling of clouds instead of steel beams and reinforced concrete. Smaller activity areas can also be created with wood and cloth.

Many Steiner/Waldorf kindergartens are painted a light rose colour that Steiner called 'peach blossom.' It is a colour that reflects the lightness of young children, who have not yet fully arrived on earth. A special way of painting called lazuring uses washes of various colours on a wall to give an impression of depth on a flat surface. Through this technique, murals or images can be painted to suggest forms in a very soft, beautiful way.

The room is decorated with seasonal motifs, such as a nature table, tissue paper pictures on the windows, and decorated branches. The attention to detail and beauty will be reflected in the mood of the children and the quality of their play.

The toys are made from natural materials and are arranged in activity areas or little scenes that invite imaginative interaction.

The Role of the Teacher

Steiner/Waldorf nurseries and kindergartens often appear deceptively simple. Everything flows so easily and looks so effortless. The tremendous amount of work by the teacher is mostly invisible, except as it is felt by those who know children and who can sense the mood the teacher creates. Someone from another preschool program visited our preschool home and was surprised by how peaceful it was with twelve children in such a small space. She said to her assistant, 'Can you imagine Jane [one of their teachers] here? It just wouldn't be the same.' The being of the teacher and the physical and emotional environment she or he creates are what really nourish the children.

Because the teacher is constantly an example for the children, she pays special attention to the quality of her movements and the tone of her voice. She does many things with the children, such as preparing the snack, telling a story, or leading the circle games. But she also does a great deal just by her being, by who she is. She tries to put aside her own problems and emotional upsets so that she is as clear as possible when she is with the children. She needs to get enough sleep and to have her own meditative practices to remain centered in the classroom and to keep the rest of her life in order. Her role with the children is similar to a meditative state of awareness: she is aware of everything, totally in the present moment, not thinking about other things – just there with and for the children. Being with young children often involves more being than doing. It's hard to make everything simple enough. We tend to think that we have to stimulate and provide things for the children, when our more difficult task is to provide them with the space to be themselves, to experience and grow and try on the world and its activities within the guidance and protection provided by the adults.

The teacher's attitude of warmth and love provides a calm and healthy atmosphere for the young child. Steiner describes it as follows:

> The joy of the child in and with his environment must be reckoned among the forces that build and mould the physical organs. He needs people around him with happy looks and

manners and, above all, with an honest, unaffected love. A love which fills the physical environment of the child with warmth may literally be said to 'hatch out' the forms of the physical organs. The child who lives in such an atmosphere of love and warmth and who has around him really good examples for his imitation is living in his right element. One should therefore strictly guard against anything being done in the child's presence that he must not imitate.[16]

Because the young child is an imitative being, the teacher simply begins each activity, and the children follow along. She doesn't announce, 'Now it's story time,' or 'Let's take hands for circle games.' Instead, she simply takes two children's hands and starts singing and moving with the intention that everyone will join in, and they do. Story time may begin with the same song every day, or the teacher may light a candle or put on a special storytelling hat and play a few notes on the kinderharp; whatever she has chosen, the children soon learn what will follow.

During the children's free play, the teacher can provide an example of work from real life – sawing wood, gardening during outside play, making something for the preschool. The children can often help with the activity itself, like cutting fruit for snacks or winding yarn. The activity will also appear transformed in their play. For example, if the teacher is sewing, a few children will want to get out their sewing basket, while another might go off and pretend to sew something with her fingers.

The warmth and love of the teacher for the children involves really taking on their care as a trust, in conjunction with the parents. Thus the teacher needs as complete a picture as possible of each child before accepting him or her into the program. She will observe the child if possible and have an in-depth interview with the parents – how was her birth; how did she develop; what does she like to play; are their any health problems; has she been in other daycare or preschool programs; what are the parents' expectations? The teacher needs to feel that she can really take on this child, and that she can work together with the parents for the child's growth and well-being. The parents also need to evaluate the teacher and the program and make sure that this is where they want their child to be.

Once a child has been accepted, the teacher tries to visit the family at home to get a picture of the child in his own surroundings, to meet any brothers and sisters or pets, and to see the child's room. In addition to helping the teacher better understand the context in which the child lives, such a visit provides a wonderful link for the child between home and school, a sense of interpenetration of the two worlds that is very supportive.

The teacher's work does not stop when the children go home. There is not only cleaning up and preparing for the next day's activities, but there is also work with the parents through parent evenings, conferences, toymaking workshops, and so forth. At night the teacher visualizes each child and takes the image into her sleep. This practice not only supports the child and his connection with the teacher, but can provide the teacher with inspiration if a child is having particular difficulties.

The Training of a Steiner/ Waldorf Early Childhood Teacher

The attitude of the teacher and the understanding gained by working out of the indications that Rudolf Steiner gave about the developing human being are the most important elements of a Steiner/Waldorf preschool. Simply having dolls without faces or block-shaped crayons does not make a Steiner/Waldorf program! The activities suggested in this book are appropriate for all children and really fit the young child. They can be incorporated into home life and into existing daycare and preschool programs with very positive results. But one needs to distinguish between 'a bit of this and a bit of that' and a full Steiner/Waldorf program. For such a program, trained Steiner/Waldorf teachers are the essential element; addresses of training programs are listed in Appendix D.

However, it is often impossible for someone with a spouse and small children to move near a training center for one or two years. It is sometimes possible to do home study while apprenticing as an assistant in an existing Steiner/Waldorf school, and there are programs that meet over three or four summer sessions. There are also several short courses and workshops available for parents, daycare providers, and new teachers; they are listed in Appendix E.

Steiner/Waldorf Early Childhood Education in the Home

Many mothers who are trying to incorporate these ideas and recommendations about young children into their home life find themselves wanting to start parent and child groups with other parents who share the same interests and ideals. If there is a group of interested mothers, you can take turns being with the children while the other mothers discuss questions they are having about their children and share resources. It is also possible to share craft and festival ideas and to select a book for study and discussion. Several recommended titles are listed at the end of this chapter. If you find yourself alone in working with these ideas, you will need to keep studying and find support through networking while you are looking for more like-minded people. The book called *The Parent and Child Group Handbook – A Steiner/Waldorf Approach* may be a helpful resource.

In many places in the US, Waldorf early childhood teachers have founded what could be called Waldorf preschool homes, in which a full Waldorf program is offered to a small group of children in teachers' homes. Many times such programs have grown up around an existing Waldorf school, forming a network of preschool homes that provide support for parents who are interested in Waldorf education.

Our experience has been that children in these programs have the best of both worlds – a full Waldorf early childhood program in a home environment with from six to twelve children. It is a very gentle first introduction to 'school' for the young child. It is also ideal for the teachers, both financially and in terms of the minimal amount of administrative work required.

In our community, mothers who have been associated with the school for several years began to offer Waldorf-oriented daycare in their homes, and this is also happening in many other communities. The need for quality daycare still far exceeds the supply and there remains much room for growth in this area.

Many women start taking this approach to early childhood with a group of children in their home, because they want this kind of experience for their own children. When there is no Waldorf School in your area, such a group can also evolve into a 'Saturday Club,' which provides some of the enriching activities of Waldorf education for older children who are in other schools or who are being taught at home.

In the UK there are an increasing number of child-minders who are working with the Steiner/Waldorf approach and occasional examples of child-minder practises, with two trained adults taking six children at one time using the home-based Steiner/Waldorf kindergarten model. The 'Saturday Club' idea for older children, however, has been adopted in some Steiner/Waldorf initiatives in the UK.

Steiner/Waldorf education was started for the children of the workers in a factory in Stuttgart in 1919; it embraces children of all economic and intellectual levels and welcomes children from all cultural backgrounds. The principles of Steiner/Waldorf education are not elitist and reserved for the relatively small number of children who live near Waldorf schools. Its principles are universal and can be applied to all children. In many states in the US Waldorf-oriented charter schools are arising, and many parents are using a Waldorf approach to home schooling. At the Rudolf Steiner College in California and Sunbridge College in New York, there are also summer courses for public school teachers who want to re-enliven their teaching within the public school system.

In our highly technological western world, the view of child development and the principles of education initiated by Rudolf Steiner (and further developed by thousands of Steiner/Waldorf teachers over the past eighty-plus years) need to become known to more and more parents for the healthy development of young children. The quality of life in the home and the preschool environment is perhaps more important than what kind of school the child attends.

When Is Your Child Ready for School?

Due to the downward shift of the curriculum over the past thirty years, it is even more important that children today be developmentally ready for school as well as chronologically ready.

The developmental age of a child can be six months to a year or more away from his or her chronological age. Developmental age is measured by how closely the child's social, emotional, physical, and perceptual maturity corresponds to the norm for his age. Just as babies crawl, teethe, walk, and become toilet-trained at different ages, older children too remain on their own individual timetables. There is not necessarily any correlation between developmental age and intelligence; a child with a high IQ can be developmentally delayed.[17]

Although it is the studies and research from the US which are described here, the findings are relevant and pertinent to the UK, where children start formal learning a year earlier than in the US.

For example, in 'Pupil Age at School Entrance – How Many Are Ready for Success?' James Uphoff and June Gilmore report marked differences in school performance and emotional adjustment between children with summer and autumn birthdays, who were less than five years and three months of age when they entered kindergarten, and those children with summer birthdays who were given an extra growth year and were as much as six years and three months when they entered kindergarten.

Uphoff and Gilmore summarize their research as follows:

1. The chronologically older children in a class tend to receive many more above-average grades from teachers than do younger children in that class.
2. Older children also are much more likely to score in the above-average range on standardized achievement tests.
3. The younger children in a class are far more likely to fail at least one grade than are older children.
4. The younger children in a class are far more likely to be referred by teachers for learning disabilities testing and subsequently be diagnosed as being learning disabled than are older students in a class.
5. The academic problems of younger children who were developmentally unready at school entrance often last throughout their school careers and sometimes even into adulthood.[18]

The Gesell Institute of Human Development in New Haven, Connecticut, is a leading advocate of slowing down the accelerated pace of childhood. Their studies found that only about one-third of the children they tested between the ages of 5 and 8 years old were ready for the class in which their age had placed them. The readiness of another third was questionable, and the final third definitely were not ready. Their recent studies compiled from school districts across the country indicate that as many as 50 percent of students with school problems today have them because of overplacement.[19]

Regardless of a school system's cut-off dates, parents together with teachers must decide if an individual child is really ready for formal school learning. Giving a child who has a summer or autumn birthday an extra growth year can be a lifelong gift that may put him at the head of the class instead of scrabbling to keep up intellectually or socially. This is true for children in the UK as well as the US. If a child is kept out of school an extra year, in no way should the parents regard the child as a failure or learning disabled. Remember that developmental maturity has no correlation with IQ. If the parents feel positive about the change and take responsibility themselves, the child can adapt well and the change can have positive benefits. Parents sometimes find it hard to explain to grandparents why they are keeping their child out of formal schooling for a year, but the advantages for the child are worth the effort if you are feeling pressured to keep your child going through the system when he is showing signs of not being ready.

What Happens Around Age Seven?

Between five and seven you will see many dramatic changes in your child. In terms of the development of memory, your child may say something like, 'I can see grandma anytime I want to now,' referring to an emerging ability to call on mental images at will. He may also tell you more of his dreams.

You will see a kind of logic appearing in speech that represents a new level of thinking and is expressed in words like *because, so, if,* and *therefore.* This new ability is expressed in creative play by the love of tying things together with string, like linking one thing to the next with logic. A growing grasp of, and interest in, time will also be apparent.

In play you may also see intention manifested as things are built for other things, as with a sand structure now being built as a garage for a car rather than for the activity itself. An authoritative element enters into group play at this age, with a child sometimes directing and sometimes being told who or what he will be.

In the sphere of drawing, the individualizing element expresses itself in the use of the diagonal line: triangular designs, a ladder leaning against a tree, the stair going up inside the house, or the appearance of the arching rainbow.

Physically you will first see the differentiation of the chest or 'middle sphere' around age five – the child suddenly loses its round 'Buddha belly' and acquires a waist and a neck, showing how the life forces have completed their work in the rhythmic system. As the shift of the growth forces is made to the limbs, the arms will lengthen during this time. This is why an older child will be able to reach directly over his head and touch his ear, while a younger or less-developed one will not. Finally the growth shifts into the legs, and the child will also often start to eat more and will sometimes increase his awareness of digestion (expressed in the frequent stomach aches of some children at this age). At the same time the growth forces are moving into the legs, the features of the face become more individualized and the milk teeth begin to loosen.

In the area of brain development, the changes are so great that Healy says this time is commonly termed the 'five to seven year shift.' She explains, 'From ages five to seven or eight the brain is in one of its most dynamic states of change as it practices combining sensory patterns from different modalities. Maturation of a small part of the parietal lobe, at the junction where all the senses come together, is one development that makes many kinds of new learning possible, but there is enormous variability in the age when it occurs… Only now does it make sense to ask a youngster to look at a series of written letters and 'sound out' a word, to coordinate motor programs and visual skills such as in catching or kicking a ball, or later, reading music while playing an instrument.'[20]

The child starts to have real friendships and likes to make and give surprises. He likes to play with words and create rhymes, to play riddle and guessing games, to whisper and to giggle. Meyerkort says, 'He feels the future dawning, the new stage coming; he says, "I hope…"'[21]

All of the changes discussed here should be allowed to become consolidated in a play-oriented early childhood setting before the child is called upon to exercise the new faculties that are used in formal learning.

Steiner explains the changes around the age of seven as resulting from the life forces completing their work of individualizing the child's physical body: first the head between birth and age three, then the middle sphere between ages three and five, and finally the limbs and hard, bony teeth. Once finished, the forces are freed for development of the memory and school work. According to Steiner, the way to teach the child between the change of teeth and puberty is with images and pictures, through which the child is allowed to take guidance from the inner meaning she discovers for herself in the pictures and allegories. What the child sees and perceives with the eye of the mind is a more appropriate means of education than abstract conceptions.

It is upon this ground of imagination that the later powers of intellect, judgment, and critical thinking will be based. Therefore, all of the subjects – from reading to mathematics to physics – are taught in an imaginative and artistic way in Steiner/Waldorf schools, providing a rich and nourishing foundation for the faculty of analytical thinking that arises and can be developed in puberty.

Beginning Academic Work: The Steiner/Waldorf Approach

In Steiner/Waldorf schools, reading, writing, and maths are started when the child is 6-7 years old. By starting academic tasks when they are developmentally more mature, such children do not fall behind peers who start earlier in other school systems. In fact, there are definite advantages in delaying instruction in the Three R's until around the age of seven.

Writing is taught in the first year of a Steiner/Waldorf school through stories and pictures, and then the children learn to read from what they have written themselves. Just as humanity first wrote through picture glyphs before developing the alphabet, so the young child develops the forms and the sounds of the letters through stories and pictures provided by the teacher. In this way the letters and their sounds 'live within the child' as vibrant pictures. One morning when she was in her first year of school, my daughter said, 'I dreamed about the letter A. There were all these A's...' The children progress to writing from verses that they know and then 'reading' from what they have written themselves. Thus the more abstract work of reading begins toward the end of first year, and the transition to printed books is generally not made until the second year.

Some people have the mistaken idea that there are no books in a Steiner/Waldorf school. This is far from true! In the first year of school children learn to read from what they have written themselves, books with real literary content are introduced from second year on, and children are never given anything that is condescending in tone or that has been predigested especially for children. Real literature is always used in the classroom, selected according to reading level and inner maturity level of the children. Steiner/Waldorf schools have libraries for children's reading pleasure and for doing research in the upper classes.

Although reading is taught more slowly in the Steiner/Waldorf curriculum, maths is not. Nothing is done until the first year of school, but then all four processes – addition, subtraction, multiplication, and division – are introduced. This is possible because the concepts are introduced imaginatively. For example, there might be a story about four gnome brothers: Mr. Plus is fat and jolly with stuffed pockets; Mr. Minus is thin and sad, and all of his jewels keep falling out of a hole in his sack, and so forth. The children work from the whole to the part, first using chestnuts or shells to see that 8 is 1 plus 7; 8 is 2 plus 6; and so on. They also walk various rhythms and verses that help to make the multiplication tables much easier to learn. When mathematics is made concrete and imaginative, children take to it with delight.

A complete listing of the Waldorf curriculum for grades 1-8 can be found in Appendix B.

What About the Advanced or Gifted Child?

Waiting until a child is 6/7 years old before starting academic work has obvious advantages for an average or slow child, who needs the extra neurophysiological maturity before beginning tasks such as reading and mathematics. However, what about the bright child, who wants to start writing letters or learning to read at age three or four, or certainly the age of 5? As children become more aware of the world around them, they want to imitate and learn, and many children will show interest in these activities by age five. Reading and writing are the way of the future for children, so you want to share their enthusiasm and eagerness, but it doesn't mean that it's time to start doing worksheets. Often teaching them to print their name will satisfy them for quite a while. You can also share their enthusiasm and say, 'You will learn more about how to do that when you are in first grade!' But it is still too soon to exercise the memory or the intellect directly with lessons. There is no critical window when you have to teach a child to read or risk his not being interested later on. On the contrary, telling a child, 'That's what you'll learn when you go to the big school,' develops eagerness and anticipation, and keeps the young child learning through imitation rather than through direct lessons.

By not being taught to read before the age of 6-7 years old, children miss several years of early readers (which isn't missing much), and they are given the gift of the final year or more of early childhood. Direct cognitive work wakes the child up and brings her out of the magical world of early childhood. Children grow out of these years soon enough on their own. Allowing your child to stay in the magical realm of early childhood without pushing cognitive development provides a sound basis for later health and creativity.

Especially with bright children, it is important to emphasize balance. It is possible to teach them intellectual skills at a young age and to put them into academically advanced programs from preschool or kindergarten on. But the result is often the production of a 'forty-year-old' in a five-year-old body. Advanced intellectual development in childhood is usually at the expense of the artistic/emotional sphere or the healthy development of the body. School education should appeal so much to the child's imagination that the gifted child still feels fully interested and engaged. If that kind of creative education isn't available for the very bright child, you may face some hard choices.

You will need to investigate educational approaches and make your own decisions for your child. I felt it was important to work toward a balanced development of the heart forces, the head forces, and the body/will forces, so that a whole human being would emerge who would be able to lead a fruitful life and act in service to humanity. The danger in education that emphasizes only intellectual development is in turning out thinkers and scientists who are emotionally divorced from humanity and from the consequences of their work for the world. For this reason, I chose for my children an approach to education that emphasized balance, rather than a program designed specifically for gifted children.

Many parents are turning to home schooling as a viable alternative, or some combination of school and enrichment at home. Making decisions about your child's education is an ongoing adventure, but one that is worth the effort.

Recommended Reading

Brain Development and Academics

Endangered Minds – Why Children Don't Think and What We Can Do About It by Jane M. Healy, Ph.D. (Simon & Schuster).
Failure to Connect: How Computers Affect Our Children's Minds – for Better and Worse by Jane M. Healy, Ph.D. (Simon & Schuster).
The Hurried Child by David Elkind (Knopf).
Miseducation: Preschoolers at Risk by David Elkind (Knopf).
Set Free Childhood by Martin Large (Hawthorn Press).
Your Child's Growing Mind – A Practical Guide to Brain Development and Learning from Birth to Adolescence by Jane M. Healy, Ph.D. (Doubleday).

School Readiness

Better Late Than Early by Raymond and Dorothy Moore (Reader's Digest Press).

The Hurried Child by David Elkind (Knopf).

Miseducation by David Elkind (Knopf).

'Pupil Age at School Entrance – How Many Are Ready for Success?' by James K. Uphoff and June Gilmore. Authorized copies are available from the Waldorf Early Childhood Association, 285 Hungry Hollow Rd., Spring Valley, NY 10977.

Ready to Learn by Martyn Rawson and Michael Rose (Hawthorn Press).

School Can Wait by Raymond and Dorothy Moore (Brigham Young University Press).

US Videos on Steiner/Waldorf Education

(There is nothing like seeing Waldorf principles in action, in a variety of settings. And what a bargain – all are sold for $20-$40 by the Rudolf Steiner College Book Store!)

Reviving the Art of Education (20 minutes)

Taking a Risk in Education – Waldorf Inspired Public Schools (48 minutes)

Urban Waldorf – A Day in the Life of a Milwaukee Public School (20 minutes)

Waldorf Education – A Vision of Wholeness (16 minutes)

The Waldorf Promise (53 minutes)

Videos available in the UK from the Steiner Waldorf Schools Fellowship. Kidbrooke Park, Forest Row, East Sussex RH18 5JB
Tel no. 01342 822115   www.steinerwaldorf.org.uk. Email: mail@swsf.org.uk

Awakening to Tomorrow – A film about Waldorf Education following five Waldorf pupils from around the world.

Time to Learn – classic documentary by leading film maker Jonathan Stedall. 110 mins.

Journals on Waldorf Education

Gateways, Newsletter of the Waldorf Early Childhood Association of North America, 285 Hungry Hollow Rd., Spring Valley, NY 10977; published twice a year.

Kindling – The Journal for Steiner Waldorf Early Childhood Care and Education, 3 Church Lane, Balsham, Cambridge, UK
Tel No. 01223 890988

The Peridot, PO Box 97, Gainesville, FL 32602; Waldorf-oriented newsletter.

Renewal, A Journal of Waldorf Education from the Association of Waldorf Schools of North America, 3911 Bannister Rd., Fair Oaks, CA 95628; published twice a year.

Steiner Education, semiannual journal. Inquire from The Secretary, Steiner Education, The Spring, Ashdown Road, Forest Row, East Sussex RH18 5BN, England; can be paid for in US dollars.

Books for Beginning Study Groups

Beyond the Rainbow Bridge by Barbara Patterson and Pamela Bradley (Michaelmas Press). Discusses nurturing our children from birth to age seven, creating balance in family life, and how Waldorf education supports the development of the whole child.

Lifeways by Gudrun Davy and Bons Voors (Hawthorn Press). Chapters deal with issues of family life. Excellent for a mothers' group.

Waldorf Education – A Family Guide by Pamela Fenner and Karen Rivers (Michaelmas Press). Deepens understanding and enriches family life.

Waldorf Parenting Handbook by Lois Cusick (Rudolf Steiner College). An introduction to some of the ideas behind Waldorf education from birth through high school.

Waldorf Schools – Volume I, Kindergarten and the Early Grades. Thirty-three articles are compiled and edited by Ruth Pusch (Mercury Press).

You Are Your Child's First Teacher. Share it with friends!

Books on the Steiner/Waldorf Parent and Child Groups and Preschool

Collected articles from the Waldorf Kindergarten Newsletter: Vol. I: *An Overview of the Waldorf Kindergarten* and Vol. II: *A Deeper Understanding of the Waldorf Kindergarten* (Waldorf Early Childhood Association).

Early Childhood Education and the Waldorf School Plan by Elizabeth Grunelius (Rudolf Steiner College).

Free to Learn – Introducing Steiner Waldorf early childhood education by Lynne Oldfield (Hawthorn Press).

Nurturing Children and Families: One Model of a Parent/Child Program in a Waldorf School by Sarah Baldwin (Waldorf Early Childhood Association of North America)

The Parent and Child Group Handbook – A Steiner/Waldorf Approach by Dot Male (Hawthorn Press)

Work and Play in Early Childhood by Freya Jaffke (Anthroposophic Press).

Steiner/Waldorf School Education

Education Towards Freedom by Frans Carlgren (Lanthorn Press/ through Anthroposophic Press).

Kindergarten Education by Betty Peck (Hawthorn Press).

Kingdom of Childhood by Rudolf Steiner (Anthroposophic Press).

More Lifeways edited by Patti Smith and Signe Eklund Schaefer (Hawthorn Press).

School as a Journey by Torin Finser (Anthroposophic Press).

Waldorf Education – A Family Guide by Pamela Fenner and Karen Rivers, Eds. (Michaelmas Press).

Resources for Steiner/Waldorf Home Schooling

Live Education! offers a Waldorf curriculum and advising for grades K-8, PO Box 306, Aptos, CA 95001. (408/457-4243); www.live-education.com.

Rudolf Steiner Library, 65 Fern Hill Rd., Ghent, NY 12075; offers extensive lending services.

Parents may attend summer programs on teaching in the grades that are offered by: The Waldorf Institute, 260 Hungry Hollow Rd., Spring Valley, NY 10977; Rudolf Steiner College, 9200 Fair Oaks Blvd., Fair Oaks, CA 95628; Rudolf Steiner Institute, PO Box 207, Kensington, MD 20895; and Gradalis Seminars, PO Box 1095, Boulder, CO 80306.

'Waldorf Methods and Home Schooling' – annual conference offered by Informed Birth & Parenting, PO Box 1733, Fair Oaks, CA 95628. (916/961-6923).

Waldorf Without Walls, quarterly journal for home schoolers, from Barbara Dewey, 89900 Mill Hill Rd., Bowerston, OH 44695. www.waldorfwithoutwalls.com

W.I.S.H. – newsletter for Waldorf Inspired Students at Home, P.O. Box 1034, Bellevue, WA 98009.

www.waldorfhomeschoolers.com

CHAPTER 13

More Parenting Issues

When I speak with parents , similar issues come up again and again as parents consider the approach to the young child suggested in this book. By sharing some of these questions and the reasoning behind my answers, I hope this chapter will spark your own questions and your search for the answers that are most nurturing to you and your family.

> Even if I wanted to provide an idyllic world for my young child, I don't think I could do it. Modern life is just too fast-paced and stressful. Children need to adjust to the realities of today's world.

The best way to prepare your children for the stresses of today's world is not to expose them to problems early in their life, but to provide them with an environment that is warm and nurturing and that shelters them when they are young from as many of the problems of the adult world as possible. Child psychologist David Elkind has discussed at length the difficulties children encounter when they are hurried to grow up and face adult choices too soon, or when they are subjected to miseducation in academic subjects, swimming, gymnastics, ballet, and so forth.[1]

The rushed lives that most of us live make it difficult to provide children with an ideal world for their early childhood years. We tend to move frequently or travel a lot, to work full time or part time, to be 'too busy' for the tempo of our children. Divorce, single parenting, and blended families add to the stresses of a child. And, with the best intentions, many parents push their children to achieve at an early age or to be grown-up emotional companions for them.

Yet there is a great deal parents can do for their children by providing an environment filled with love and warmth. By understanding a young child's development and his complete openness to his surroundings, we can do our best to provide a stable and nurturing environment within our current living situation. Children are, fortunately, very giving and forgiving – and fairly resilient.

Now that we have recognized some of the ways in which children differ from adults, how can we let them be children in a world in which changing family, social, and academic pressures make them deal with the adult world earlier than ever before? Most of us can't radically change our life situations, even if we wanted to. For the most part we are members of our highly technological, urban, material-minded society. Yet no matter where we find ourselves, ways to meet the real needs of the young child have been suggested in this book. In summary:

- Attend to your own life and emotions. The emotional environment you create for your child is far more important than the material environment.
- Honor the spiritual element in life, especially as it is brought to you by your children.
- Work toward rhythm in family life that can support you and your children.
- Remember that imitation and repetition are the keys to discipline with the young child, not reasoning or punishment.
- Set limits and consistently enforce them; accept that you are the parent.
- Allow plenty of time for your child's creative free play as well as musical and artistic play. Include time for just being home and 'doing nothing.'
- Buy or make childlike toys, ones that encourage imaginative play.
- Avoid pressuring your child to be an early achiever in academics, sports, or the arts.

- Continue to pay attention to what your child experiences, limiting overstimulation from loud music, films, and television.
- Avoid concerning your child with adult problems through news broadcasts, conversations, and so forth. Even eight and nine year olds don't yet need to be taught about AIDS or substance abuse, as they have no way of comprehending such things!

Your description of a play-oriented kindergarten leaves me wondering whether it really prepares children for the high-tech world in which we live. What about computer literacy? I want my child to have a competitive edge, not be behind the times.

Every parent should read Jane Healy's extensively researched book *Failure to Connect: How Computers Affect Our Children's Minds – for Better and Worse*. She reviews all the studies to date about what is and isn't working with educational software, both at home and in the schools. She provides recommendations for evaluating games and educational programs before purchasing them and gives vital guidelines for parents in starting and guiding their child's computer use at home. She also shares her understanding, as a learning specialist and developmental neuropsychologist, of the effects that video games and extensive computer use may be having in actually changing children's 'wiring' through hours of rapidly changing visual images. And she makes recommendations for protecting children's health, pointing out that if employers let people use computers under the conditions found in most schools in the US, they would be investigated by OSHA (Occupational Safety and Health Administration). In fact, the American Academy of Pediatrics has recently expressed concern about how much time children spend in front of various types of screens, and recommends that a 'media history,' including amount and type of computer, television, and video use, be taken by physicians as a routine part of a child's media record for diagnosis of media-related problems – physical, academic, and emotional.[2]

Precisely because computers are changing our world so rapidly, what children will need most in the future is the ability to think creatively. Most of the jobs that your children will be entering don't even exist today! The qualities that children will need as 'skills for the future' are not technical skills, but mental habits like analytic thinking and problem-solving, communication abilities, imagination, values, persistence, creativity, kindness, and tolerance. Todd Oppenheimer (investigative journalist) reported in the renowned US literary cultural magazine *Atlantic Monthly* in an article called 'The Computer Delusion,' that even high-tech corporations who are seeking creative employees rarely hire people who are primarily computer experts. Rather, they look for innovation, teamwork, flexibility, and innovative thinking, qualities they often find lacking in many 'technology nerds.'[3]

As with other forms of instruction, there is no demonstrated advantage for a child starting to use computers in preschool over a child who begins at age twelve or fourteen. Computers, as word processors and vehicles for logical thinking through programming, are suited to the realm of the adolescent, not the preschool-age child! Computers as toys are inappropriate, because they present a two-dimensional abstraction of the world to the young child, who should be moving and playing and acquiring a broad base of experiences of the physical world and the world of imaginative play. The visual image on the computer screen is especially hard on the developing eyes of the young child.

Because children's senses and brains are developing throughout childhood, Healy states that 'Age-appropriate computer use may help establish some forms of connections, but inappropriate use may also build resistant habits that interfere with academic learning. Once set into the brain's connectivity, such patterns are hard to break.'[4] Parents, like educators in the nation's schools, are jumping on the band wagon that every child should be computer literate and be on the Internet, without sufficiently investigating the nature of brain development, how children learn, and what is necessary for healthy development at various ages.

Most of the educational programs for young children try to teach concepts at too young an age. Remember that the young child needs to be addressed through movement and imitation. Steiner comments: 'Have we the right to believe that with our intellectual mode of knowledge we can ever participate in the experience of the outer world which a child has, the child who is all sense-organ? This we cannot do.... It is immensely important that we do not consciously or unconsciously call upon the child's intellect prematurely, as people are so prone to do today.'⁵

We need to remember how the fantasy and play of the young child transform into the artistic imagination of the primary-school child, the questioning of the teenager, and the rational thinking of the young adult. Then we will have confidence that fantasy and imagination, which are so natural for the young child, form a better foundation for later creative thinking than early learning. Creative thinking is more needed in our highly technological world than four-year-olds who can push the buttons and manipulate the mouse of a computer.

> My five-year-old has always been precocious and already reads. And he can outreason me in getting what he wants. If we want to try to encourage balanced development, what can we do now? He can't go back to early childhood!

In working toward balanced development, it is necessary to have a picture of your child that includes more than intellectual achievements. What is he like emotionally? Is he happy being a child? Does he relate well with other children, or almost exclusively with adults? What is he like physically? Is he at home in his body and well-coordinated? Does he have frequent illnesses and require antibiotics frequently?

Many times early intellectual awakening can result in a weakening of the child's vital forces, manifesting in frequent colds or other illnesses. The dreamy state of early childhood is an essential element in the healthy formation of the physical body during the first seven years. The intellect is crystalline and hardening in its effect. When it is engaged prematurely, it can inhibit the proper development of the physical organs and the unfolding of the fluid emotions. Steiner even relates some illnesses in later life to influences in the first seven years:

> Whoever studies the whole course of a man's life from birth to death, bearing in mind the requirements of which I have spoken, will see that a child who has been exposed to things suitable only to grown-up people and who imitates these things will in his later years, from the age of about 50, suffer from sclerosis... Illnesses

that appear in later life are often only the result of educational errors made in the very earliest years of childhood.[6]

Because the job of the intellect is to analyze and exercise critical judgment, very bright children tend to have difficulty relating emotionally with other children, a problem that can intensify as the child becomes older.

While an awakened child cannot go back to the dreamy world of early childhood, imaginative play and the arts can have a healing influence on the child's life forces, helping to 'reweave the web' that protects the child during the first seven years. Images from fairy tales are also nurturing to the unconscious elements of the young child.

While you can't go back in time and do things differently with your child, it is also important not to feel guilty about choices you have already made. You were just as good a parent then as you are now. You made the best decisions you could then, based on your knowledge and perceptions of your choices. Guilt only takes us out of the present moment and makes us less able to see what is needed now, thus perpetuating problems rather than leading to meeting the present creatively. If there is going to be the possibility of healing, it must take place in the present. We make the best choices we can for our children in each moment, just as our parents did for us.

> Why do you suggest eliminating television for young children? We only let Jessica watch educational programs and she loves them!

Probably anyone who is reading this book is concerned enough about their children's development that they think seriously about television watching and have probably limited it in some ways to only certain programs, a certain amount of time, or watching programs together and talking about them, for example. However, the problem is twofold. First, television watching, including videos, is very seductive and the time children spend doing it expands the moment your awareness drops. This is because it entertains the child and buys time for you as a parent; creative play does the same thing, but television watching tends to squelch imagination and free play, leaving only bored children and more need for TV or another video!

Secondly, any amount and any kind of screen time – TV, video,

video game, or computer – is not healthy for the young child, regardless of the content of the program. The American Academy of Pediatrics recommended (in 1999) that children under the age of two not watch any television for healthy development. This was done in the face of statistics that show two-year-olds spend an average of twenty-seven hours a week watching television. There has also been recent heavy marketing of television programs designed for toddlers under the age of two. For example, six more programs are in production by the makers of the Teletubbies, and Disney's toddler programs have taken off. The doctors also recommended that older children not have televisions in their bedrooms.

I was delighted that the Academy finally took the most rudimentary stand for child health, developmentally appropriate activities, and brain development with regard to the media. And I was astounded that they took so much criticism for it, from editorials in the *New York Times* to the *Sacramento Bee*. The primary criticisms were that their recommendations were dogmatic, unrealistic, and unscientific, since studies of the effects of TV viewing on infants and toddlers haven't been done yet. When the 'experts' finally recommend something sensible, society discredits them as 'unscientific.'

Television is an important source of information and diversion for most adults. But children are not in the same stage of development as adults. The lack of movement and the poor quality of the sensory stimulation from the television screen make television watching problematical for all children. In an article on 'Children and Television,' John Rosemond suggests that you look at your child next time he is watching television and ask yourself what he is doing – or better yet, what he is not doing. He states:

In answer, the child is not:

- scanning
- practicing motor skills, gross or fine
- practicing eye-hand coordination
- using more than two senses
- asking questions
- exploring

- exercising initiative or motivation
- being challenged
- solving problems
- thinking analytically
- exercising imagination
- practicing communication skills
- being either creative or constructive

Also, because of television's insidious 'flicker,' television does not promote long-term attention.

Lastly, because the action shifts constantly and capriciously backward, forward and laterally in time, not to mention from subject matter to subject matter, television does not promote logical, sequential thinking.[7]

Rosemond notes that the deficiencies listed above are characteristic of learning disabled children, 'children who don't seem to 'get it all together' when it comes to learning how to read and write.' While television is not the only cause of the learning problems plaguing our schools, we need to look at the fact that learning disabilities have become epidemic, and functional illiteracy among 17-year-olds has steadily risen since television became a mainstay of our culture in 1955.

In her article 'Movement or Television,' special education expert Audrey McAllen also reports that kindergarten teachers of long experience observe that children today have less initiative than formerly, and expect grown-ups to start something. They wait passively for something to stimulate them when indoors. Their play lacks the imaginative inventiveness children once had.[8] Rosemond reports the same phenomena: 'Veteran teachers consistently report that today's children are less resourceful, imaginative, creative and motivated than pre-television generations. They also comment that the average child's attention span seems to have shortened mysteriously since 1950.'[9]

Jane Healy found the same phenomena in interviewing teachers and in her own work with children over the past twenty-five years as a learning specialist. She found through her research in brain development that 'fast-paced, nonlinguistic, and visually distracting television may literally have changed children's minds, making sustaining attention to verbal input, such as reading or listening, far less appealing than faster-paced visual stimuli. (This thesis is explored in depth in my book *Endangered Minds*.)'[10] Healy also reported that optometrists and other specialists have found an increase in vision problems among children due to the two-dimensional nature of the images, the flicker, and the lack of eye movement involved in watching TV and videos.[11] And in 1997 more than 650 viewers ages three to twenty fell ill in Japan with nausea or seizures from the flashing lights in a Pokemon cartoon; 150 were still hospitalized the following day.

Healthy development for the young child must engage all the senses. The young child wants to run and jump in space, touch and grasp with his hands, hold his breath for the fun of it, jump with joy, experience the world for himself with all his senses. 'Can I see it?' means 'Can I touch it?' The child is hungry to experience everything as fully as possible. Dr. Ann Barber, a developmental optometrist in Santa Ana, California, explains:

> When the child is born the wiring is all there, the light hits the retina but he makes no sense of it. He needs to learn by touching, putting things in his mouth, moving around, and then he has to integrate all this with vision and the other senses to make an intelligent child that's ready for school. There are about eight or ten perceptual processes developing in the preschool years that go beyond the eyeball, and so much... is done with the body, manipulating objects, dropping toys to learn about distance and develop visual convergence, practicing how to catch or kick a ball, hit a target. The child also must learn to focus on what's important and make sense out of the world. How can you understand 'above, below, inside, outside' if you're not crawling into the cardboard box and seeing and feeling it? But today we see so many kids are delayed in these skills – six-, seven-, eight-year-olds who are more at a four-year-old-level.[12]

And yet *Sesame Street* makes parents wonder if their preschooler will learn 'above' and 'below' or will somehow be behind if she doesn't watch Grover and company teach it.

Marie Winn, in her book *The Plug-In Drug*, again emphasizes, 'It isn't what your children watch on TV but the act of watching that harms them.' She states that with heavy television viewing, the right hemisphere of the brain is developed at the expense of the left. The left hemisphere controls the verbal, rational thought – the ability to read and write, to reason, to organize ideas and express them in speech and writing. Television viewers are bombarded with images that don't require them to think, or even give them time to.[13]

With the popularity of children's programming on cable stations, children's viewing is steadily increasing. More than 40 percent of children aged six to eleven have televisions in their bedroom to watch on their own; nearly a quarter of toddlers aged two to five also have their own TVs.[14] By the time most children leave school they will typically have spent 35,000 hours in front of a television set, compared with only 11,000 hours in the classroom. If you subtract hours for sleeping and doing homework, children are left with relatively few hours spent in reading, playing, and doing the other creative activities of childhood. Radically limiting your child's television watching before the age of ten or eleven is probably one of the most far-reaching gifts that you can possibly give him or her developmentally. This may mean putting the television set in your bedroom, if there are shows that you or your partner watch regularly while the children are up, or finding another way to keep it covered or inaccessible if your child is a button pusher. You will probably need to put more time into family activities when you first get rid of the television, but then you will find that the children become self-motivating and that you, as well as they, will have more time to do things alone as well as together. The world without television is very different and very much more in keeping with the developmental needs of the young child.

> I want to change the kind of toys my child plays with, but she always
> pesters me to buy her the other ones when we go to the shops. I can't just
> throw everything out. Where can I start?

At first it may be difficult to step outside of the chrome and plastic world of high-tech toys, but as you and your daughter begin to experience more alternatives, it will become easier. Certainly you won't want to take away favorite toys and create lots of strife! Possibly you can make a start by eliminating toys she doesn't play with now. That will clear out some of the clutter and make some space. Then make something, or buy an imaginative toy, and have a special place in her room where it lives or is played with. Invest some energy into the imaginative aspect of it, and make sure that it is put away each day in an attractive manner, ready for the new day. Gradually add other toys of the type that encourage imagination, while you phase out old ones that are no longer played with. You will find that costumes and toys that invite imaginative play in little scenes will easily become favorites.

Increase the kinds of toys you want your child to have by requesting that appropriate catalogs be sent to grandparents and others who send gifts. Some parents have a 'rainy day box' for gifts and toys that don't match their values for daily play, but that can be a fine adventure for a rainy day.

Sometimes it is necessary to go cold turkey, as when we decided to get rid of our television set. We did it at a time when we were moving anyway, so it didn't become associated with patterns in the new house. And I was amazed that the children didn't even complain. (I had been braced for a loud wail!) At first we replaced television time with activities the children were doing at school – knitting, singing, playing recorder, and reading stories out loud so they wouldn't go around asking what to do now that they couldn't watch television. We also tried to keep television from becoming forbidden fruit by telling the oldest child that he could watch certain events like special football games at the neighbors if invited. With the younger children, we told the neighbors that we didn't have a television, so they should tell our girls their daughter couldn't 'play' if she wanted to watch television instead. I found being tolerant and avoiding being 'holier than thou' helped things to go smoothly without a lot of emotional upset.

Sometimes parents are discouraged by their children's playing with neighbors who have different values. You can't continually police your child when he is out of the house, so have faith that your values make the strongest impression on your child. What you can do most effectively is to make your own rules at your house, and then make your house sufficiently attractive that your children and their friends will play there much of the time.

The issue of play with guns, for example, is one that parents need to discuss together and decide for themselves. I still don't have any clear philosophical or psychological answers as to what parents should do on this issue and why; I just knew that I wouldn't buy guns and my children learned that no gun play was allowed in our house. That limited their access without bringing up long discussions or making neighbors wrong. Children can accept that there are different rules in different places. 'This is the way we do it at our house,' is enough of an answer to many a why from a young child. Similarly, in the kindergarten, children were told that certain play was all right at home, but not there. They didn't have any problem with that.

> Ryan loves his Nintendo games so much – he'd play through meals, if we let him. I'm thinking about some of the things you've said about passive screen time, but video games are more active and encourage eye-hand coordination, don't they?

Video games have become big business in the US. Professor Dale Mann of Teacher's College of Columbia University points out that the entertainment industry has now replaced the U.S. defense industry as the main developer of technology, and at least half as much again is spent on entertainment as on education in the U.S.15 While it is true that video games improve the kind of coordination needed by airplane pilots (hence the value of flight simulators in training), they were also used by the military to desensitize recruits to actually firing and killing another person in training during the Vietnam War (this was reported by a high-ranking former Army officer in an article in *Time* after the killings at Colombine High School in May, 1999). As the analysts have said, all television, videos, and video games are educational; the question is, what are they teaching? Consider this development:

> Setting the stage for an unprecedented collaboration between the Pentagon and Hollywood, the U.S. Army will announce the formation of a major research center today at the University of Southern California to develop core technologies that are critical to both the military and to the entertainment industry.
>
> The primary goal of the new Institute for Creative

Technologies is to allow the Army to create highly realistic training simulations that rely on advances in virtual reality, artificial intelligence and other cutting-edge technologies. The entertainment industry is expected to use the technology to improve its motion picture special effects, make video games more realistic and create new simulation attractions for virtual reality arcades.[16]

Jane Healy found in her research that because video games strongly engage the player, they have more profound effects (good or bad) than viewing TV. They also 'decrease the psychological distance' between the child and the medium, especially as games become increasingly sophisticated and realistic. Healy asks that we consider what behaviors and world views certain games might be conveying (such as, 'this is a violent place where I can't trust anyone'). She also found that the hyperactivation of the adrenaline response that accompanies most video games and even some 'educational' computer games may, with repeated experience, become an ingrained physical habit. Measurements of blood pressure, heart rate, and even brain waves during virtual interactions mirror those that would be present in a real-life situation – all without conscious control or being discharged through movement.[17]

Video games prior to the age of seven, when the child is so open in the realm of the senses, simply can't be considered healthy for children. Although video-game-related seizures (called VGRS by neurologists) are rare, a recent study indicated they can occur in youngsters without previous seizure difficulties. Nintendo now attaches a warning of epilepsy-like symptoms triggered by the games' optical stimuli after a handful of teenagers suffered seizures while playing Nintendo video games several years ago. Symptoms include stiffening, shaking, or even losing consciousness for a few seconds, or may be less dramatic and involve merely staring for a few seconds and then 'coming back' with a start. Less dramatic symptoms may also occur as a result of such overstimulation. Robert W. Kubey of Rutgers University, New Jersey, US, reported, 'I have many parents report to me that, short of seizures their children have become nauseated, tired or listless, or experience headaches during and after playing a video game.'[18]

The later you can postpone the world of video games for your children, the better. If you already have them, or you are going to introduce them into your home, Healy provides valuable 'Guidelines for Video Game Use' in her book *Failure to Connect.*[19]

What about vaccinations? I've heard some people say that childhood illnesses could be beneficial. How could this be?

While no one wants their child to become ill, many parents today question whether it is necessary to immunize their children with the standard array of vaccinations, and at what age the immunizations should be given. Many opposing views exist on the subject, and parents need to do their own research and make responsible decisions.

The doctors in Germany who are working out of the indications of Rudolf Steiner will not immunize infants until they are one year old, and then will only immunize for the more serious illnesses such as polio, diphtheria, and tetanus. They feel that the childhood illnesses such as measles, mumps, chicken pox, and even whooping cough can have beneficial effects. By activating the immune system in a natural way, childhood illnesses strengthen it and can help to prevent susceptibility to other illnesses in later life.[20]

Most childhood illnesses are characterized by fevers, which not only activate the immune system, but can have developmental benefits as well. Pediatrician Uwe Stave reports: 'Fever attacks can affect children in quite a positive way. Even though his physical strength is reduced, the child may disclose a wealth of new interests and skills. He may find new and advanced ways to communicate, think, and handle situations, or display a refinement of his motor skills. In short, after a fever, the child reveals a spurt of development and maturation. Parents, frequently surprised, fail to mention their observation of such development to their physicians.'[21]

Dr. Stave explains this observation by referring to the effect of warmth on the process of incarnation:

Fever acts by shaking and loosening up the physical body. Activation by heat can help the Ego form and reshape the physical organization of the young child. In addition, the

physiological and biochemical functions of organs and systems
are assisted in the maturation process through febrile illness, and
inner forces gain strength and become more differentiated.
Although the pediatrician often shares parental concern that
repeated feverous infections overstress the young child's fragile
organism, fever most often supports development and
individualization, although it is sometimes a warning signal,
indicating weakness in the child's defense against his
environment. As children grow older and learn how to control
the will, gradually an 'inner fire' replaces the 'developmental
fever' of a young child.[22]

Many of the childhood illnesses that involve fever, such as measles,
chicken pox, and mumps, have nearly become anachronisms
through routine immunization of infants. Parents who choose not
to have their children vaccinated for some or all illnesses need to
appreciate the seriousness of the diseases and the child's special need
for strict home care and medical help in mustering her forces to
overcome the illness. Measles can't be treated like a common cold or
flu – it can develop into pneumonia, or worse. Whooping cough
requires weeks of convalescence and may require medicine or other
remedies to help fight the illness successfully.[23]

On the other hand, if you do immunize your child, you need to
recognize that introducing the illness through the vaccine is a
powerful shock to the body. Dr. Wilhelm zur Linden states that the
reason vaccinations are given to babies and infants is because older
children can react with cramps, fever, vomiting, and confusion. He
states, 'It is not known that small children react so mildly because
they do not yet possess sufficient strength with which to counteract
the vaccination.'[24] Dr. zur Linden suggests that the homeopathic
remedy Thusa 30X given morning and evening starting on the day
of vaccination can help to protect the child when vaccinations are
given. Whether or not to immunize a child, for which illnesses, and
at what age, is an individual decision parents must make for their
children, weighing the pros and cons as best they can.

In order to make informed decisions for your children, you need
to gather information on all sides of the issues. The 'pro' side is
readily available from your pediatrician or health department. But

you need to realize there are other forces at work in public health than wanting what is best for your individual child. Many of these issues are discussed in detail in the books listed at the end of this chapter.

You have the ultimate responsibility for your child's health and well-being. You – not your doctor – will live with and be responsible for the consequences of your decision. Work in conjunction with your health care provider to assess what is best for your individual child. Don't be intimidated by medical personnel and forced into a vaccination decision before you are comfortable with your decision. On the other hand, don't let your child come down with whooping cough because you haven't got around to figuring out whether or not you're vaccinating! It's a lot of work to take responsibility for your child's birth, health, and education, but somebody's got to do it.

How should I care for my child when he is sick?

Before talking about how to care for a sick child, it is necessary to emphasize how important it is *that* you care for a sick child. A child needs time and rest to fight off an illness and to consolidate the physical and developmental changes that may be occurring. If given insufficient time to recuperate, the child's system will become weaker and more prone to complications or future infections. Many young mothers are so harried that they don't think to call everything to a halt and get help (with taking the other child to school or going shopping) so they can keep the sick child at home and really attend to his needs. Mothers who have to work are often tempted to give antibiotics immediately (suppressing symptoms) so the child can be back in preschool within twenty-four hours, not realizing that he needs quiet time to regroup his inner forces and to heal. Or working mothers must take their children to unfamiliar daycare centers for sick children if they can't use their own sick days in order to stay home with a child. Clearly our culture is not set up to meet the needs of children and working parents!

When a child is sick, with whatever illness, certain principles need to be kept in mind. The most important is that the child needs less stimulation so that the forces of the body and of the Ego can fight off the illness and go through whatever changes are necessary. This means quiet play, staying in bed if necessary, eating lighter foods (usually less meat or egg during an illness – most sick children know this naturally). Television is especially to be avoided when the child is sick. It is amazing how most hospitals not only pay so little attention to the environment, but also expect patients to get well while watching 'General Hospital' on the television!

Once you recognize the importance of home care for a sick child, what should you do? One important thing is to observe your child, both physically and intuitively. With an infant, note how he holds his body when he cries; observe the breathing and the nature of the cough; note the child's eyes and facial expression. Try to feel what is happening and whether the child is getting better or worse. All good pediatricians will ask the mother for her observations and intuitions about a sick child and will take them seriously. It is important to try to find a doctor with whom you can develop a relationship of trust, feeling that you are both working toward healing of the whole person.

The health and vitality of your children are a responsibility shared by you and your children in conjunction with healthcare providers when they are ill. In the US, we are a nation prone to the 'quick fix.' But, if we can take the time for real healing with our own and our children's illnesses, we will have gained a great deal. As parents, there is a great deal we can do to help members of our family when they are ill. Compresses and poultices, herbal teas, and therapeutic touch are all home measures that can be learned to comfort a sick person and aid in healing.

One of the best books on taking care of your family (and yourself) is *Healing at Home* by Sandra Greenstone with Clinton L. Greenstone, M.D. In addition to providing a thoughtful overview of the healing process, the authors give a detailed and well-organized guide to recognizing symptoms and things you can do at home to aid the healing process – as well as telling you how to recognize when something is serious and requires a visit to your healthcare provider. This book and other valuable resources are listed at the end of this chapter.

My husband and I don't go to church, but we want to do something with our child in terms of religious instruction or upbringing. We don't just want to send her off to Sunday School, but what can we do that is meaningful and appropriate?

Having children usually brings up questions about one's own experiences with religion as a child, one's current spiritual orientation, and what one wants for the children. Many times children lead parents back into a relationship with the religion of their childhood, which they rediscover with new depth and meaning. Because the expression of spiritual beliefs is so individual, I encourage you and your partner to discuss them together and to work toward finding or creating an appropriate expression of your beliefs that is suitable for your children as they grow.

It is our job as parents to acclimatize the child to this new land, this new condition of life on earth, but to do this in such a way that the child is not driven into forgetfulness of his true origin and ultimate goal. How can we help our children develop their innate religious sense? How can we feed their spiritual hunger? How can we assist them in developing their spiritual nature? These questions are addressed in *The Spiritual Hunger of the Modern Child*, a compilation of ten lectures by notable speakers representing a variety of religious perspectives including Judaism, Christianity, Subud, and Buddhism.[25] In great depth the writers discuss the nature of children, the effect of the home environment, the use of prayer, the power of attraction, heredity, and conscience.

All of the writers agree that who you are and what you do around young children are more important than religious dogmas or indoctrination. Reviewer René Knight-Weiler summarized the book's common theme as: 'Religion must be caught, not taught, and indeed it cannot be caught from someone who doesn't truly have it. It will be caught through practice, feeling, symbolism, image and spirit in the home.'[26]

In one of the essays, the Reverend Adam Bittleston of the Christian Community speaks on the ideas of Rudolf Steiner and echoes the theme that the real work of early childhood is work on oneself: 'That is really the fundamental thing to satisfy the spiritual hunger of the child – that the grown-up does not stop working upon himself, that no day does he stop working on himself.'[27]

Joseph Chilton Pearce, in *The Magical Child Matures,*[28] emphasizes this same theme: In order for the child to be whole, he must have a model who is whole. While none of us qualify as fully realized human beings (and our children must have known this!), the fact of our striving and our efforts, our awareness and our yearning communicate to the child, and are far more valuable than either complete materialism or sanctimonious piety, both of which children can see through and reject as false.

From the *Well-Springs of the Soul: Religious Instruction for the Child* by Herbert Hahn[29] and *Celebrating the Festivals with Children* by Friedel Lenz[30] provide information for parents on a Christian orientation that is consonant with Steiner's understanding of child development. Principles to keep in mind include not calling on the intellect or giving moral exhortations, but providing stories and images that awaken in the child a feeling for the holidays or the qualities one is trying to convey.

Because of the imitative nature of the young child, the child's experiences during any kind of Sunday School will have a deeper effect than the words that are spoken, just as what you are and what you do speaks more clearly than your words. Thus it is important to give attention to the quality of this experience in your church, temple, or mosque. Is there an atmosphere of calm and warmth in the preschool classes? Do the activities and methods fit the nature of the young child? You may find that you have to become a teacher yourself !

According to Steiner, the imitative nature of the young child has a spiritual basis. In speaking of the young child, Steiner says, 'He is still filled with the devotion that one develops in the spiritual world. It is for this reason that he gives himself up to his environment by imitating the people around him. What then is the fundamental impulse, the completely unconscious mood of the child before the change of teeth? This fundamental mood is a very beautiful one, and it must be fostered in the child. It proceeds from the assumption, from the unconscious assumption, that the whole world is of a moral nature.'[31]

The child gives himself over to the people and objects of the world with the assumption that they are good, and then imitates them. Steiner states, 'The child is completely given up to his environment. In adult life the only parallel to this devotion is in religion, expressed in the soul and spirit of man... [The adult's] own soul and spirit are given up to the divine spirit of the world. The child gives up his whole being to his environment. In the adult the activities of breathing, digestion and circulation are within himself, cut off from the outside world. In the child all these activities are given up to his environment and are therefore by nature religious. This is the essential feature of the life of the children between birth and the change of teeth; his whole being is permeated by a kind of 'natural-religious' element, and even the physical body is in a religious mood.'[32]

In another lecture, Steiner clarifies, 'It is not the soul of the child that is given up to the environment, but its blood circulation, its breathing activities and processes of nourishment through the food it takes in. All these things are given up to the environment. The blood circulation, the breathing and the nourishment processes are praying to the environment. Naturally, such expressions seem paradoxical, but in their very paradox they present the truth. If we observe such a thing with our whole being and not with the theoretical intellect...' then we will develop an attitude or mood in being with young children that Steiner calls 'priestly.'[33] Thus parents, daycare providers, and early childhood teachers are like 'caretakers of the divine' as they recognize it in the child and introduce him or her to earthly life through the sacred qualities of rhythm, beauty, and love.

While I feel it is beneficial to recognize the importance of our role with young children, I am the first to admit shortcomings in my attitudes and actions in bringing up my own children and in being with young children in many given moments. However, we not only try to do the best we can, but we can also strive to do better, for the most important work of the parent with young children is inner work on oneself. The young child accepts us as perfect and good; once he becomes older and sees our imperfections, the most important thing is that the child sees we are striving to do better. Our desire for inner growth (or our complacency) is perceived by the child and has a very deep effect on him.

How can we help the child's natural development of religious feeling? Because the child is so given over to the environment, we help the child by furthering an attitude of gratitude in ourselves and hence in the child for all that the world gives us. 'If he sees that everyone who stands in some kind of relationship to him in the outer world shows gratitude for what he receives from this world; if, in confronting the outer world and wanting to imitate it, the child sees the kind of gestures that express gratitude, then a great deal is done towards establishing in him the right moral human attitude. Gratitude is what belongs to the first seven years of life.'[34]

Reverence is another attitude important to foster in early childhood. Steiner writes: 'If one observes children who, by a right upbringing, have developed a natural reverence for the grownups in their surroundings, and if one follows them through their various stages of life, one can discover that their feelings of reverence and devotion in childhood are gradually being transformed during the years leading to old age. As adults such persons may have a healing effect upon their fellow-men so that by their mere presence, or through the tone of their voice, or perhaps by a single glance they can spread inner peace to others. Their presence can be a blessing because as children they have learned to venerate and to pray in the right way. No hands can bless in old age, unless in childhood they have been folded in prayer.'[35]

However, qualities such as reverence and prayer cannot be taught to a young child through doctrine or exhortation. They must live within the parents. If prayer is a living reality for the mother or father, then he or she can communicate that to the child and teach him, through example, about prayer. Think about your own childhood. What experiences brought you closer to God? Which people seemed to have a special quality? Looking at spiritual questions can be a great gift that your children bring to you.

Conscious parenting seems like a tall order! What can help us on the way?

Conscious parenting involves keeping perspective – that we don't let ourselves become so bogged down in the day-to-day task of raising our children that we neglect to focus on the larger picture. Part of our task is to see the spiritual in the mundane, to recognize the inner light in a child, or the ways in which a child's drawing, for instance, might give us a picture of his emerging consciousness. Another part of our task is to let the events or experiences of the everyday world lead us to questions and experiences of the divine. As we come to see the relationship of microcosm to macrocosm, to 'see a world in a grain of sand... and eternity in an hour,' we will find ourselves transformed in the process.

Certainly we all have shortcomings and failings; there wouldn't be any growth if we didn't. But we need to have patience and kindness toward our own development and not be self-critical. Practicing kindness toward one's own shortcomings is as important as developing patience with others.

Parenting takes a tremendous amount of energy. If you don't keep your energy replenished, you become frazzled, harried, short-tempered, and otherwise hard to be around. Especially while your children are young, you need to make sure that you get adequate sleep. It helps to have some kind of meditation or practice or prayer, even five minutes a day, that can help to keep you centered. Creative activities such as art, music, sculpture, or dance are also unique in actually replenishing the kind of energy that children demand. Being in nature also does this. When you're taking the baby out for a walk or taking your two-year-old to the park, cherish this time as something that can help renew your energy as well.

Taking parenting seriously can also remind you that what you are doing is important and worthwhile. Because women's work is undervalued and underpaid, we can fall into the same trap of undervaluing it, unless we put intentionality into what we are doing. Peggy O'Mara, editor of *Mothering*, states very clearly:

> I believe, however, that women will never be satisfied with a life that is an economic imitation of mens' lives. Women must find a new way, a way of the spirit, and they must insist on an economic reality that acknowledges the concerns of the heart. If women are satisfied only to find success as men have found it, in the traditional marketplace separate from the home, we will never create a better world. When women polarize over daycare and at-home mommies, they polarize over a male model of the separation of work and family that has not worked for men and

is not now working for women. It doesn't work, not because we need more daycare centers, but because the current social reality we emulate has no heart.

We must seek broader solutions to the economics of family life, and we must be very careful not to fall into the trap of defining ourselves solely by the values of a society in transition.[36]

Viewing parenting as part of the path of love and service can also help get you through the rough spots. Having children certainly opens your heart and makes you stretch, through constantly having to consider the needs of another person who is dependent on you – and whom you must gradually release. Parenting can be a rich source of life experiences in the course of one's development as a human being, if you use what is given to you for self-knowledge and transformation. In her article, 'An Ethic of Parenting,' O'Mara describes the inner work of parenting as follows:

> In our society, we are not accustomed to the surrender and service required by the human infant. In order to sustain an ethic of parenting that honors the necessity of surrender and service, we will have to surround ourselves with the kind of support and information that will enable us to overcome the limitations…
>
> Serve your child – for in serving your child, in trusting your child, you serve yourself and give yourself an opportunity to be reparented and reloved. The greatest kept secret of the world is the personal transformation inherent in developing an ethic of parenting that is truly in keeping with the nature of the child. Parenting with this type of ethic releases the full potential of the human being, a force greater than anything we have yet to see on this planet.[37]

In Conclusion

All parents want what is best for their child. But most first-time parents know very little about children or parenting (I certainly didn't!). Learning as you go is often uncomfortable, but it can provide many opportunities for growth for parents as well as children. As our children's first teachers, we can and must provide the love and warmth, calm and rhythm, interest and enthusiasm vital to their growth. And, they provide us with new areas of study, work, and self-examination as we come up against our shortcomings and the dilemmas our children present to us.

What is needed today is not another expert, some new authority to follow or to reject, but a new way of seeing the human being that takes into account all aspects of development – physical, emotional, intellectual, and spiritual – so we and our children can meet the challenges of our changing world and fulfill the purposes of our time on earth.

We are living in a time of transition, a time in which the old patterns of society no longer hold us. We are being called upon to approach all aspects of our lives with new awareness. Life in our families, cities, churches, and schools is changing at an ever-increasing rate as we struggle to establish or maintain equilibrium and then to create something new.

We can't go back to a 'milk-and-cookies' mentality that denies the changes that have led to the present. But we need to recognize that the world of the young child is critically endangered today, as more and more children are placed in daycare beginning in infancy, and academics are pushed onto younger and younger children. It has become even more urgent that we understand that children are not little adults. They do not think, reason, feel, or experience the world as an adult does. Instead they are centered in their bodies, and in the will which manifests in such powerful growth and need for movement in the first seven years. They learn primarily and more appropriately through example and imitation. Repetition and rhythm are also vital elements in the healthy world of the young child and need to be emphasized by parents and others responsible for the care of young children.

The young child takes everything in without blocks or filters, and for this reason we must put special attention into the quality of the environment and the experiences that come to her. There needs to be a balance between stimulating and protecting the baby's and young child's senses. Stimulation from artificial sources (films, recordings, synthetic fabrics) has a different impact on the young child than stimulation from your own voice or objects from nature. Because the young child is all sense-organ, we need to be selective in what is experienced and help guard against violating the young child's natural dreamy state.

Everything of life is taken in so deeply by the young child, to be transformed and come out again in creative play. Providing time and appropriate materials for this kind of play helps the child to work his way into earthly life by imitating through his play everything that he experiences. Allowing this natural impulse of creative imagination to flourish is one of the greatest gifts parents can give their child between birth and first grade.

The young child also has a natural artistic and musical ability, which can be furthered by allowing its free expression without lessons or pressure to produce something in a certain way. Songs, rhythmical movement, and circle games all speak to the magical world of early childhood.

Just as it is developmentally important that children crawl before they walk (and do not skip steps), so it is important that children not be prematurely awakened from the dreamy, imaginative world of early childhood before the natural time for this, around the age of six or seven. Lessons, workbooks, and academic tasks not only take the child away from movement and valuable play, but they also accelerate the child's change of consciousness and rob him of the last valuable years of early childhood – years that are vital to a person's later physical health as well as mental development. Trying to speed up development in young children places them at risk, with no apparent gain to justify such risks.

As our children's first teachers, there is much we can do, and much that is better if we don't do! It is my hope that this book will contribute to parents' understanding the special nature of the young child and his or her unique needs. If we can take both knowledge and practical experience into our hearts, we will have increased confidence as we develop our own ethic of parenting and make our own best choices for our children. The challenges are great, but so are the growth and the rewards!

Recommended Reading

(Because many of these titles are difficult to find, check with the mail order book services listed in Appendix A or see if your local bookstore can order them.)

Health and Illness

The practice of medicine directly inspired by Steiner's work has developed more extensively in continental Europe, with only a handful of practitioners in North America. These doctors and nurses work out of an inner effort to understand the entire human being and the meaning of illness, utilizing many things in addition to standard techniques: nutrition, massage, painting, eurythmy, sculpture, music, baths, herbal oils, and so forth. Further reading about this approach can be found in:

Caduceus – Health and Healing Magazine www.caduceus.info
Caring for the Sick at Home by Tineke van Bentheim et al. (Steiner Books)
A Guide to Child Health by Michaela Glöckler and Wolfgang Goebel (Floris Books)
Healing at Home. A guide to using Alternative Remedies and Conventional Medicine that will change your approach to Illness by Sandra Greenstone with Clinton L. Greenstone. (Healing at Home Publishing)
Healing for Body, Soul and Spirit. An Introduction to Anthroposophical Medicine by Michael Evans and Iain Rodger. (Floris Books)
'Illness' by Gudrun Davy and 'A Sick child in the Hospital' by Stephanie Westphal, in *Lifeways – Working with Family Questions* by Bons Voors and Gudrun Davy. (Hawthorn Press)
An Introduction to Anthroposophical Medicine. Extending the Art of Healing by Victor Bott. (Rudolf Steiner Press).
A Child is Born by Wilhelm zur Linden M.D. (Healing Art Press)

Park Attwood Clinic. Anthroposophical Clinic. Trimpley Lane, Bewdley, Worcestershire DY12 1RE Tel no. 01299 861444 www.parkattwood.org

Weleda – Homoeopathic medicines and list of UK Anthroposophical Doctors. Heanor Road, Ilkeston, Derbyshire DE7 8DR Tel no. 0115 944 8200 www.weleda.co.uk

Vaccinating your Children

A Guide to Child Health by Michaela Glöckler and Wolfgang Goebel (Floris Books)

How to Raise a Healthy Child in Spite of your Doctor by Robert Mendelson (SOS Free Stock)

The Immunization Resource Guide. Where to Find Answers to All your Questions about Childhood Immunizations by Diane Rozario. (Patter Publications).

The Informed Parent – information on immunization choices. PO Box 4481, Worthing, West Sussex BN11 2WH
Tel no. 01903 212969 www.informedparent.co.uk

NHS – Information Service www.immunisation.nhs.uk

Vaccination. A Guide for Making Personal Choices by Hans-Peter Studer et al. (Floris Books)

The Vaccination Bible edited by Lynn McTaggart (What the Doctors don't tell you Books).

'Vaccination: The Issue of Our Times'. Articles, research, references, and resources by physicians, public health workers, and parents from *Mothering Magazine*. Available from the US. www.mothering.com

Media and Children

Amusing Ourselves to Death by Neil Postman (Viking)

The Child and the Machine – Why Computers Put Children's Education at Risk by Alison Armstrong and Charles Casement (Roundhouse Publishing)

Failure to Connect: How Computers Affect Our Children's Minds – for Better and Worse by Jane M. Healy (Simon and Schuster)

Four Arguments for the Elimination of Television by Jerry Mander (William Morrow Publishing)

The Plug-in Drug by Marie Winn (Viking/Penguin)

Set Free Childhood – Parents Survival Guide for Coping with Computers and TV by Martin Large (Hawthorn Press)
Unplugging the Plug-in Drug by Marie Winn (Viking/Penguin)
Who's bringing them up? by Martin Large (Hawthorn Press)

Religious Life

All Year Round by Ann Druitt, Christine Fynes Clinton and Marije Rowling (Hawthorn Press). Explanation and ideas for celebrating festivals with children.
Celebrating the Festivals with Children by Friedel Lenz (Anthroposophic Press)
Festivals Family and Food – Guide to seasonal celebration by Diana Carey and Judy Large (Hawthorn Press).
In the Light of a Child by Michael Burton. Fifty-two verses for children inspired by Rudolf Steiner's *Calendar of the Soul* (Hawthorn Press).
The Mystery of Growing up by Evelyn Francis Capel (Temple Lodge Publishing)
Prayers for Mothers and Children by Rudolf Steiner (Rudolf Steiner Press)
The Radiant Child by Thomas Armstrong (Quest Books)
The Spiritual Hunger of the Modern Child: A Series of Ten Lectures by John G. Bennet et al (Claymont Communications US)

Sources for Steiner Books

US

Anthroposophic Press, 3390 Route 9, Hudson, NY 12534
(518) 851-2054

AWSNA Publications, 3911 Bannister Rd., Fair Oaks, CA 95628
(916) 961-6923

Mercury Press, 241 Hungry Hollow Rd., Spring Valley, NY 10977
(914) 425-9356

Rudolf Steiner College Book Store, 9200 Fair Oaks Blvd., Fair
Oaks, CA 95628, (916) 961-8729

Rudolf Steiner Library, 65 Fern Hill Rd., Ghent, NY 12075
(518) 672-7690

UK

Helios Foundation, 7 Grassmarket, Edinburgh 0131 229 7884
www.helios-foundation.co.uk

Rudolf Steiner Books, Well Spring Book Shop, 5 New Oxford
Street, London WC1A 1BA 0207 405 6101
www.rudolfsteinerbooks.co.uk

Skylark Books, 30 Elphinstone Road, Hastings East Sussex
TN34 2EQ 01 424 441487 www.skylarkbooks.co.uk

Steiner House Bookshop, 35 Park Road, London NW1 6XT
0207 723 4400
Steiner Waldorf Schools Fellowship Publications, Kidbrooke Park,
Forest Row, East Sussex RH18 5JB Tel no. 01342 826004
www.steinerwaldorf.org.uk

Publishers of Anthroposophical and related books

Floris Books, 15 Harrison Gardens, Edinburgh E11 1SH
Tel no. 0131 337 2372   www.florisbooks.co.uk
Hawthorn Press, Hawthorn House, 1 Lansdown Lane, Stroud,
Glos.GL5 1BJ Tel no. 01453 757040   www.hawthornpress.com
Rudolf Steiner Press, Hillside House, The Square, Forest Row, East
Sussex RH18 5ES Tel no. 01342 824433
www.rudolfsteinerpress.com

Rudolf Steiner
and Waldorf Education

Rudolf Steiner (1861-1925) spent his early adult years preparing the scientific writings of Goethe for republication. A. P. Shepherd, a canon of the Anglican Church, says of him, 'Steiner thought, spoke and wrote as a scientist... Although his own investigations carried him into fields far beyond the range of physical science, he always carried into these investigations, and into the application of them to physical phenomena, the concepts and methods of scientific thought.'

At the beginning of this century, Steiner began to lecture and write extensively, imparting a knowledge about the realms beyond the physical and our connection with them. During the last six years of his life, he was active in applying his spiritual scientific knowledge in various fields such as education, agriculture, arts, medicine, theology, and so forth. To help carry on his work as a force for personal and cultural renewal, he founded the Anthroposophical Society ('anthroposophy' comes from the roots 'anthropos,' meaning 'man,' and 'sophia,' meaning 'wisdom'). The society now has working groups and branches all over the world.

Steiner turned his attention to education after the First World War at the request of Emil Molt, who helped him found a school for the children of the factory workers at the Waldorf-Astoria cigarette factory in Stuttgart in 1919. The impulse for 'Waldorf education,' as it came to be called, spread throughout Europe, with the first school in America being founded in New York City in 1928, and the first one in the English speaking world founded in Forest Row, East Sussex, UK in 1925. In the UK the education became known as 'Steiner Education'.

Steiner was a pioneer in the area of developmentally based, age-appropriate learning, and many of his indications were later borne out by the work of Gesell and Piaget and by later brain research in the 1990s. In addition, he sought to develop a balanced education for the 'whole child,' one which would engage the child's feeling and willing, as well as thinking, and would leave his or her spiritual nature acknowledged, but free. From preschool through the whole of school, the goal of Steiner/Waldorf education is the same, but the means differ according to the changing inner development of the child. According to Steiner, 'Our highest endeavor must be to develop free human beings, who are able of themselves to impart purpose and direction to their lives.'

Because of this emphasis, Steiner/Waldorf schools were closed by the Nazis during World War II, but soon re-opened and have spread in the last two decades to such troubled areas as South Africa, Palestine, Eastern Europe, and Russia. Waldorf has become the largest private school movement in the world. In 1994 there were 640 schools, 1087 kindergartens, more than 300 curative (special education) centers, and 60 teacher training institutes in 46 countries that are based on Rudolf Steiner's pedagogical impulse. Growth of the movement in the US and the UK has been very rapid since the 1980s.

During the early childhood years, the child is surrounded by a homelike environment that encourages imaginative free play and artistic activity. Steiner recognized that the young child learns primarily through example and imitation, with an emphasis on the importance of movement, rhythm, fairy tales, and oral language. Steiner felt that it is not healthy for children to concentrate on cognitive skills, such as reading, writing, and maths, until the body has reached a certain level of maturity, freeing the forces of growth for cognitive work. Typical daily activities in the preschool/kindergarten include free play, movement games, story circle, and a craft or artistic activity (watercolour painting, beeswax modeling, colouring with beeswax crayons, baking, and so forth). Puppet plays, nature walks, and celebrating the festivals are frequent events throughout the year.

In the lower school (ages 7-14), all of the subjects are presented in a lively and pictorial way, because Steiner found the elementary-school child learns best when information is artistically and imaginatively presented. The same teacher stays with the children from Class 1 through to Class 8, teaching the 'main lesson' subjects, which include language, arts, mathematics, history, and the sciences. Main lesson is taught during the first two hours of the morning in blocks of three to six weeks per topic. Students create their own 'main lesson books' as artistic records of their learning, rather than using textbooks or worksheets. During the rest of the day special subject teachers fill out the curriculum with two foreign languages, orchestra, singing, arts, crafts, gardening, eurythmy (a movement art developed by Steiner) and physical education (see the chart,

The Steiner/Waldorf Curriculum

Class 1	Class 2	Class 3	Class 4
Language Arts	Language Arts	Language Arts	Language Arts
•writing	•extend skills	•extend skills	•grammar
•phonics	•legends &	•grammar	•drama
•reading	fables	•letter writing	•Norse myths
•fairy tales	Mathematics	•Old Testament	Mathematics
Mathematics	•+, −, x, ÷	stories	•adv. skills
•add./subt.	•telling time	Mathematics	•fractions
•mult./div.	•money	•extend skills	German
German*	German	•measurement	French
French*	French	German	Zoology
Beeswax	Beeswax	French	Local History
Modelling	Modelling	Farming	Geography
Painting	Painting	Painting	Embroidery
Knitting	Crochet	Crafts	String or Wind
Recorder	Recorder	Recorder	Instr.
Phys. Ed.	Phys. Ed.	String Instr.	Phys. Ed.
		Phys. Ed.	

Quoted in Joan Salter, *The Incarnating Child* (Glouc., UK: Hawthorn Press, 1987, p. 146)
*Languages may vary, including Spanish, Russian etc.

below).

The adolescent's emerging powers of analytical thinking are met and developed in the Waldorf upper school, where subjects are taught by specialists in their fields. The role of the teacher is seen as helping the students to develop their own thinking powers. A key to this process is presenting students with an immediate experience of phenomena, such as hands-on experiments or primary sources in literature and history – instead of predigested work from textbooks or anthologies. The rapidly changing psychological nature of the adolescent is addressed through each year's studies being tailored to the central 'questions' that live in the hearts of the students of that grade level.

A complete list of Steiner/Waldorf schools in the UK can be obtained from the Steiner Waldorf Schools Fellowship, Kidbrooke Park, Forest Row, Sussex RH18 5JB, UK.

Class 5	Class 6	Class 7	Class 8
Language Arts	Language Arts	Language Arts	Language Arts
•extend skills	•biography	•biography	•biography
•stories of	Pre algebra	•drama	•drama
ancient cultures	Geometry	Algebra	Algebra
and Greece	German	Geometry	Geometry
Mathematics	French	German	German
•adv. skills	Greek and Latin	French	French
•decimal	Physics	Greek and Latin	Greek and Latin
fractions	Roman History	Physics	Physics
German	World Geog.	Chemistry	Chemistry
French*	Woodworking	Astronomy	Physiology
Botany	Recorder	Med./Ren. Hist.	Modern History
Greek History	Orchestra	World Geog.	World Geog.
Geography of	Choral Singing	Woodworking	Woodworking
Country	Gardening	Sewing	Sewing
Crafts	Phys. Ed.	Recorder	Recorder
Recorder		Orchestra	Orchestra
Orchestra		Choral Singing	Choral Singing
Phys. Ed.		Gardening	Gardening
		Phys. Ed.	Phys. Ed.

Alliance for Childhood

www.steinerwaldorf.org.uk

The Alliance for Childhood was formed in February 1999 and publishes the following concerns and invitation to join in their work:

Research and experience have identified many social factors that create stress in children and contribute to a range of physical, emotional, and mental illnesses. Children have a right to a basically sound and healthy childhood but need increased protection in today's world if they are to have one.

The concerns of the Alliance are:

1. ***Protection of Childhood.*** Children have natural and inherent gifts such as openness, creativity, wonder, and trust. In adulthood these can be transformed into interest, initiative, respect, self-confidence, and flexibility if they are allowed to mature at their own pace and in a secure and loving environment. If we lose the wisdom of our early childhood development we forfeit an element of our humanity that will be increasingly essential in coping with and understanding a rapidly changing and turbulent world.

2. ***Poverty and abuse***, violence and neglect, child prostitution, pornography, and child labour have such a severe impact on

children that they intractably undermine the quality of life and need to be addressed with utmost urgency. Children have a right to be protected from conditions that endanger their lives.

3. *Changes in Family Life and Child Care.* Today's children are frequently asked to adjust to divorce, shared custody, and fragmented or combined families. In addition, growing numbers of families are dependent on childcare that is often of variable quality. At the same time, modern homes tend to be hurried places, filled with modern labour-saving technology, yet surprisingly little real contact takes place between adults and children.

4. *Early Academic Pressure.* Over the years, the assumption has grown that if children would stop playing and learn to read, write, and do arithmetic before the age of six, they would be better prepared for life. Early academics have not yielded long-term gains, however, and have been firmly associated with increased stress in childhood. By the age of nine, children from play-oriented kindergartens have been shown to surpass those from academic kindergartens in physical, social, emotional, and mental development.

5. *Media, Computers, and Video Games.* These have become major influences in the lives of many children and are generally viewed as benign or even positive influences. However, recent research shows they can have a negative impact on the physical development of children, as well as on their emotional, social, and mental development.

6. *Commercialism.* This is a growing influence as nearly every children's television show has a product line connected with it. It used to be thought inappropriate to advertise directly to children. This is no longer the case, as advertisers battle to gain product loyalty by the time a child is five or six years old. The pressure this brings to parents and therefore to family life is often disregarded and is an added source of stress.

7. *Diet and Health.* Children's diets are increasingly filled with

processed foods and food additives. Many of these additives have been linked to obesity, asthma, allergies, and behavioral problems. In the health field, advances that have been viewed as a help to children, such as inoculations and antibiotics, are now being questioned as to whether they are being over-used and thereby becoming a source of illness in children.

An Invitation:

There are many individuals and organizations committed to relieving the plight of children today. Yet the problems grow greater year by year, like a tide that cannot turn by itself. To turn the situation around requires an alliance of individuals and organizations working together in communities, in nations, and worldwide.

We would like to propose an Alliance for Childhood, which would bring together parents, teachers, doctors, therapists, researchers, and politicians with a wide range of child-oriented organizations to identify causes of this health crisis and to work together for social change.

The Alliance seeks to become a broadly-inclusive, independent nonprofit organization. We invite you to participate. For more information, please contact:

In North America:
Alliance for Childhood, P.O. Box 444, College Park, MD 20741.

In the UK:
Christopher Clouder, Chair, European Council of Steiner/Waldorf Schools, Kidbrooke Park, Forest Row, Sussex RH18 5JB, UK.

In continental Europe:
Jürgen Flinspach, Internationale Vereinigung der Waldorfkinder-gärten, 11 Heubergstrasse, D-70188, Stuttgart, Germany.

Steiner/Waldorf Teacher Training Programs and School Associations

Programs in English-speaking countries include:

Canada
Rudolf Steiner Centre, 9100 Bathurst St., #4, Thornhill, ON L4J 8C7

US
Association of Waldorf Schools of North America (AWSNA), 3911 Bannister Rd., Fair Oaks, CA 95628

Rudolf Steiner College, 9200 Fair Oaks Blvd., Fair Oaks, CA 95628. Also offers an extension program in San Francisco.

Antioch/New England Waldorf Teacher Training, 40 Avon St., Keene, NH 03431

Waldorf Institute of Sunbridge College, 260 Hungry Hollow Rd., Spring Valley, NY 10977

Arcturus Rudolf Steiner Education Program, PO Box 607116, Chicago, IL 60626

Waldorf Institute of Southern California, 17100 Superior St., Northridge, CA 91325

Waldorf Teacher Development Association, 2555 Burns, Detroit, MI 48214

Kula Makua – Adult Waldorf Education, 350 Ulua St., Honolulu, Oahu, HI 96821

Waldorf Teacher Training, 3976 Oak St., Eugene, OR 97405

UK

Emerson College, Forest Row, Sussex RH18 5BN, England

Steiner Waldorf Schools Fellowship, Kidbrooke Park, Forest Row, Sussex RH18 5JB, England

Australia

Renate Breipohl, 5 Trevose St., The Gap, QLD 4061

South Africa

Mary G. Haupte, 68 Peninsula Rd., Zee Koeulie 7945, Cape Town

New Zealand

Preparatory Course for Rudolf Steiner School Teachers, Taruna, P.O. Box 8103, Havelock North

Federation of Rudolf Steiner Schools in New Zealand, P.O. Box 888, Hastings, Hawke's Bay 4201

Steiner/Waldorf Early Childhood Education – Trainings and Seminars

US

Waldorf Early Childhood Association of North America (WECAN)
www.waldorfearlychildhood.org
285 Hungry Hollow Rd., Spring Valley, NY 10977 Provides information on centres for Early Childhood Teacher Training, Childcare Provider Training and other courses in US and Canada.

UK

Steiner Waldorf Schools Fellowship (SWSF)
www.steinerwaldorf.org.uk
Kidbrooke Park, Forest Row, East Sussex RH18 5JB
01342 822115 Provides information on Early Years Teacher Training courses and parenting workshops.

Notes

Chapter 1
You Are Your Child's First Teacher

1. Barbara Kantrowitz, 'Off to a Good Start,' in 'Your Child From Birth to Three,' *Newsweek* Special Edition, Spring/Summer 1997, p. 8.
2. Burton L. White, *The First Three Years of Life* (New York, NY: Prentice-Hall Press, 1985, p. 4)
3. Ibid., p. 5.
4. Ibid., p. 90.
5. 'The Missouri Project,' *American Baby*, April 1986, p. 43.
6. Rudolf Steiner, 'The Child Before the Seventh Year,' Dornach, December 23rd, 1921. Reported by Albert Steffen, *Lectures to Teachers* (London, England: The Library of the Anthroposophical Society in Great Britain, 1948, p. 39).
7. *Newsweek*, op. cit.
8. David Elkind, *The Hurried Child* (New York, NY: Alfred A. Knopf, 1984).
9. David Elkind, *Miseducation: Preschoolers at Risk* (New York, NY: Alfred A. Knopf, 1987).
10. Rudolf Steiner, quoted by Werner Glas in lectures at the Waldorf Institute, October 1980.
11 Betty Friedan, *The Second Phase* (MA: Harvard University Press, 1981, Rev. Ed. 1998).
12. Fern Schumer Chapman, 'Executive Guilt: Who's Taking Care of the Children?' *Fortune*, Feb. 16, 1987.
13. LynNell Hancock and Pat Wingert, 'The New Preschool,' *Newsweek* Special Edition, op. cit., pp. 36-37.
14. Ibid.
15. David Elkind, op. cit., p. 120.
16. Rudolf Steiner, *Philosophy of Freedom* (Spring Valley, NY: Anthroposophic Press, 1964).

17. For accounts of the spiritual aspects of conception and pregnancy, see Jeannine Parvati Baker, et al., *Conscious Conception* (Monroe, UT: Freestone Publishing Company, 1986) and Murshida Vera Justin Corda, *Cradle of Heaven* (Lebanon Springs, NY: Omega Press, 1987).

18. Quoted in Sharon Begley, 'How to Build a Baby's Brain,' in *Newsweek* Special Edition, op. cit., p. 30.

19. Ibid., p. 31.

20. Ibid.

21. Quoted in Jerry Adler, 'It's a Wise Father Who Knows... ,' *Newsweek* Special Edition, op. cit., p 73.

Chapter 2
Receiving and Caring for the Newborn

1. Frederick Leboyer, *Birth Without Violence* (New York, NY: Alfred Knopf, 1975).

2. Hugo Lagercrantz and Theodore A. Slotkin, 'The 'Stress' of Being Born,' *Scientific American*, April 1986, pp. 100-107.

3. Werner Hassauer, *Die Geburt der Individualität* (Stuttgart, Germany: Verlag Urachhaus Johannes M. Mayer GmbH, 1984, p. 57).

4. Ibid., p. 97.

5. Ibid., p. 65. For further information on Steiner's use of the terms body, soul, and spirit, see Rudolf Steiner, *Theosophy* (Spring Valley, NY: Anthroposophic Press, 1971).

6. Karl König, *Eternal Childhood* (N. Yorkshire, England: Camphill Press, 1994), pp. 44-45.

7. Ibid., p. 36.

8. Ibid., p. 92.

9. Rudolf Steiner, *The Kingdom of Childhood* (London, England: Rudolf Steiner Press, 1974, p. 22).

10. König, op. cit., p.33.

11. Leboyer, op. cit.

12. See Thomas Verny, M.D., *The Secret Life of the Unborn Child* (New York, NY: Dell Publishing Company, 1981) or contact the Association for Pre- and Perinatal Psychology and Health, PO Box 994, Geyserville, CA 95441.

13. Rudolf Steiner, course of lectures given in Torquay, England, Summer, 1924. Quoted in Elisabeth Grunelius, *Early Childhood Education and the Waldorf School Plan* (Englewood, NJ: Waldorf School Monographs, 1974, p. 42).

14. Rudolf Steiner, *The Spiritual Ground of Education* (London, England: Rudolf Steiner Press, 1947, p. 38).

15. Begley, op. cit., pp. 30-31.

16. Debra Rosenberg and Larry Reibstein, 'Pots, Blocks & Socks,' *Newsweek* Special Edition, op. cit., p. 34.

17. Joseph Chilton Pearce in a lecture at the Magical Years Conference, Ann Arbor, MI, April 3, 1987.

18. Tom McNichol, 'The Power of Touch,' *USA Weekend*, Feb. 6-8, 1998, p. 22.
19. Ibid.
20. Mariana Caplan, *Untouched: The Need for Genuine Affection in an Impersonal World* (Prescott, AZ: Hohm Press, 1998), p. 145.
21. Reported in *Lancet*, Vol. 2, 1983, p. 1014.
22. White, op. cit., p. 19.
23. Rudolf Steiner, *The Education of the Child* (London, England: Rudolf Steiner Press, 1965, p. 24).
24. White, op. cit., p. 15.
25. Leboyer, op. cit.
26. Lark Bergwin-Anderson, 'Letters from Readers,' *Waldorf Kindergarten Association of North America Newsletter*, Spring 1990, p. 30.
27. White, op. cit., p. 29.
28. Joan Salter, *Mothering with Soul* (Gloucestershire, UK: Hawthorn Press, 1998, pp. 43-52).
29. Karl König, op. cit., p.63.
30. Aletha Jauch Solter, *The Aware Baby* (Goleta, CA: Shining Star Press, 1984).
31. Rudolf Steiner in a lecture given January 30, 1913, and quoted in *The Waldorf Kindergarten Newsletter*, Winter, 1987, p. 15. For an inspiring description of one mother's work with this picture, see Joan Salter, op. cit., pp. 17-21.
32. White, op. cit., pp. 24-27.
33. For further information on the Pikler method, contact Resources for Infant Educarers, 1550 Murray Circle, Los Angeles, CA 90026.

Chapter 3
Growing Down and Waking Up

1. Jane Healy, *Your Child's Growing Mind* (NY: Doubleday, 1994), p. 30.
2. Jean Ayers, *Sensory Integration and Learning Disorders* (Los Angeles, CA: Western Psychological Services, 1973).
3. White, op. cit., p. 60.
4. *Pediatric Notes*, March 26, 1987, p. 46, summarized in *Pediatrics for Parents*, Vol. 8, Issue 6, June 1987.
5. *Canadian Medical Association Journal*, January 1, 1987, p. 57, summarized in *Pediatrics for Parents*, ibid.
6. *Pediatric Notes*, op. cit.
7. White, op. cit., p. 80.
8. Rudolf Steiner, lectures given in Dornach, Switzerland, April 15-22, 1923, reported by Albert Steffen in Swiss Teachers' Course (London: The Library of the Anthroposophical Society in Great Britain, na).
9. Rudolf Steiner, *Pneumatosophy*, 'The Riddles of the Inner Human Being,' lecture given in Berlin, May 23, 1923 (New York, NY: Anthroposophic Press, p. 2).

10. Rudolf Steiner, reported by Steffen, loc. cit.
11. Geoffrey Cowley, 'The Language Explosion,' *Newsweek* Special Edition, op. cit., p. 17.
12. Ibid., pp. 16-17.
13. Candy Verney, *The Singing Day* (Gloucestershire, UK: Hawthorn Press, 2004).
14. Rudolf Steiner, reported by Albert Steffen, loc. cit.
15. Cowley, op. cit., p. 20.
16. Sharon Begley, op. cit., p. 31.
17. Donna Tommelleo, 'Toddlers not chatty? That's OK, experts say,' *Ann Arbor News*, December, 1997, 'Connection Section.'
18. Cowley, op. cit., p. 21.
19. Karl König, *The First Three Years of the Child* (Spring Valley, NY: Anthroposophic Press, 1969, p. 24).
20. Daniel Udo de Haes, *The Young Child* (Spring Valley, NY: Anthroposophic Press, 1986, p. 24.).
21. Ibid.
22. Steiner, *Pneumatosophy*, op. cit., p. 3.
23. Unsigned, 'A baby's 'ga-ga' speaks volumes, *Los Angeles Times*, carried in the *Sacramento Bee*, January 1, 1999, p. A8.
24. Cowley, op. cit., p. 21.
25. Ibid.
26. Reported in 'The Calling,' PO Box 162, Mikado, MI 48745, Spring, 1998, p. 12.
27. Reprinted from p. 19 of the *Waldorf Parenting Handbook* by Lois Cusick by permission of the publishers, St. George Publications, Spring Valley, NY 10977.
28. White, op. cit., p. 157.

Chapter 4
Helping Your Baby's Development in the First Year

1. Helle Heckmann, *Nøkken: A Garden for Children* (Wilton, NH: A Center for Anthroposophy, 1998, p. 4).
2. Ibid., p. 16.
3. References quote in Robert B. McCall, 'Support Thy Wife,' *Parents*, July 1987, pp. 168-169.
4. See work by Audrey McAllen, available through the Remedial Research Group, 9200 Fair Oaks Blvd., Fair Oaks, CA 95628.
5. Joseph Chilton Pearce, *The Magical Child* (New York, NY: E. P. Dutton, 1977).
6. White, op. cit., p. 102.
7. Healy, *Your Child's Growing Mind*, op. cit., pp. 47-48.
8. White, op. cit., p. 88. More recent studies with visual habituation have shown that when balls are rolled behind a screen and babies become bored, they become agitated when the screen is removed and

the balls aren't there, leading scientists to believe that 'object permanence' is established earlier than previously thought.

9. Healy, op. cit., pp. 29 & 39.
10. White, op. cit., p. 106.
11. Ibid., p. 91.
12. Healy, op. cit., p. 33.
13. Anne Scott, *The Laughing Baby* (South Hadley, MA: Bergin & Garvey, 1987).
14. Heckmann, op. cit., p. 18.
15. White, op. cit., pp. 282-294 and write for further information from The Center for Parent Education, 55 Chapel St., Newton, MA 02160.

Chapter 5
Helping Your Toddler's Development

1. Elkind, op. cit.
2. Begley, op. cit., p. 31.
3. White, op. cit., p.176.
4. Ibid., p. 151.
5. Ibid., p. 181.
6. Udo de Haes, op. cit.
7. Ibid., p. 61.
8. Ibid.
9. Ibid., p. 65.
10. Ibid., p. 72.
11. Steiner, *The Education of the Child*, op. cit., p. 26.
12. Heidi Britz-Crecelius, *Children at Play* (New York, NY: Inner Traditions International, 1986, pp. 94-96).
13. Steiner, op. cit., pp. 25-26.
14. For detailed directions on making knot dolls, see Susan Smith, *Echoes of a Dream* (London, Ontario: Waldorf School Association of London, 1982) or Freya Jaffke, *Toymaking with Children* (UK: Floris, 1988).
15. Verney, op. cit.

Chapter 6
Parenting Issues of the First Three Years

1. Rudolf Steiner, *Knowledge of Higher Worlds: How Is It Achieved?* (London, England: Rudolf Steiner Press, 1969).
2. Evelyn Thoman and Sue Browder, *Born Dancing* (New York: Harper & Row, 1987).
3. Tine Thevenin, *The Family Bed* (Garden City, NY: Avery, 1987).
4. Norbert Glas, *Conception, Birth and Early Childhood* (Spring Valley, NY: Anthroposophic Press, 1972).
5. Salter, op. cit., pp. 49-52.
6. Wilhelm zur Linden, *When a Child Is Born* (New York, NY: Thorsons

Publishers, Inc., 1984).

7. Write to Rudolf Steiner College Book Store or Anthroposophic Press (see Appendix A) for titles by Steiner on nutrition.

8. Aletha Jauch Solter, 'Exercises in Self-Awareness for New Parents' (Goleta, CA: Shining Star Press, 1984).

9. Aletha Jauch Solter, *The Aware Baby*, op. cit.

10. Vimala Schneider, 'Crying,' *Mothering*, Spring 1987, p. 23.

11. David Sobel, *Waldorf Teacher Training Newsletter*, Spring 1987, p. 5.

12. Heckmann, op. cit. pp. 10-12.

13. Melissa Healy, 'Study links good day care, success in early grades,' *Sacramento Bee*, June 9, 1999, p. A5.

14. Melissa Healy, 'Study: Day care doesn't harm cognitive growth,' *Ann Arbor News*, April 4, 1997.

15. T. Berry Brazelton, *Working and Caring* (Reading, MA: Addison-Wesley, 1985).

16. White, op. cit., p. 267.

17. Ibid.

18. Elkind, op. cit.

19. White, op. cit., p. 272.

20. Susan Reimer, 'It's time to review more True Facts,' *Ann Arbor News*, August 5, 1997.

21. Rahima Baldwin Dancy and Terra Palmarini Richardson, *Pregnant Feelings* (Berkeley, CA: Celestial Arts, 1986).

22. T. Berry Brazelton, *Infants and Mothers: Differences in Development* (New York, NY: Dell, 1986).

23. Rudolf Steiner, *The Four Temperaments* (Hudson, New York: Anthroposophic Press, 1967).

24. Kim Boatman, 'Parenting guru's push for bigger diapers embraced by consumers,' *Sacramento Bee*, January 2, 1999, Scene 7.

25. Ibid.

Chapter 7
The Development of Fantasy and Creative Play

1. Caroline von Heydebrand, Childhood: *A Study of the Growing Soul* (London: Anthroposophic Publishing Company, 1946, p. 60).

2. Britz-Crecelius, op. cit., p. 7.

3. Caroline von Heydebrand, 'The Child at Play,' in Paul M. Allen (Ed.), *Education as an Art: Rudolf Steiner and Other Writers* (Blauvelt, NY: Steinerbooks/Multimedia Publishing Corp., 1970, p. 89).

4. Britz-Crecelius, op. cit., p. 32.

5. Ibid., p. 40.

6. Bruno Bettelheim, *The Uses of Enchantment* (New York, NY: Alfred A. Knopf, 1975, p. 46).

7. von Heydebrand, op. cit., p. 95.

8. Britz-Crecelius, op. cit., pp. 79-101.

9. Ibid., p. 92.

10. Bruno Bettelheim, 'The Importance of Play,' *Atlantic Monthly*, March 1987, p. 40.
11. Britz-Crecelius, op cit., p. 97.
12. Ibid.
13. Bettelheim, op. cit., p. 37.
14. Ibid., p. 36.
15. Ibid., p. 37.
16. Helle Heckmann, 'Imagination Surpasses Reality – Also When it Comes to Toys,' unpublished handout at her lecture, April, 1998, Ann Arbor, MI.
17. Dr. Gilbert Childs and Sylvia Childs, *Your Reincarnating Child* (London: Rudolf Steiner Press, 1995, p. 89).
18. Ibid., p. 107.
19. Quoted in Britz-Crecelius, op. cit., p. 81
20. Heckmann, loc. cit.
21. Barbara Dewey, 'Play with Your Child?' *Herb 'n Home Newsletter*, July 1998, p. 8.
22. Ibid.
23. Rudolf Steiner, *The Child's Changing Consciousness and Waldorf Education* (NY: Anthroposophic Press, 1988, pp. 79-81).

Chapter 8
Nourishing Your Child's Imagination

1.   Dr. Karen N. Olness, 'Little People, Images and Child Health,' *Amer. J. of Clinical Hypnosis*, Vol. 27, No. 3, January 1985.
2.   Rudolf Steiner, *The Arts and Their Mission*, Lectures given in Oslo, May 27-June 9, 1923 (New York: Anthroposophic Press, 1964, p. 108).
3.   Rudolf Steiner, course of lectures delivered at Ilkey, Yorkshire, England, August 1923 and quoted in Grunelius, op. cit., pp. 42-43).
4.   Olness, op. cit.
5.   Olness, op. cit., p. 173.
6.   Barry Sanders, *A Is for Ox* (NY: Pantheon Books, 1994, p. 243).
7.   Eileen Hutchins, 'The Value of Fairy Tales and Nursery Rhymes,' *Child and Man Extracts* (Sussex, England: Steiner Schools Fellowship, na, p. 173).
8.   Robert Carter, *The Tao and Mother Goose* (Wheaton, IL: The Theosophical Publishing House, 1988, pp. 65-66).
9.   Joan Almon, 'Choosing Fairy Tales for Young Children,' *Waldorf Kindergarten Newsletter*, Fall 1985, p. 7.
10. Quoted by Mary Jo Kochakian in 'Fairy tales allow kids to grapple with good and evil, says psychologist,' *Ann Arbor News*, July 5, 1987.
11. Kornei Chukovsky, *From Two to Five* (Berkeley, CA: University of California Press, 1963).
12. See Helmut von Kügelgen, 'Fairy Tale Language and the Image of

Man,' *Waldorf Kindergarten Newsletter*, Fall 1986 and Rudolf Steiner, *The Interpretation of Fairy Tales* (Spring Valley, NY: Anthroposophic Press, 1943).

13. Miriam Whitfield, *Fairy Stories... Why, When, How* (Boulder, CO: The Juniper Tree, 1986).
14. Ibid., p. 22.
15. Ibid., p. 23.
16. Linda Pritzker, *The Princess Who Wept Pearls* (self-published, 1998, p. 12). Available for purchase from Rudolf Steiner College Book Store, 9200 Fair Oaks Blvd., Fair Oaks, CA 95628.
17. Diana Hughes, 'Fairy Tales: A Basis for Moral Education,' *Ethics in Education*, Vol. 6, No. 4, March 1987, p. 11.
18. Ibid., p. 12.
19. Bettelheim, *Uses of Enchantment*, op. cit., p. 9.
20. Hughes, op. cit., p. 11.
21. Bettelheim, op. cit.
22. Neil Postman, *The Disappearance of Childhood* (New York, NY: Dell Publishing, 1982, pp. 93-94).
23. Udo de Haes, op. cit., p. 49.
24. Almon, op. cit.
25. Ibid.
26. Udo de Haes, op. cit., p. 52.
27. Steven Spitalny, 'Diversity and the Story in the Kindergarten,' *Gateways, Waldorf Kindergarten Association Newsletter*, Issue 33, Autumn 1997, pp. 7 10.
28. Bronja Zahlingen, *Plays for Puppets and Marionettes* (Silver Spring, MD: Acorn Hill Children's Center, 1983).
29. Bronja Zahlingen, 'The Pedagogical Value of Marionette and Table Puppet Shows for the Small Child,' *Waldorf Kindergarten Newsletter*, Fall 1982.
30. Helmut von Kügelgen, 'Marionette Theaters: Posing a Task for Socially Oriented Education,' *Waldorf Kindergarten Newsletter*, Fall-Winter 1982.
31. Ibid.

Chapter 9
Developing Your Child's Artistic Ability

1. Rauld Russell, 'Wet-on-Wet Watercolor Painting,' *Mothering*, Summer 1987, p. 89.
2. Rudolf Steiner, *The Education of the Child*, op. cit., p. 27.
3. Johann Wolfgang von Goethe, *Theory of Colours* (Totowa, NJ: Biblio Distribution Center, 1967).
4. Rudolf Steiner, *Practical Advice for Teachers* (London, England: Rudolf Steiner Press, 1970, p. 11).
5. Brunhild Müller, *Painting with Children* (Edinburgh, UK: Floris Books, 1987, p. 11).

6. Russell, op. cit., p. 90.
7. Ibid., p. 89.
8. Caroline von Heydebrand, 'The Child When He Paints,' in Allen (ed.) op. cit., p. 86.
9. Freya Jaffke, 'About Painting and Human Development Through Art' translated from *Plan und Praxis des Waldorf-kindergartens* printed in the *Waldorf Kindergarten Newsletter*, Fall 1984.
10. Ibid.
11. Ibid.
12. Michaela Strauss, *Understanding Children's Drawings* (London, England: Rudolf Steiner Press, 1978).
13. Ibid., pp. 22 and 29.
14. Ibid., p. 47.
15. Ibid., p. 62.
16. Isabel Wyatt, *Seven-Year-Old Wonder-Book* (San Rafael, CA: Dawn-Leigh Publications, 1978).
17. Julia Cameron, *The Artist's Way* (NY: Putnam's Sons, 1992).

Chapter 10
Your Child's Musical Ability

1. Julius Knierim, *Quintenlieder* (Echzell, Germany: Verlag Das Seelenpflegebedürftige Kind, 1982, pp. 3-4).
2. Rudolf Steiner, *Practical Course for Teachers* (London: Rudolf Steiner Press, 1937, pp. 18-19).
3. Vadim Prokhorov, 'Will Piano Lessons Make My Child Smarter?' *Parade Magazine*, June 14, 1999, p. 15.
4. Quoted in Pamela G. Kripke, 'Get the Beat, Baby,' *American Baby*, February, 1998, p. 51.
5. Rudolf Steiner, *The Kingdom of Childhood*, op. cit., p. 110.
6. Knierim, loc. cit.
7. Hutchins, op. cit., p. 44.
8. Rosemary Gebert, in a lecture at the Waldorf Institute, Oct. 1981.
9. Jane Winslow Eliot, *From Ring Around the Roses to London Bridge Is Falling Down: Some Incarnating Games* (New York, NY: Rudolf Steiner School Press, 1982, p. 1).
10. Steiner, *Education of the Child*, op. cit., p.29.
11. 'Mood of the Fifth' is a special kind of pentatonic music that is discussed in Julius Knierim's book *Quintenlieder: Songs in the Mood of the Fifth*, translated by Karen and Peter Klaveness. Readers interested in the healing and other esoteric aspects of music are referred to Rudolf Steiner's work *The Inner Nature of Music and the Experience of Tone* (Spring Valley, NY: Anthroposophic Press, 1983).
12. Rudolf Steiner, course of lectures delivered at the foundation of the Waldorf School in Stuttgart, August 21-September 5, 1919, and quoted in Grunelius, op. cit., p. 45.

13. Elkind, op. cit.
14. 'Head trauma questions,' in *USA Weekend*, January 3, 1999.

Chapter 11
Rhythm and Discipline in Home Life

1. Margret Meyerkort, 'Creative Discipline,' in Davy and Voors (eds.), op. cit., pp. 214-223.
2. Rudolf Steiner, *Soul Economy and Waldorf Education* (Spring Valley, NY: Anthroposophic Press, 1986, p. 121).
3. Ibid., p. 115.
4. Grunelius, op. cit., p. 29.
5. Ibid., p. 28.
6. Rudolf Steiner, *Signs and Symbols of the Christmas Festival* (Spring Valley, NY: Anthroposophic Press, 1969).
7. Grunelius, op. cit., p. 27.
8. Ibid.
9. Andrea Gambardella, 'Rhythm in Home Life,' *Waldorf Kindergarten Newsletter*, Fall 1984, p. 10.
10. Bons Voors, 'Family Meals,' in Davy and Voors (eds.), op. cit., pp. 154-160.
11. Margret Meyerkort, 'Sleeping and Waking,' in ibid., pp. 142-153.
12. Ibid., p. 150.
13. Rudolf Steiner, *Prayers for Mothers and Children* (London: Rudolf Steiner Press, 1983, p. 50, translated from the German).
14. Friedel Lenz, *Celebrating the Festivals with Children* (Spring Valley, NY: Anthroposophic Press, 1986).
15. Diana Carey and Judy Large, *Festivals, Family and Food* (Gloucester, UK: Hawthorn Press, 1982).
16. Margret Meyerkort (ed.), *Spring* (Gloucester, UK: Wynstones Press, 1983). Available from Rudolf Steiner College, 9200 Fair Oaks Blvd., Fair Oaks, CA 95628.

Chapter 12
Cognitive Development and Early Childhood Education

1. Elkind, *Miseducation*, op. cit., pp. 119-122.
2. Grunelius, op. cit., p. 26.
3. 'Kids Need Time to Be Kids,' *Newsweek*, Feb. 22, 1987, p. 57.
4. Steiner, *Education of the Child*, op. cit., p. 21.
5. Healy, op. cit., pp. 49-50.
6. Ibid., p. 238.
7. Ibid., p. 240.
8. Ibid., p. 265.
9. Healy, *Failure to Connect* (NY: Simon & Schuster, 1998), p. 241.

10. Healy, *Your Child's Growing Mind*, op. cit., p. 63.
11. S. W. Haughland, 'The Effect of Computer Software on Preschool Children's Developmental Gains,' *Journal of Computing in Childhood Education*, 3(1), 1992, pp. 15-30.
12. 'Kids,' op. cit., p. 58.
13. Ibid., p. 56.
14. Ibid., pp. 57-58.
15. Joan Almon, 'What Are the Needs of the Five-Year-Olds?' *Leading Forth, Journal of the Waldorf School of Baltimore*, Spring 1988, No. 4, pp. 5-6.
16. Steiner, op. cit., pp. 28-29.
17. Diana Loercher Pazicky, 'Just because a child is the right age doesn't mean he's ready for school,' *Philadelphia Inquirer*, April 22, 1984.
18. James K. Uphoff and June Gilmore, 'Pupil Age at School Entrance – How Many Are Ready for Success?' *Educational Leadership*, September 1985, pp. 86-90.
19. Pazicky, loc. cit.
20. Healy, *Your Child's Growing Mind*, op. cit., p. 55.
21. Audrey McAllen, 'On First Grade Readiness: An Interview with Margret Meyerkort,' *Bulletin of the Remedial Research Group*, No. 5, August 1986 (Fair Oaks, CA: Remedial Research Group at the Rudolf Steiner College, pp. 12-15).

Chapter 13
More Parenting Issues

1. Elkind, *The Hurried Child* and *Miseducation*, op. cit.
2. Healy, *Failure to Connect*, op. cit., p. 110.
3. Todd Oppenheimer, 'The Computer Delusion,' *Atlantic Monthly*, July 1997, pp. 45-62.
4. Healy, op. cit., p. 133.
5. Rudolf Steiner, from a course of lectures delivered in Oxford, England, in the summer of 1922, quoted in Grunelius, op. cit., p. 43.
6. Rudolf Steiner, *Human Values in Education*, lectures given in Arnheim, Switzerland, July 17-24, 1924 (London: Rudolf Steiner Press, 1971, p. 55).
7. John Rosemond, 'Children and Television,' *Boston Globe*, Jan. 3, 1984.
8. Audrey McAllen, 'Movement or Television,' *Bulletin of the Remedial Research Group* (Fair Oaks, CA: Rudolf Steiner College, na).
9. Rosemond, op. cit.
10. Healy, op. cit., p. 32.
11. Ibid., pp. 112-115.
12. Ibid., pp. 114-115.
13. Marie Winn, *The Plug-In Drug* (New York, NY: Viking, 1985).
14. Study by BJK&E Media Group of Manhattan, reported in David

Bauder, 'Children today watching more and more TV, study shows,' *Ann Arbor News*, December 30, 1997.

15. *Education Week*, February 14, 1996, p. 32; quoted in Healy, op. cit., p. 104.
16. Karen Kaplan, 'Army, Hollywood to co-star in research,' *Sacramento Bee*, Aug. 18, 1999, p. A4.
17. Healy, op. cit., p. 180.
18. Robert W. Kubey, Letter to the editor, *New York Times*, December 25, 1997, p. A14.
19. Healy, op. cit., pp. 158-159.
20. See Otto Wolff, 'Childhood Diseases as a Source of Development,' *Weleda News*, Vol. 4, 1983, pp. 14-15.
21. Dr. Uwe Stave, 'Reflections on Fever in Childhood,' *Journal for Anthroposophy*, No. 42, Autumn 1985, p. 9.
22. Ibid., p. 10.
23. In addition to Western allopathic medicine, other systems such as homeopathy, naturopathy, anthroposophical or ayurvedic medicine also can provide helpful approaches.
24. zur Linden, op. cit., pp. 163-164.
25. J. G. Bennett, et al., *The Spiritual Hunger of the Modern Child* (Charles Town, WV: Claymont Communications, 1984).
26. René Knight-Weiler, *Spiritual Mothering Journal*, pp. 28-29.
27. Ibid.
28. Joseph Chilton Pearce, *The Magical Child Matures* (New York: Bantam, 1986).
29. Herbert Hahn, *From the Well-Springs of the Soul: Religious Instruction for the Child* (Forest Row, England: Rudolf Steiner Schools Fellowship, 1966).
30. Friedel Lenz, *Celebrating the Festivals with Children* (Hudson, NY: Anthroposophic Press, 1986).
31. Rudolf Steiner, *Study of Man* (London: Anthroposophic Press, 1947, p. 138).
32. Rudolf Steiner, *The Roots of Education* (London: Rudolf Steiner Press, 1968, pp. 37-38).
33. Rudolf Steiner, *The Essentials of Education* (London: Rudolf Steiner Press, 1948, p. 29).
34. Steiner, *Human Values in Education*, op. cit., p. 125.
35. Rudolf Steiner, *The Renewal of Education* (Forest Row, UK: Steiner Schools Fellowship Publications, 1981, p. 65).
36. Peggy O'Mara McMahon, 'An Ethic of Parenting,' *Mothering*, No. 47, Spring, 1988, p. 6.
37. Ibid., p. 7.

Bibliography

Almon, Joan, 'Choosing Fairy Tales for Young Children.' *Waldorf Kindergarten Newsletter,* Fall, 1985.

Baker, Jeannine, et al. *Conscious Conception.* (Monroe, UT: Freestone Publishing Company, 1986).

Baldwin Dancy, Rahima, *Special Delivery.* (Berkeley, CA: Celestial Arts, 1986).

Baldwin Dancy, Rahima and Richardson, Terre Palmarini. *Pregnant Feelings.* (Berkeley, CA: Celestial Arts, 1986).

Bennett, John, et al. *The Spiritual Hunger of the Modern Child.* (Charles Town, WV: Claymont Communications, 1984).

Bettelheim, Bruno. *The Uses of Enchantment.* (New York, NY: Alfred A. Knopf, 1975).

___'The Importance of Play.' *Atlantic Monthly*, March 1987.

Bettelheim, Bruno and Zelan, Karen. 'Why Children Don't Like to Read.' *Atlantic Monthly*, November 1981.

Brazelton, T. Berry. *Infants and Mothers: Differences in Development.* (New York, NY: Dell, 1986).

___*Working and Caring.* (Reading, MA: Addison-Wesley, 1985).

Britz-Crecelius, Heidi. *Children at Play.* (New York, NY: Inner Traditions International, 1986).

Cameron, Julia. *The Artist's Way.* (NY, NY: Putnam's Sons, 1992).

Caplan, Mariana. *Untouched.* (Prescott, AZ: Hohm Press, 1998).

Carey, Diana and Large, Judy. *Festivals, Family and Food.* (Gloucester, UK: Hawthorn Press, 1982).

Carlgren, Frans. *Education Towards Freedom.* (East Grinstead, UK: Lanthorn Press, 1976).

Carter, Robert. *The Tao and Mother Goose.* (Wheaton, IL: The Theosophical Publishing House, 1988).

Childs, Dr. Gilbert and Childs, Sylvia. *Your Reincarnating Child.* (London: Rudolf Steiner Press, 1995).

Chukovsky, Kornei. *From Two to Five*. (Berkeley, CA: University of California Press, 1963).

Cooper, Stephanie, et al. *The Children's Year*. (Gloucester, UK: Hawthorn Press, 1987).

Corda, Murshida Vera Justin. *Cradle of Heaven*. (Lebanon Springs, NY: Omega Press, 1987).

Cusick, Lois. *Waldorf Parenting Handbook*. (Spring Valley, NY: St. George Publications, 1984).

Davy, Gudrun and Voors, Bons (Eds.). *Lifeways*. (Gloucester, UK: Hawthorn Press, 1983).

Eliot, Jane Winslow. *From Ring Around the Roses to London Bridge Is Falling Down*. (New York, NY: Rudolf Steiner School Press, 1982).

Elkind, David. *The Hurried Child*. (New York, NY: Alfred A. Knopf, 1984).

___*Miseducation: Preschoolers at Risk* (New York, NY: Alfred A. Knopf, 1987).

Gabert, Erich. *Punishment in Self-Education and the Education of the Child*. (Forest Row, UK: Steiner Schools Fellowship Publications, 1972).

Glas, Norbert. *Conception, Birth and Early Childhood*. (Spring Valley, NY: Anthroposophic Press, 1972).

Glöckler, Michaela and Goebel, Wolfgang. *A Guide to Child Health*. (Hudson, NY: Anthroposophic Press, 1984).

Grunelius, Elizabeth. *Early Childhood Education and the Waldorf School Plan*. (Englewood, NJ: Waldorf School Monographs, 1974).

Hahn, Herbert. *From the Well-Springs of the Soul*. (Forest Row, UK: Rudolf Steiner Schools Fellowship, 1966).

Harwood, A. C. *The Recovery of Man in Childhood*. (Spring Valley, NY: Anthroposophic Press, 1958).

Hassauer, Werner. *Die Geburt der Individualität*. (Stuttgart, Germany: Verlag Urachhaus Johannes M. Mayer GmbH, 1984).

Healy, Jane. *Endangered Minds*. (New York: Simon & Schuster, 1990).

Healy, Jane. *Failure to Connect*. (New York: Simon & Schuster, 1998).

Healy, Jane. *Your Child's Growing Mind*. (New York: Doubleday, Rev. 1994).

Heckmann, Helle. *Nøkken: A Garden for Children*. (Silver Spring, MD: Waldorf Early Childhood Association, 1998).

Hughes, Diana. 'Fairy Tales: A Basis for Moral Education.' *Ethics in Education*, Vol. 6, No. 4, March 1987.

Hutchins, Eileen, 'The Value of Fairy Tales and Nursery Rhymes.' *Child and Man Extracts*. (Sussex, UK: Steiner Schools Fellowship, na).

Jaffke, Freya. 'About Painting and Human Development through Art.' *Waldorf Kindergarten Newsletter*, Fall 1984.

___*Toymaking with Children*. (Edinburgh, UK: Floris, 1988).

___*Work and Play in Early Childhood*. (Hudson, NY: Anthroposophic Press, 1996).

Knierim, Julius. *Quintenlieder*. (Echzell, Germany: Verlag Das Seelenpflegebedürftige Kind, 1982).

König, Karl. *The First Three Years of the Child.* (Spring Valley, NY: Anthroposophic Press, 1969).

___*Eternal Childhood.* (North Yorkshire, UK: Camphill Books. 1994).

Lagercrantz, Hugo and Slotkin, Theodore. "The 'Stress' of Being Born." *Scientific American*, April 1986, pp. 100-107.

Leboyer, Frederick. *Birth Without Violence.* (New York, NY: Alfred A. Knopf, 1975).

Lebret, Elisabeth. *Pentatonic Songs.* (Toronto, Ontario: Waldorf School Association of Toronto, 1985).

Lenz, Friedel. *Celebrating the Festivals with Children.* (Hudson, NY: Anthroposophic Press, 1986).

Masters, Brien, Ed. *Rudolf Steiner Waldorf Education.* (Spring Valley, NY: Steiner Schools Fellowship, 1986).

Meyer, Rudolf. *The Wisdom of Fairy Tales.* (Edinburgh, UK: Floris Books, 1987).

Montagu, Ashley. *Touching.* (New York, NY: Columbia University Press, 1971).

Moore, Raymond, and Moore, Dorothy. *Better Late Than Early.* (New York: Reader's Digest Press, 1975).

___*School Can Wait.* (Provo, UT: Brigham Young University Press, 1979).

Müller, Brunhild. *Painting with Children.* (Edinburgh, UK: Floris Books, 1987).

Neuschütz, Karin. *The Doll Book.* (Burdett, NY: Larson Publications, 1982).

Olness, Karen N. 'Little People, Images and Child Health,' *American Journal of Clinical Hypnosis*, Vol. 27, No. 3, January 1985.

O'Mara McMahon, Peggy. 'An Ethic of Parenting,' *Mothering*, No. 47, Spring 1988.

Pearce, Joseph Chilton. *The Magical Child.* (New York: E. P. Dutton, 1977).

___*The Magical Child Matures.* (New York, NY: Bantam, 1986).

Pritzker, Linda. *The Princess Who Wept Pearls: The Feminine Journey in Fairy Tales.* (Boulder, CO: Self-published, 1998).

Querido, René. *Creativity in Education: The Waldorf Approach.* (San Francisco, CA: H.S. Dakin Company, 1985).

Russell, Rauld. 'Wet-on-Wet Watercolor Painting.' *Mothering*, Summer, 1987.

___*How to Do Wet-on-Wet Watercolor Painting and Teach Your Children.* (Coos Bay, OR: The Iris, 1987).

Russ, Johanne. *Clump-a-Dump and Snickle-Snack.* (Spring Valley, NY: Mercury Press, na).

Salter, Joan. *The Incarnating Child.* (Gloucester, UK: Hawthorn Press, 1987).

___*Mothering with Soul.* (Gloucester, UK: Hawthorn Press, 1998).

Sanders, Barry. *A Is for Ox.* (NY: Pantheon Books, 1994).

Schmidt-Brabant, Manfred. *The Spiritual Tasks of the Homemaker.* (London, UK: Temple Lodge, 1996).

Scott, Anne. *The Laughing Baby.* (South Hadley, MA: Bergin & Garvey, 1987).

Segal, Marilyn. *Your Child at Play: Birth to One Year.* (New York: Newmarket Press, 1985).

Segal, Marilyn and Adcock, Don. *Your Child at Play: One to Two Years.* (New York: Newmarket Press, 1985).

Siegel, Richard. *The First Jewish Catalog.* (Philadelphia, PA: The Jewish Publication Society of America, na).

Smith, Susan. *Echoes of a Dream.* (London, Ontario: Waldorf School Association of London, 1982).

Solter, Aletha Jauch. *The Aware Baby.* (Goleta, CA: Shining Star Press, 1984).

___*Exercises in Self-Awareness for New Parents* (Goleta, CA: Shining Star Press, 1984).

Stave, Uwe. 'Reflections on Fever in Childhood.' *Journal for Anthroposophy*, No. 42, Autumn, 1985.

Steiner, Rudolf. *The Arts and Their Mission.* (New York: Anthroposophic Press, 1964).

___*The Cycle of the Year.* (Spring Valley, NY: Anthroposophic Press, 1984).

___*The Education of the Child.* (London, UK: Rudolf Steiner Press, 1965).

___*The Essentials of Education.* (London, UK: Rudolf Steiner Press, 1948).

___*The Four Temperaments.* (Hudson, NY: Anthroposophic Press, 1987).

___*Human Values in Education.* (London, UK: Rudolf Steiner Press, 1971).

___*The Interpretation of Fairy Tales.* (London, UK: Rudolf Steiner Press, 1971).

___*An Introduction to Waldorf Education.* (Spring Valley, NY: Anthroposophic Press, 1985).

___*The Kingdom of Childhood.* (London, UK: Rudolf Steiner Press, 1974).

___*Lectures to Teachers.* (London, UK: Rudolf Steiner Press, 1974).

___*Pneumatosophy.* (New York: Anthroposophic Press, na).

___*Practical Advice for Teachers.* (London, UK: Rudolf Steiner Press, 1970).

___*Practical Course for Teachers.* (London, UK: Rudolf Steiner Press, 1937).

___*Prayers for Mothers and Children.* (London, UK: Rudolf Steiner Press, 1983).

___*The Renewal of Education.* (Forest Row, UK: Steiner Schools Fellowship Publications, 1981).

___*The Roots of Education.* (London, UK: Rudolf Steiner Press, 1968).

___*Signs and Symbols* of the Christmas Festival. (Spring Valley, NY: Anthroposophic Press, 1969).

___*Soul Economy and Waldorf Education.* (Spring Valley, NY: Anthroposophic Press, 1986).

___*The Spiritual Ground of Education.* (London, UK: Rudolf Steiner Press, 1947).

___*Study of Man.* (London, UK: Anthroposophic Press, 1947).

___*Swiss Teachers' Course.* (London, UK: The Library of the Anthroposophical Society in Great Britain, na).

Strassford, Michael. *The Jewish Holidays*. (New York, NY: Harper & Row, 1985).

Strauss, Michaela. *Understanding Children's Drawings*. (London, UK: Rudolf Steiner Press, 1978).

Thevenin, Tine. *Mothering and Fathering. The Gender Differences in Child Rearing*. (Garden City Park, NY: Avery Publishing, 1993).

Thoman, Evelyn and Browder, Sue. *Born Dancing*. (New York, NY: Harper and Row, 1987).

Udo de Haes, Daniel. *The Young Child*. (Spring Valley, NY: Anthroposophic Press, 1986).

Uphoff, James and Gilmore, June. 'Pupil Age at School Entrance—How Many are Ready for Success?' *Educational Leadership*, September 1985, pp. 86-90.

van Bentheim, Tineke, et al. *Caring for the Sick at Home*. (Edinburgh, UK: Floris Books, 1987).

von Heydebrand, Caroline. 'The Child at Play' and 'The Child When He Paints' in Allen, Paul (Ed.). *Education as an Art: Rudolf Steiner and Other Writers*. (Blauvelt, NY: Steinerbooks, 1970).

___*Childhood: A Study of the Growing Soul*. (London, UK: Anthroposophic Publishing Co., 1946).

von Kügelgen, Helmut. 'Fairy Tale Language and the Image of Man.' *Waldorf Kindergarten Newsletter*, Fall, 1986.

___ 'Marionette Theaters. Posing a Task for Socially Oriented Education.' *Waldorf Kindergarten Newsletter*, Fall 1982.

Watson, Clyde. *Catch Me & Kiss Me & Say It Again*. (New York, NY: Philomel Books, 1978).

White, Burton L. *Educating the Infant and Toddler*. (Lexington, MA: D.C. Heath and Co., 1988).

___*The First Three Years of Life* (New York, NY: Prentice Hall, 1986).

Whitfield, Miriam. Fairy Stories... *Why, When, How*. (Boulder, CO: The Juniper Tree, 1986).

Winn, Marie. *The Plug-In Drug*. (New York, NY: Viking, 1985).

Zahlingen, Bronja. 'The Pedagogical Value of Marionette and Table Puppet Shows for the Small Child.' *Waldorf Kindergarten Newsletter*, Fall, 1982.

___*Plays for Puppets and Marionettes*. (Silver Spring, MD: Acorn Hill Children's Center, 1983).

zur Linden, Wilhelm. *When a Child Is Born*. (New York, NY: Thorsons Publishers, 1984).

Index

Other books from Hawthorn Press

The Parent and Child Group Handbook
A Steiner/Waldorf approach

DOT MALE

Regular contact with other families can be a vital lifeline for parents with young children. Dot Male's lively, accessible guide to running a thriving parent and child group expains how to: create a calm, harmonious space; use rhythm and ritual to structure a session; devise appropriate toys, crafts, games and outdoor play; celebrate seasonal festivals and the cycle of the year; fulfil key health, safety and legal requirements.

256pp; 246 x 189mm; 1 903458 46 3/978-1-903458-46-4; pb

Jabulani!
Ideas for making music

CAROL SHEPHARD AND BOBBIE STORMONT

Jabulani! has all the tools you need to enjoy creating music – without having to read music or follow a song-sheet. The activities are suitable for all ages and abilities, including those with special needs. This user-friendly guide and CD includes: instructions for making drums, shakers and other instruments from scrap materials; how to organise and lead a music session; activities, case studies, useful tips and techniques; ideas for using music with story-telling, drama and sports.

128pp; 246 x 189mm; 1 903458 51 X/978-1-903458-51-8; pb/CD

The Birthday Book
CELEBRATIONS FOR EVERYONE

ANN DRUITT, CHRISTINE FYNES-CLINTON
AND MARIJE ROWLING

Everything you need for celebrating birthdays in enjoyable ways. There are suggestions for 'oldies', for teenagers, 18th and 21st parties as well as children's parties. You will find unusual celebrations for those on holiday, ill in bed, at Christmas or for rainy days.

256pp; 250 x 200mm; 1 903458 01 3; pb

The Well Balanced Child
Movement and early learning

SALLY GODDARD BLYTHE

'Learning is not just about reading, writing and maths,' says Sally Goddard Blythe. 'A child's experience of movement will help play a pivotal role in shaping his personality, his feelings and achievements.' Her book makes the case for a 'whole body' approach to learning which integrates the brain, senses, movement, music and play.

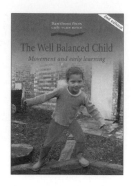

304pp; 216 x 138mm; 1 903458 63 3; pb

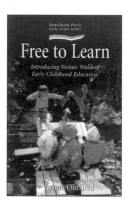

Free to Learn
Introducing Steiner Waldorf early childhood education

LYNNE OLDFIELD

Free to Learn is a comprehensive introduction to Steiner Waldorf kindergartens for parents, educators and early years' students. Lynne Oldfield illustrates the theory and practice of kindergarten education with stories, helpful insights and lively observations.

256pp; 216 x 138mm; 1 903458 06 4; pb

The Genius of Play
Celebrating the spirit of childhood

SALLY JENKINSON

The Genius of Play addresses what play is, why it matters, and how modern life endangers children's play. Sally Jenkinson's amusing, vivid observations will delight parents and teachers wanting to explore the never-ending secrets of children's play.

224pp; 216 x 138mm; 1 903458 04 8; pb

Set Free Childhood

Parents' survival guide to coping with computers and TV

MARTIN LARGE

Children watch TV and use computers for five hours daily on average. The result? Record levels of learning difficulties, obesity, eating disorders, sleep problems, language delay, aggressive behaviour, anxiety – and children on fast forward. However, *Set Free Childhood* shows you how to counter screen culture and create a calmer, more enjoyable family life.

240pp; 216 x 138mm; 1 903458 43 9; pb

The Singing Day

Songbook and CD for singing with young children

CANDY VERNEY

Singing with babies is one of the joys of being a parent. It is a lifetime gift from you that children love. This easy to use songbook and CD offer practical help for singing with young children from birth to 4 years old.

160pp; 250 x 200mm; 1 903458 25 0; pb/CD

The Children's Year

Seasonal crafts and clothes

STEPHANIE COOPER, CHRISTINE FYNES-CLINTON, MARIJE ROWLING

You needn't be an experienced craftsperson to create beautiful things! This step by step, well-illustrated book with clear instructions shows you how to get started. Children and parents are encouraged to try all sorts of handwork, with different projects relating to the seasons of the year.

192pp; 250 x 200mm; 1 903458 59 9; pb (new edition)

Storytelling with Children

NANCY MELLON

Telling stories awakens wonder and creates special occasions with children, whether it is bedtime, around the fire or on rainy days. Nancy Mellon shows how you can become a confident storyteller.

192pp; 216 x 138mm; 1 903458 08 0; pb

Making Waldorf Dolls

(formerly Kinder Dolls)

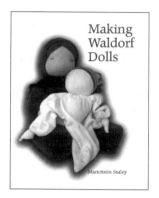

MARICRISTIN SEALEY

This comprehensive, well illustrated book will give even the most nervous beginner the confidence to produce a unique, handcrafted toy from natural materials. Once you have mastered the basic baby dolls, you can progress to a more ambitious limbed or jointed doll.

This new edition is published with a completely revised resource list.

**160pp; 246 x 189mm; 1 903458 58 7/
978-1-903458-58-7; pb**

The Winding Road

Family treasury of poems and verses

COMPILED BY MATTHEW BARTON

Celebrate each age and stage of your child's life with this poetic travelling companion. *The Winding Road* offers over 200 poems on the theme of childhood and growing up by writers ancient and modern — from Gaelic blessings to Navajo prayers, from William Blake to Eleanor Farjeon and Billy Collins. This rich treasury of poems, verses, blessings and meditations reflects a child's journey from baby to teenager, from first milestones to leaving home.

224pp; 210 x 148mm; 1 903458 47 1; pb

Stargazers' Almanac

Monthly guide to the stars and planets

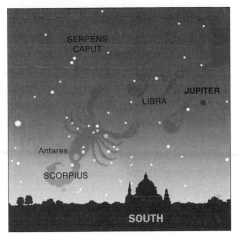

Explore the wonders of the night skies with the *Stargazers' Almanac* – no telescope required! Track the planets, locate the Milky Way, discover the heavenly Giraffe, Orion's dogs and Draco the dragon, recognise the signs of the zodiac and watch meteor showers and other planetary phenomena. The beautiful, easy to use colour charts make this a great introduction to astronomy, perfect for beginners, children and back-yard stargazers.

Each monthly chart features two views of the night sky looking north and south; a visual guide to the phases of the moon; and key planets and other objects. The observing notes include fascinating insights into the science, history, folklore and myths of the stars and planets.

Stargazers' Almanac also includes:
- Advice on how to navigate the night sky
- Overhead map of the sky
- Reference plan of constellations
- Guide to the signs of the zodiac and how they relate to the stars
- Glossary of constellations and Latin names; glossary of brightness of stars
- Information on the British Astronomical Association's Campaign for Dark Skies

Art and Science series; 32pp; 420 x 297mm landscape; pb

PUBLISHED ANNUALLY
Printed on environmentally friendly paper and packaged in an attractive gift box, *Stargazers' Almanac* is an ideal Christmas gift which will last the whole year!

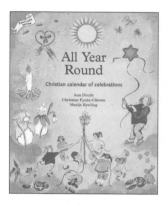

All Year Round

Christian calendar of celebrations

ANN DRUITT, CHRISTINE FYNES-CLINTON, MARIJE ROWLING

All Year Round is brimming with things to make; activities, stories, poems and songs to share with your family. It is full of well-illustrated ideas for fun and celebration: from Candlemas to Christmas and Mid-summer's day to the Winter solstice.

320pp; 250 x 200mm; 1 869 890 47 7; pb

Festivals, Family and Food

Guide to seasonal celebration

DIANA CAREY AND JUDY LARGE

This family favourite is a unique, well-loved source of stories, recipes, things to make, activities, poems, songs and festivals. Each festival such as Christmas, Candlemas and Martinmas has its own, well-illustrated chapter.

224pp; 250 x 200mm; 0 950 706 23 X; pb

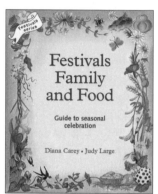

Ordering books

If you have difficulties ordering Hawthorn Press books from a bookshop, you can order direct from:
Booksource, 32 Finlas Street, Glasgow G22 5DU
Tel: (08702) 402182 Fax: (0141) 557 0189
E-mail: orders@booksource.net
or you can order online at **www.hawthornpress.com**

For further information or a book catalogue, please contact:
Hawthorn Press, 1 Lansdown Lane, Stroud,
Gloucestershire GL5 1BJ
Tel: (01453) 757040 Fax: (01453) 751138 E-mail:
info@hawthornpress.com
Website: www.hawthornpress.com

Dear Reader

If you wish to follow up your reading of this book, please tick the boxes below as appropriate, fill in your name and address and return to Hawthorn Press:

☐ Please send me a catalogue of other Hawthorn Press books.

☐ Please send me details of Early Years events and courses.

Questions I have about Early Years are:

Name

Address

Postcode   Tel. no.

Please return to:

Hawthorn Press, 1 Lansdown Lane, Stroud, Gloucestershire.
GL5 1BJ, UK
or Fax (01453) 751138

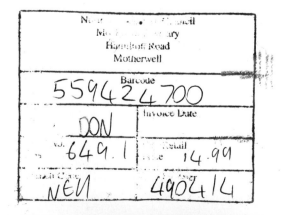